T0413732

The Ruby Rosary

Kyabje Dudjom Jigdral Yeshe Dorje Rinpoche

Kyabje Thinley Norbu Rinpoche

Shambhala Publications gratefully acknowledges the generous support of the Tsadra Foundation in sponsoring the translation and preparation of this book.

The Ruby Rosary Joyfully Accepted by Vidyādharas and Ḍākinīs as the Ornament of a Necklace

Thinley Norbu

TRANSLATED BY

Heidi Nevin

FOREWORDS BY

Dudjom Yangsi Rinpoche and Alak Zenkar Rinpoche

INTRODUCTION BY

Lama Tharchin Rinpoche

SHAMBHALA

Shambhala Publications, Inc.
2129 13th Street
Boulder, Colorado 80302
www.shambhala.com

© 2022 by the Estate of Kyabje Thinley Norbu Rinpoche

Cover art: Courtesy of Robert Beer
Cover design: Gopa & Ted2, Inc.

All rights reserved. No part of this book may be reproduced in any form or by any means, electronic or mechanical, including photocopying, recording, or by any information storage and retrieval system, without permission in writing from the publisher.

9 8 7 6 5 4 3 2 1

First Edition
Printed in the United States of America

Shambhala Publications makes every effort to print on acid-free, recycled paper.

Shambhala Publications is distributed worldwide by Penguin Random House, Inc., and its subsidiaries.

LIBRARY OF CONGRESS CATALOGING-IN-PUBLICATION DATA
Names: Thinley Norbu, author. | Nevin, Heidi, translator.
Title: The Ruby Rosary: joyfully accepted by Vidyadharas and Dakinis as the ornament of a necklace / Thinley Norbu; translated by Heidi Nevin; forewords by Dudjom Yangsi Rinpoche and Alak Zenkar Rinpoche; introduction by Lama Tharchin Rinpoche.
Description: First edition. | Boulder, Colorado: Shambhala Publications, Inc., 2022. | Includes bibliographical references and index.
Identifiers: LCCN 2019012650 | ISBN 9781559394574 (hardcover: alk. paper)
Subjects: LCSH: Rnying-ma-pa (Sect)—Prayers and devotions. | Prayer—Buddhism. | Rnying-ma-pa lamas—Biography. | Rdzogs-chen. | Bdud-'joms 'Jigs-bral-ye-śes-rdo-rje, 1904–1987.
Classification: LCC BQ7662.6 .T55 2022 | DDC 294.3/9230922—dc23
LC record available at https://lccn.loc.gov/2019012650

Contents

Foreword by Dudjom Yangsi Rinpoche ix

Foreword by Alak Zenkar Rinpoche xi

Introduction by Lama Tharchin Rinpoche xiii

About the Translation xxv

The Root Text. ***The Pearl Necklace: A Prayer to the Emanations*****,** by Kyabje Dudjom Jigdral Yeshe Dorje Rinpoche 1

A Commentary on ***The Pearl Necklace*****, Called** ***The Ruby Rosary Joyfully Accepted by Vidyādharas and Ḍākinīs as the Ornament of a Necklace*****,** by Kyabje Thinley Norbu Rinpoche 9

How the Buddha's Teachings Came to Exist in Our World 13

The Coming of Buddha Śākyamuni 19

The Three Councils 32

The Spread of the Mahāyāna Teachings 36

The Vajrayāna: How the Secret Mantra Teachings Came to This World 65

A Brief History of the Successive Rebirths of Kyabje Dudjom Rinpoche 141

Nuden Dorje Chang 142

Śāriputra 145

Saraha 153

Kṛṣṇadhara 157

Hūṃkāra 158

Drogben Khyeuchung Lotsawa 159

Smṛtijñāna 160

Rongzom Chökyi Zangpo 162
Katok Dampa Deshek 173
Lingje Repa 183
Drogön Chögyal Phagpa 186
Kharnakpa of Drum 188
Hepa Chöjung 189
Tragtung Dudul Dorje 190
Gyalse Sönam Detsen 194
Dudul Rolpa Tsal 195
Garwang Dudjom Pawo (Dudjom Lingpa) 197
Jigdral Yeshe Dorje: A Brief Biography of the Great Treasure Revealer Dharma King 209
Dorje Nönpo 249
Möpa Taye (Buddha Adhimukta) 252
Concluding Verses of Aspiration 257

Concluding Verses 261

Notes 267

Bibliography 301

Index 323

Foreword

Dudjom Yangsi Sangye Pema Shepa

The first volume of Kyabje Thinley Norbu Rinpoche's *Collected Works* is comprised of commentaries on writings by the Great Treasure Revealer Dudjom Jigdral Yeshe Dorje, including a supplication prayer to the successive lifetimes of Dudjom Rinpoche, entitled *The Pearl Necklace*, as well as a "Calling the Lama from Afar" prayer.* The American woman Sangye Pal Lha [Heidi Nevin] has translated this volume into English, which is wonderful. Our world has many different ethnicities and languages, yet we all share the common wish for happiness. By relying upon the sublime life stories of this holy master, which are free from exaggeration and understatement, and upon his sacred writings, we will be able to follow his example and train in the precious Buddha Dharma, which is the source of every happiness and benefit. For this and many other reasons, I feel that this translation will be of value, so I rejoice with full heart.

This was written by Sangye Pema Shepa, the one bearing the title "Dudjom Incarnation," on Ḍākinī Day in the eighth month of the Tibetan Earth Dog year [October 4, 2018].

*The commentary on the "Calling the Lama from Afar" prayer was not translated for this volume.

Foreword

Alak Zenkar Rinpoche Tupten Nyima

Geuter Tragtung Dudjom Lingpa, the banner of whose renown flies high above the three planes of existence, effortlessly opened the hundred gateways to profound hidden treasures, including the body of teachings on the inconceivable secret of the three yogas of the Early Translation (Nyingma) school. His immediate reincarnation was the king of scholars, Dudjom Tulku Jigdral Yeshe Dorje, who freely expounded the sūtras, tantras, and sciences, unaided by others. He was the sovereign of the Nyingma teachings and a mighty siddha of the Luminous Great Perfection and the level of great-bliss unity, which is achieved through the swift-messenger path of Secret Mantra. Dudjom Rinpoche's sublime natural and heart-son was the great tantric Vidyādhara Dungse Thinley Norbu Rinpoche. He was learned in Sūtra, Mantra, and the conventional sciences, and through the swift path of profound, secret instructions, he held the throne of mighty yogins who have realized the dissolution of delusion. Thinley Norbu's compositions are eloquent, profound, easy to understand, and concise, and they draw forth the key points in clear progression. He elucidates the major topics of texts through the stainless path of scripture and reasoning, creating treatises that both heal [the ills of the three poisons] and protect [from the sufferings of cyclic existence and the lower realms]. His lucid writings, which captivate the mind the moment they are heard, were written exclusively to benefit his followers. Therefore, the effort to publish and distribute them widely is an excellent one, and as I see it, such actions can only bring benefit to the Dharma and beings. In this case as well, I join my palms before my heart and with deep sincerity, I scatter a rain of joyful flowers to celebrate the fine people who have worked to publish and distribute Thinley Norbu's

Collected Works [which includes the present commentary]. I pray that your efforts may be swiftly and excellently accomplished.

This was offered by Tupten Nyima on March 10, 2019, in Hong Kong.

Introduction

Lama Tharchin Rinpoche

Sovereign of the hundred Buddha families, glorious holy Guru, at your feet I bow!

Here I shall offer a brief biography of the supreme sovereign master Dudjom Jigdral Yeshe Dorje, entitled "Treasury of Gems of the Threefold Faith."

> Oṃ svasti!
> From the spacious expanse of the sky, free of constructs, the primordially pure inner lucidity of the youthful vase body,
> The spontaneously accomplished outer lucidity amasses as dense clouds of unobstructed dynamic energy,
> From which the sweet, nourishing rain of compassion pours down, enriching the vital essence of the definitive secret Dharma and beings.
> May the sovereign master Dudjom Drodul Lingpa be victorious over existence and quiescence!
> The limits of the sky of your three secrets' enlightened qualities
> Are impossible to measure—how dare I attempt to describe them?
> However, please grant your permission
> For me to write whatever fits through the needle hole of my mind.

With this offering of reverence and request for permission, I shall begin.

The embodiment of all the Buddhas of the three times and ten directions, the great glorious master of Oddiyana, Padmasambhava himself, enthroned, empowered, and confirmed as his representative by vajra decree the great emanated treasure revealer and sovereign master Dudjom Jigdral Yeshe

Dorje Drodul Lingpa Tsal. Kyabje Dudjom Rinpoche is widely praised and prophesied in many ancient revealed Treasure teachings as the Dharma King of the Three Realms and the crown jewel of all the Great Secret Early Translation teachings. Completely without rival throughout the past, present, and future, Kyabje Rinpoche is like the newly dawning sun amidst the constellation of starlike Vidyadhara siddhas and scholars in the snowy land of Tibet. The renown of his name reverberates unceasingly throughout all the regions of this great Earth. In incomparable kindness, this supreme master accepted the role of holy protector and supporter of the Buddhist teachings and living beings in this degenerate era. I will briefly narrate his story.

From the beginningless beginning, great beings have been propelled by the power of their intense compassion to enter the realms of sentient beings, never once hesitating or forgetting. From the perspective of ultimate truth, such beings have been naturally free since the very beginning, embodying the youthful vase body of the blissful Dharmakāya, the nonconceptual wisdom of all Buddhas' enlightened mind, in the expanse of Samantabhadra's awareness. They arise in the form of the original protector Glorious Heruka or other principal deities in the immense ocean of maṇḍalas, amidst a boundless retinue of self-appearing wisdom manifestations, dwelling throughout the four times without transition or change. Never wavering from this state, they emanate an inconceivable illusory display of self-emerging magical manifestations in harmony with the situations and perceptions of infinite living beings.

Speaking generally about Nirmāṇakāya emanations, there are emanations who continuously take birth one after the next, emanations who appear simultaneously, emanations who are consecrated emanations, and so on. Such emanations do not appear in any consistent, fixed manner, but rather, just as the reflection of the moon's compassionate form appears in the water vessel of each and every disciple, they are limitless and immeasurable. Therefore, my mind, which is limited to my own experience, is incapable of fathoming or identifying this supreme master's incarnations and naming them as this one or that one.

Nevertheless, here I will share the stories of his succession of lifetimes in consecutive order as they are traditionally presented. The Great Treasure Revealer and Dharma King of the Three Realms himself composed a root text supplication to his succession of lifetimes, entitled *The Pearl Necklace*, for which there is an extensive one-volume commentary, entitled *The Ruby*

Rosary Joyfully Accepted by Vidyādharas and Ḍākinīs as the Ornament of a Necklace, written by Kyabje Dudjom Rinpoche's son, the sovereign master Jigme Thinley Norbu Gelek Nampar Gyalwede, whose wisdom realization is one taste with his father's. In addition, the Great Treasure Revealer's foremost disciple, the great learned siddha of the true meaning, Venerable Chatral Sangye Dorje, wrote a brief supplication entitled *Seed of the Three Faiths: A Supplication to* [Dudjom Rinpoche's] *Liberated Life*. Furthermore, this supreme Nirmāṇakāya emanation and Great Treasure Revealer, Dudjom Jigdral Yeshe Dorje, has included colophons and histories within the treasure texts he revealed. I urge you to study all of these closely.

Here I will write a brief explanation of a single-stanza supplication made in this Great Treasure Revealer's own vajra speech.

> In the past, you were the powerful Vidyādhara Nuden Dorje.
> In the future, you will be the Buddha of Boundless Dedication.
> At present, you are the Lotus Born's regent, Drogben incarnate.
> Jigdral Yeshe Dorje, to you I pray.

The first line states:

> *In the past, you were the powerful Vidyādhara Nuden Dorje.*

Our present era, in which 1,002 Buddhas will accept disciples and light the lamp of the Holy Dharma, is known as the age of illumination or the fortunate eon. The individual who, through profound aspirations, conferred empowerments, made prophecies, granted blessings, and placed seals of entrustment upon each of the 1,002 Buddhas of this fortunate eon was the head of the 1,000 Buddhas' family, the Lord of Yogins, Nuden Dorje Chang, Powerful Vajradhara. This was the first in the Great Treasure Revealer's series of lifetimes.

Later, during the time of our Teacher, Buddha Śākyamuni, [the Great Treasure Revealer was reborn as] Noble Śāriputra, whose wisdom realization became equal to the Buddha's, and who was foremost among Buddha's heart-disciples in sublime knowledge. This was the second of Kyabje Rinpoche's lifetimes.

Among the masters known as the Eighty-Four Mahāsiddhas of India, Brahmin Saraha, who gained supreme accomplishment, was the third of his lifetimes.

During the reign of Indrabhūti, king of the noble land of India, the great Buddhist minister Kṛṣṇadhara was the fourth of his lifetimes.

The great master Hūṃkāra, renowned throughout the breadth of India and Nepal, was the fifth of his lifetimes.

In Tibet, Guru Rinpoche's closest heart-disciples were known as the King and Twenty-Five Subjects. Among them, Drogben Khyeuchung Lotsawa, the Boy Translator of the Drogmi Clan, gained wisdom realization equal to the Guru's. He was the sixth of the Great Treasure Revealer's lifetimes.

The great paṇḍita from the noble land of India, Lord Smṛtijñāna, was the seventh in his series of lifetimes.

The foremost among all learned and accomplished masters throughout noble India and Tibet, known as Mahāpaṇḍita Rongzom Chökyi Zangpo, was the eighth in his series of lifetimes.

The Lord of the Teachings at the great Victorious Katok Monastery, home to more than 80,000 monks, was Dampa Deshek, the ninth in his series of lifetimes.

Drogön Pagmo Drupa's chief heart-disciple, Glorious Lingje Repa, who was renowned for his high realization, was the tenth in his series of lifetimes.

During the great reign of the glorious Sakyapas, a Bodhisattva dwelling upon the highest bhūmis appeared in the form of a human king, Drogön Chögyal Phagpa, and exercised power all across Tibet. He was the eleventh in the series of lifetimes.

Karnakpa of Drum, a mighty treasure revealer with mastery over miraculous powers, was the twelfth in his series of lifetimes.

Hepa Chöjung, who possessed the power to annihilate demonic forces through the enlightened activity of direct wrathful intervention and liberate them into the state of everlasting happiness and ultimate excellence, was the thirteenth in his series of lifetimes.

The Great Treasure Revealer Dudul Dorje, who was an emanation of Drogben, became the teacher of all the famous, learned, and accomplished Nyingma masters throughout Tibet, and he revealed countless treasures, including treasure wealth, Treasure teachings, and treasure substances. He was the fourteenth in the series of lifetimes.

Dudul Dorje's subsequent emanation, Gyalse Sönam Detsen, preserved the traditions of teaching and practice at Victorious Katok Monastery through the three spheres of a teacher's activity [teaching, accomplishment, and activities of a teacher]. He was the fifteenth in the series of lifetimes.

Gyalse Sönam Detsen's reincarnation was the Great Treasure Revealer

Dudul Rolpa Tsal, who inherited the great secret Dharma treasury of the Ḍākinīs' heart essence and raised the victory banner of the Victorious Katok teachings. He was the sixteenth in the series of lifetimes.

Dudul Rolpa Tsal's reincarnation, the Great Treasure Revealer Garwang Dudjom Lingpa, did not need to rely upon the arduous and limited process of training and purification in his lifetime, but instead received the ultimate lineage transmission from nonhuman teachers and spontaneously released the seal of the space of Samantabhadra's wisdom mind, the great treasury of the spacious expanse of Dharmatā. He was the seventeenth in the series of lifetimes.

Thus, the words "in the past" are used to connote all those lifetimes that preceded the present lifetime, although Nuden Dorje Chang is the only one who is explicitly mentioned. This concludes my short explanation of the first line of Kyabje Dudjom Rinpoche's autobiographical supplication.

The second line states:

In the future, you will be the Buddha of Boundless Dedication.

As this expresses, in the future, as well, this great being will continue to appear spontaneously, without hesitation or effort, as artisan Nirmāṇakāyas, incarnated Nirmāṇakāyas, and supreme Nirmāṇakāyas, in order to work for the benefit of sentient beings. This is caused both by blessing waves of compassion and by the expansion of beings' positive actions, similar to the threefold interaction between water, the moon's reflection, and the moon: just as the moon has the ability to leave a reflection, the moonlike Sambhogakāya has the ability to appear as Nirmāṇakāya emanations in the perception of disciples. Likewise, just as water has the ability to reflect, when a disciple has the merit to perceive a Nirmāṇakāya emanation, the reflection of the autumn moon will effortlessly appear in the water vessel of disciples' minds, never veiled for even an instant. Thus, the dance of this protector's emanated magical displays will continue uninterrupted until the ocean of saṃsāra runs dry.

Specifically, among the six regions of this world, Jambudvīpa, the northern kingdom of Shambhala is an especially sublime area, where Bodhisattvas on the tenth bhūmi appear as a series of kings. Kyabje Rinpoche will take rebirth in the lineage of Kalkī kings as Raudra Cakrin, "Fierce Iron Wheel Holder," an emanation of Mañjuśrī. He will defeat the barbaric forces that constantly destroy beings' peace and happiness with their evil schemes and savage, hostile behavior, and will guide them along the path to peace and enlightenment.

Furthermore, long ago, when the Buddhas of this fortunate eon were each making their respective vows and aspirations for the benefit of beings, the youngest of these 1,000 guides, Lodrö Taye, said: "The Buddha's teachings are like the sky, and sentient beings, too, will never end. So I shall make the aspiration to have your combined life spans and other qualities, and to perform deeds equal to all your deeds combined." As soon as he had spoken, the voice of the gods rang out from space, "May it be so!"

By the power of this prayer, the last of the 1,000 buddhas, the Bliss-Gone Buddha named Adhimukta, Boundless Light of Wishes [Möpa Taye], will definitely be a future emanation of the Great Treasure Revealer, Kyabje Dudjom Rinpoche himself.

This concludes my very brief explanation of the meaning of the second line in the stanza.

The third line states:

At present, you are the Lotus Born's regent, Drogben incarnate.

As this line expresses, our supreme, incomparable guide, Dharma King of the Three Realms, the sublime Dudjom Jigdral Yeshe Dorje, is the body emanation of Drogben Lotsawa; the speech emanation of the Queen of Space, Yeshe Tsogyal; and the mind emanation of the King of Victorious Ones, Padmasambhava. In accordance with the prophetic praises of the Great Master of Oḍḍiyāna and Dudjom Lingpa, among others, found in numerous ancient treasure texts, the lotus of Kyabje Rinpoche's perfect physical form, adorned with all the marks and signs of a Nirmāṇakāya emanation, bloomed afresh in the hidden land of Pemakö in the Wood Dragon year [1904], to a father whose blood lineage traced back to King Trisong Detsen and a mother whose blood lineage traced back to Ratna Lingpa.

Right from his early youth, his noble propensities were awakened, and Guru Rinpoche and his consort revealed themselves to him. They empowered him as the master of their profound treasures and enthroned him as Guru Rinpoche's regent, giving him the name Orgyen Garwang Drodul Lingpa Tsal. He drank deeply of the nectar of ripening, liberating, and supportive transmissions from many great, authentic, learned, and accomplished masters until his thirst was quenched and his mindstream was deeply enriched. His innate supreme knowledge and ability to discern the key points of view, meditation, and philosophical systems spontaneously overflowed, and he became universally renowned as a king of scholars, unrivaled in past, present, or future.

As a great Bodhisattva, Kyabje Rinpoche relied upon the six transcendent perfections and the four ways of gathering disciples to lead beings to the temporary goodness of liberation and the ultimate exaltation of full awakening. He had no need for the path of expedient meaning and hardship and went directly onto the path of the absolute meaning, the short path of Ati's Luminous Essence. He reached a high level of accomplishment, and his enlightened qualities of manifest realization blazed forth all at once. Wisdom Ḍākinīs actually came and offered him scrolls of yellow parchment containing treasure inventories and other items, and the Dharmapālas and guardians watched over him like their own child. His mastery of the three blazes and the three gatherings made him worthy of gracing the crowns of all beings, regardless of status.

During these degenerate times, Kyabje Rinpoche's profound aspiration to prevent the decline of the teaching and practice of the Early Translation school and to spread them in one hundred directions led him to establish Buddhist communities on a vast scale. Rather than exerting himself to reveal his allotment of earth treasures, he decided to focus his attention on the greater purpose of preserving the Nyingma and Kagyu teachings. He raised the victory banner of the teachings that unite all transmission lineages, such as Jamgön Kongtrul's *Five Great Treasuries*, high in the skies over the four continents. In order to help beings of this degenerate age accumulate merit through making offerings, Kyabje Rinpoche built a replica of the structure and contents of the great palace of Lotus Light on the Glorious Copper-Colored Mountain [Zangdok Palri] on Tail-Fan Island [Ngayab Ling], with a conjoined retreat center. He thereby completely reversed the decline of the Dharma and beings. Moreover, Kyabje Rinpoche produced inconceivable numbers of the three sacred supports [statues, stūpas, and scriptures], such as printing extremely rare ancient texts, and he was thereby single-handedly responsible for bringing about the revival of the Buddhist teachings and restoring happiness and well-being to the three regions of Tibet. His enlightened activities truly fulfilled and proved true the prophecies identifying him as Guru Padmasambhava's regent.

This great being's reincarnation is the supreme Nirmāṇakāya emanation Sangye Pema Shepa Drodul Rigdzin Trinley Drupe De, also known as Pema Ösel Pal Zangpo. His father was the great holy Treasure Revealer's own son,

Dola Choktrul Jigme Chökyi Nyima, and his mother is Pema Khandro, who has all the marks and signs of a Ḍākinī. In the year of the Iron Horse [1990], the lotus of his perfect form blossomed anew amid many amazing, auspicious signs. Right from his early youth, his excellent propensities awakened, igniting the dynamic power of his innate supreme knowledge, an experience unique to the extraordinary liberated lives of great noble beings. Thus, he was able to read and write merely by glancing at words and letters. He received Kama and Terma empowerments, reading transmissions, and pith instructions from numerous learned and accomplished holy lineage masters, including the supreme sovereign master Kyabje Jigme Tsewang Thinley Norbu, who was his paternal uncle [the Treasure Revealer's son], as well as the most senior of all of Kyabje Dudjom Rinpoche's disciples, Kyabje Chatral Sangye Dorje and Gonjo Tulku Orgyen Chemchok. Sangye Pema Shepa Rinpoche drank deeply of this nectar until his thirst was quenched. The force of his recollection of past lives has given him prodigious knowledge of boundless gateways to the Dharma of scripture and realization. His qualities of scholarship, discipline, and kindness are completely unrivaled, and his enormously powerful enlightened activities are flourishing in every direction. He has accepted his role as a holy and courageous protector of the Great Secret Early Translation teachings and beings.*

Kyabje Dudjom Jigdral Yeshe Dorje's feet touched the ground of every part of this great Earth, including all over Tibet and the regions of Greater Tibet, Bhutan, Nepal, India, China, North America, and Europe. He guided all those connected to him through receiving his teachings and sacred elixirs, seeing his face, hearing his voice, or speaking with him, without a single exception, to the Land of Lotus Light on Tail-Fan Island, thus fulfilling all the prophecies made about him.

Moreover, even though the greatest, most learned and accomplished lamas and high-ranking kings, ministers, and officials bowed their heads at his feet, Kyabje Rinpoche had no pride or arrogance and regarded the eight worldly concerns with equanimity. He maintained the fearless conduct of an ordinary, hidden yogi throughout his life. He visited the pure lands of innumerable Buddhas, had countless visions of deities and spiritual masters, received prophecies from Ḍākinīs, and had untold other pure perceptions,

*This introduction was written in 2005. Dudjom Yangsi Rinpoche (b. 1990) passed into parinirvana on February 14, 2022.

yet he kept all of these tightly sealed in secrecy, without ever praising himself, showing off, or feeling superior.

When his disciples' karma and aspirations came to fruition, the seal on the vast treasury of his luminous wisdom mind was naturally released. His mind-treasure cycles—the outer, inner, secret, and innermost secret Three Roots sādhana practices, including their Dharmapāla rituals, activity practices, precious guidance texts, and so on—flooded forth like the pure, distilled essence of the Ḍākinīs' heart-blood: pithy, clear, drenched with the blessings of the ultimate lineage, granting swift accomplishment, and so on. Like quintessential nectar, these profound teachings satisfy all those who connect with them. Once Kyabje Rinpoche had decoded them, he granted their oral instructions and reading transmissions in full to his prophesied doctrine holders and karmically destined lineage holders. As he spread these profound Dharma practices throughout all the regions of the world, he became known as the universal monarch of all accomplished treasure revealers.

Furthermore, Kyabje Rinpoche organized, revised, and clarified numerous ancient treasures, such as the trio of the Guru Sādhana, Great Perfection, and Avalokiteśvara and the trio of the Eight Herukas, Master's Realization, and Vajrakīlaya, which delighted the learned and prevented the unsuspecting from misperforming rituals with omissions or additions by arranging them in an easy, straightforward manner. For his own New Treasure tradition and for ritual arrangements of ancient treasure cycles, he composed outlines, recitation manuals, activity practices, instructional commentaries, and appendixes; vast and profound guidance texts conjoined with the procedures for conferring the four empowerments in concise and elaborate form; histories of Tibet, Buddhism, and the Nyingma School; a record of the teachings he received; and supplemental writings. In total, his collected works comprise twenty-five volumes. Moreover, he collected scattered ancient texts from the Nyingma Kama, proofread them, produced definitive versions, and organized them in a total of over 50 volumes.

In brief, his preservation of the Nyingma Kama and Terma texts exemplifies the manner in which Kyabje Rinpoche supported, elucidated, and propagated the teachings that lead to maturation and liberation. He is truly unique in the history of both India and Tibet, and nowadays he is renowned as the second Guru Padmasambhava. His kindness restored the precious teachings of the Great Secret Luminous Essence from their very foundation. When his enlightened activity had reached its perfect conclusion, in the year of the Fire Tiger [1986], the display of his miraculous illusory form dissolved into space, and the basis of his Nirmāṇakāya emanation merged into the expanse of Samantabhadra Guru Padmasambhava's heart, as one taste. This concludes the commentary on the meaning of the third line.

The fourth line states:

Jigdral Yeshe Dorje, to you I pray.

Jigdral Yeshe Dorje is one of this Great Treasure Revealer's names. In fact, there is a prayer composed by him, *Prayer with the Various Names of Dudjom Tulkus*, that lists his many names. One stanza reads:

To your holy lord father, Jampal Norbu, a royal descendant,
A Ḍākinī said, "A son greater than his father will appear."
As prophesied, your name was given before your birth.
To you, the one known as Yeshe Dorje, Vajra Wisdom, I pray.

As this describes, before Kyabje Rinpoche was born, his father, Katok Tulku Jampal Norbu Tenzin, who was descended from the Divine Flower of Brahmā [King Trisong Detsen], received a prophecy from the Ḍākinīs, in which they named the child "Yeshe Dorje." I have heard it told that it was the Karmapa [the sixteenth Gyalwa Karmapa, Rangjung Rigpe Dorje] who added "Jigdral." That is the sublime name by which this master is most widely known.

When you pray to the supreme refuge who bears this name, lord of our Buddha family, with the conviction that he embodies all Buddhas, and ask him to bless you and all sentient beings, your devotion will join with his compassion, and your minds will merge inseparably. As the fruit of dwelling on the ground of primordial being, the true Lama—your own vajra wisdom [yeshe dorje]—will manifestly awaken, and you will attain Buddhahood in the inner space of the youthful vase body, the deep and luminous Dharmakāya.

This concludes my brief explanation of this four-line stanza. May it spread far and wide!

This was composed by the decrepit vagabond Tsedrub Tharchin of Repkong, the most wretched among the students of the Great Treasure Revealer Dudjom Rinpoche and his son, based upon both their writings. May all those who read this become disciples of this sublime sovereign master!

About the Translation

The Ruby Rosary Joyfully Accepted by Vidyādharas and Ḍākinīs as the Ornament of a Necklace was published in Tibetan with the title *rig 'dzin mkha' 'gro dgyes pa'i mgul rgyan pad ma ra ga'i do shal*. It is an elaborate commentary on a supplication prayer by Kyabje Dudjom Jigdral Yeshe Dorje Rinpoche, entitled *The Pearl Rosary: A Prayer to the Emanations* (*sku 'phreng gsol 'debs mu tig ka'i do shal*). The prayer invokes and pays homage to the "pearls" of Kyabje Dudjom Rinpoche's twenty successive incarnations, beginning with the yogin Nuden Dorje Chang, who, countless ages ago, vowed to appear as Buddha Adhimukta (Möpa Taye), the final Buddha of this fortunate eon. Dudjom Rinpoche's illustrious line includes famous masters such as Śāriputra, Saraha, Hūṃkāra, and the wild yogin Dudjom Lingpa, the first of three emanations bearing the name Dudjom.

The root text appears first in the book in its entirety and is repeated verse by verse in the commentary by Kyabje Thinley Norbu Rinpoche. The commentary is divided into three main sections, beginning with an extensive overview of Buddhist history adorned with colorful stories and anecdotes. The second section contains a series of brief biographies of Dudjom Rinpoche's successive emanations, following the style of a word commentary on the root text. The book concludes with a concise biography of Kyabje Dudjom Jigdral Yeshe Dorje Rinpoche. Throughout the section entitled "A Brief History of the Successive Rebirths of Kyabje Dudjom Rinpoche," boldface type is used to highlight words drawn from the root text that are repeated in the commentary.

A few elements not present in the original Tibetan work were added by the translator and editors. These include a few simple English subheads as well as verse numbers for the root text, as a convenience for study. Endnotes were added to provide linguistic information, definitions, and other explanations. Occasional editorial interpolations appear in the text within square brackets. Lifetime dates for major figures were inserted where possible. Tibetan years and dates are indicated in some places; the rest of the dates are of the Common Era.

Style and terminology choices for the English translation reflect, wherever possible, preferences expressed by Kyabje Thinley Norbu Rinpoche during his lifetime. As in the author's previous publications, titles of works have been mostly given in English. These are not the titles of published English versions, but simply translations of Tibetan and Sanskrit titles cited by the author. To help readers identify these works, a bibliography was compiled containing Wylie transliterations for the corresponding Tibetan titles and Sanskrit titles romanized according to a modified IAST system. Most Tibetan names of Indian masters in the text have been back-translated into the original Sanskrit, but in some cases, where reconstructions were not possible, names have been left in Tibetan.

A few comments on pronunciation may be helpful for the nonspecialist reader. In Sanskrit words, both the retroflex *ṣ* with underdot and the palatal *ś* with acute accent may be pronounced like English *sh*. The letter *c* represents the sound *ch* as in *church*, for example in *cakra* (spelled *chakra* in English dictionaries). The letter *ṛ* with underdot may be pronounced like English *ri*, as in *Kṛṣṇa* ("Krishna") and *amṛta* ("amrita").

The Sanskrit language contains several aspirated consonants, represented by an *h* following the consonant, for example in sounds such as *bha*, *kha*, and *tha*. The *h* in these sounds is like a small puff of air following the consonant sound. For instance, the *tha* sound is pronounced like the *th* in *hothouse* and not like the *th* in *that* or *thin*.

Tibetan also has aspirated sounds usually represented in phonetic spelling by the letter *h* following some consonants. In this book, the letter *h* is omitted from aspirated consonants where it might be misleading to English-speakers, notably in *pha*, *tha*, and *tsha*. Thus, the spellings *pa* (instead of *pha*), *ta* (instead of *tha*), and *tsa* (instead of *tsha*) are used in order to avoid the mispronunciation of names such as Pagpa, Tröma, and Tsogyal. The exceptions are proper nouns whose phonetic spellings have already been established with *h*, such as the author's name, *Thinley*.

Finally, the letter *e* at the end of Tibetan words in phonetic spelling should be pronounced like *é* or *ay*. The many examples include *Dorje*, *Rinpoche*, *Yeshe*, *tigle* (pronounced *tig-lay*), and *Trime* (*Tree-may*).

The Root Text

The Pearl Necklace: A Prayer to the Emanations

Kyabje Dudjom Jigdral Yeshe Dorje Rinpoche

1
In the sky of unchanging Dharmadhātu, the bliss and emptiness of
Samantabhadrī,
You gather wisdom clouds of boundless omniscience and love
And skillfully shower us with a compassionate rain of virtue and goodness.
Supreme Lord Guru, to you I pray.

2
Here in this illumined realm in what is known as the fortunate eon,
You are the crown of all thousand Buddhas.
Manifesting in the form of a supreme powerful yogin,
Nuden Dorje Chang, to you I pray.

3
When the beings of this age of strife, abandoned by other Buddhas,
Were embraced by the Kin of the Sun, Buddha Śākyamuni,
You appeared with supreme sublime knowledge, no different from
Buddha himself.
Noble Śāriputra, to you I pray.

4
Completely intoxicated with indestructible, flawless youth,
With the wisdom arrow of all appearances arising as great exaltation,
You sealed the life force of all beings of the three realms.
Brahmin Saraha, to you I pray.

5
Adorned with the garland of the fortunate sole king Indrabhūti's command,
You served as an honest minister, enacting the king's laws
To bring about benefit and happiness.
Buddhist minister Kṛṣṇadhara, to you I pray.

6
With the magical, blissful dance of the Glorious Heruka,
You manifested unchanging, supreme wisdom.
Awareness Holder of Viśuddha Mind,
Ācārya Hūṃkāra, to you I pray.

7
In the presence of the Lotus-Born Second Buddha,
You appeared as one who attained tantric accomplishment, with wisdom realization equal to his.
Your mere gaze drew birds from the sky.
Drogben Khyeuchung Lotsawa, to you I pray.

8
Guided by the actual presence of Mañjuśrī, Lion of Speech,
You saw all phenomena exactly as they are,
And you liberated beings through skillful means, O Brave Heart.
Lord Smṛtijñāna, to you I pray.

9
Through your mastery of all ten sciences,
The sun of the Buddha's teachings shone with glory.
Great Paṇḍita of Tibet, Land of Sal Trees,
Rongzom Chökyi Zangpo, to you I pray.

10
From the Supreme Conqueror Padmasambhava's ocean of compassion,
You arose radiant with the thousandfold light of sublime activity.
Sun of the Nyingma teachings, founder of Katok,
Dampa Deshek, at your feet I pray.

11
Heart-son of Deshek Phagmo Drupa,
You perfected your realization through the inner path.
Supreme Heruka of the saints of Snowland,
Glorious Lingje Repa, to you I pray.

12
By the thousandfold light of your sublime wisdom and love shining,
The lotus grove of benefit and happiness bloomed instantly in the cool land of Tibet.
Mañjuśrī in the form of a divine human king,
Drogön Chögyal Phagpa, to you I pray.

13
Seeing Dharmatā just as it is, free from elaboration, supreme ultimate truth,
You were liberated from the chain of existence
And attained the kingdom of unwavering Dharmakāya.
Kharnakpa of Drum, to you I pray.

14
Through vast, fearless wisdom activity and fulfilled aspiration prayers,
You have the power of the one who wielded the Yogurt Drinker's vajra
To dash the brains of the unruly and vicious.
Hepa Chöjung, at your feet I pray.

15
Great master of marvelous holy places and hundreds of treasures,
Including hidden lands, teachings, wealth, samaya substances, and others,
Lord of the ten bhūmis, sovereign among saints,
Tragtung Dudul Dorje, to you I pray.

16
The actual emanation of Pema Dragpo is Longsal Nyingpo.
As his descendant and lineage holder of his teachings,
You illuminated the tradition of the essence of the absolute meaning.
Gyalse Sönam Detsen, to you I pray.

17
Cared for and blessed by your Yidam deity,
You held the Ḍākinīs' secret treasury through the power of your previous fortunate karma,
And led all those connected to you to the pureland of Lotus Light.
Dudul Rolpa Tsal, to you I pray.

18
Having received the father's gift from self-appearing nonhuman spiritual teachers,
The treasures of Samantabhadra's wisdom mind overflowed from your expanse.
Yogin of space, you are truly the crazed King of Wrath,
Garwang Dudjom Pawo, to you I pray.

19
From the continent of Cāmara, the Guru and Consort
Bestowed on you the warmth of their wisdom, and from this confidence
You raised aloft the victory banner of the Great Secret Vajrayāna teachings in all directions.
Jigdral Yeshe Dorje, to you I pray.

20
Furthermore, according to beings' natures, faculties, wishes,
And different fortunes,
You appear in whatever ways are necessary to subdue them.
To your infinite manifestations, I pray.

21
Eventually, when barbarians try to harm the Buddha's teachings,
You will be the one called Dorje Nönpo in Shambhala,
Taking rebirth as the Kalkī king.
To you who will defeat the enemy armies, I pray.

22
In the future, as the final guide of this fortunate eon,
You will arise in the form of Sugata Möpa Taye.

With the four limitless ways of subduing beings,
You will dredge the depths of the realms of beings—to you, I pray.

23
By the power of praying with unshakable heartfelt devotion,
Throughout all my lifetimes, may I never be separate from you, Sovereign Protector.
By always worshipping you as my Crown Jewel,
May I have the good fortune to enjoy the amṛta of your wisdom speech.

24
By the power of your boundless great loving compassion,
You accepted me as a child of your heart.
May I awaken to my courageous and virtuous nature
So I can spread your enlightened activities in a hundred directions.

25
In the unexcelled Palace of Lotus Light,
In the one taste of the indivisible wisdom mind of the Guru and retinue,
May I attain fully manifest Buddhahood and become a Supreme Guide
For all infinite sentient beings throughout the far reaches of space.

In response to the insistent requests of a few earnest, devoted individuals, who over the years have expressed a need for a prayer to my successive rebirths, I, Jigdral Yeshe Dorje, wrote this based upon prophetic treasure texts and the writings of past Vidyādharas. May it bring virtue and excellence!

A COMMENTARY ON *THE PEARL NECKLACE*, CALLED *THE RUBY ROSARY* *JOYFULLY ACCEPTED BY VIDYĀDHARAS AND ḌĀKINĪS AS THE ORNAMENT OF A NECKLACE*

KYABJE THINLEY NORBU RINPOCHE

OM SVASTI ŚRĪ VIJAYANTU! May all be auspicious and always victorious!

In the palace of perfectly pure self-appearances of Dharmakāya, you sit unwavering on the exalted throne of flawless precious qualities.
In the city of pure and impure beings to be subdued, you emanate messengers to subdue each one at the perfect moment.
Proclaiming the four seals[1] of the Buddha's teachings to the ears of infinite beings of the three planes,[2] you enforce the law of constant bliss.
Peerless throughout all existence, you are the Dharma King, Omniscient Kin of the Sun, Buddha Śākyamuni; I speak and bow reverently to you, always in all ways.

The successive waves of conceptual characteristics are completely pacified on the divine lake of Samantabhadra, where the glory of infinite Kāyas and wisdoms,
The natural radiance of the spontaneously present Sambhogakāya, becomes clearly visible.
In the field of the natural Nirmāṇakāya, with clouds of the five inexhaustible wheels of ornaments[3] densely gathering,
A rain of compassion showers down to quell the feverish torment of beings' karma and passions.
As soon as the thunderous name of the Lotus-Born falls upon our ears like amṛta, we beings to be subdued, like a gathering of peacocks, delight in a dance of the three faiths,[4] rejoicing in all things in every way.

You liberated the demon of conditioned existence, born from dualistic grasping and fixation, with the realization of selflessness in the space of great nondual wisdom.
At the feast celebrating his defeat in the battle of saṃsāra, your mouth of natural Dharmatā wrathfulness **drank**[5] his **blood** [Tragtung] and, fully inebriated, your crazed form
Blazed with radiant splendor, **annihilating** all four classes of **demons** [Dudjom] and filling the entire billionfold universe.
Supreme lord of siddhas, you are truly the one who wields the vajra weapon, Dorje Drolö, manifesting in human form. I bow down to you.
Utterly **free** of all **fears** [Jigdral] that come from clinging to phenomena of saṃsāra and enlightenment, passionately cherishing the face of the consort, emptiness that is supreme in all aspects,
With a body of supreme flawless **wisdom** [Yeshe], in the bloom of blissful youth, you are the venerable, all-powerful, wish-fulfilling jewel king,
Lord Padmasambhava, master of those who fly through the sky, crown ornament of every Awareness Holder saint's high topknot,
Returning in the guise of a **vajra** [Dorje] master—Supreme Refuge, I rely upon you from the depths of my heart. Please care for me until enlightenment.

The speech of the Buddha, abiding nowhere,
Is inconceivably secret.
From that, any speech can arise.
May this precious speech grant auspiciousness.

This book contains the life and liberation of the Great Treasure Revealer and all-victorious Dharma King Jigdral Yeshe Dorje. It will only cover parts of his oceanic biography, just enough to moisten the tip of the kuśa grass of devotion and cause the lotus ears of fortunate disciples to bloom.

There will be three sections, beginning with how the Buddha's teachings came to exist in our world; followed by each of the Great Treasure Revealer Dharma King's lifetimes in sequence, a subject too vast to be covered; and particularly, a concise biography of the great master Jigdral Yeshe Dorje.

How the Buddha's Teachings Came to Exist in Our World

As it says in the *Sūtra of Inconceivable Secrets: The Arrangement of the Three Jewels*:

> Wherever space pervades,
> Enlightened body also pervades.
> Wherever enlightened body pervades,
> Light also pervades.
> Wherever light pervades,
> Enlightened speech also pervades.
> Wherever enlightened speech pervades,
> Enlightened mind also pervades.

So it is. That which is completely free of elaboration, such as bounds and directions, restrictions and biases, time and place, edge and center, is the final sublime destination, the place of the Dharmakāya Buddha, which is called the "ultimate true Akaniṣṭha." As it says in the *Tantra of the All-Doing Great King*:

> The place of the Dharmakāya Buddha
> Is the palace of Dharmadhātu, Akaniṣṭha.
> It is called the ultimate true Akaniṣṭha.

Akaniṣṭha is defined as "never inferior" or "below nothing,"[6] meaning that it is above all and unsurpassable. Since the essence of Dharmakāya does not have an iota of conceptually characterized substantiality, it is impossible to define or describe it in any way. However, using the example of the sky, which is the basis for the arising of the other elements, or the example of a stainless mirror, which is the basis for the arising of various reflections, the Dharmakāya is the basis for the arising of the two Rupakāyas:[7] the Sambhogakāya and the Nirmāṇakāya. In the words of Omniscient Longchenpa [1308–1363]:

> Saying that the place is the pureland[8] of Dharmakāya, the teacher is the Self-Recognizing King of Awareness, the retinue is the ocean of wisdom, the time is unchanging Dharmatā, and the teaching is the Great Perfection, is an effort to express that which is inexpressible beyond language, names, and words. These are just designations for the basis of nonduality, the primordial abiding nature; there are no actual five perfections to define. That is the characteristic of the Dharmakāya.

As for the characteristics of the Akaniṣṭha of the Sambhogakāya, first there is the *certain place*: the light from the natural radiance of the Dharmakāya's Luminous Vajra Essence, and that which is made out of that light, such as purelands and palaces, splendid adornments and their arrangements, the five male and female Buddhas with their self-manifesting retinues, the boundless maṇḍalas of victorious peaceful and wrathful deities, and all the infinite sublime riches throughout the farthest reaches of space. When there is mastery over this always continuous maṇḍala, it is called "the place of the Supreme Master."

The *certain perfect time* is beyond the three times of past, present, and future. It is the time of originally pure evenness.

The *certain teacher* is the glorious originally pure Buddha Samantabhadra, with the magnificent qualities of the thirty-two major and eighty minor marks of sublime excellence, or in the naturally occurring aspects of the nine signs of a wisdom body of peaceful deities, and the nine expressions of dance of wrathful deities.[9]

The Great Omniscient Longchenpa says:

> The Akaniṣṭha of the Sambhogakāya is the self-arisen appearance of great wisdom from the space of the Dharmakāya, appearing as palaces of light, each with its principal Buddha and retinue, the forever unchanging, naturally fulfilled[10] five wisdom families.

As it says in the *Magical Vajra* [*Mirror of All the Vajrasattva Magical Infinity Tantras*]:

> Leaving the pure abodes,[11]
> And in the supreme place of the Great Akaniṣṭha,[12]
> The spontaneously present wisdom form of the Lord of the Family,
> Completely free of being "one" or "many,"
> Is the embodiment of all Buddhas.
> Since this wisdom form is the primordial treasure of the Mahāyāna,
> Disciples who clear all obscurations
> Will perceive it in a single instant.

Here, "leaving the pure abodes" means going beyond those realms. The Great Akaniṣṭha is superior to worldly phenomena, but it does not always have to be above the pure abodes, since it appears naturally wherever Buddha abides.

Likewise, as it says in the *Prayer for Excellent Conduct*:

> On one particle, there are immeasurable particles with inconceivable Buddhas . . .

Do not mistake this to mean that Buddhas do not also abide *inside* those most minute particles; the Rich Adornment pureland appears unceasingly within them as well. Therefore, there is no need to search for particular locations in a limited, intellectual way. Whatever distinctive qualities appear through the power of the stainless space of Dharmatā should be recognized as the maṇḍalas of the Victorious Ones. Such places are called "the Great Akaniṣṭha." This is because these are the Buddhas' own emanated manifestations, and no one other than Buddhas can enjoy this. Specifically, they are Vairocana of the Buddha family, Akṣobhya of the Vajra family, Ratnasambhava of the Ratna family, Amitābha of the Padma family, and Amoghasiddhi of the Karma family, with their own naturally appearing, self-accomplished gatherings of maṇḍala that extend boundlessly throughout the far reaches of space. Perceived Kāyas and appearances of wisdom are not the same, because they appear variously;

> nor are they different, because they are the self-manifestation of a single Sambhogakāya. Such appearances of purelands, Kāyas, and wisdoms are the embodiment of Sambhogakāya, the self-manifestation of all Buddhas, which cannot be experienced by everyone. It is shared only by Sambhogakāya Buddhas. These appearances of principal Buddhas and retinues are the unique treasury of the Mahāyāna teachings, because this is the nature of Sambhogakāya Buddhas.

The *certain perfect retinue* is the assembly of the five noble regents of the Victorious Ones and the fulfilled male and female Bodhisattvas.[13]

The *certain perfect teaching* is the Great Perfection, which teaches that all phenomenal existence is beginninglessly enlightened. As indicated by the quotation "The Tathāgata explained the teachings to himself . . . ," teacher and retinue have the same inseparable wisdom mind, and the teachings are spoken in that manner.

For further reference, various explanatory commentaries give very clear and detailed descriptions of the Sambhogakāya purelands, palaces, splendid adornments, and their manifestations. The *Account of the Great Caitya of Thimbu* [by Kyabje Thinley Norbu Rinpoche] also offers clear descriptions. Those who prefer visual replicas may look at drawings or models, which will make it easy to gain an understanding.

More challenging to understand than these drawings and images are the descriptions of the marks and signs of a supreme Nirmāṇakāya Buddha found in the teachings common to all vehicles [yānas], and in the teachings of the extraordinary, unsurpassed Secret Mantra. According to the tradition of the common vehicles,[14] the thirty-two major marks of excellence are as follows: the palms and soles are adorned with wheels; the soles of the feet resemble the belly of a tortoise; the fingers and toes are webbed like those of a duck; the arms and legs are smooth and youthful; the seven parts of the body—the two soles, two palms, two shoulders, and nape of the neck—are without indentations and elevated; the fingers and toes are long; the heels are broad; taller than average, the body is seven cubits in height and perfectly erect; the kneecaps and ankles are not protruding; the hairs on the body grow in an upward direction; the lower legs are like those of a deer; the arms are so long they reach the knees; the genitalia are withdrawn and concealed; the skin is glossy and golden; the skin is soft and smooth; each hair grows in a right-spiraling coil; the point between the eyebrows is adorned with a tuft of soft white hair; the torso is lionlike; the tops of the shoulders are broad and round; the upper back—the area between the shoulder blades and neck—is expansive; even if consuming poor-tasting food, the taste becomes sublime; the body is perfectly proportioned and resembles a banyan tree; the head is crowned with a right-spiraling, four-inch uṣṇīṣa;[15] the tongue is long; the voice is melodious and Brahmā-like; the cheeks are round; the teeth are white; the teeth are uniform and not too big or small; the teeth have no gaps; the teeth number forty in total; the eyes are deep sapphire-blue; and the eyelashes are long like those of a king bull.

The eighty minor marks of excellence are as follows: the Sambhogakāya Buddha's nails are red like copper; the nails are glossy; the nails are raised and free of indentations and ridges; the fingers are rounded; the fingers are fleshy; the fingertips are tapered; the veins of the body are not visible; the subtle channels have no knots; the ankle bones are delicate and not visible; the feet are the proper size, not too long or too short; the way of walking is majestic with the gait of a lion; straight with the gait of an elephant; soars into the sky with the lift of a swan; leads the nose rope of sentient beings with the gait of a king bull; to the right, following the path of circumambulation; elegant and beautiful; straight and even, without wavering; the body is fleshy and muscular, poised, resplendent, and graceful; the body is clean and pure, as if freshly bathed and polished; the body is perfectly proportioned and erect, firm and wholesome; the body, because it is perfectly pure, is clean; the body is smooth to the touch; the body is free of odors and defilements; the body has all thirty-two major marks of excellence; with its very broad frame, the body is powerful and well built; the gait is even and balanced; the eyes are clear and free of defilement; the body is extremely smooth, lithe, and youthful; the flesh is not sunken or dull; the flesh is extremely well developed and full-bodied; the body is very firm and taut, not flabby or sagging; the fingers, toes, and limbs all have the proper length and thickness, not protruding or bulbous, and are fully extended; the vision is perfectly clear and free of any visual impairment; the waist and buttocks are rounded and even; the waist and hips are distinct and curved; the waist is not overly long, and the hips are balanced; the belly is flat, neither too high nor too low; the navel is deep and long; the navel's design coils to the right; every aspect of the conduct is elegant and beautiful; body, speech, and mind are always engaged in pure conduct; the body is free of moles and discoloration; the hands are soft as cotton balls; the lines on the palms are lustrously clear; the lines on the palms are deep and visible from a great distance; the lines on the palms are long; the face is evenly shaped and not overly long; the lips are as red as a bimba fruit and shiny; the tongue is agile and supple; the tongue is slender and delicate as a lotus petal; the tongue is red; the voice is deep and thunderous; the voice is melodious, agile, and soft; the incisors are round; the incisors have sharp points; the incisors are white; the incisors are neither too long nor too short; the incisors are tapered from top to tip; the nose is high and prominent; the nose is immaculate and free of mucus; the eyes are long and wide; the eyelashes are thick; the eyes, like lotus petals, are beautiful and perfect; the eyebrows are connected and long; the eyebrows are soft to the touch; the eyebrows have a shiny color; the eyebrow hairs are of equal length; the hands are long and fully formed; the ears are equal in size; the faculty of the ears functions evenly when engaging with sound; the hairline above the forehead is well defined; the forehead is broad and expansive like a parasol; the hair is black and shiny like a silverstone,[16] thick and unparted; the hair is soft to the touch; the hair is untangled; the hair is smooth and streams upward; the hair has a delicious scent and is attractive to everyone; the thumbs and big toes are adorned with vajra-like endless knots; the palms and soles are adorned with square-patterned auspicious signs; and the ring fingers are adorned with seven right-spiraling svāstikas.[17] These physical characteristics are illustrations to help others understand the precious qualities of the Buddhas' inner wisdom mind, which is why they are called minor or "illustrative" marks.

The uncommon Secret Mantra Vajrayāna has its own unsurpassed tradition of major and minor marks, which consist primarily of the sixteen male Bodhisattvas, who are the manifestations of the five Buddhas' sixteen moments of wisdom, as well as their consorts, the sixteen female Bodhisattvas, who are the power of the sixteen states of Dharmadhātu. Together they make up the thirty-two major marks of excellence. Each of the sixteen male Bodhisattvas as well has the individual marks of the five wisdoms—the wisdom of Dharmadhātu, the mirrorlike wisdom, the wisdom of discernment, the wisdom of equanimity, and all-accomplishing wisdom—representative of the five Buddhas that ornament their crowns, making eighty in all.

Regarding this, Omniscient Longchenpa says:

> The sixteen female consorts do not have crown ornaments, for they represent the Dharmadhātu. Major and minor marks are assigned to them, because perfect retinues beautify and complete

the principal figure, just as the anthers and petals beautify the design of a flower.

Even though this would be the time to briefly explain the wrathful deity maṇḍala, which is the self-appearing, unobstructed power of the vajra expanse maṇḍala of the spontaneously existing peaceful Sambhogakāya, this will not be elaborated on here since it is explained in detail in the main texts of the three inner Yogatantras.

The Akaniṣṭha of the natural Nirmāṇakāya is characterized first by the appearance of five purelands of Rich Adornment in the center, Manifest Joy in the east, Endowed with Glory in the south, Lotus Mound or Great Bliss[18] in the west, and Supreme Perfect Activity in the north; second, of their five Buddhas, Vairocana in the center, Vajrasattva or Akṣobhya in the east, Ratnasambhava in the south, Amitābha in the west, and Amoghasiddhi in the north; third, of their retinues, composed of male and female Bodhisattvas abiding on the highest Bodhisattva stage, or bhūmi;[19] fourth, the teachings they give do not manifest in words, as in the common and uncommon Mahāyāna teachings, but only manifest from the tips of the light rays emitted from their mouths and tongues; and fifth, merely by seeing the stainless mirrorlike wisdom form of Buddha that reflects with brilliant clarity whatever residual obscuration remains in them, the retinue achieves realization, their obscurations are purified, and they attain unsurpassed enlightenment.

The Nirmāṇakāya's Akaniṣṭha of the Pure Abodes is characterized by the fact that its realm, palace, and so forth are made entirely of pure light and adorned with inconceivable varieties of ornaments and designs. Here, the Buddha, resplendent with the precious qualities of the thirty-two major and eighty minor marks of excellence, reveals his form and subdues his retinue, composed of infinite gods, siddhas, and powerful mantra holders, with the teachings of many vehicles, such as Kriyāyoga, Upayoga, and Yogatantra.

It was just such a Buddha, who, with the precious qualities of the Three Kāyas,[20] while never wavering in the three times from the timelessness of Dharmadhātu, took compassionate birth in this world for a brief time to benefit others. Here is how it happened.

The Coming of Buddha Śākyamuni

Many eons ago, when Buddha Mahā-Śākyamuni, an earlier Buddha, came to this world, our Teacher, Buddha Śākyamuni, was born as a potter's son named Luminous One.[21] He made a flower offering of parasols, sandals, and five hundred cowrie shells and said:

> Sugata, may I attain a body,
> Retinue, life span, purelands,
> And excellent noble marks
> Exactly the same as yours.

This was how supreme bodhicitta arose in his mind, which was the first step.

Then, during the first of three countless eons, he developed the powerful strength of the two accumulations[22] and attained the paths of accumulation and joining by relying on the empowering conditions of 55,000 Buddhas, such as Vināyaka Dhṛtarāṣṭra. During the second of these countless eons, he made offerings to 66,000 Buddhas, such as Vināyaka Sādhukāra, and progressed from the first to the seventh Bodhisattva bhūmi.[23] During the third of these countless eons, from the time of Buddha Dīpaṃkara to Buddha Kāśyapa, he developed his accumulation of virtue from 77,000 Buddhas[24] and actualized the three pure Bodhisattva levels.[25] Thus, gathering the accumulations over three countless eons was the second or middle step.

Finally, he manifested full and perfect Buddhahood. According to the philosophical views of the Śrāvakas, such as in the main texts of the Sthavira school and others, our Teacher, the Fourth Guide [of the 1,002 Buddhas of this fortunate eon],[26] was a gifted individual in his final ordinary lifetime before attaining enlightenment. The scriptures of the Bodhisattvayāna, one of the causal Vehicles of Characteristics,[27] assert that Buddha Śākyamuni first attained Buddhahood in Akaniṣṭha and then attained Buddhahood in this world.

As it says in the *Fully Enlightened Buddhahood Sūtra of Dharma and Enjoyment*:

> Beautifully adorned with various gems,
> The sublime realm of Akaniṣṭha, joyous and delightful,
> Exists above the pure abodes.
> It was there that the perfect Buddha attained enlightenment,
> And here in this world, his emanation attained Buddhahood.

By way of a brief summary, from the *Dharma History of the Early Translation School*:

Here, according to the view of the unsurpassed essence of absolute truth, our Teacher, Buddha Śākyamuni, has been liberated in the wisdom of self-awareness and fully enlightened in the basis of primordial space since beginningless time. In the pureland of luminous Dharmatā, in the nature of the indivisible Kāyas and wisdoms, without ever wavering from the one taste of the wisdom mind of all Buddhas, infinite Tathāgata Nirmāṇakāya emanations manifest for the benefit of sentient beings. Through their infinite enlightened activity that establishes beings at the three stages of enlightenment,[28] they subdue beings, each according to his or her unique karmic destiny. As it says in the *Tantra of the Adornment of Wish-Fulfilling Jewels*:

> Having reached Buddhahood before anyone,
> Victorious Vajra Holder of the Great Secret,
> You manifest in infinite purelands,
> Time and time again, countlessly, at all times,
> Appearing in infinite peaceful and wrathful forms,
> As hunters, prostitutes, and so on,
> Benefitting beings in various ways.
> And even now, in this fortunate eon,
> You will be a thousand Guides,
> Likewise assuming various forms,
> To benefit countless beings.

Also, it is said in the *Guhyagarbha: The Root Tantra*:

> The awareness beings, who are the six Buddha Munis[29] called the Blessings of Great Compassion, emerge from the wisdom body, speech, and mind of the Tathāgata. When they emerge, each of these great Buddha Munis benefits the five types of beings[30] through the four ways of subduing beings,[31] in each of the infinite, limitless, billionfold universes in the ten directions[32] of the six worlds[33] of beings who, due to their karma, move with their heads held horizontally, such as animals; beings who move with their heads upright, such as humans, asuras, and gods; and beings who move with their heads positioned downward, such as pretas and hell beings.

Such descriptions are found not only in the tantras of the Secret Mantrayāna but also in the profound sūtras, with which these teachings accord. The *Sūtra of the White Lotus of Sublime Dharma* says:

> During the unfathomable billion eons
> That never, ever end,
> I will attain supreme enlightenment.
> Also, I will always teach the Dharma.

As it says in the *Sūtra of the Meeting of Father and Son*:

> Great Hero, skilled in means,
> In order to fully ripen sentient beings,[34]
> For a billion eons,
> Victorious One, you have manifested as Buddhas.
> Again and again, O Guide,
> You will reveal yourself as many more Buddhas.

To further classify these Nirmāṇakāya emanations, which appear according to beings' phenomena, it says in the *Ornament of the Mahāyāna Sūtras:*

> Countless emanations of Buddha
> Are held as Nirmāṇakāya.
> The perfection of the two benefits[35]
> Abides in the omniscient Buddha.
> Through creations, chosen rebirths, and great
> enlightenment,
> Ceaselessly revealing enlightenment,
> The Buddha's Nirmāṇakāya form
> Is the great means for perfect liberation.

As explained, Nirmāṇakāya emanations arise infinitely as reflections of various animate and inanimate forms, yet they are said to be mainly synthesized into the three categories of creations, chosen rebirths, and supreme emanations. Of these three, as to the ways in which a supreme Nirmāṇakāya emanation reveals enlightened activities, the *Root Tantra of Magical Infinity* says that beings are benefitted through four ways of subduing: through the great merit of wisdom body, starting from the moment the supreme Nirmāṇakāya emanation enters the womb until displaying parinirvāṇa; through awareness of wisdom speech, revealing limitless Dharma teachings; through the direct realization of wisdom mind, the total omniscience that results from the six clairvoyant realizations;[36] and through inconceivable wisdom miracles revealing infinite body, speech, and mind emanations in various forms that precisely accord with beings' needs, which is the performance of enlightened qualities and activities.

Regarding the activities of subduing through the great merit of wisdom body, the way in which the Nirmāṇakāya Buddha Śākyamuni reveals his enlightened activities is inconceivable so it cannot be identified with certainty in a limited way, through numbers or anything else. Also in the Mahāyāna sūtras, there are variations in the number of these activities, and one should not try to find any contradictions. Here, considering how Buddha benefitted this world primarily through the twelve deeds of a Buddha,[37] *Unsurpassed Continuity* says:

> Without ever wavering from the Dharmakāya,
> By the varied nature of Nirmāṇakāya emanations,
> You take actual rebirth,
> Descend from Tuṣita Heaven,
> Enter the womb and are born,
> Become skilled in the arts,
> Delight in the company of royal consorts,
> Develop renunciation and practice austerities,
> Proceed to Bodhgayā,
> Defeat Māra's armies and become fully enlightened,
> Turn the Dharma Wheel of enlightenment,
> And pass into parinirvāṇa.
> Such deeds will be revealed
> In all impure realms
> As long as saṃsāra remains.

So it is.

In the sūtras, it also states:

> Our own Guide, Buddha Śākyamuni, took birth in the excellent realm of Tuṣita Heaven as a devaputra, son of the

gods, named Sublime Svetaketu, and taught the Dharma to the gods while residing there with them.

Here is a brief summary from this account. Lord Buddha, the Blessed One, took birth in Tuṣita Heaven in the form of the great Bodhisattva Svetaketu, and from a Dharma throne he gave teachings to the gods. While he was there, from the sound of celestial music came this verse:

With your vast accumulation of one hundred merits, powerful remembrance,
Infinite intelligence, brilliant sublime knowledge,[38]
Incomparable strength, and vast ability,
Please consider the prophecy of Dīpaṃkara.[39]

This story, from long ago when Buddha Śākyamuni in the form of Svetaketu developed supreme bodhicitta and Tathāgata Dīpaṃkara made his prophecy, spontaneously resounded from celestial music. Buddha Śākyamuni [as Svetaketu] then appointed Maitreya as his regent and looked upon this world of Jambudvīpa,[40] where beings must rely on karma. He looked upon a time when many were deeply weary and disillusioned, wrong views were minimal, teaching the Dharma would be meaningful, and life spans were 100 years. Even though Buddha had no pride whatsoever about race or class, ordinary individuals were strongly fixated on these distinctions. During that time, royalty was held to be superior, so he looked upon the race known as the Ikṣvakus. He then looked upon his future father and mother, the parents of all Buddhas of the fortunate eon. His father was King Śuddhodana, and his mother was the sublimely beautiful Queen Māyādevī. These five are known as the five visions.[41] Then, as praised in traditional Brahmin Vedas, Buddha assumed the form of a white elephant with six tusks, and on the full moon of the fourth lunar month, he entered Queen Māyādevī's womb through the right side of her body, while she was engaged in poṣadha purification.

After residing in her womb for ten months, symbolic of the ten Bodhisattva stages, Buddha was born in the Lumbinī Grove from his mother's right side, causing her no pain. As soon as he was born, he took seven steps in each of the four cardinal directions, to indicate that his mind was turned toward the path of the four boundless wishes: loving-kindness, compassion, joy, and equanimity. Every place he set his foot, a lotus bloomed. The earth quaked, and brilliant light rays were pervasive. He spoke the words "I am supreme in this world . . ."[42] and so forth, and the gods offered this praise:

Supreme Among Humans, when you were born,
You took seven steps upon this great earth,
Proclaiming, "I am supreme in this world."
Homage to you, O Wise One!

Also at that time, King Mahāpadma of Magadha had a son named Bimbisāra, King Brahmadatta of Kośala had a son named Prasenajit, King Nabhika Ananta of Takṣilā had a son named Pradyota, and King Śatānīka of Vaiśālī had a son named Udāyana. Thus, four princes were born in the four surrounding kingdoms. At the same time, 500 young Śākya boys, including Prince Siddhārtha's half brother Nanda; 800 girls, including Prince Siddhārtha's wife Yaśodharā; 500 attendants, including Candaka; and 500 supreme steeds, including the All-Knowing Kanthaka, Prince Siddhārtha's horse, were also born. The Bodhi Tree at the center of the continent, along with 500 gardens and 500 treasuries, also came into being, effortlessly fulfilling all of King Śuddhodana's wishes. As a result, he named his son Siddhārtha, meaning "Fulfillment of All Wishes." Since he was seen as capable of outdoing the other young Śākyas, he was called the Capable Śākya.

Then the baby was shown to a Brahmin astrologer, who prophesied that if Siddhārtha chose not to renounce worldly life, he would become a universal monarch,[43] whereas if he chose to renounce worldly life, he would become a Buddha. At the time, in the direction of Mount Meru, there lived an ascetic named Kāḷadevala, also known as Asita, who, upon seeing various extraordinary signs through his clairvoyance, used miraculous means to reach the king's palace. There, after examining the prince's marks and signs, he determined that the earlier astrologer had been mistaken and said:

In these times of strife, he shall not become a universal monarch.
This Supreme One, victorious over all faults,
Shall become a self-arisen Buddha for the benefit of beings.

Seven days after Siddhārtha's birth, his mother passed away. Thereafter, he was entrusted to the care of thirty-two nursemaids, including his aunt Mahāprajāpatī Gautamī,[44] who raised him. In the presence of Viśvāmitra and Rakṣasavarma, among others, he learned reading and writing, archery, sports, and so forth, and excelled in the arts. His cousin Devadatta and his half brother Nanda challenged him to an archery contest, in which they were to shoot through seven banana trees with a single arrow, then seven iron bricks, and then seven iron pots. The Bodhisattva Prince Siddhārtha pierced all sets of seven targets. He was unrivaled in all sixty-four skills of a Bodhisattva, including elephant riding and swimming across great rivers like a swan.

He then took Gopa, Yaśodharā, and Mṛigajā as his wives, each with a retinue of 20,000 attendant women, and all of these 60,000 sublime ladies served as his royal consorts. With them, he partook of the illusory pleasures of the senses. In the words of Omniscient Jigme Lingpa [1729–1798]:

> Without being conquered by the lasso of ordinary desire,
> To please your sole, honorable father,
> You watched the magic of the queen from your magic point of view.
> I prostrate to you, the one who succeeded in ruling your kingdom.[45]

As this praise explains, Prince Siddhārtha took great pleasure in his retinue of royal consorts, until one day the power of his prayers from previous lifetimes was awakened and the sound of cymbals filled him with renunciation. With Candaka as his charioteer, he visited the four directions of the city to console himself, but there he clearly saw the four great rivers of human suffering,[46] which sent him further into despair, and he resolved to renounce his kingdom. After removing the barrier of his parents' disapproval, he mounted his horse, Kanthaka, and the Four Great Kings[47] reverently appeared from the sky. Then Siddhārtha rode before the Stūpa of Great Purity[48] and cut off his hair. He exchanged his fine linen clothing for saffron robes, thus discarding all the signs of a householder. From Ārāḍa Kālāma and Udraka Rāmaputra, he learned the samādhi of nothingness and the samādhi of the peak of existence.

When King Śuddhodana learned that his son had gone off wandering without any servants, he dispatched 300 attendants. Likewise, when the Śākya king Suprabuddha[49] heard this, he sent 200 attendants, bringing the total to 500 attendants. From each hundred, one attendant was selected to remain—Kauṇḍinya, Aśvajit, Bhadrika, Vāṣpa, and Mahānāma—and the rest returned home. These five attendants would later become the Buddha's first disciples.

The six of them, master and friends, then went to the banks of the Nerañjanā River and undertook six years of meditative austerities. For each of the first two years, they had one grain of rice a day; for each of the next two years, they had one drop of water; and for each of the final two years, they had nothing at all. Finally, for the benefit of all beings, the Buddhas, male and female Bodhisattvas, and gods throughout the ten directions awakened him from the lower path and urged him to seek the essence of enlightenment. In order to relieve his fatigue and exhaustion, he accepted a little solid food, and when his five friends witnessed this, they lost faith in him and left for Vārāṇasī.

Siddhārtha then set out for Bodhgayā in Magadha. Along the way, a Brahmin girl named Sujātā offered him a bowl of milk, the pure quintessence of 500 cows, sweetened with vital honey, and his body instantly shone like a polished gold door bolt.

He then accepted a handful of kuśa grass from a grass seller named Sotthiya and proceeded to Bodhgayā, the Vajra Seat[50] spontaneously arisen from the blessings of all Buddhas. In the shade of a bodhi tree, he spread the kuśa grass as a mat and sat on top of it with crossed legs. Then he made this vow:

> Even if my body should wither away,
> Even if this heap of skin and bones should fall apart,
> Until I reach the enlightenment I have sought for eons,
> I will not move from this seat.

At dusk, he settled into the concentration that conquers all māras, so that the māras were intimidated and humbled. When the moment came for the fruit of many eons of accumulated merit and wisdom—the actual attainment of full enlightenment—and Siddhārtha asked the Earth Goddess Tenma[51] to bear witness to this truth, Māra, the Evil One, became deeply humiliated[52] and returned to his abode, where he summoned his billion-strong legions of māras. As they advanced for battle, Buddha settled into the concentration of great love, and their rain of sharp weapons fell as a rain of soft, delicate flowers. Their raucous curses became melodious praises, and the Evil One and his vicious armies were completely defeated. Then the Evil One's seven daughters disguised themselves as ravishingly beautiful women with deeply passionate expressions, but when they tried to seduce the Buddha, he blessed them, and they turned into seven hideous hags. Filled with remorse, they begged his forgiveness, whereby his great, desireless compassion restored them to their former selves.

The moment of manifest enlightenment had come. In the middle of the night, he reached the meditation of the fourth samādhi.[53] In the early dawn, with divine vision and stainless clairvoyance, he reached a perfect understanding of the Four Noble Truths[54] and attained complete and perfect Buddhahood. The earth quaked violently, and all dualistic elements without exception were purified into the space of the clear light Dharmakāya, the central channel free of dualistic extremes. This caused a full eclipse of the moon, and Rāhula and Ānanda were also born at this time.[55]

Seven weeks after the Buddha's enlightenment, two merchants named Trapuṣa and Bhallika offered him honey, and because of that, the Four Great Kings offered the Buddha four begging bowls made of materials ranging from precious gems to stone. As a sign of his renunciation, Buddha accepted the bowl of stone and spoke words of auspiciousness. Because the profound nectar of the Holy Dharma, which cannot be understood through conceptual analysis, is not the domain of intellectuals, Buddha spoke this verse:

> I have found a very profound, peaceful, free-from-mental-activity
> Unconditioned luminosity, a nectarlike Dharma.
> Even though I teach this for all, no one will understand,
> So I'd better stay silently under the leaves of the forest.

Buddha then displayed the manner of one who lives at ease. Brahmā, remembering Buddha's earlier aspirations, went before the Tathāgata, scattered sandalwood powder, and said:

> Sun of Speech, why do you now rest in evenness?
> Please beat the great drum of the Holy Dharma!
> Please blow the conch of the Holy Dharma!

Then Brahmā summoned Indra, who came bearing a right-spiraling white conch and precious jewels. He offered this to the Buddha, saying:

> Just as the full moon has escaped from Rāhu,[56]
> Capable One, your heart has been completely liberated.

Please arise, Victorious in Battle.
Please shine your light of wisdom on the darkness of the world.

But Buddha refused and thought, "If Brahma made repeated requests to teach, he would perfect the great accumulation of merit and wisdom." Again, Brahma offered Buddha a thousand-spoked golden wheel with a verse requesting the Buddha to turn the Wheel of Dharma. Buddha accepted the wheel and spoke thus:

Brahmā, for the beings of Magadha
Who are endowed with ears, faith, and sublime knowledge,
And spend their lives listening to spiritual teachings,
I will open the door of amṛta.

As soon as this was spoken, the sound of the words "the Tathāgata will turn the Wheel of Dharma!" was heard all the way to Akaniṣṭha, and the gods arrived bearing multitudes of offerings. Buddha knew that his former teachers Ārāḍa Kālāma and Udraka Rāmaputra would be worthy recipients of his teachings, but they were no longer alive. Recalling his former aspirations and remembering the Five Noble Ones,[57] Buddha set off for Vārāṇasī [to teach them]. There the Five Noble Ones said in disgust, "The monk Gautama is not being diligent, is eating so much, and has fallen from his renunciation!" They were determined not to show him any respect.

On the road [to Vārāṇasī], Buddha met a babbling Brahmin named Upajīvaka, who asked, "Gautama, from whom did you take your vows?"

Buddha replied:

I have no teacher.
There is no one like me.
I alone have reached perfect Buddhahood.
In this coolness, I have exhausted all defilement.

When Buddha had answered three such questions, he continued on to Vārāṇasī. Just as the sun's brilliance outshines all other stars, the Five Noble Ones found themselves unable to withhold respect when Buddha approached. Seeing Buddha as an equal, they said, "Living One, Gautama, your faculties are clear and your skin is completely pure! Isn't that an indication of your wisdom realization?"

The Buddha replied, "Do not address the Tathāgata as 'Living One,'[58] or you will suffer for a long time. I have found amṛta. I have reached Buddhahood. I have gained omniscience."

With this, Buddha dispelled whatever doubts and confusion they had. In that place [where all the thousand Buddhas of this fortunate eon first turn the Wheel of Dharma], 1,000 jeweled thrones appeared. Śākyamuni bowed in homage to those belonging to the three previous Buddhas and sat down resplendently upon the fourth throne. Instantly, the other thrones disappeared from view. For the Five Noble Ones, joined by 80,000 gods, Buddha turned the Wheel of Dharma of the Four Noble Truths, repeating each one three times, in twelve aspects.[59] The Five Noble Ones thus spontaneously received full ordination and became the great Saṅgha, the assembly of fully ordained monks, peerless throughout the world. The entire retinue perceived the truth. Buddha went on to teach the Vinaya of the Vinaya Piṭaka, which mainly revealed the higher training of moral discipline with the detailed classifications of nonvirtue resulting from violating Buddha's instructions and by naturally nonvirtuous actions; the Sūtra of the Vinaya Piṭaka, with its detailed classification of samādhis; and the Abhidharma of the Vinaya Piṭaka, with its elaborate explanation of the higher training of sublime knowledge, and so forth.

Then, at the excellent place of Vulture Peak[60]—before an extraordinary retinue composed of an assembly of about 5,000 Arhats, including Śāriputra and Maudgalyāyana; 500 fully ordained nuns, including Queen Mahāprajāpatī Gautamī; an assembly of male and female lay practitioners, including the householder Anāthapiṇḍada[61] and the laywoman[62] Sagama; and an enormous number of Bodhisattvas residing on the higher bhūmis, including Bhadrapāla, Ratnasambhava, and Jaladatta—Buddha Śākyamuni turned the Wheel of Dharma of the Absence of Characteristics, known as the intermediate set of teachings. Here Buddha taught the Vinaya of the Sūtra Piṭaka, the detailed classifications of the Bodhisattva's trainings or discipline; the Sūtra of the Sūtra Piṭaka, the profound and vast samādhis; and the Abhidharma of the Sūtra Piṭaka, all the many divisions of the levels, paths, dhāraṇī mantras, and samādhis.

In the various places of gods, nāgas, and other beings, Buddha addressed an ordinary fourfold retinue composed of fully ordained monks and nuns and male and female novices, along with innumerable gods, nāgas, and Bodhisattvas, teaching them the Vinaya of the Abhidharma Piṭaka, containing the undemanding and easily applied skillful means for subduing the passions; the Sūtra of the Abhidharma Piṭaka, on the entry into the absolute nature; and the Abhidharma of the Abhidharma Piṭaka, which contains various divisions and subdivisions, including the aggregates,[63] elements, sense sources, and consciousnesses, as well as the naturally pure sphere of Buddha nature.

In summary, these are renowned as the Three Turnings of the Wheel of Dharma, which are heard in stages by those who understand gradually and are heard immediately by those who understand all at once. The limitless Dharma classifications, stages of the vehicles, methods of taming, and distinctions of earlier or later teachings are all infinite manifestations and expressions arising from the inconceivable secret of Buddha's wisdom speech. As Buddha says in the *Sūtra of the Ornament of Qualities*:

> I say nothing at all,
> Yet sentient beings perceive infinite teachings.
> When beings wish to proceed gradually,
> That is exactly how it happens for them.
> Those who wish to proceed all at once
> Perceive all the categories of the Dharma in their entirety.
> The fulfillment of all hopes and wishes
> Is the greatness of wisdom speech.

Thus, through an infinite ocean of Dharma methods, Buddha made the support for the path, the path, and the result of the path vividly manifest for all sentient beings.

Then, with the wisdom thought of performing his final deed, Buddha journeyed to the city of Kuśinagarī. There, from the throat of his glorious wisdom body, pleasing to behold, a sneeze came forth, and Queen Mahāprajāpatī Gautamī prayed, "May Buddha remain with us for three incalculable eons!" Her prayer resounded from the Earth all the way to Akaniṣṭha, and all who heard it repeated the prayer.

At this, the Tathāgata said, "Queen, because you failed to say, 'May the teachings endure for a long time!' this created a condition of obstacles to accomplishing Dharma for many lazy beings." In order to beg his forgiveness, the Queen, along with 500 female Arhats, passed into nirvāṇa.

Around that time, Śāriputra and Maudgalyāyana journeyed to the hell realms and encountered the nihilist teacher Pūrṇa Kāśyapa, who was experiencing the full ripening of his karma. He made this request: "When you return to the world, please give my followers the message that our doctrine is terribly wrong and they should follow the Buddha!" Heeding his request, Śāriputra delivered the message, but because he had no karmic flesh debts,[64] they did not hear him.

Afterward, when Maudgalyāyana said, "Your late master is languishing in the Hell of Ultimate Torment and sent you this message," they screamed, "This man is not only condemning us, he is condemning our master and teachers, too! Get him!" And they beat him to a bloody pulp, as if they were thrashing reeds. Wrapping him in his Dharma robes, Śāriputra carried him to the town of Shingtakchen. He knew that Maudgalyāyana would not survive, and said, "If even hearing that my friend is dying is unbearable, how can I stand to witness it?" He then left for Glorious Nālandā. The next morning, Śāriputra and 80,000 Arhats passed into nirvāṇa. In the evening of that same day, Maudgalyāyana and 70,000 Arhats passed into nirvāṇa. Like a fire that has run out of firewood, many other Arhats as well entered parinirvāṇa.

Then the Tathāgata entrusted the care of his teachings and fourfold retinue to the elder monk Mahākāśyapa. Taking off his upper robe, Buddha said, "Monks, gaze upon the Tathāgata's body. It is rare to gaze upon a Tathāgata, as rare as seeing an uḍumbara flower![65] Monks, do not speak. Like this, all that is compounded is destructible." With this cause for renunciation, Buddha encouraged lazy beings to practice the Dharma.

Then, reclining on the ground between two sal trees, Buddha passed into parinirvāṇa. Mahākāśyapa then came from the realm of the nāgas. When he prayed to the precious body, it spontaneously began to burn, and the precious remains disintegrated. They were divided into eight portions according to particular karmic fortunes and housed in eight reliquary stūpas.

The Three Councils

In this way, the Buddha's teachings were entrusted to the Sixteen Great Arhats, and to the Seven Patriarchs of the Teachings, including Mahākāśyapa. The Sixteen Arhats were Panthaka, who lives in the Heaven of the Thirty-Three;[66] Abhedya in the Land of Snows [Tibet]; Kanaka on the western continent, Bountiful Cow [Aparagodaniya]; Bakkula on the northern continent, Ominous Sound [Uttarakuru]; Bhāradvāja on the eastern continent, Noble Body [Pūrvavideha]; Mahākālika in Tāmradvīpa; Vajraputra in Sri Lanka; Rāhula in Priyangudvipa; Śrībhadra on an island in the Yamuna River; Gopaka on Mount Bihula; Nāgasena on Mount Vipulaparṣva; Vanavāsin on Mount Saptaparṇi; Cuḍapantaka on Vulture Peak; Kanakavatsa in Kashmir; Aṅgaja on Mount Kailash; and Ajita in Ṛṣi Crystal Forest. Each abides with a large retinue of Arhats. In China, during the reigns of Emperor Taizong of the Tang dynasty, Kublai Khan, and the Yongle Emperor, some say the Arhats actually appeared, visible to everyone. Others say that the common folk could not see them, their bodies being rainbowlike. As it says in the *Biography of Joyous Countenance*:

> Wherever a new temple of the Three Jewels[67] is constructed, the Sixteen Great Arhats will send their emanations to bless it. Finally, when human life spans extend to 600 years, they will gather in the central land,[68] make offerings to the Buddha's reliquaries, and pass beyond sorrow into pure space where nothing remains.

On the other hand, the Seven Patriarchs came gradually. Mahākāśyapa was born in answer to a prayer made to the god of the nyagrodha [banyan] tree by his father, the Brahmin Nyagrodhaketu, and was thus called Nyagrodhaja [Banyan-Born] or Kaśyapa, his family caste name. Kaśyapa entrusted the teachings to Ānanda, the son of Buddha's paternal uncle Amṛtodana. Ānanda entrusted them to Śāṇavāsika, who in turn entrusted them to Monk Upagupta, the son of Guhya, an incense seller. He entrusted them to Ārya[69] Dhītika, who in turn entrusted them to Ārya Kṛṣṇa. Ārya Kṛṣṇa entrusted them to Sudarśana and entered final nirvāṇa.

There are varying opinions as to how the teachings spoken by the Buddha—the holy Dharma—were compiled. According to the common vehicles, there were what are called the Three Councils.

Not long before our guide, Buddha Śākyamuni, passed on, Śāriputra with 80,000 Arhats, and Maudgalyāyana with 70,000 Arhats, passed beyond suffering. Then, the Blessed One himself entered nirvāṇa with 80,000,000 Arhats, and at that time, the gods scoffed, "All the mighty monks have passed into nirvāṇa and the Holy Dharma is nothing more than smoke left from a dead fire. There is not even any sound of the Tripiṭaka[70] coming from the monks!" To dispel this criticism, in Rājagṛha, at the Nayagrodha Cave during the summer rainy season retreat, in the year following the parinirvāṇa of the Buddha, with King Ajātaśatru as the patron, Upāli compiled the Vinaya Piṭaka, Ānanda compiled the Sūtra Piṭaka, and Mahākāśyapa compiled the Abhidharma Piṭaka, in their entireties. The gods exclaimed in praises made to be heard all the way to the Akaniṣṭha Heaven, "The gods shall increase! The asuras shall diminish! The teachings of Buddha shall long endure!"

One hundred and ten years after the First Council was convened, the fully ordained monks of Vaiśālī were engaging in the ten points, or transgressions [in *Minor Transmissions of the Vinaya*]:

> Allowing *hulu hulu* and rejoicing,
> That which everyone uses, pot, and salt,
> Road, two fingers, stirring, and mat,
> And gold.
> These are held to be the ten transgressions.[71]

In order to rid the Saṅgha of this corruption, 700 Arhats, such as Yaśas, gathered together under the patronage of the Buddhist emperor Aśoka, and eradicated the ten points. They performed one entire recitation of the Tripiṭaka and also held a restoring and purifying ceremony for harmony and propitiousness.

Beginning with the reign of King Vīrasena, who was the great-grandson of Dharma Emperor Aśoka and the son of Vigataśoka, monks appeared one after another who were blessed by demons: Mahādeva, Bhadra, the elder Nāga, and Sthiramati. In five points they proclaimed this false doctrine:

> Arhats can respond to others, be unknowing,
> Have doubts, rely upon others,
> And take care of themselves.
> This is the Buddha's teaching.

Because of that, disputes were caused among the Saṅgha during the reigns of four kings—the last half of King Vīrasena's life, the entire lifetimes of both Nanda and Mahāpadma, and the first half of Kaniṣka's life. Since the Buddha had not given permission for the Vinaya to be put into writing, after many years passed, differing styles of reciting the *Prātimokṣa Sūtra* caused the Saṅgha to split into eighteen divisions. It happened like this: The elder monk Nāga caused more disputes, which caused the Mahāsāṃghikas, Sthaviras, and Saṃmitīyas to split off from the Mūlasarvāstivāda tradition, thereby forming four main divisions. Later, Sthiramati caused an extensive dispute, and the four divisions gradually split into eighteen. Apparently, the Mūlasarvāstivāda split into seven divisions, the Mahāsāṃghika into five, and the other two into three each. After that, when the disagreements among them had receded somewhat, the schools existed on their own with King Kaniṣka as the patron of a Third Council. There they proved that all eighteen schools were pure by quoting a passage from the *Sūtra of Kṛkin's Prophetic Dream* that reads:

> The complete and perfect Buddha Kaśyapa said to Kṛkin, "Your Majesty, in your dream you saw eighteen men pulling on a sheet of cloth. This means that the teaching of Śākyamuni will be split into eighteen schools, but the cloth of perfect liberation itself will never be ruined."

On that occasion, they wrote down the Vinaya Piṭaka, as well as Sūtra and Abhidharma texts that had never been written down before. Those that had been written down previously were revised. This was the significance of the Third Council.

This account is not reported in *Minor Transmissions of the Vinaya*, so opinions vary. According to the Kashmiri schools, the council was convened in the Karṇikavana Temple in Kashmir by 500 Arhats, including Ārya Pārśva; 400 fully ordained monks, including Vasumitra; and 500 Bodhisattvas. The majority of Indian scholars maintain that the council of 500 Arhats and 5,000 venerable monks convened in the Kuvana Temple of Jālandhara Monastery. The best-known Tibetan account says that 500 Arhats and either 500 or 16,000 Bodhisattvas gathered and convened the Third Council some 400 years after the Buddha's parinirvāṇa. Based upon what is said in the *Flame of Dialectics*, "Two hundred years after the Buddha's parinirvāṇa, the elder Vātsīputra compiled the teachings," the 400 years from the Tibetan account seems to have counted each six-month solstice as one year. However, if that 200-year time period is compared with the succession of kings, 200 years does not seem to be too short, but further research is needed. Also, there are many locations given for the council, such as Śrāvastī, Kusumakūṭārāma in Jālandhara, and Kuvana Monastery in Kashmir.

The Spread of the Mahāyāna Teachings

According to the uncommon tradition of the Mahāyāna, the *Flame of Dialectics* says:

> The Mahāyāna was taught by the Buddha, as evidenced by the fact that the original compilers were Samantabhadra, Mañjuśrī, Vajrapāṇi, Maitreya, and others.

In the *Sūtra of Inconceivable Secrets*, Vajrapāṇi is named the compiler of the teachings of the thousand Buddhas. An early annotation says that one million Bodhisattvas assembled on Vimalasvabhāva Mountain, south of the royal city of Rājagṛha, where it is known that Maitreya compiled the Vinaya, Mañjuśrī the Sūtras, and Vajrapāṇi the Abhidharma. Also, in the Mahāyāna Sūtra Piṭaka, it says that the sections on the Profound View were compiled by Mañjuśrī and those on Vast Conduct by Maitreya.[72]

After the Buddha's parinirvāṇa, countless sublime beings who were like Buddha came to guard the teachings: great Śrāvakas, a gathering of Arhats such as Uttara and Yaśas, a community of fully ordained monks such as Kāśyapa, a community of great Brahmins such as King Sujaya and Kalyāṇa, and many others. All of these glorious masters who came and served the teachings were learned, pure, and kind, and attained immeasurable qualities of realization. Even so, according to the Śrāvaka followers of the Sautrāntika school, the true charioteers of the *Śāstra* tradition[73] had to have been the Arhats who composed the *Great Treasury of Detailed Explanations*. But according to the Mahāyāna, they were Maitreyanātha and Nāgārjuna, and this is because all other commentators relied upon śāstras that followed the traditions established by these two.

In accordance with the Buddha's own prophecies, the charioteer of the Profound View tradition was none other than the Second Buddha, Nāgārjuna, the disciple of the Great Brahmin Saraha. He was prophesied by the Buddha in the sūtra *Gone to Laṅka*:

> In the southern land of Vidarbha,
> The famous Glorious Monk, Śrīman,
> Called by the name Nāga,
> Will destroy the extremes of existence and nonexistence.
> He will teach my vehicle in this world,

The unsurpassed vehicle.
Attaining the level of Supreme Joy,
He will go to the pureland of Great Bliss.[74]

Also, the *Root Tantra of Mañjuśrī* says:

When four hundred years have elapsed
After I, the Tathāgata, pass beyond,
The monk called Nāga will appear.
He will have faith in and benefit the teachings.
He will attain the level of Supreme Joy
And live for six hundred years.
The Peacock Queen of Awareness, Mahāmāyūrī,
Will be realized by this Great Being as well.
He will realize the meaning of many śāstras,
The truth of insubstantiality.
When the time comes to cast off his body,
He will be reborn in the pureland of Great Bliss.
Finally, in the state of absolute certainty,
He will attain perfect Buddhahood.

Such was the prophecy about the coming of Nāgārjuna, the founder of the tradition of the Profound View, or the Middle Way free of extremes.

Four hundred years after the Buddha's parinirvāṇa, in the South Indian kingdom of Vidarbha, there lived a Brahmin of high caste who was as wealthy as a king but had no son. One night, the Brahmin dreamed that the gods prophesied that if he invited one hundred Brahmins to a religious feast, a son would be born to him. Accordingly, he offered a great feast, and ten months later a beautiful young son was born. The sound of "Nāgārjuna" resounded from the heavens, so that is what he was named. The baby was shown to a soothsayer, who said, "Though he has noble marks, this child will not live for more than seven days."

"Is there nothing we can do?" the parents asked.

"If you invite one hundred Brahmins for a feast, he will live for seven months. If you invite one hundred monks for a feast, he will live for seven years. Beyond this, there is nothing to be done," the soothsayer replied.

His parents followed the instruction, and as Nāgārjuna's seventh birthday approached, knowing they would be unable to bear the sight of their son's corpse, they sent the boy and his servants away on a long journey. Eventually, he arrived at the door of Rāhulabhadra, the abbot of Nālandā University. There Nāgārjuna recited the Vedas, and the abbot called him inside and questioned him. The boy gave an explanation and the abbot asked, "Are you able to take monastic ordination?"

"I am able," the boy replied, and he was ordained. His Yidam deity was found to be the Peacock Queen, Mahāmāyūrī, and the night before his seventh birthday, he chanted her long-life dhāraṇī all night long and accomplished[75] the deity. Thus, the auspicious circumstances for a lifetime of six hundred years were aligned. Nāgārjuna attained the common accomplishments and in the presence of the abbot, he received full ordination. Ārya Mañjuśrī took him under his care, and Nāgārjuna became a supreme scholar in all fields of study.

After that, the abbot undertook a twelve-year retreat, during which he entrusted the care of the Saṅgha to Nāgārjuna. Once during that period, Nāgārjuna failed to offer a meal to Śrī Virūpa, and as a result, a terrible twelve-year famine ensued. The majority of people perished, but Nāgārjuna was able to sustain the Saṅgha by making gold through alchemy and selling it. With that, he was able to protect them from harm.

When the abbot finished his retreat, he saw heaps of human bones and asked, "What has happened?" Nāgārjuna explained how he had protected the Saṅgha from harm. The abbot replied, "You need not have done that. I have a much better skill!" He milked a drawing of a cow and received an inexhaustible supply of milk. "You have established a wrong livelihood for the Saṅgha," he told Nāgārjuna. "To purify this negativity, you must build one hundred and eight monasteries and ten million stūpas."

Almost everyone says that Nāgārjuna was exiled from Nālandā at that point. But this is not correct, since it ignores the fact that not long after that, the abbot undertook the fearless conduct of a yogin and became known as Saraha, and he entrusted the abbotship of Nālandā to Nāgārjuna. Nāgārjuna guarded the teachings there for a long time afterward.

Gelong Deje composed a major text called *Ornament of Awareness* in 1,200,000 lines, which defeated the views of everyone, both Buddhist and non-Buddhist, and he in turn was subdued by Ācārya Nāgārjuna, who defeated them all in debate. Ācārya Nāgārjuna constructed 108 monasteries and entrusted them to 108 Dharma Protectors.

One time, when Ācārya Nāgārjuna gave the Dharma teachings, two young boys came. Watching where they went afterward, the Ācārya saw that they went underground. When he questioned them, they said, "We are nāgas." Nāgārjuna asked them to bring him some mud from the land of nāgas, which they agreed to do. The two boys put this request to Nāga King Takṣaka, who invited Nāgārjuna to come as a doctor to cure his ills. Nāgārjuna, recognizing a special purpose, went there and cured the Nāga King's illness. In gratitude, the Nāga King brought the section of teachings called the *Prajñāpāramitā* and offered it to Nāgārjuna, requesting him to return in the future. Accepting the scripture, Nāgārjuna promised to return after he had constructed ten million stūpas, and the Nāga King retained the last part of the *Prajñāpāramitā* as a security. Nāgārjuna constructed nearly all the stūpas using mud from the land of the nāgas, but there was not enough mud [to complete them all].

In Bodhgayā, Nāgārjuna built a stone wall with latticework encircling the Bodhi Tree. Swayambhunath and other stūpas are also counted among his legacies. The Nepalese say that Nāgārjuna went to the land of nāgas from Swayambhunath.

Beginning with the development of bodhicitta, which is great compassion adorned with nondual wisdom and is the primary cause for the arising of the Tathāgatas' wisdom, Nāgārjuna eventually gained irreversible realization of the nature of sublime knowledge. Through the five sciences,[76] he brought his disciples to perfect ripening. According to the Sūtra tradition, Nāgārjuna attained the eighth Bodhisattva level[77] within his lifetime. In particular, he elucidated the *Prajñāpāramitā*, which had been like a nugget of gold lying in darkness, with his *Collection of Discourses*, *Collection of Logical Arguments*, *Collection of Hymns*, and *Collection of the Natural State*. His main disciple was Śākyamitra, to whom he entrusted the care of Nālandā University before departing for Śrī Parvata.[78]

In addition, this master's writings include his famous *Collection of Six Texts on Reasoning*, consisting of *Root Verses on the Middle Way Called "Sublime Knowledge," Refutation of Objections*, *Seventy Stanzas on Emptiness*, *Sixty Stanzas on Reasoning*, *Crushing to Fine Powder*, and *Precious Garland*.

Lord Maitreya's disciple was Noble Asaṅga [4th–5th c.], who spread the tradition of Vast Conduct throughout Jambudvīpa.

The holy teachings of the Abhidharma experienced enemy opposition on three occasions in India. First, an old lady with tīrthika[79] views said, "I heard the word 'Conquer!' resound from the Buddhist gong. We must find out if they are planning to harm us!" They investigated this and heard:

> By beating the gong of the Three Jewels,
> Venerated by gods, nāgas, and yakṣa spirits,
> The deranged brains of tīrthikas are smashed to pieces.

When they realized this, they drew up their armies and suppressed the teaching.

When the teaching had reemerged and spread to some degree, the king of Central India [Magadha] sent the king of Persia a gift of clothing made from seamless cotton fabric. There was a footprintlike image on the heart area. After seeing this, the Persian king said, "They cast an evil spell on us," drew up his armies, and suppressed the teaching.

After that, when the Dharma had once again reemerged and spread to some degree, a beggar with tīrthika views arrived at a Buddhist temple to beg for alms. When he was sprinkled with ablution water at the temple, he became enraged. He accomplished the practice of worshipping the deity Sūrya, and then he burned the temple to the ground, suppressing the teaching.

At that point, a Brahmin girl named Prasannaśīla thought to herself, "The root of the Buddha's teaching is the Abhidharma, and enemies have thrice attacked and suppressed it. I don't see anything that will enable it to spread. I, being female, am also unable to do anything. If only I could give birth to a boy who would spread the teaching!" From her union with a Kṣatriya, Asaṅga was born, and from her union with a Brahmin, Vasubhandu was born. As soon as they were born, she wrote AH syllables on their tongues with yellow pigment, and she trained them until their minds were sharp and clever. When they were fully grown, they asked, "Mother, what work do our fathers do?" Their mother answered, "That is not why you were born. Study hard and spread the teaching of the Abhidharma."

She sent the younger brother, Vasubandhu, to Kashmir to study with Saṅghabhadra. The elder brother, Asaṅga, thought to himself, "I shall meditate on Buddha Maitreya and spread the Mahāyāna Abhidharma," and he went to a cave on Kukkuṭapada Mountain. He practiced for three years without achieving a single sign of success. Saddened, he came outside. There sat an old man rubbing an enormous iron bar with a soft cotton cloth.

"What are you doing?" Asaṅga asked him.

"I'm making a needle," he replied.

"How can you possibly make a needle from a solid iron bar with a soft piece of cotton?" Asaṅga asked.

The man replied:

> For those with courage and determination,
> There is nothing that cannot be achieved.
> If one never gives up, no matter the difficulty,
> Even mountains can be reduced to dust.

At this, Asaṅga thought, "I only stayed for a short time," and he practiced for another three years. That yielded no signs either, so he came back out. This time he saw a boulder being eroded by drops of water, so he practiced for another three years. Still there were no signs. When he emerged a third time, he saw a man wearing away a boulder with a pigeon feather, so he practiced for another three years. Yet even after twelve years of practice, he did not experience any signs. Utterly dejected, he left his cave. He then encountered a dog with her hindquarters crawling with maggots. The dog tried to bite him as she dragged herself along on her forelegs. Seeing this, he was overcome with compassion and thought, "If I clean her wounds, the maggots will die. If I don't, the dog will die. I'll cut some flesh from my own body and let the maggots eat that." He made his way to the town of Ajanta, giving his monk's staff as a guarantee in order to borrow a golden razor, and sliced a piece of flesh off his body. Fearing that he might kill the maggots if he removed them with his fingers, he shut his eyes and bent down to remove them with his tongue. The dog vanished, and in its place stood Lord Maitreya in a sphere of light.

Seeing him, Asaṅga cried reproachfully:

> Alas, Sole Father, my refuge!
> I faced so much pain, yet I had no results.
> Why is it that your massive ocean of rain clouds
> Leaves me sweltering and thirsty?
> I have practiced so hard—how unkind of you to give me no signs!

Lord Maitreya replied:

Even if the king of gods showers down rain,
Rotten seeds will not sprout.
Likewise, even when the Buddhas come,
Those lacking merit will not experience their excellence.

Maitreya continued: "I have been with you from the beginning, yet your obscurations prevented you from seeing me. The great compassion you just felt washed away your obscurations, and now you can see me. If you don't believe me, carry me on your shoulder and show me to people."

Asaṅga carried him to the middle of the marketplace and showed him to people. One old lady whose karma had been slightly purified saw the corpse of a dog on his shoulder, and everyone else saw nothing. Asaṅga then believed him.

"What do you need?" Maitreya asked him.

"Please, I would like to spread the Mahāyāna," Asaṅga replied.

"Hold on to my robe," Maitreya said, and they journeyed to Tuṣita Heaven. It is said that Asaṅga stayed there for one mealtime of a god, which is about fifty or fifty-three human years. According to the annotations in Asaṅga's *Treatise on the Yogācāra Levels*, he stayed and received teachings for six months. While there, he received the *Prajñāpāramitā Sūtra*, the *Levels of Yogic Practice*, numerous Mahāyāna sūtras, and the *Five Treatises of Maitreya*. The famous *Five Treatises of Maitreya* consist of *Ornament of Manifest Realization*, *Ornament of the Mahāyāna Sūtras*, *Unsurpassed Continuity*, *Distinguishing between Dharma and Dharmatā*, and *Distinguishing between Middle and Extremes*.

When Asaṅga returned to the human world, he composed numerous works, including his *Five Treatises on the Yogācāra Levels*, containing *Treatise on the Yogācāra Levels* and so on, that systematize the Mahāyāna Tripiṭaka, as well as his two collections [*Mahāyāna Samucchaya* and *Abhidharma Samucchaya*][80] and others. This master attained the Samādhi of the Dharma Stream. As it says in the *Commentary on the "Earlier Bhūmis"*:

Homage to Asaṅga, who, to benefit the entire world,
By the power of his Dharma-Stream Samādhi, drank the amṛta of Dharma
Poured from the vase of Lord Maitreya's mouth

Into the cupped hands of his ears.
Homage to he who partook of this.

That is his story.

Ācārya Dignāga [480–540], founder of the tradition of reasoning by the power of fact, was taken under the care of Mañjuśrī and attained the special accomplishment of perfect victory in all directions. He was of the Brahmin caste and received ordination from Jinendra, an abbot of the Vātsīputrīya school. He trained to mastery in the worldly sciences, such as grammar and logic, and requested from the abbot oral instructions on meditation for abandoning the passions.

"Meditate on the inexpressible nature of the self, which is neither the aggregates themselves, nor other than the aggregates," the abbot said.

Dignāga meditated accordingly, and finding no self, he wondered if perhaps this self was obscured by inner or outer circumstances. He lit four butter lamps in the four directions, stripped himself naked, opened his eyes wide, and searched everywhere, yet still he could not find a self.

A friend witnessed this and told the abbot.

"Why are you doing that?" the abbot asked Dignāga.

"I'm searching for the self," Dignāga replied.

"You are disproving your own doctrine, so you should leave," the abbot said.

"Logic can certainly disprove it, but that's not appropriate," Dignāga thought to himself, and he left for Nālandā. He apprenticed himself to Vasubandhu and became learned in the three yānas. Dignāga was particularly skilled in Mind Only [Cittamātra] philosophy and logic,[81] on which he composed 108 separate śāstras. In the wake of Vasubhandhu's passing, Dignāga stayed on the face of Mount Vindhya with the intention of combining his miscellaneous śāstras. He wrote this verse with alabaster on the wall of his cave:

Always truthful, with the wish to benefit beings,
Prostrations to the Teacher, the Bliss-Gone Buddha,[82] the Protector.
In order to establish logic, I shall hereby combine
All my miscellaneous writings into one.

Instantly, many amazing signs occurred: the earth quaked, lights shone, loud sounds resounded, and tīrthika teachers were paralyzed with fear.

Nearby, there lived a tīrthika teacher named Munīndrakṛṣṇa [Tubgyal Nagpo]. Using his slight clairvoyance, he looked and discovered that it was Dignāga's power that had caused these omens to occur. "What is this all about?" the tīrthika wondered. Looking, he saw that Dignāga's great śāstra would harm the tīrthikas. When Ācārya Dignāga went out for his alms round, Munīndrakṛṣṇa went and erased the verse. Twice he did this, and when Ācārya Dignāga had written it for a third time, he added these lines at the end: "Who is erasing my verse? If it is for fun and jest, please don't! There is a vast need for it. If it is out of jealousy, know that it is within my mind, so you cannot erase it. If you think the words and meanings are confused, come here in person and debate me!"

Once again, as soon as Dignāga had finished writing, the amazing signs occurred as before. Munīndrakṛṣṇa came to erase it, but when he saw the words "debate me!" he refrained and sat down to wait. When Ācārya Dignāga returned from his alms round, the two met and placed a wager with each other to hold three debates [agreeing that the loser should renounce his position]. Ācārya Dignāga won all three of these. However, he was still unable to convert the tīrthika teacher to Buddhism.

Finally, fire erupted from Munīndrakṛṣṇa's mouth and burned up Ācārya Dignāga's supplies and possessions. The Ācārya thought, "If I cannot tame even one tīrthika, how can I possibly tame all sentient beings? As soon as this chalk hits the ground, I shall abandon my bodhicitta!" and he threw it to the ground.

Lord Mañjuśrī appeared in the sky and said, "Son, don't do that, don't do that! Exposure to the lower vehicles will only increase negative understanding. The tīrthikas cannot harm your śāstra. Until you have reached the Bodhisattva levels, I shall be your spiritual guide. In future times, this will become the sole eye of all śāstras." This is the famous wisdom permission[83] Dignāga received. Accordingly, Ācārya Dignāga combined all his writings on valid cognition, as *Compilation of All Teachings on Logic*, and composed an autocommentary on it, thus thoroughly defeating all tīrthikas. Dignāga's principal disciple was Paṇḍita Īśvarasena, who also wrote a commentary on *Compilation of All Teachings on Logic*.

As such, the Glorious Protector Nāgārjuna, Noble Asaṅga, and Ācārya Dignāga are known as the "three authors of fundamental texts."

Nāgārjuna's disciple was Ācārya Āryadeva. Āryadeva was born about 500 years after the Buddha's parinirvāṇa in a lotus grove belonging to King Pañcaśṛṅga. He appeared miraculously in the form of an eight-year-old child.

It is said that because it was not appropriate for him to be touched by those who were born from the womb, Āryadeva was wrapped in the folds of pañcalika[84] silken brocades and received into the world. On the road, the boy asked, "Where is Ārya Nāgārjuna?"

"He is still staying in Jambudvīpa. He does not live in this region," they replied.

The king took him as his son and cared for him for many years. Āryadeva grew up quickly. He begged his parents for permission to take ordination in the presence of Nāgārjuna, which they granted. He traveled to Śrī Parvata and took monastic vows. He meditated on the Lord of Speech, Protector Mañjuśrī, and became extremely learned in all Buddhist and non-Buddhist scriptural traditions.

At that time, in South India, a son named Maticitra [Aśvagoṣa] was born to a Brahmin named Varyamavyitakraya. From a young age, the boy did whatever his mother asked. Since he acted like a servant to his mother, Maticitra was called Makhol, "Mother's Servant." After being fully educated in the tīrthika tradition of Śiva, Maticitra left for western India and settled near the Maheśvara Temple. Vowing that he would not get up until he received the siddhi of becoming an all-victorious supreme debater, he lay down by the pool in front of the temple and recited the mantra of Maheśvara [Śiva] for seven days.

On the morning of the eighth day, Śiva appeared to him in a vision and asked, "What special attainment do you wish?"

"Please, I would like to be all-victorious in debate," Maticitra replied.

"I can bring about defeat for those who took womb birth, but if someone has taken miraculous birth, it will be extremely difficult." Śiva then summoned Brahmā to the scene and ordered, "When this person engages in debate, you must turn yourself into a parrot scholar and help him." He summoned Viṣṇu and said, "You must turn yourself into a chalk scholar[85] and help him." He summoned the goddess Umā and said, "You must turn yourself into a sister scholar and help him." Then he promised Maticitra, "I myself will enter your body and make you victorious." Maticitra went south and east, defeating everyone in debate, both Buddhist and non-Buddhist, except for those of his own sect, the tīrthika Śiva worshippers. He converted everyone to his beliefs.

Maticitra returned home to see his mother, who was offering a maṇḍala to the goddess Tārā. She venerated the followers of the Buddha. "Where are others who practice in this way?" he asked her.

His mother wondered if Maticitra could be subdued by the learned paṇḍitas living in Central India. She replied, "In East and South India, the number of Buddha's followers are like the hairs in the mane of a white horse. In Central India, there are as many as there are hairs on a horse's body."

"I will defeat them all," he thought. In the middle of washing his feet, he stopped and set off in the direction of Nālandā.

When he was nearly there, he came to a fork in the road, where a girl named Sapadini sat eating a piece of fruit. "Which road leads to Nalandra?" he asked her.

"Ignorant, uncivilized man who cannot speak our language, it is pronounced *Nā-lan-dā*." She showed him the way, and his hair stood on end. She was an emanation of the goddess Tārā. He went in that direction and arrived at the glorious Nālandā University, known in Tibetan as Gyunter, "Continuously Giving." There were fourteen large temples, eighty-four smaller temples, and numerous consecrated holy objects, with 500 scholars surrounded by many Mahāsiddhas. Not one of them was able to successfully debate him. Every morning, Maticitra came among the monks and tapped his own head with a stick. "Monks, where did this head come from? When I stand on the threshold, am I going out or coming in?" he asked. Holding a bird in his hand, he asked, "Will it die or not?"

No one could answer him.

At this, the monks met and decided, "No one but Nāgārjuna living on Śrī Parvata can defeat this man in debate." They all understood how extremely far away Nāgārjuna lived and how difficult it would be to get there. One night, the abbot dreamed of a large black man who said, "The tīrthika blessed an acacia-wood dagger with one hundred thousand recitations of Kṣitigarbha's mantra and placed it on the top of my head, so all my power has been crushed. To remove the curse, you must chant the mantras of Cakrasaṃvara and Mahākāla many times and perform ablution, so that a raven will come out of my heart center. Tie your letter of invitation around its neck, and it will fly to Śrī Parvata to invite Nāgārjuna."

The abbot did as he was instructed, and everything happened just as it was foretold it would. On a banana leaf, he wrote:

> Alas! Is your flawless Mahāyāna practice being disturbed by your focus on individual liberation only?
> There is no one more capable than you are—swiftly pull the chariot with the sunken wheels!

All of us are fatigued by the burden too difficult to bear at this time,
and even the best among us are praying to you.
It is your responsibility to protect the gods and humans long residing
in this place, so please shoulder the burden!

He tied the message around the raven's neck, and the raven flew away and landed on Nāgārjuna's torma offering table. It croaked and caught Nāgārjuna's attention. Āryadeva untied the message and read it. They understood that a tīrthika teacher had debated the Buddhists at Nālandā, and they were requesting Nāgārjuna to come defeat him. "I will go," Nāgārjuna said.

"If this is something I can do, I will go," Āryadeva said. "Ācārya, please do not worry."

In a trial debate, Ācārya Nāgārjuna took the tīrthika position and Āryadeva took the Buddhist position. Āryadeva won and shouted, "Take that, you evil tīrthika!" and threw his sandal at the Ācārya. When Āryadeva regained his senses, he was filled with remorse and asked to be punished.

"No wrong has been done," said Ācārya Nāgārjuna.

"I will do whatever you ask," Āryadeva insisted.

"Well, then, along the way to Nālandā there are a hundred thousand tīrthika Śiva devotees. Defeat them and convert them to Buddhism," Ācārya Nāgārjuna said.

Along the way, Āryadeva met a blind tree goddess and offered her one of his eyes. Then, in accordance with the Ācārya's orders, he debated groups of Śiva devotees, defeated them, and converted them to Buddhism. Then, at Nālandā, he stuffed his clothing into his begging bowl and hid the begging bowl inside a bundle of wood. He covered his body with ashes, disguised himself as a wood seller, and walked along beside a cowherd. There stood the tīrthika teacher Maticitra, who was not allowing any Buddhists to leave or any tīrthikas to enter the monastery. Āryadeva said, "I am a wood seller. If you don't let me in, I will starve." At that, Maticitra allowed him to pass.

Once inside, Ācārya Āryadeva took out his Dharma robes and begging bowl and said, "Ācārya Nāgārjuna has not come. His disciple Āryadeva has come and is here before you." The Nālandā residents were overjoyed and welcomed him with parasols, victory banners, and all manner of musical instruments.

In the morning, they offered him a large bucket of water for bathing and fifty grams of butter for massage. Āryadeva returned three liters of water and half the butter, saying, "I am so reluctant to waste the belongings of the Saṅgha." At this, they realized that he was a Bodhisattva skilled in means.

Ācārya Āryadeva sat down at the end of the row of monks, and Maticitra arrived and repeated his earlier questions. Āryadeva took him by the hand and said, "This head comes from your neck."

Maticitra said, "Hey, this one-eyed man wasn't here before!"

At this, the Ācārya replied:

> Indra is endowed with a thousand eyes, yet he does not see the true essence.
> Rudra is endowed with three eyes, yet he does not see the true essence.
> Brahmā sees the world, yet how could he possibly see the true essence?
> Āryadeva has just one eye, and with it
> He sees the true essence of everything throughout the three planes of existence.

Maticitra stood upon the threshold and repeated his earlier question.

"That depends on what you want," Āryadeva replied.

At that, Maticitra said, "You and I shall have a debate! Whoever loses shall abandon his position."

Next to the debating arena, seats were set up for the witnesses to judge the defender and the challenger. Āryadeva gathered oil, a cat, a naked black Brahmin, and rotten leather in preparation. The witnesses included the king, three Buddhist scholars, and three tīrthika scholars, and a large assembly gathered to cheer the victor and insult the loser.

When the time came for the debate to begin, Maticitra transformed his chalk into a chalk scholar who could answer any question. But because Āryadeva had rubbed oil on the brick courtyard, the chalk made no marks. Then Maticitra brought forth the parrot, and the cat broke its neck. At this, he said to Āryadeva, "Evil will come to you!"

Āryadeva replied, "I know a great meditator in Śrī Parvata who will purify this sin for me."

"If he purifies sin from there, will your sin be purified?" Maticitra demanded.

"In that case, if a cat kills a parrot, will any evil come to me?" Āryadeva challenged.

Maticitra had no reply. He brought forth the sister scholar, but when the naked black Brahmin pursued her, she was embarrassed and ran away.

Maticitra, unable to win the debate, hoped that Śiva would enter his body, but he did not. Knowing he would lose, Maticitra looked up and saw the rotten leather beneath the parasol. He tore it off and threw it away, whereupon Śiva entered his body and the debate continued. At the beginning, those gathered there could understand. In the middle, they could understand only a fraction of what was being said. In the end, the material they debated had never been heard before, so that even when Ācārya Āryadeva won, no one realized it.

Maticitra transformed himself into Indra with a thousand eyes, and the Ācārya transformed himself into Avalokiteśvara with a thousand arms and eyes and overpowered him. Maticitra made flames erupt from his mouth, and the Ācārya brought forth water from his feet and extinguished it. The Ācārya was praised as the victor, and Maticitra said, "Your witnesses are slanted! You need to debate this Śiva-devotee cowherd!" Hoping that the cowherd would take his side, the Ācārya hypnotized the cowherd with the sound of a fife and was pronounced the victor once more.

Maticitra tried to flee into the sky, but Āryadeva chased after him, saying, "Do not fly too high! There is a wind called Sword that will slice your body to bits!"

"How do you know?" said Maticitra.

Āryadeva replied, "Cut off a piece of your dreadlocks and throw it upward!"

When Maticittra did this, his hair exploded into tiny particles. Seeing this, Maticitra was terrified and returned to the ground. Had he not done so, he would have gone higher and higher until he reached the realm of Brahmā. Back on the ground, the king caught and imprisoned him, along with his retinue, in an enclosed chamber on the roof of the palace. Maticitra thought of killing himself.

Maticitra opened a single volume of scripture to an explanation of the great benefits of reciting Acalā's ten-syllable mantra. "That much benefit is not feasible," he thought.

Just as that thought arose in him, Acalā's deity form appeared before him and said, "You still do not believe the truth of Dharma?" He slapped him across the face, and Maticitra fell down unconscious. When Maticitra regained his senses, he untied many volumes of scriptures and gradually read through them. When he came across the sūtra on the prophecies of Makhol,

Maticitra realized that he was the disciple described in the sūtra. Great faith in the Buddha's teachings arose in him, and he asked Āryadeva to grant him ordination. Āryadeva took him to Ācārya Nāgārjuna, in whose presence he became ordained. His powerful knowledge of tīrthika logic and linguistics enabled him to learn the major Buddhist texts with almost no difficulty, and he became a very learned scholar.

Then, one night, Maticitra dreamed that a Ḍākinī sitting by the roadside in a Bengali city would bless him. He traveled there and found an old woman on the verge of death, gasping for air. When he prostrated to and circumambulated her, she gave him her excrement and urine and told him to eat it. She floated up into the sky and transformed into a cat-faced Ḍākinī. Her lice and lice eggs transformed into bone ornaments. She granted him her blessing, and all at once he perfectly understood all the teachings of the vehicles of Buddhism and the non-Buddhist schools simultaneously. He is known by many names, including Bhavila, Sura, and Aśvagoṣa, among others.

As such, Ācārya Sura's, or Aśvagoṣa's, teacher was Ācārya Āryadeva, who composed numerous clear explanations, such as the *Four Hundred Stanzas on the Middle Way*, and vastly spread the teachings.

Asaṅga's younger brother, the prodigious scholar Ācārya Vasubandhu [4th–5th c.], learned 9,900,000 verses of scripture by heart and thus crossed the ocean of learning. Due to the power of his aspiration to spread the Abhidharma teachings, he left at a young age for Kashmir to study with the great Ācārya Saṅghabhadra. There he trained in the sciences in general and specifically in the Abhidharma, focusing on works composed by Arhats such as Upagupta, who wrote the *Great Treasury of Detailed Explanations*, and on the seven sections of Abhidharma,[86] and so on. These he learned without difficulty, and he prepared to return to India. On the way, a Kashmiri tax collector seized the sacred objects he was carrying and sent him back three times. When he had nothing valuable left to confiscate, since they could not take away the Dharma that was in his mind, Vasubandhu was permitted to pass and travel to Nālandā.

When Vasubandhu learned that his elder brother Asaṅga had composed numerous śāstras, he said:

> Alas! Asaṅga spent twelve years
> In the forest practicing samādhi.
> Failing to accomplish it, he created a doctrine
> With enough volumes to load up an elephant.

When his elder brother heard that Vasubandhu was rebuking the Mahāyāna and its followers, he knew that Vasubandhu's practice had been wrong and in vain. In order to reverse this, Asaṅga had two of his disciples memorize the *Dhāraṇīs of the Ten Bhūmis* and the *Sūtra of Inexhaustible Intelligence*. Asaṅga then told them to recite these two in the vicinity of Vasubandhu, at dusk and dawn, respectively.

Upon hearing their recitations, Vasubandhu said at dusk, "This Mahāyāna has an excellent cause, but the result seems a little scattered."

At dawn, he said, "Both the cause and result are excellent, and my tongue is responsible for blasphemy. Cut it off!"

When he began searching for a razor, the two disciples cried, "You do not need to destroy your tongue. Your brother has the means to purify this obscuration. We can go to him."

Vasubandhu agreed and went with them. He listened extensively to Asaṅga's teachings, and during the elaborate teachings and discussions, the younger brother was quick-witted, while the elder brother was extremely slow but had excellent responses.

"How do you come up with such excellent answers? Is there a reason for that?" Vasubandhu asked.

Asaṅga replied, "You have been a scholar for five hundred lifetimes, so you were born with superior intelligence. I don't have such an intellect, so I actually asked my Yidam deity for the answers, and he responded."

"Will you please show me your deity?" asked Vasubandhu.

"I will ask Lord Maitreya," replied Asaṅga. This is the message he received:

> You are an ordinary being, and because you have slandered the Mahāyāna, you lack the fortune to see me in this lifetime. In order to purify your obscuration, compose numerous sūtra commentaries. Recite the mantra of Uṣṇīṣavijayā[87] and in your next life you will see me.

At this, Vasubandhu's faith in his elder brother grew even stronger, and he said:

> My elder brother is like a nāga.
> I am like a bird wishing for rain.
> Even when the Nāga King sends down rain,
> It does not enter the bird's throat.

In order to accomplish what Maitreya had said, Vasubandhu rewrote his *Treasury of Abhidharma* as a root text in verse and sent it to Saṅghabhadra, whose disciples exclaimed, "For shame! He's insulting our philosophy by using critical phrases such as 'It is merely said to be so'!"

Saṅghabhadra replied, "No, he is adept at composing śāstras. His words are like adornments!" Saṅghabhadra was extremely pleased, and he himself wrote a commentary consistent with the sūtras.

Ācārya Vasubandhu served as abbot of Nālandā University, and also continued to uphold the Mahāyāna Abhidharma teachings after Asaṅga passed away. Because he was able to memorize 9,900,000 verses of scripture and recite them continuously for twelve days while covered in oil, Vasubandhu was renowned as a Second Buddha.

After Vasubandhu composed the *Treasury of Abhidharma* in verse, he wrote an autocommentary on it and sent it to Saṅghabhadra, who was greatly upset. "Now I will defeat him with quotations and logic, and make him erase this with his own hands," Saṅghabhadra said, and he set out for India, surrounded by monks whose radiant saffron robes cast a golden hue on the sky.

When Vasubandhu heard about this, he announced, "Ācārya Saṅghabhadra is versed in the Vaibhāṣika school of philosophy, so he will be difficult to convince. Even if he is defeated, it is meaningless. I will go instead to see the self-arisen stūpa in Nepal."

Accordingly, Vasubandhu entrusted Nālandā to Śrī Dharmapāla and left for Nepal. Soon afterward, Saṅghabhadra arrived at Nālandā and passed away there at the age of 300. As soon as Vasubandhu, who was 200 years old, reached Nepal, he saw someone named Hadu dressed in monk's robes yet disregarding his vows and lifting a pitcher of beer. Witnessing this, Vasubandhu was filled with sadness. He recited the Uṣṇīṣavijayā mantra backward and passed away. Upon his passing, a stūpa was built.

Glorious Dharmakīrti [ca. 600–660], who instantly made all tīrthikas lose their confidence, was a disciple of the disputant Īśvarasena, who in turn was a disciple of Dignāga. Dharmakīrti was born into a tīrthika Brahmin family in South India, in the kingdom of Cūḍāmaṇi. He became thoroughly learned in language at a young age. His maternal uncle was a tīrthika teacher named Kumārila, who had a young consort. Dharmakīrti took ordination from his uncle, but his uncle disparaged him in many ways and forced him to leave.

Dharmakīrti thought to himself, "I shall bring about the defeat of all tīrthikas." He took Buddhist ordination and began his training. In particular, when he first heard teachings on logic from Ācārya Īśvarasena, Dharmakīrti's understanding became equal to his. When Dharmakīrti received the same teachings for a second time, his realization became equal to that of Dignāga.

When Dharmakīrti requested the same teachings a third time, Ācārya Īśvarasena said, "Dignāga had no other student like me, and I have no other student like you. There is no precedent for teaching this more than once, and I have already taught you twice. It is not enough for me to only give this teaching. I must engage in other activities as well, so prepare an oil lamp and I will teach you this evening."

Dharmakīrti did as he was told. He gained a vivid understanding of results in relation to particular causes, and when he explained all this to the Ācārya, he was immensely pleased. "Now, with my mistakes as the basis of your refutation, write a commentary on *Compilation of All Teachings on Logic*," the Ācārya said, granting his permission.

Then, in order to understand the secret language of Sāṃkhya dialectics, Dharmakīrti disguised himself as a servant and attended his maternal uncle's wife, pleasing her with his service.

"I need you to ask your husband some questions about the key points of Sāṃkhya philosophy," Dharmakīrti said.

"I will ask him while we're making love, and you memorize the answers," she said. So Dharmakīrti tied a string to her foot and lay down beneath their bed. Whenever something was difficult to understand, he tugged on the string, prompting her to seek clarification until he became well versed. When he had extracted all the key points and knew he had fully mastered them, he ran away.

He made a public announcement that all learned tīrthika scholars should come debate him, and most of them fled elsewhere. Those who did engage him in debate were soundly defeated and converted to the Buddhist doctrine. As it is said:

> If the sun of Dharmakīrti's
> Speech were to set,
> The Dharma would either sleep or die.
> Anti-Dharma beliefs would eventually rise up.

This master was a yogic practitioner of Cakrasaṃvara who ultimately attained the Greater Khecara[88] within his lifetime. He was prophesied in the *Mañjuśrī Root Tantra*:

> The renunciate monk called by the letter DHA,
> Renowned [kīrti] in the south,
> Will not only defeat his opponents
> But will also accomplish Secret Mantra practice.

In summary, Āryadeva, Vasubandhu, and Dharmakīrti are known as the "three commentators."

Guṇaprabha [7th c.], singularly learned in the Vinaya, was Ācārya Vasubandhu's disciple, born into a Brahmin family in Central India. He attended the fully ordained monk Vasubandhu, and when he had crossed over the oceans of learning in his own and others' doctrines, his faculty of sublime knowledge fully blossomed with the distilled nectar of the Vinaya, the Dharma of the Sugatas. Guṇaprabha became the crown jewel of all the noble Sarvāstivādin Vinaya holders who diligently accomplished the essence of the Tathāgata's holy teachings. King Śrī Harṣa of Central India, recognizing him as supreme among all scholars, relied upon him as his royal court guru. Guṇaprabha composed the *Vinaya Sūtra* and *One Hundred and One Formal Ecclesiastical Acts*. He lived and sustained the Buddha's teachings for 400 years.

In *Prabhāvati* [*Luminosity*], Śākyaprabha [8th–9th c.] writes:

> My teacher, who resided in Magadha and gained renown as its ornament,
> Is Puṇyakīrti, from whom I heard the Vinaya teachings.
> I composed this commentary on my own Vinaya ritual text
> With threefold knowledge,[89] revealing it as a basis for studying the Vinaya.

Also:

> With the wish that my guru, Śāntiprabha, who lives far away and is extremely renowned,
> Will hold me in his compassion, I have written this commentary clarifying the meaning.

Later, Śākyaprabha, who was the disciple of Puṇyakīrti and Śāntiprabha, composed the *Vinaya in Three Hundred Verses* root text and its commentary, *Prabhāvati*.

Thus, Āryadeva, Vasubandhu, Dignāga, Dharmakīrti, Guṇaprabha, and Śākyaprabha are known as the "six ornaments of Jambudvīpa," and Nāgārjuna and Asaṅga are known as the "two supreme ones." They are collectively referred to as the "six ornaments and two supreme ones."

Śāntideva [8th c.], one of the "two excellent masters," was a disciple of Jayadeva. He was renowned as the "great scholar with seven wondrous anecdotes":

> The pleasing of his supreme Yidam deity;
> The perfect deeds at Nālandā;
> The healing of a conflict; and the taking as disciples those with
> bizarre views,
> As well as beggars, unbelievers, and a tīrthika king.

As for the first of these:[90] Śāntideva was born in the southern country of Saurāṣṭra, as the son of King Kalyāṇavarman. His given name was Śāntivarman. Right from his early youth, Śāntideva became expertly trained in all the arts and sciences. In particular, he meditated on the *Sādhana of Keen Mañjuśrī* and beheld Mañjuśrī in a vision. After a time his father passed away, and it was decided that the royal power should be conferred on Śāntivarman, and a great throne made of precious substances was duly set in place. But in his dreams that night, the prince saw Bodhisattva Mañjughoṣa [Mañjuśrī] sitting on the very throne that he himself was to ascend the following day. Mañjughoṣa spoke to him and said:

> My dear son, this is my seat,
> And I am your spiritual friend.[91]
> You and I sharing the same seat
> Would not be right at all.

With that, Śāntivarman woke from his dream and understood that it would be wrong for him to assume the kingship. Feeling no desire for the great wealth of the realm, he departed and entered the glorious monastery of Nālandā, where he received ordination from Jayadeva, the chief of its 500 paṇḍitas, taking the name Śāntideva.

Regarding his inner spiritual life, Śāntideva received the teachings of the entire Tripiṭaka from Ārya Mañjuśrī. He meditated on them and condensed their precious contents into two śāstras: the *Collection of All Trainings* and the *Collection of Sūtras*. But though he gained boundless qualities of abandonment and realization, the other monks knew nothing of this; and since to all outward appearances his behavior seemed to be restricted to the activities of eating [*bu*], sleeping [*su*], and defecating [*ku*], they gave him the nickname Three-Thoughts Busuku. Such was their estimate of his outward conduct. "This man," they complained, "performs none of the three duties required of the monks of this monastery. He has no right to enjoy the food and alms offered by the faithful to the Saṅgha. We must drive him away!"

Their plan was to take turns expounding the scriptures, so that when Śāntideva's turn came around he would be embarrassed and run away. They then requested Śāntideva to teach the sutras, and when Śāntideva accepted they were thrown into confusion. The next day, they set up an enormously high lion throne in the midst of a large congregation of people. Śāntideva [miraculously] ascended the throne by pressing it down with his hand.

"Would you like me to recite some well-known teaching of the Buddha?" Śāntideva asked. "Or would you prefer something you have never heard before?"

Everyone was thunderstruck. "Please tell us something completely new," they said.

Śāntideva then recited the *Way of the Bodhisattva*. He came to the verse that reads:

> When tangible and intangible conceptions
> Are not appearing in the mind,
> At that time, there are no other forms.
> Aimlessness is great peace.[92]

At that moment, his body rose higher and higher into the sky, until at last he vanished altogether. His voice continued to resound until the teaching was complete, and then he departed.

Those monks who possessed perfect memory retention wrote down everything they remembered, but they produced texts of varying lengths:

some with 700 verses, some with 1,000 verses, and some with even more. Disagreement and uncertainty reigned. Moreover, they did not know the texts Śāntideva had referred to in the course of his recitation:

> Over and over again,
> Consult the *Collection of All Trainings.*

And:

> Otherwise, for a time,
> Consult the summary, the *Collection of Sūtras.*

Eventually, they learned that Śāntideva was residing at Śrīdakṣiṇa Stūpa in the south, and they sent two monks to invite him back to Nālandā. When the monks met with him, they asked about his teachings. Śāntideva told them that his *Collection of All Trainings* and *Collection of Sūtras* were hidden above a roof beam in his room at Nālandā, written in a fine paṇḍita script. He explained that his complete *Way of the Bodhisattva* was indeed 1,000 verses. He also gave them the scriptural transmissions authorizing them to study and practice these texts.

Śāntideva then traveled east, where he resolved a serious conflict and restored harmony between the contending parties.

Just west of the country of Magadha, there lived 100 holders of a bizarre tīrthika view, and Śāntideva joined their entourage. After a time, there was a terrible natural disaster, and they ran out of food and water and were tormented by misery. It was decided that whoever could gather the most alms would be appointed as spiritual master, and everyone would obey that person's command. Ācārya Śāntideva received a full begging bowl of cooked rice, and by blessing it, he was miraculously able to feed and satisfy everyone. This enabled him to turn them away from their bizarre views and guide them on the Buddhist path.

During a subsequent famine Ācārya Śāntideva provided nourishment to 1,000 beggars who were emaciated and dying of starvation, taught them the Dharma, and restored them to health and happiness.

The king of Ariviśana in the east was threatened by the villagers of Macala, who lacked sufficient resources for survival. They demanded money, saying that they would kill the king if he did not give it. Śāntideva acted as the king's bodyguard, but when the others saw that he was armed only with a wooden sword, symbolic of the sword held by Mañjuśrī,[93] they said to the king, "This man is an imposter! Look what he has in his hand!"

This enraged the king. "Take out your sword!" he commanded Śāntideva. Śāntideva declined, saying that it would harm the king if he did so.

"Take it out anyway, even if it harms me!" commanded the king.

"In that case, please cover one of your eyes with your hand and look with only one eye," Śāntideva requested.

The king did so, and Śāntideva drew his sword. It was so bright that it blinded the king's exposed eye. He begged Śāntideva's forgiveness, requested refuge, and entered the Dharma.

Then Śāntideva traveled south of Śrī Parvata Mountain and joined a group of people displaying "Ucchuṣma conduct," wandering as naked beggars who lived on food scrapings from dishes. The king of Karivihara's servant girl, Kacalaha, noticed that when she threw out the dishwater, it boiled when it touched Ācārya Śāntideva.

At the time, there lived a tīrthika teacher named Śaṅkaradeva, who appealed to the king and issued the following challenge. The tīrthika said that he would draw the maṇḍala of Maheśvara in the sky, and that if the Buddhists were unable to destroy it, then all Buddhist images and writings should be burned and the Saṅgha would be obliged to convert to his religion.

The king gathered the monks together and explained the situation, but the monks could not promise they would be able to destroy the maṇḍala. The king was deeply troubled, but when the servant girl told him what she had seen, he ordered that Śāntideva be summoned. They searched everywhere for him and eventually found him sitting under a tree. They explained the situation to him, and he assured them that he would be able to help them, telling them that they would need to prepare a vase full of water, two pieces of cotton cloth, and fire. They did as they were told.

On the evening of the following day, the tīrthika yogin drew some lines on the sky and departed. Everyone began to feel afraid. Early the next morning, he began drawing the maṇḍala, but no sooner had he finished the east gate than Śāntideva entered a profound samādhi. A great hurricane surged forth and swept everything away. Trees and towns lay flattened or were about to collapse. The people assembled there were scattered, and the tīrthika teacher was swept clean away. A great darkness fell over the land.

Then a light shone from Śāntideva's brow showing the way for the king and queen. They had been stripped of their clothes and were coated with dust. He bathed them with the water, dressed them in the clean cotton cloth, and warmed them with the fire, setting them at ease. After that, the tīrthika temples were demolished, and everyone converted to Buddhism. Even now, that region is known as the region where a false doctrine was defeated.

The Great Ācārya Buddhapālita composed *Commentary on "Root Verses on the Middle Way Called 'Sublime Knowledge,'"* on Nāgārjuna's classic work on Mother Prajñāpāramitā, according to teachings Buddhapālita received from Nāgārjuna himself.

After a while, there came a great scholar named Bhāviveka, who claimed to be a skilled professor of dialectics. He read Buddhapālita's commentary and composed a commentary criticizing it, called *Lamp of Sublime Knowledge*, with the intention of preventing the truth of the Middle Way from becoming corrupted. Previous Tibetan writers have said that Ācārya Buddhapālita and Bhāviveka debated in person and that Buddhapālita could not defeat Bhāviveka. They said that Buddhapālita prayed that he would be victorious in his next life and was reborn as Candrakīrti, who debated Bhāviveka and won, whereupon Bhāviveka became Candrakīrti's disciple. That account is not accurate at all, as Candrakīrti writes in his *Clear Words*:

> Upon seeing the commentary composed by Buddhapālita and Bhāviveka's writings in response,
> Which were all transmitted to me from the lineage that goes from one teacher to the next,
> I have thoroughly analyzed them and combined all my findings,
> Which I present here to delight those with great minds.

Ācārya Candragomin [ca. 600–650] was constantly engaged in debate with a tīrthika propounder of nihilism. Known as Paṇḍita Candra at the time, he argued that past and future lives exist, and the tīrthika argued that they do not, but the debate always ended in a draw. So Paṇḍita Candra said, "I will personally show you my future life. Next month I will die and be reborn as the son of Paṇḍita Dharma Das in the city of Vareṇdra. The sign that it is really me will be a moon-shaped mole between my eyebrows, and my name will be Candra ['Moon']. When I am seven, I shall debate you!"

That all happened, and as soon as Paṇḍita Candra was reborn, he said, "Mother, was [my birth] difficult?

"Hush!" said his mother. He obeyed his mother's word and said nothing. He was given the name Candra.

Later, in order to avoid receiving homage from the monastic Saṅgha or sitting at the head of a row of monks, Candra took vows in the Gomi upāsaka[94] tradition, whereupon he became known as Candragomin. The nihilist gave Candragomin's father a śāstra on grammar that was all mixed up and said, "If you cannot elucidate this, you must convert to our nihilist view."

Candragomin's father could not understand the text, so he asked other scholars about it and even paid some tīrthikas to explain the text, but to no avail. He memorized the most difficult points and went to ask about them, leaving the text behind. In his absence, his son arranged the text in order and read through it, adding notes as he read. When his father returned, just by looking at the text, he understood its meaning.

"Who has been here?" he asked.

"No one has been here," his wife replied. "Only our silent son."

When his father asked Candragomin, the boy pointed to his mother.

"Say something!" his mother demanded. "Why don't you ever say anything?"

"Mother, you told me to hush," Candragomin explained. "I've only been doing what you asked."

On the full moon of the following month, the day of the debate, the young boy said to his father, "Put me on your lap and let me debate."

When his father told the tīrthika to debate his son, the tīrthika retorted, "That young boy will never be able to debate me!"

To this, the boy replied:

> A lamp may be small, yet it dispels darkness.
> A hook may be small, yet it can tame an elephant.
> A boy may be small, yet he can defeat a tīrthika.
> Did I not promise you this before?

Just this was enough to shatter the tīrthika's confidence and make him speechless, and all the tīrthikas converted to Buddhism. The king of Vareṇdra came to pay homage as well and offer him his princess daughter's hand in marriage. Later, when a maid called the princess "Goddess Tārā," Candragomin realized it would be disrespectful to have a wife with the same name as his Yidam deity, so he asked for the king's forgiveness for being unable to accept the princess. Thereupon the king commanded that Candragomin be thrown in the Ganges River.

Ācārya Candragomin prayed to Tārā, and an island formed in the middle of the Ganges. He sat upon it, and it became known as Candra Island. He was rescued by a fisherman, and even the king was filled with faith and honored Candragomin as his guru.

Later, Candragomin traveled to Nālandā University and, carrying a parasol, he went to the place where Ācārya Candrakīrti was teaching the Dharma. "That person over there looks like someone who would like to debate me," Candrakīrti remarked. "Ask him what Dharma he knows."

When asked, Candragomin replied, "I know these three: *Pāṇini's Grammar*, *One Hundred and Fifty Verses of Praise*, and *Revealing the Names of Mañjuśrī*."

Realizing that this was a great scholar, the Nālandā Saṅgha asked him to leave briefly, in order to be able to welcome him properly from a distance of one league away. Candragomin thought to himself, "It is not right for a layperson like me to receive such a welcome from so many fully ordained monks." He decided to offer this welcome to the Three Jewels instead, so he asked that a statue of Mañjuśrī be placed in a chariot. Ācārya Candragomin offered praise while fanning the statue, and the statue actually tilted its head toward him to listen. That song of praise is called *Praise to Mañjuśrī with the Tilted Head*, which is considered the first of the four great praises in Jambudvīpa.[95]

While Candragomin was engaged in debate with Ācārya Candrakīrti, he responded to Candrakīrti's questions the day after they were asked. Suspecting that Candragomin was consulting with someone, Candrakīrti spied on him and found him in the Kharsapaṇi Temple listening to a statue of Avalokiteśvara, who had released his mudrā of supreme generosity and was pointing his finger and speaking.

"Will you look at that, even tenth-level Bodhisattvas are biased," thought Candrakīrti. "Ārya, quit playing favorites!" he told the statue, and it promptly stopped speaking, its finger still poised in the air.

Candrakīrti supplicated the statue with the hymn called *Praise to the Pointing Avalokiteśvara*, which is renowned as the second of the four great praises of Jambudvīpa. In the early dawn, Avalokiteśvara appeared in Candrakīrti's dream and said, "I have a special connection with Candragomin because a monk and the three of us gave rise to bodhicitta at the same time in the past, and Candragomin accomplished me as his Yidam deity. Your special deity is actually Mañjuśrī."

Avalokiteśvara told Candragomin to compose many Mahāyāna śāstras, and as a result, Candragomin wrote numerous works, including *Commentary on the "Moon Lamp Sūtra"* and *Entering the Three Kāyas*. A monk of the Kṣatriya caste became his disciple, and Candragomin was able to successfully subdue the monk's negative conduct by composing *Letter to a Disciple* and *Candra's Grammar* along with its subsidiary text.

Ācārya Candrakīrti composed a beautiful text in verse called the *Samantabhadra Grammar Sūtra*, and when Candragomin read it, he was so ashamed of his own book that he threw it down a well. The well, known as Candra Well, is always wreathed in rainbows, and whoever drinks its water pacifies their illnesses and sharpens their sublime knowledge. Avalokiteśvara said, "You wrote that book with pure intention, and it will benefit many beings. Pull it out of the well and show it to others." Candragomin's book is renowned even today.

In India, rumor had it that *Candra's Grammar* was unpopular and the *Samantabhadra Grammar Sūtra* had been widely favored, so Candragomin said, "Please make my book more popular." From that moment, the Samantabhadra book stopped circulating and Candragomin's book became widespread. At that, Ācārya Candrakīrti was filled with despair and threw his own book down a well, which also became known as Candra Well. Later, a stūpa was said to have been built on that spot.

Another time, a poor Brahmin came to Ācārya Candragomin begging for money. The Ācārya had nothing to give, but he was overcome with compassion and drew an image of Tārā on the wall. Beneath it, he wrote a song of praise to the great glorious Tārā. When he had written just over half of it, a dazzling ray of light emerged from the jewel drawn on Tārā's foot bangle and grew brighter and brighter. When he finished writing, an actual jewel emerged from the wall and dropped into his hand. He gave it to the Brahmin, thereby ending his poverty. This mural was said to contain great blessing.

The third of the four great praises is the hymn *Praise to the Tathāgata Who Surpasses Worldly Gods*, reputed to have been written by Ācārya Bhatasiddhi. In Prajñāvarman's *Extensive Commentary on "Praise to the Exalted,"* he tells of two brothers, Bhatasiddhi and Camkarapati, who realized that Buddha is supreme upon seeing Śiva make offerings to the Arhats on Mount Kailash and being instructed by Śiva to worship Buddha. When they returned to their homeland, the brothers understood that the Buddhist teachings were faultless and uncorrupted, and they cast away the words of the Vedas like straw. They took Buddhist ordination and composed *Praise to the Exalted* and *Praise to the Tathāgata Who Surpasses Worldly Gods*. Other than this, no further explanation is given.

However, in Prajñāvarman's *Extensive Commentary on "Praise to the Tathāgata Who Surpasses Worldly Gods,"* he states that Bhatasiddhi wrote the *Praise to the Exalted* in praise of Buddha Śākyamuni, and Camkarapati praised the Buddha with the *Praise to the Tathāgata Who Surpasses Worldly Gods*. Since both commentaries cite only two brothers and there is no mention of a third brother, it appears that Prajñāvarman does not want to mention that the two brothers were in fact two elder brothers who were initially Hindu devotees. The existence of a third, younger brother is clearly mentioned in authentic historical accounts of Bodhgayā, which can be understood by consulting the genuine, reliable history of the Mahābodhi Temple.

The fourth of the great praises is a hymn called *Praise to Tārā Who Holds a Flower Garland*. One night, King Lalitavajra of Kashmir dreamed of making offering tormas according to instructions given by the gods, whereby the Temple of Powerful Strength was erected in a dry lake. There, 300,000 monks made thrice-daily offerings to a stūpa, until one day, on top of the parasol crowning the stūpa, there appeared a beautiful newborn baby boy wrapped in silk. He was crying, and the monks fetched him from the top of the stūpa, knowing that he was a very special child deserving reverence. They entrusted him to the care of a nursemaid and oversaw his education. The boy became a great learned scholar and became known as Ācārya Sarvajñānamitra, "All-Knowing Friend." He extracted a sādhana from the *Hundred Thousand Verses of Tārā's Perfect Renunciation*, and when he practiced it, he was graced with a vision of Tārā herself. He gave away all his material belongings without a trace of attachment and became known as Ācārya Sarvaprada, "He Who Gives Away All." There were many beggars in need, but he had nothing left to give, so he traveled to Magadha. Along the way, he met a blind Brahmin being led by his son and daughter.

"These two have nothing with which to make a home. We are going to Kashmir to beg from Ācārya Sarvaprada," said the blind Brahmin.

"I am Ācārya Sarvaprada," the Ācārya declared, and the Brahmin fainted. The Ācārya was filled with great compassion and wished he could sell his body and give the money to the Brahmin. He sold himself to King Brahmadatta, who was planning to burn 108 servants as a sacrificial offering and needed one more human. The Ācārya received his weight in gold, which he then gave to the Brahmin, ending his poverty. The king threw the Ācārya into a pit and said, "Now that I have the full number, I shall burn all of you."

Inside the pit, everyone wailed in terror. The Ācārya, overwhelmed with compassion, recited the *Praise to Tārā Who Holds a Flower Garland*, and a rain of amṛta poured from Tārā's body, filling the pit and transforming it into a pool of lotuses. The prisoners, radiant and gleaming, appeared on top of the lotus flowers, and the king, wonderstruck, set them all free.

Soldiers surrounded the Ācārya and held him captive. Witnessing these sinful actions, the Ācārya was filled with despair and prayed to Ārya Tārā that he might return to his homeland. He grabbed hold of Tārā's silken scarves, and when he opened his eyes again, a different Kashmiri king sat upon the throne. Tārā said, "You were born as the son of this king, and immediately after your birth, as you lay sleeping in the shade of a tree and your attendants were distracted, a vulture swooped down and carried you off. Planning to eat you once you had died, the vulture deposited you on top of a stūpa. According to your prayer, I have brought you back to your homeland."

The Ācārya served as head of both temples and acted as court guru to both kings. Later, through the practice of this Tārā sādhana, many beings beheld Ārya Tārā in visions, and she saved the life of the great Kashmiri paṇḍita Śākyaśrī [Śākyaśrībhadra]. Once, there was a man who had to work as a servant to pay off a debt of 500 gold coins. He painted an image of Tārā surrounded by depictions of the Ācārya's life story, and as he worked, he recited Tārā's sādhana. One night in a dream, he received a prophecy that he would find a vase filled with pearls, which he actually did find. He was then able to pay off his debt and grow rich. There are many other stories like this of people attaining siddhis through practicing Tārā's sādhana.

Ārya Nāgārjuna and his spiritual heir, Āryadeva, are known as followers of the main Madhyamaka śāstras, and the holders of their lineage, such as Buddhapālita and Candrakīrti, are known as Prāsaṅgika Mādhyamikas, who accept relative truth according to worldly perception. Bhāviveka and those like him were Svātantrika Mādhyamikas, and in particular, Jñānagarbha and Śrī Gupta were Sautrāntika Mādhyamikas. There were also Yogācāra Mādhyamikas, such as Śāntarakṣita, Kamalaśīla, and Haribhadra. All of these Madhyamaka variations explain the view of the noble father and son, Ārya Nāgārjuna and Āryadeva.

To explain in further detail: Ācārya Candrakīrti, disciple of the Glorious

Protector Nāgārjuna and proponent of his Prāsaṅgika philosophy, was born in Mandya in South India. He had been a scholar for 500 lifetimes, and when Mañjuśrī took him into his care, his scholarship became unrivaled. Candrakīrti composed the *Catuḥśataka Ṭīkā*, a commentary on Āryadeva's *Four Hundred Stanzas on the Middle Way*, as well as what are known as his "Two *Clears*," which consist of *Clear Words*, a commentary on Nāgārjuna's *Root Verses on the Middle Way Called "Sublime Knowledge,"* and *Clear Lamp*, a commentary on the *Guhyasamāja Tantra*. The latter two are his principal works and are as renowned as the sun and moon.

While Candrakīrti was in residence at Nālandā University, all 500 resident scholars were followers of Cittamātra, the Mind Only school. He alone was a follower of Prāsaṅgika Madhyamaka.

One time, as Candrakīrti was walking out into the courtyard, he bumped his head on a stone pillar.

"You say all phenomena lack inherent existence, so surely you can make the pillar and your head nonexistent!" his companions teased.

"What pillar?" Candrakīrti asked, and he passed his hand through the pillar as if it were a ray of sunshine.

Another time, there was a huge thunderstorm, and the Saṅgha's water buffalo were scattered throughout the forest. Left without a source of milk, the monks said to Candrakīrti, "You claim that all appearances are lacking true existence yet appear as truly existing. Well, if that's the case, then draw a picture of a cow and milk it for us!" So he did. He drew a picture of a cow, milked it, and served the Saṅgha.

All told, a limitless number of spiritual teachers with mastery of the true meaning of the Buddha's teachings have come, and they have all mainly elucidated the teaching of Prajñāpāramitā.

The Vajrayāna: How the Secret Mantra Teachings Came to This World

There are varying accounts among the Early Translation and New Translation[96] schools as to how the tantras of the Secret Mantra emerged, both during the time when the complete teachings were given in the noble land of India as well as how they later spread and declined in response to particular circumstances.

According to what is known in the Secret Mantra New Translation tradition, the Buddha entrusted the tantras to King Indrabhūti of Oḍḍiyāna, although some claim that it was Vajrapāṇi who entrusted them. Whatever the case, King Indrabhūti made the tantras into a book and showed it to his people, whereupon all the living creatures in his kingdom, right down to the tiniest insect, attained spiritual accomplishments and vanished in the Rainbow Body.

Then the empty land of Oḍḍiyāna transformed into a lake, which was filled with nāgas. The Lord of Secrets, Vajrapāṇi, taught them the tantras and ripened them. Eventually, they became human beings, who settled on the edges of the lake. They put the teachings into practice and attained accomplishment. Their sons and daughters became Ḍākas and Ḍākinīs, and the place became known as Oḍḍiyāna, Land of Ḍākinīs.

In time, the lake dried up and a Heruka temple spontaneously appeared there. The temple treasury contained all the volumes of the tantric scriptures, and it was from there that future Mahāsiddhas retrieved nearly all their tantras: King Vasukalpa the *Guhyasamāja Tantra*, Nāgārjuna the *Hevajra Tantra*, Kukkuripa the *Mahāmāyā Tantra* and the *Vajrabhairava Tantra*, and so on.

Similarly, some say that Tsilupa and others brought the Kālacakra from the land of Shambhala,[97] or from various other places. Such stories abound, each with its own slight variations.

Regardless, we know that numerous Mahāsiddhas, wondrous beyond words, did appear. There were the Eighty-Four Mahāsiddhas, such as Glorious Saraha; the Twelve Masters renowned at Vikramaśīla University,[98] such as Jñānapada; the Six Scholarly Gatekeepers[99]; and the Elder and Younger Kālacakrapadas.[100] It was primarily by means of the Mahāyāna Secret Mantra that these masters set innumerable fortunate disciples on the path of ripening and liberation.

The Secret Mantra teachings of the Early Translation school abide within three main lineages of transmission: the Wisdom Mind Lineage of the Victorious Ones, the Gesture Lineage of the Vidyādharas, and the Lineage of Personally Heard Teachings Given by Voice.[101]

As explained above, the Wisdom Mind Lineage of the Victorious Ones consists of the Glorious Sovereign of all saṃsāra and enlightenment, Samantabhadra, the all-pervading Lord of the Sixth Buddha Family.[102] He appears in the form of Vajradhara with complete marks and signs of Buddhahood in the perfect pureland of self-manifesting space, the unexcelled and indestructible Great Akaniṣṭha; and by the blessing of his absolute wisdom mind, the abiding nature of inconceivable pure phenomena that is inexpressible through words or language, his retinue—the Teachers of the five Buddha families, who are the regents of the Conqueror, or the countless self-appearing maṇḍalas of peaceful and wrathful Buddhas, whose nature is indivisible with Vajradhara—realizes the meaning, so therefore this is designated as the speech of Dharmakāya. As it says in commentaries on the *Secret Essence Tantra*:[103]

> The Teacher, the Dharmakāya, displays a sign to the assembly,
> the ocean of wisdom, through unborn ultimate speech.

As for the aspects of the profound and vast pith of the Luminous Vajra Essence,[104] the place, teacher, retinue, and teaching emanate from the wisdom of self-occurring awareness, the sphere of precious spontaneous presence, the vast and expansive nature of the self-manifest array of the Three Kāyas, and so forth. They are united in a single taste in the great evenness of Dharmatā, the true nature beyond the domain of word and thought, never wavering from the turning of the Wheel of Dharma.

From this, great sublime beings who have reached the culmination of the ten Bodhisattva levels perceive Extraordinary Akaniṣṭha, a Sambhogakāya pureland of complete and perfect abundance. Here, Samantabhadra, in the form of Vajradhara, the Lord of the Sixth Buddha Family, and the forms of the Teachers of the five Buddha families[105] continuously turn the Wheel of Dharma of the inexpressible vehicle of Unsurpassed Yoga [Anuttarayoga tantra] teachings. They transmit wisdom through gestures to an assembly of great Bodhisattvas who possess extraordinary awareness, such as Vajrapāṇi, Avalokiteśvara, and Mañjuśrī, resultant Bodhisattvas,[106] who are themselves the pure appearances of the sense faculties [male resultant Bodhisattvas] and sense objects [female resultant Bodhisattvas].

In the same way, in Just Barely Akaniṣṭha, which appears to those on the ninth Bodhisattva bhūmi; in Akaniṣṭha in Name Only, which appears to those on the eighth bhūmi; and in the palace of great liberation, Dharmadhātu, the womb of the Vajra Queen, where there are Mahottara Heruka, Kumāravīrabalin, Padmanarteśvara, and others who appear to the sense consciousnesses of malicious beings, such as Rudra and Bhairava; and also, there are Hevajra, Cakrasaṃvara, Kālacakra, and other deities: whatever vajra purelands these deities reveal, their maṇḍalas manifest in the aspects of the principal deities and their expressions as the retinues, turning the Wheel of Dharma through the sound of the indestructible nāda.[107] As it says in the *Root Tantra of the Gathering of the Sugatas*:

> I am the king of the great.[108]
> I am both teacher and listener.

Similarly, in relative places such as Tuṣita, the summit of Mount Meru, Oḍḍiyāna, and Shambhala, the Buddha also taught the Kriyā, Caryā, and Yogatantras, either in the guise of a passionless monk or as a universal monarch. As it says in the *Guhyagarbha Tantra*:

> When appearing in various forms,
> Corresponding to different beings,
> Buddha never wavers from the essential nature,
> Yet appears variously through the power of beings' karma.

As for how all of these teachings of Buddha Vajradhara have been compiled, in most of the Unsurpassed Yogatantras, the compiler is shown to be separate from the main deity. However, in many of the truly secret tantras, such as the *Guhyagarbha Tantra*, the wisdom mind of the teacher and that of the retinue are explained as being inseparable. In the *Guhyagarbha Tantra* one finds the words "Thus I have explained," and in the *Cakrasaṃvara Root Tantra* "Now I shall explain what is secret." These words indicate that the compiler is none other than the Teacher himself. As it says in the *Accomplishment of Secrets*:

> The Teacher of Tantra is vajra mind.[109]
> The Teacher is also the compiler.

Furthermore, most tantras, such as those of the Great Perfection, were compiled by Bodhisattvas like the Lord of Secrets Vajrapāṇi, Vajradharma, Vajragarbha, Mañjuśrī, Avalokiteśvara, and the Nirmāṇakāya emanation Garab Dorje, as well as by a host of Ḍākas and Ḍākinīs, such as Ḍākinī Pūrṇopasanti, and by an assembly of various disciples, such as devas, nāgas, and yakṣas.

It has been said that the Lord of Secrets alone collected all the tantras, but those who requested particular tantras also became their compilers. Thus, the *Kālacakra Tantra* was compiled by Sucandra,[110] the *Hevajra Tantra* by Vajragarbha, the *Saṃvarodaya Tantra* by Vajrapāṇi, and the *Vajraḍāka Tantra* by Vārāhī.

An emanation of Buddha Vajradhara appeared as Mañjuśrī, in the youthful and handsome form of Vajratīkṣṇa, who taught the deva Yaśasvī Varapāla in the realm of the gods. He, in turn, taught the deva Brahmāratnaprabha, who then taught Prajāpatibrahmā, who taught Brahmāsarvata, who taught Brahmāsikhandara, who taught the lord of the devas, Indra, who taught a mass of one hundred thousand deva Vidyādharas.

Avalokiteśvara appeared in the form of the deity Amṛtabhaiṣajya and taught Nāga King Kālagrīva in the domain of the nāgas. He, in turn, taught the nāginī Khandulma, who taught the nāginī Dultsangma, who taught the nāga Manorathanandin, who taught the nāga Takṣaka, who taught a mass of one hundred thousand nāga Vidyādharas.

Vajrapāṇi appeared in a terrifying, threatening form and taught the yakṣa Samantabhadra in the domain of the yakṣas. He, in turn, taught the yakṣa Vajrapāṇi, who taught the yakṣa Yaśasvī Varapāla, who taught the yakṣa Ulkamukha, who taught a mass of one hundred thousand yakṣa Vidyādharas. Each of these, in turn, taught their own congregations, and they and all their hundred thousand disciples attained the state of Vajradhara.[111]

In the *Sūtra of Wisdom Prophecies*, the Buddha is asked:

> O Transcendent Conqueror, you have indeed taught
> The three guiding vehicles.[112]
> Why, then, do you not teach the certain vehicle,[113]
> In which cause and result are enjoyed as self-accomplished
> And Buddhahood is not searched for elsewhere?

To this, Buddha replied:

> I have turned the wheel of the Vehicle of Cause
> For those who believe in a cause;
> The swift path of the Vajrayāna
> Will appear at a future time.

Accordingly, twenty-eight years after the supreme Nirmāṇakāya of the Teacher [Buddha Śākyamuni] passed into nirvāṇa, five eminent ones of noble birth—namely, the deva Yaśasvī Varapāla, Nāga King Takṣaka, the yakṣa Ulkamukha, the rakṣa Matyaupayika, and the human Vidyādhara Vimalakīrti of the Licchavi clan—came to know through clairvoyance that the Protector of the World had passed into parinirvāṇa. They arose from their inner samādhis and traveled by miraculous means to the peak of Mount Malaya in Laṅka, where they assembled and cried out a lamentation in twenty-three verses, beginning thus:

> Alas! When the light from the Teacher's lamp
> Has vanished from the universe,
> Who will dispel the darkness of the world?

And they wept to the point of exhaustion.

The Transcendent Conqueror had prophesied that the Secret Mantra would resound throughout the world at some future time, and when that time came, Vajrapāṇi, the Lord of Secrets, actually appeared there, for he had been empowered by the Buddha to reveal the Secret Mantra. Vajrapāṇi instructed those of the five lineages,[114] as well as most of the community of Vidyādharas, repeating the teachings of the Secret Mantrayāna that the Buddha had previously conferred in the Akaniṣṭha realm and elsewhere. The rakṣa Matyaupayika inscribed them on golden paper with liquid lapis lazuli, and by the seven pure wisdom thoughts he concealed the book, invisibly sealing it in space.

The seven pure wisdom thoughts are: the wisdom thought of golden paper as the perfect writing material; the wisdom thought of liquid lapis as the perfect ink; the wisdom thought of jewel-encrusted treasure chests as the perfect vessel; the wisdom thought of space, which the four elements cannot destroy, as the holy abode for treasures; the wisdom thought of mamos[115] and Ḍākinīs[116] who possess eyes of wisdom as the special treasure-guardians; the wisdom thought of King Ja as the holder of the teaching, a destined one with superior acumen, who achieved simultaneous realization and liberation; and King Ja's realization that there would be ordinary and sublime beings, Bodhisattvas, and others as lineage holders who would spread and propagate his teachings.

While the Lord of Secrets turned the Dharma Wheel of the Secret Mantra for the five sublime beings on Mount Malaya, King Ja of Sahor, who was engaged in practicing the tantras of the Secret Mantra at the time, had seven wondrous signs appear in his dreams:

Signs of enlightened body, speech, and mind dissolved into his body,
speech, and mind,
Precious scriptures descended,
He had Dharma discussions,
All proclaimed him as sublime,
He was worshipped with great offerings,
A rain of jewels fell,
And a prophecy was made that he would attain Buddhahood.

Buddha made predictions about King Ja in many different sūtras and tantras. The *Later Tantra of the Coming of Cakrasaṃvara* says:

When I have disappeared from here,
After one hundred and twelve years,
A holy, quintessential teaching
Renowned throughout the three heavens[117]
Will be revealed by the Lord of Secrets,
Who will appear to the one named King Ja
From the eastern border of Jambudvīpa,
Through the power of his great merit.

The *Embodiment of Wisdom Mind* also contains quotations like this.

While King Ja, who was the middle Indrabhūti,[118] sat meditating on the yoga of the lower tantras, a volume of scripture containing the great collection of Secret Mantra teachings, including the *Buddhasamāyoga*, and a cubit-high statue of the Lord of Secrets actually fell upon the royal palace, just as in his dream. Praying to them, King Ja realized the meaning of the chapter called "Vision of Vajrasattva" from the *Mirror of All the Vajrasattva Magical Infinity Tantras*, and with this and the Vajrapāṇi statue as his supports, he practiced for seven months. He had a vision of Vajrasattva and received from him the wisdom empowerment, through which he came to understand all the words and meanings of the entire volume of scripture.

Simultaneously, the collection of Anuyoga teachings descended in Sri Lanka. The fifth chapter of the *Tantra That Contains the Supreme Path of Skillful Means for Clearly Revealing the Wisdom of Samantabhadra* contains this prophecy:

The Mahāyoga tantras will fall upon King Ja's rooftop.
The Anuyoga tantras will appear in the forests of Sri Lanka.

King Ja then taught the scriptures to Ācārya Uparāja, whose vast scholarship was renowned throughout the land of Sahor, but he failed to grasp their symbolic and ultimate meanings. After that, the king taught them to Ācārya Kukkurāja, who understood the chapter "Vision of Vajrasattva." When Kukkurāja practiced this, Vajrasattva appeared before him and spoke this prophecy: "Now the Lord of Secrets will reveal the meaning of the Tantra." Kukkurāja continued to practice, and the Lord of Secrets actually appeared before him, gave the complete empowerment of the ultimate teaching and all the vehicles, and instructed him to request a teaching on the words from Vimalakīrti of Licchavi. Heeding the Lord of Secrets' orders, Ācārya Kukkurāja divided the Mahāyoga teachings into the eighteen great Mahāyoga tantras and expounded them to King Ja, who later wrote in his *Array of the Path of the "Magical Infinity"*:

In Indrabhūti's eastern kingdom,
At Vajrakūṭa in India,
I, Indrabhūti, of noble birth,
Practiced the *Magical Infinity*,
Directly taught to me by the Lord of Secrets,
And fully accomplished Vajrapāṇi,
Along with a retinue of fifty thousand.
Empowered in the fearless activity of abandoning and accepting,[119]
I upheld virtue and was free of negativity.
I then attained the bhūmis.

Although the king himself had already attained realization, in order to stop charlatans from entering the path at will, he apprenticed himself to Kukkurāja and demonstrated the traditional process of gaining realization.

The eighteen great Mahāyoga tantras are as follows.[120]

The five root tantras:

1. Body Tantra: *Union of All Buddhas*
2. Speech Tantra: *Secret Moon Essence*
3. Mind Tantra: *Gathering of Secrets*

4. Qualities Tantra: *Glorious Supreme Beginning*
5. Activity Tantra: *Garland of Activity*

The five manifestation tantras that show how to practice the sādhanas:

6. Heruka: *Tantra of the Manifestation of the Heruka*
7. Hayagrīva: *Tantra of the Manifestation of Hayagrīva*
8. Yamāntaka: *Tantra of the Manifestation of Compassion*
9. Amṛtakuṇḍalī: *Tantra of the Manifestation of Amṛtakuṇḍalī*
10. Vajrakīlaya: *Tantra of the Manifestation of Kīlaya*

The five branch tantras on conduct:

11. *Arrangement Like a Mountain Tantra*
12. *Magnificent Wisdom Lightning Tantra*
13. *Arrangement of Samayas Tantra*
14. *One-Pointed Samādhi Tantra*
15. *Rampant Elephant Tantra*

The two subsequent tantras:

16. *Magical Infinity of Vairocana*, which is the branch for engaging in the activity of the maṇḍala as an amendment
17. *Lasso of the Ārya's Method Called "Garland of Lotuses,"* which is the concise branch for the accomplishment of siddhi

And the tantra that summarizes the meanings of all the others:

18. *General Tantra of Magical Infinity*, also known as the *Guhyagarbha*. The *Glorious Secret Essence That Ascertains the Absolute Nature Just As It Is* consists of Eight Sections:
    1. *Magical Infinity of Vajrasattva*
    2. *Magical Infinity of Vairocana*, which gives an elaborate explanation of activity practices
    3. *Magical Infinity of Mañjuśrī*, which gives a complete explanation of all the piṭakas

4. *Vast Magical Display*, which gives an elaborate explanation of maṇḍalas
5. *Tantra in Forty Stanzas*, which gives an elaborate explanation of enlightened activity
6. *Guru Tantra*, which primarily explains empowerment
7. *Tantra in Eighty Stanzas*, which gives a thorough explanation of precious qualities
8. *Supplementary Tantra*, which explains samayas as supreme

Ācārya Kukkurāja, or Kutarāja, whose name means "King of Dogs," taught thousands of Ḍākas and Ḍākinīs, all of whom were in the form of dogs during the daytime. At night, he went with them to sacred charnel grounds and engaged in ganacakra offerings and other samaya practices. This went on for twelve years, until finally he attained the siddhi of Mahāmudrā.

Some say that while the Ācārya was engaged in these practices, he traveled to Oḍḍiyāna and gave another vast explanation of the five inner tantras,[121] *Union of All Buddhas* and others, from within the eighteen great Mahāyoga tantras, and ultimately attained supreme accomplishment by relying upon the *Secret Moon Essence*.

Ācārya Kukkurāja particularly emphasized the *Union of All Buddhas* tantra and composed numerous śāstras, including the *Six Arrays of Secret Meaning* and the *Fivefold Ritual for Entering All Maṇḍalas*.

Kukkurāja passed his teachings to Śakraputra, the younger Indrabhūti, who in turn transmitted them to Siṃharāja, who passed them to Śakrabhūti, also known as Uparāja, who then taught them to Princess Gomadevī. Through the path of accomplishing the swift accumulation of merit and wisdom, they each, along with their retinues, reached the level of Vajradhara. As it says in *Stages of the Path*:

> Then, above Bodhgayā,
> On the eastern border of Jambudvīpa,
> In a precious holy palace
> Within an auspicious sublime shrine,
> Kukkurāja, Indrabhūti,
> Siṃharāja, Uparāja,
> Princess Gomadevī, and others
> Received the empowerment of the *Magical Infinity*,

Practiced the maṇḍala of the Deity Assembly,
And actually attained the state of Vajradhara.

Princess Gomadevī passed the teachings of karmamudrā to King Ja and Kukkurāja, who in turn taught them to Ācārya Vilāsavajra and Ācārya Buddhaguhya.

Ācārya Vilāsavajra[122] [8th c.] was born in the land of Ṣaṃṣara.[123] He took ordination in the land of Oḍḍiyāna and trained in the Tripiṭaka. He was especially well versed in Asaṅga's philosophical principles, and he knew all of the common sciences as well. Vilāsavajra practiced *Revealing the Names of Mañjuśrī* on the island of Madhima in Oḍḍiyāna. When he came close to accomplishment, rays of light emerged from the face of a drawing of Mañjuśrī and illumined the island for a long time. Because of that, he was given the name Sūryavat, "Like the Sun."

At another time, a practitioner of a wrong view, who needed the five sense organs of a Buddhist paṇḍita as ritual substances to support his practice, came to kill Vilāsavajra. The latter transformed himself into myriad forms of an elephant, horse, boy, girl, buffalo, and peacock. Not knowing which of these was the master, the man left. Vilāsavajra thereafter became known as Viśvarūpa, "Having Myriad Forms."

In his later life, Ācārya Vilāsavajra benefitted the beings living in the country of Oḍḍiyāna in a vast way. He became very learned and accomplished in all the tantras, and especially in the *Magical Infinity*. He wrote and gave detailed explanations of many śāstras, including the *Sādhana of Spontaneous Presence* and works on other tantras; the *Parkhab Commentary on the "Guhyagarbha Tantra"*; and many long and short works related to the *Magical Infinity*. Ultimately, he attained the Vajrakāya.[124]

Buddhaguhya was born in the central land of India, and became ordained at Nālandā University. One day, while he was engaged in the practice of Ārya Mañjuśrī in one of the holy places in Vārāṇasī, a painting of Mañjuśrī smiled; the ghee obtained from the milk of a red cow, which was an accomplishment substance, boiled; and some old, wilted flowers blossomed anew. Although he knew these were signs of accomplishment, he remained doubtful for some time as to whether he should first offer the flowers or enjoy the ghee. A yakṣinī interrupted him by slapping him in the face, and he fell unconscious for a while. When he regained consciousness, he saw that the painting was covered with dust, the flowers had wilted, and the ghee had spilled. However, he cleaned the dust away, placed the flowers on top of his head, and drank the remaining ghee. Because of that, his body became free of illness, he grew strong, he gained intelligence, and he mastered clairvoyance.

Around that time, Buddhaguhya journeyed to Oḍḍiyāna and met with Ācārya Vilāsavajra, from whom he received teachings on Yogatantras and the five sections of unsurpassed inner Anuttaratantras, and became especially learned in the *Magical Infinity*.

At another time, he went with Buddhaśānti to Mount Potalaka to meet with Ārya Avalokiteśvara. At the base of the mountain, they saw Ārya Tārā giving teachings to an assembly of nāgas; at the middle of the mountainside, Frowning Yellow Tārā [Bhṛkuṭi] was giving teachings to an assembly of asuras and yakṣas; and on the mountain peak was Ārya Avalokiteśvara. All appeared as they actually are.

While there, Buddhaguhya attained various siddhis, including the ability to walk without his feet touching the ground. In a prophecy, Ārya Tārā told him to go to the snowy Himalayas and practice at Mount Kailash.

When the two returned, Buddhaguhya gave teachings in Vārāṇasī and other places for many years. Once more, Ārya Mañjuśrī appeared and urged him to heed the prophecy he had received from Ārya Tārā. He then traveled to Mount Kailash and engaged in practice. He had visions of the great Vajradhātu maṇḍala[125] many times and was able to speak with Mañjuśrī as if he were communicating with another human being. Nonhumans attended him as well.

This master was extremely prolific. His many works include the *Analytical Commentary on the "Secret Essence Tantra," Stages of Vajra Activity*, and *Stages of Realization of Peaceful and Wrathful Deities*. On Yogatantra, he wrote *Introduction to Yoga*, the skillful means to accomplish the Vajradhātu maṇḍala, *Concise Commentary on "Vairocana's Awakening,"* and the *Expanded Commentary on the "Later Concentrations,"* among many others. Tibet is deeply indebted to him.[126]

King Ja and Kukkurāja also taught Zombie Sukhasiddhi [Garab Dorje] and Ṛṣi Bhāṣita. Zombie Sukhasiddhi then taught Vajrahāsya, and Ṛṣi Bhāṣita and Vajrahāsya both taught King Prabhāhasti of Sahor. King Prabhāhasti received ordination from Ācārya Śāntiprabha and the great Vinaya master Puṇyakīrti, and was named Śākyaprabha. When he entered the Vajrayāna, he received the name Prabhāhasti. Buddhaguhya and the Great Ācārya Padmasambhava both received teachings from him, and Padmasambhava also received teachings from King Ja. The Great Ācārya

Padmasambhava, known as Guru Rinpoche, was prophesied in the *Magical Infinity of Mañjuśrī*:

> The glorious Buddha born from a lotus
> Is an omniscient treasure holder of wisdom,
> King of various magical manifestations,
> Great Buddha, lineage holder of Vajrayāna.

In truth, Padmasambhava is an emanation of Buddha Amitābha, embodiment of all the Tathāgatas' vajra speech, but he is seen in various ways by beings due to their particular karmic fortunes and faculties. According to the history of Kīlaya within the Kama[127] teachings and in some Indian versions, Padmasambhava is said to have been born the son of the king of Oḍḍiyāna or of one of the ministers. Some claim that he appeared in a flash of lightning on the meteorite peak of Mount Malaya. Here I will present the most famous version of his life story found in the revealed treasures and other sources, which mention only his miraculous birth.

In the western land of Oḍḍiyāna, there were three great lakes to the east, south, and north. On an island in a lake to the southwest, quite close to the land of rakṣasas, a lotus bud with multicolored petals arose from the blessings of the Buddhas. A golden vajra marked with a HRĪ syllable emanated from the heart of Buddha Amitābha, lord of the Sukhāvatī pureland, Great Bliss, and alighted upon the center of the lotus flower. The HRĪ-marked vajra instantly transformed into an eight-year-old boy, adorned with all the major and minor marks of Buddhahood, who sat holding a vajra and a lotus, teaching the profound Dharma to the gods and island Ḍākinīs.

At the time, the king of that land, Indrabhūti, who was without a son, had emptied his royal treasury by making offerings to the Three Jewels and giving alms in hopes of gaining a son. Indrabhūti then went to an island to bring back a wish-fulfilling gem, and on his way home, his Dharma minister, Kṛṣṇadhara, first saw the boy. The king then saw him and invited him to the palace, adopting him as his son. He offered the boy the names Padmākara ["Lotus-Born"] and Saroruhavajra ["Lake-Born Vajra"], and invited him to sit upon a jeweled throne, which arose from the power of the wish-fulfilling gem.

A rain of food, clothing, and jewels pleased everyone, and through his youthful play he ripened an infinite number of disciples. He brought the Ḍākinī Prabhāvatī to the palace and ruled the kingdom of Oḍḍiyāna in harmony with the Dharma. Thus, he became known as King Śikhin, "King with a Topknot."

At this point, Padmasambhava knew that by reigning over the kingdom, it would not bring great waves of benefit for others. Even after asking his father about this, he was not granted permission to leave. He then performed a playful dance, feigning that his khatvanga slipped from his hand, whereby the son of an evil minister was ejected into space. As a sentence for killing the son, Padmasambhava was banished to the charnel grounds. There he engaged in fearless activity in the charnel grounds of Śītavana, Nandanavana, and Sosadvipa, where the Ḍākinīs Mārajitā and Śāntarakṣita gave empowerments and blessings. When Padmasambhava brought all the charnel ground Ḍākinīs under his power, he became known as Śāntarakṣita, Guardian of Peace.

Then he traveled to Dhanakośa Island, where he practiced Secret Mantra in the Ḍākinīs' symbolic language and brought the island Ḍākinīs under his power. When he engaged in yogic conduct in Parūṣakavana, Vajravārāhī appeared before him and gave her blessing. He bound all nāgas of the ocean and spirits of stars and planets under oath. All the Vīras and Ḍākinīs of the three abodes[128] granted him siddhis, and he became known as Dorje Dragpo Tsal, Wrathful Vajra Power.

Padmasambhava then traveled to Bodhgayā and displayed many different miracles, causing others to ask who he was. "I am a self-occurring Buddha," he replied. Disbelieving him, they disparaged him, and he realized for various special reasons the need to journey to the land of Sahor and receive monastic ordination from Ācārya Prabhāhasti. He then became known as Śākyasiṃha, "Lion of the Śākyas."

Padmasambhava listened to the Yogatantra teachings eighteen times and had visions of each of their deities. The Ḍākinī Guhyajñāna appeared in the aspect of the nun Ānanda, and when he requested empowerment, she transformed him into a HŪṂ syllable and swallowed him. With him inside her belly, she bestowed the complete outer, inner, and secret empowerments and then sent him forth from her lotus, purifying the three obscurations.[129]

Padmasambhava studied with many learned and accomplished Ācāryas of India, principally the Eight Great Realized Masters, from whom he received the Eight Sādhana Teachings;[130] Buddhaguhya, from whom he received the *Magical Infinity*; and Śrī Siṃha, from whom he received the Great Perfection. He listened to teachings on all the sūtras, tantras, and sciences, and through demonstrating the process of training, he understood them perfectly after practicing each one only once. Even without practicing, he had visions of deities. He became known as Guru Mativat Vararuci, known in Tibetan as Loden Chokse, "Intelligent One Who Yearns for Supreme Knowledge," and showed the way to attain perfection as a Fully Ripened Vidyādhara.[131]

After that, Padmasambhava summoned Princess Mandāravā, daughter of King Arśadhara of Sahor, who had the signs of a Ḍākinī, and brought her to Maratika Cave, where she acted as his wisdom consort to support his practice. They engaged in longevity practice for three months, whereupon Buddha Amitāyus actually came and bestowed empowerment. He blessed them, and they became one with him. He bestowed upon them one billion longevity tantras, and they attained the accomplishment of the Immortal Vidyādhara.[132] Having accomplished the vajra body beyond birth and death, Padmasambhava went to subdue the kingdom of Sahor. When the king and his ministers tried to burn him alive, he arose atop a lotus blossom in the center of a lake of sesame oil. By his miraculous display, he established them in faith, and everyone converted to Buddhism and reached the irreversible stage.[133]

Then Padmasambhava returned once more to the kingdom of Oḍḍiyāna. In order to subdue the people there, he set off on an alms round, but they recognized him, and the wicked ministers and others tried to burn him alive on a pile of sandalwood. Both Padmasambhava and his consort miraculously appeared upon a lotus flower at the center of a lake. Padmasambhava wore a garland of skulls signifying that he had liberated sentient beings from saṃsāra, and he became known as Padma Tötreng Tsal, "Powerful Lotus-Born with a Skull Garland."

Padmasambhava acted as the king's revered guru for thirteen years, and during that period he established the entire kingdom in the Dharma. He granted the ripening empowerments and liberating instructions for the *Ocean of Dharma That Embodies All Teachings*, and the king and queen, as well as all other karmically destined beings, attained the level of Supreme Vidyādhara. He became known as Padmarāja [or Pema Gyalpo], "Lotus King."

As prophesied in the *Sūtra of the Magical Emanation of the Bodhisattva's Sphere of Activity*, Padmasambhava took the form of a fully ordained monk named Indrasena in order to subdue the Emperor Aśoka, inspiring irreversible faith in him. In the span of a single night, the Emperor erected ten million stūpas throughout Jambudvīpa, each containing sacred relics of the Tathāgata.

Padmasambhava exorcised and skillfully subdued several powerful tīrthika kings harmful to the Buddhist teachings, transferring their consciousness to higher rebirths. One of these kings served him poison, and when it failed to harm him, the king threw him into the Ganges River. Padmasambhava made the water flow upstream and danced in the sky. He became known as Khyeuchung Khadingtsel, the "Boy With the Power to Soar in the Sky."

Also, Padmasambhava revealed himself in many other physical manifestations and under many other names, such as Ācārya Saroruha, who brought forth the *Hevajra Tantra*, the Brahmin Saraha, Ḍombi Heruka, Virūpa, and the great Kṛṣṇācārya. Padmasambhava visited the great charnel grounds, such as Kula Dzogpa,[134] and taught the Secret Mantra to the Ḍākinīs. He seized the vital life force[135] of all the outer and inner haughty spirits[136] and appointed them as guardians of the Buddhist teachings. Performing these deeds, he became known as Sūryaraśmi, "Rays of the Sun."

When 500 tīrthika teachers began attacking the Buddhist teachings in Bodhgayā, Ācārya Padmasambhava was victorious in a competition of debate and magical powers. When their followers cursed him with evil mantras, he reversed their curses with a wrathful mantra offered to him by Ḍākinī Mārajitā, "Demon-Tamer Ḍākinī." He brought down a great bolt of lightning that liberated[137] the tīrthika teachers and set their city ablaze. He converted whomever was left to Buddhism and raised the victory banner of Dharma high in the sky. When this happened, Padmasambhava became known as Siṃhanāda, "He Who Roars Like a Lion." At this point, he had fully traversed the supreme path that exhausts the three defilements[138] and lived as a Vidyādhara with Power Over Life.

Then, Padmasambhava practiced the glorious Yangdak Heruka in Yangleshö Cave, near the border of India and Nepal, with the Nepalese princess Śākyadevī, daughter of the Nepalese king Puṇyadhara, as the support for his practice. When he was about to attain supreme accomplishment, three powerful demons created obstacles: for three years, no rain fell, and epidemics and famine were widespread. He sent for teachings from his gurus in India to dispel the obstacles, and they sent back two porters bearing the Vajrakīlaya tantric scriptures. As soon as these arrived, the obstacles naturally subsided. Rain began to fall and the epidemics and famine ended. The tantric consorts attained supreme accomplishment and manifested in the form of Mahāmudrā Vidyādharas.

Yangdak Heruka grants great accomplishments, but like merchants [who travel over treacherous lands to sell their wares], practitioners face many obstacles. Realizing that the Kīlaya practice would be indispensable, like an escort or bodyguard, Guru Padmasambhava composed many sādhanas that combined the practices of Yangdak Heruka and Vajrakīlaya. He bound under oath all the male and female classes of earthly spirits, such as the sixteen Vajrakīlaya guardians, and made them guardians of the Dharma.

Also, whenever the occasion arose, Padmasambhava taught beings according to their capacities on the Oḍḍiyāna islands of Hurmudzu, Sikodhara, Dhanakośa, and Rukma, as well as in Tirahuti and other Taru kingdoms in Kamarula and elsewhere. He benefitted many beings through his common accomplishments: he brought forth water where there had been none, he made a large river flow underground, and when tīrthika deities suddenly appeared in East, South, and Central India and caused immense harm to the Buddhist teachings, he annihilated them in all three places with his Vajrakīlaya powers. When a Daruka king led his army up the River Nila to invade the land of Kanchi, where there was a flourishing Buddhist community, Ācārya Padmasambhava pointed his index finger in the threatening mudrā and 500 ships sank. After that, the Daruka attacks ceased.

It is not exactly clear when Padmasambhava visited the country of Dravida, but he did eventually subdue the Ḍākinīs and other nonhumans and humans of that region and let them build a temple there. This master's traditions of studying, teaching, and meditating on the four classes of Tantra[139]—mainly the six Anuttarayoga tantras of *Hevajra*, *Secret Moon Essence*, *Yangdak Heruka*, *Hayagrīva*, *Vajrakīlaya*, and *Mātaraḥ*—flourished there until a much later period. Legends from this region claim that Padmasambhava departed from Dravida for the southwestern continent of Cāmara, land of the rakṣasas. These accounts are from Indian sources and are quite well known, and while most claim that Padmasambhava lived in India and benefitted the Dharma and beings for 3,600 years, many scholars believe this is either a calculation based upon partial years or merely an exaggeration.

Furthermore, Padmasambhava manifested as a clairvoyant king and a powerful yogin in order to tame Turkestan and China. He appeared spontaneously in the land of Zhang Zhung as a young boy named Tavihṛca, and with the instructions he imparted from the Great Perfection Lineage of Personally Heard Teachings Given by Voice, many fortunate beings attained the Body of Light.

As all of this shows, Padmasambhava performed countless activities to subdue beings in diverse countries with diverse languages, each according to his or her needs, thus setting them all on the path to liberation. His activity is immeasurable. Indeed, all of this information derives only from biographies that mention particular aspects and names. With the mere distinction of being direct or indirect, since there is no single realm of beings that is not the domain of this particular Nirmāṇakāya manifestation, no one can possibly describe the true extent of the liberating accounts of the lives of those who dwell in the state of indivisibility.[140]

That being so, Mahāsiddhas have been known to make themselves invisible to ordinary disciples, and then after a long time, they make themselves visible and remain for a long period of time. Sometimes they are invisible in certain places but are visible in others, or they might display the process of transference[141] in one place and birth in another. Because their magical manifestations are infinite, previous saints could disappear and reappear in their same form, just as Virūpa did on three different occasions and Jālandharipa did five times. The great Kṛṣṇācārya displayed the process of dying in Devikoṭa and was cremated by his students, but he later reappeared in another place in his former body and acted for the benefit of beings. He is also reputed to have taken birth anew in other places at the same time and displayed the way of attaining supreme accomplishment. From these and other stories, it is clear that the precise conventions of time and place according to how they appear to ordinary people do not apply here, just as a commoner's concerns are never comparable to those of a king.

It is because of their power to perform miracles that sublime beings are always able to manifest according to the wishes and aspirations of sentient beings. As it says in the *Perfect Collection of All Noble Dharmas Sūtra*:

> If an eon of destruction is willed to become an eon of formation, the eon of destruction becomes an eon of formation, and those sentient beings experience it as an eon of formation. If an eon of formation is willed to become an eon of destruction, the eon of formation becomes an eon of destruction, and those sentient beings experience an eon of destruction. It is not that destruction and formation become something else; it is will that transforms them. Likewise, if an eon is willed to last for just one morning, those sentient beings experience an eon in just one morning. If one morning is willed to last an eon, this is what happens, and those sentient beings experience it as that. This is called "the miraculous ability born of the Bodhisattva's wishes."

Now that the names and stories of the oral transmission lineage of the Mahāyoga Tantra Section have been briefly introduced, the two traditions of the Mahāyoga Sādhana Section—Buddha's Speech [Kama] and Treasures [Terma] —will be explained.[142]

The Kama teachings of Yamāntaka, "Slayer of the Lord of Death," such as the *Secret Wrathful Mañjuśrī Tantra*, which belong to the Vairocana family of enlightened body, were transmitted to Ācārya Mañjuśrīmitra. He was born in the west of India in a town called Dvikrama. His father was Sadhuśāstri, and his mother was Pradīpaloka. He became so learned in the branches of the Vedas[143] that he was renowned as a scholar. From the Great Ācārya Ashen Zombie [Garab Dorje] and others, he received the outer and inner tantric empowerments, as well as all the common and uncommon precious instructions. It is said that he also received Black Yamāri, Ṣaḍānana [Six-Faced One], and Vajrabhairava from Ācārya Līlāvajra [Rolpe Dorje]. In any case, he became experienced in the common accomplishments, and when he was on the verge of reaching the state of indivisibility he left to engage in yogic conduct. On a bridge, Mañjuśrīmitra encountered a king, who was a very powerful patron of tīrthikas, riding on an elephant. When the king refused to make way for him, the master displayed the threatening mudrā, and both the king and his elephant were split in half and toppled off the bridge. At this, the king's entourage begged forgiveness from the master, who brought the king back to life and placed him in Dharma. In the Ācārya's words:

> I do not prostrate to worldly gods
> Or step aside, even for an elephant.
> I recite the king of secret mantras;
> My feet pass unhindered through rocky crags.

Eventually, Mañjuśrīmitra became one with Ārya Mañjuśrī and reached the exalted state of indivisibility. Mañjuśrī-Yamāntaka actually appeared to him, granted empowerment, and taught him all the tantras and upadeśa. Many Yamāntaka activity emanations[144] circumambulated him and offered their lives in his service. From Mount Malaya, Mañjuśrīmitra took out a golden volume of scripture written in lapis ink that contained all four activity rituals.[145] Just by looking at it, he understood it completely, so by using its wrathful mantras for subduing tīrthikas, he destroyed an entire kingdom of tīrthikas. He then made the book invisible and concealed it north of Bodhgayā.

The Kama teachings of Hayagrīva, such as *Manifestation of Hayagrīva*, which belong to the Amitābha lotus family of enlightened speech, were transmitted to Ācārya Nāgārjunagarbha [Nāgārjuna]. According to a well-known biography of this master,[146] he revealed the *Eight Mahākāla Tantras*, the *Goddess Kālī Tantra*, the *Practice Manual of Ārya Tārā Kurukullā*, and many other tantras. He received oral instructions from the wisdom Ḍākinīs, and it is said that he alone introduced sixty different sādhanas. He also accomplished many diverse powers within each of the eight common accomplishments.[147]

After spending 200 years at Śrī Parvata[148] practicing tantric conduct with a retinue of yakṣinīs, Nāgārjuna attained the vajra body.

The Kama teachings of Viśuddha Mind,[149] such as *Heruka Galpo*, which belong to the Akṣobhya family of enlightened mind, were the special transmission that was passed to Ācārya Hūṃkāra. Born in Nepal to a Brahmin family, he became extremely learned in the Vedas and so on, and also in tīrthika philosophical traditions. He developed spiritual power as well. Later, his supreme faith in the Buddha's teaching led him to Nālandā in Central India, where he received ordination from Ācārya Buddhajñānapada and Paṇḍita Rāhulabhadra. He received teachings on everything from the pāramitās to the inner and outer classes of the Secret Mantra, and with these he purified his mind. He received empowerment and all the instructions and subsequent instructions. Especially, when Hūṃkāra received empowerment into the maṇḍala of the glorious Yangdak Heruka, his flower[150] landed on the wrathful Hūṃkāra. Following his long meditation on this deity, he increased the special samādhi of the two stages.[151] Hūṃkāra realized that if he were to practice for six months, he would attain accomplishment, but he knew he needed an activity consort with skin the hue of a blue utpala flower and with all the signs of a Vajra-family spiritual consort. After an extensive search, he found one in another region. When he requested permission from her parents, they protested, saying, "Brahmin master, have you gone mad? We are outcastes! Won't we all be punished?"

"I require her assistance with my meditation practice, so the usual punishments, such as the degradation of caste, won't occur," Hūṃkāra replied.

"Well, then, we will need her weight in gold and silver," they said. At that, the master instantly brought forth a treasure from beneath the ground and gave it to them.

The master and his spiritual consort then retreated to a cave and practiced the stages of approach, close approach, and accomplishment for a period of six months. In the early dawn of the eighth day of the waxing moon, a loud HŪṂ resounded from the sky, and Hūṃkāra vividly beheld the entire maṇḍala with Vajra Heruka and the other deities. Then, through the path of the great accomplishment stage,[152] he attained the supreme siddhi of Mahāmudrā. As *Stages of the Path of Magical Infinity* explains:

> If one practices thirty times six,[153]
> Twelve, fourteen, or sixteen [months],
> This will bring about the accomplishment of the sublime sovereign of all Buddha families.[154]
> Of these, Hūṃkāra falls into the foremost.[155]

This master, Hūṃkāra, benefitted many beings through his teachings on the three stages of development, completion, and Great Perfection, as well as other Vajrayāna tantras. He composed many śāstras on the two stages as well, such as *Yangdak Rulu Golden Rosary*; *Buddhasamāyoga Upadeśa Called "Illuminating the Meaning of the Four Branches"*; and *Establishing the Authenticity of the Great Heruka Sādhana*. Ultimately, in his very body, Hūṃkāra flew like the king of garuḍas to Buddha Akṣobhya's pureland [Manifest Joy].

The Kama teachings of Vajrāmṛita, such as the *Eight Volumes of Amṛta*, which belong to the Ratnasambhava family of enlightened qualities, were transmitted to Ācārya Vimalamitra. This master was born in western India in a place called Hastivana, "Elephant Grove." He knew all the sciences and their branches, and he studied with holders of the Tripiṭaka and became well versed in the sūtras of the greater and lesser vehicles as well. From Ācārya Buddhaguhya and many other great Vajra Holders, Vimalamitra studied all the tantras, and by meditating upon them, he attained supreme Mahāmudrā accomplishment. Vimalamitra was especially adept in the *Magical Infinity* and composed many śāstras, including *Commentary on the "Guhyagarbha Tantra" Called "Illuminating Lamp of the Core Text"*; *Commentary on the "Unsurpassed Magical Infinity" Called "Dispelling Darkness"*; *Eye-Opening Commentary on the "Supplementary Magical Infinity"*; *Abridged Commentary on the "Eighty-Chapter Magical Infinity"*; *Opening the Eyes of Prajñā*; *Three Stages*; *Mudrā Concentration*; *Ritual for Fire Offerings*; *Ritual for Cremation*; *Stages of Line Drawing*; and *Short Commentary on the "Guhyagarbha."*

The Kama teachings of the Vajrakīlaya tantras, which belong to the Amoghasiddhi family of enlightened activity, were transmitted to Ācārya Prabhāhasti. Also, when the Great Ācārya Padmasambhava realized the Supreme Vidyādhara level of Mahāmudrā in Yangleshö Cave, by means of the maṇḍala of the glorious Yangdak Heruka, the minds of three spirits—an obstinate nāga, a horse-headed yakṣinī, and a celestial lightning-cloud—were filled with unbearable passion, and they undertook to destroy the master. To subdue them, Padmasambhava practiced the *Hundred-Thousandfold Supreme Awareness Tantra*, whereupon Vajrakumāra [Vajrakīlaya] appeared before him and defeated all signs of obstacles. Padmasambhava then bound the twelve Mātaraḥ[156] and the four ging spirits under oath. It is said that he later received the Yoga tantra eighteen times from Ācārya Prabhāhasti, and he became a lineage holder of the teachings.

The Mātaraḥ tantras, such as the *Hundred Thousand Quintessential Tantric Texts*, were transmitted to Ācārya Dhanasaṃskṛita. The Earthly Haughty Spirits tantras, such as *Subduing Haughty Ones*, were transmitted to Rambuguhya Devacandra. The Wrathful Mantra Incantations tantras, such as *Crystal Rosary of Wrathful Mantras*, were transmitted to Ācārya Śāntigarbha. The *Gathering of the Sugatas* tantras were transmitted through Ācārya Padmasambhava to all the masters collectively. The masters then put their respective teachings into practice and in turn taught them widely to other fortunate disciples.

The second tradition of the Sādhana Section of Mahāyoga is the Treasure tradition, the class of accomplishment. The Bodhisattva Vajradharma put the general and specific sādhana sections in writing, but at the time he saw no one in the human world to whom he could teach them. He then entrusted them to the Ḍākinī Mahākarmendraṇī, who placed the five general and ten special tantras of the Eight Sādhana Teachings[157] inside a tiny casket made of eight precious gems. She placed the special tantras in separate caskets and hid them invisibly in the Śaṅkarakuta Stūpa grove in the Śītavana charnel ground.

Later, the Eight Great Realized Masters [158] came to know of this through their clairvoyance and gathered at that place. They directed their wisdom minds by developing fearless wisdom presence; and by speaking the words of truth and using pleasing substances, they caused the worldly Ḍākinīs and haughty spirits to release the Ḍākinī seals. Through the power of their samādhi, Ḍākinī Mahākarmendraṇī actually appeared before them and revealed the caskets. She entrusted a rhinoceros hide Mahottara casket to Vimalamitra, a silver Yangdak Heruka casket to Hūṃkāra, an iron Yamāntaka casket to Mañjuśrīmitra, a copper Hayagrīva casket to Nāgārjuna, a turquoise Vajrakīlaya casket to Padmasambhava, a rhinoceros-hide Mātaraḥ casket to Dhanasaṃskṛita, an agate Worldly Worship casket to Rambuguhya, and a zi[159] Wrathful Mantra casket to Śāntigarbha. Each became learned in the meaning of his own entrusted teaching and attained tantric accomplishment. The sādhana teaching containing the tantras and upadeśa of the *Gathering of the Sugatas*, which is all eight sādhanas gathered into one, came from the casket made of eight precious gems and was given to the Great Ācārya Padmasambhava.

The Lord of Secrets, Vajrapāṇi, gave empowerment to King Ja, also known as Vyākaraṇavajra, and the king realized the meaning of all Buddhist teachings. However, in order to prevent those with narrow minds from thinking he had just arbitrarily entered the Secret Mantra, King Ja became the disciple of a human Vidyādhara, the layman Vimalakīrti of Licchavi, and received all empowerments and oral teachings from him, such as *Commentary on the "General Sūtra."* King Ja empowered his Dharma friend Ācārya Uparāja, who had studied with him under Licchavi, as well as his own three sons—Śakraputra, Nāgāputra, and Guhyaputra—into the maṇḍala that he had emanated, and taught them the precious instructions. He gave empowerment and entrusted the tantras to Uparāja at the Śrī Dhānyakaṭaka Stūpa, also called the Śrī Dakṣiṇa Stūpa, and he empowered his three sons in the town of Kṣemakara.

Śakraputra was the renowned younger Indrabhūti. It is said that when Śakraputra attained siddhi, he became well known as Ācārya Kambalapāda. The *Textual Commentary on "Establishing Simultaneous Arising"* states this as well. In any event, since Indrabhūti opened several tantric traditions, such as Cakrasaṃvara, the Brahmin Ratnavajra and others became followers of his lineal tradition. Furthermore, several later Indian gurus assert that Ācārya Kambalapāda was the son of a king and that he lived in an area within Oḍḍiyāna. Therefore, based on that, it could well have been that Śakraputra was Indrabhūti the Younger.

Śakraputra first received empowerment from a great master of mantra, meditated on his instructions, and gained realization of wisdom. Later, he went to Dhumasthira, the city of the Ḍākinīs in Oḍḍiyāna. The tīrthika Ḍākinīs placed a garland of flowers in his hands, which he took, and the Buddhist Ḍākinīs said, "Son, it was not good to take those flowers. Now, what if you have to follow the tīrthikas?" At that, Śakraputra entered samādhi, and around midnight the tīrthika Ḍākinīs caused a rain of stones to fall on him. Everything within the development-stage protective sphere he had visualized remained unharmed. "Since the development stage has so much benefit, I should demonstrate the power of the completion stage," he thought to himself. He entered into a samādhi free of characteristics, and the stones were all suspended in midair. Even today, in the land of Oḍḍiyāna, a huge boulder hangs without support above Śakraputra's practice cave. On the mirrorlike surface of a rock there, numerous stones are suspended. These are clearly visible to all.

At one time, Śakraputra fell asleep just in front of the door to the king's palace. Anyone who entered the palace without first prostrating to him had their calves stiffen, so everyone had to prostrate before proceeding. Śakraputra's sleep lasted for twelve years, but he experienced it as a single session of clear light meditation.

Another time, 500 sorceress spirits from the land of Oḍḍiyāna were plotting to create obstacles for Śakraputra, so they set out in search of him. When they reached the place where the master had been, they found only a blanket. "Oh!" they said, "Look at this monk's magic! He has transformed his body into a blanket, so let's cut it into pieces and eat them!" They proceeded to cut the blanket into 500 pieces and consume it.

Śakraputra then made his body reappear, used incantations on the sorceresses, and turned them into 500 ewes. They ran before the king and said, "That monk in charge of the charnel ground did this to us! Please find a way to free us, Your Majesty!"

The king put the request to Śakraputra, who stood up stark naked and said, "O King, your wicked sorceresses have eaten my blanket, the only thing this monk owns! Call them over here!"

The king brought them all over, and the master pointed the threatening mudrā at each one. They became beings with different kinds of heads, and each one vomited her piece of the blanket. When the bits were pieced back together, something was still not quite right. "Three are still missing," the master said. "Summon them!" The king summoned the final three from among the retinue of queens, and they were made to vomit the remaining pieces. Śakraputra wrapped the fully restored blanket around himself, and he became known as Kambalapāda, "Venerable Blanket Master."

There are so many stories about Kambalapāda, including one about how he and King Indrabhūti displayed signs of their spiritual accomplishment to people. Another describes a time when Kambalapāda and Ācārya Līlāvajra traveled together to the land of Oḍḍiyāna, after the latter had attained the common accomplishments, and competed in a contest of magical powers on Mount Muruṇḍaka.

It is said that, later in Oḍḍiyāna, King Indrabhūti and Ācārya Kambalapāda together gave teachings, and through that, everyone became a Vidyādhara and the vast country of Oḍḍiyāna became nearly empty. Presumably this story is the same as the one mentioned above about King Ja's son, Indrabhūti the Younger, who became a Vidyādhara along with his entire retinue.

Likewise, Indrabhūti the Younger gave empowerment and taught the Anuyoga tantras to Siṃhaputra and Kukkurāja the Later on an ocean shore. Kukkurāja then empowered and taught the tantras to the Great Ācārya Blissful Zombie, which is one of the names of the Nirmāṇakāya Garab Dorje.

As it is said:

> When passions overwhelm the mind; energy and power are weak;
> Karmic life spans are short; the essential meaning of the teachings has been lost;
> The essential teachings are modified by contrary schools of thought; and
> Antidotes are ineffective, making practice methods weak—then,
> At that time, the thought of awareness[160] will arise.

As this explains, when these six occasions for the arising of the Great Secret teachings arrived, the supremely secret teachings of the Great Perfection appeared. It happened like this.

At the time when the victorious Lord of Secrets, Vajrapāṇi, gave the teachings of the Secret Mantra to an assembly of Ḍākas, Ḍākinīs, siddhas, and Vidyādharas in the Blazing Mountain charnel ground north of Mount Meru, the island of Dhanakośa, in the western Indian land of Oḍḍiyāna, was filled entirely with beings called kośas—with human bodies, bear heads, and iron claws—and dense forests of sandalwood and other precious trees. Because of this, the island was given its name, which means "Treasury of Wealth."

In that land, there was a large temple called Śaṅkarakuta, surrounded by 6,800 smaller temples. Here, in this place with perfect glory and riches, there lived a king named Uparāja and a queen named Alokabhasvatī. Their daughter was named Sudharma, who became ordained as a novice, and not long afterward became a fully ordained nun. She lived just over a league away from them in a little thatched hut on an island covered with golden sand. There she practiced yoga and meditation with her attendant, Sukhasaravatī. One night, the nun dreamed that a pure, flawless man placed a crystal vase sealed with the letters OṂ ĀḤ HŪṂ SVĀHĀ upon her crown three times. Light radiated from the vase, so that she clearly beheld the three realms.[161] Shortly afterward, she gave birth to a child, who was the Bodhisattva Devaputra Adhicitta, the divine manifestion of Vajrasattva who had spread the Great Perfection in the realm of the devas.

Deeply ashamed, the nun saw this as profoundly wrong. She lamented bitterly, saying:

> What could this fatherless child be but a worldly demon?
> Is he a devil, Brahmā, or what?
> Is he a spirit—a gyalpo, a tsen, or a mu?
> In the three realms, who is this lustful one?
> But if he is a god, asura, or in some other variation of form,
> No one has ever seen anything like this!
> How is this unethical thing possible in this kingdom?
> Alas, I have pure vows and wish to transcend this world,
> Yet I will be ridiculed by corrupt beings. What nonvirtue that is!

Her attendant said, "He is the son of the Buddhas! It is not right to despair like this!" But the nun did not listen and cast the child into a pit of ashes. At that moment, sounds, lights, and other phenomena occurred.

Three days later, the nun went to look at the child and found him utterly unharmed. She knew then that he was a Nirmāṇakāya emanation, and with great reverence she carried him to the royal palace. The gods sang out from the heavens:

> Protector and Teacher, Victorious Lord!
> Illuminator of our true nature, Protector of the World!
> Grant us perfect refuge, Vajra of Space,
> We pray to you now!

Ḍākas and Ḍākinīs, devas and nāgas, yakṣas and other earthly protectors, all made elaborate offerings.

After seven years, the boy said to his mother, "Listen, Mother, will you grant me permission to discuss the Dharma with the paṇḍitas?"

His mother answered, "Son, you are so young! The paṇḍitas are so learned and brilliant that it will be much too hard for you."

But when he implored her again to allow him, she told him to go discuss the Dharma with the 500 court scholars of King Uparāja. The son then went to see the king and repeated his request. The king thought, "The boy is much too young and will have difficulty discussing the Dharma with paṇḍitas. However, given all the marks of greatness on his body, it is possible that he is a Nirmāṇakāya emanation."

He described the boy to his court scholars, but they could not reach agreement. Finally, one especially learned scholar said, "A very auspicious sign has occurred. Send the boy in, and we shall see if he is an emanation."

When the boy arrived, he prostrated himself before the paṇḍitas. They engaged in lengthy discussion and debate with him, and as a result the paṇḍitas' confidence was crushed, and they placed the boy's feet upon their crowns. They worshipped him with deep reverence and offered him the name Prajñābhāva, "Source of Knowledge." The king as well was amazed and overjoyed and named him Garab Dorje, "Indestructible Supreme Joy." Earlier, his mother, who was astonished that he had remained unharmed after she cast him into the ash pit, had called him Blissful Zombie or Ashen Zombie.

After that, Garab Dorje went north to the top of a terrifying rocky mountain called Sūryaprakāśa, where masses of pretas could actually be seen roaming about, and lived for thirty-two years in a thatched hut, absorbed in meditation. At one point, the earth quaked seven times, and a voice resounded from the sky: "The doctrine of the tīrthikas has been diminished!" The tīrthika king was about to dispatch an assassin to murder the master, when suddenly he saw Garab Dorje fly across the sky. This filled the king and his entourage with supreme faith, and they all entered the Buddhist path.

All the collected teachings of the outer and inner vehicles and, in particular, the 6,400,000 verses of the natural Great Perfection were within the enlightened mind of Garab Dorje. All of these were awakened when Vajrasattva actually appeared to him and bestowed the universal awareness empowerment, through which Garab Dorje displayed the way of attaining wisdom beyond learning, and authorized him to put the spoken tantras into writing. The master and three Ḍākinīs—Vajradhātu Ḍākinī Who

Enjoys Worldly Bliss, Bliss-Giving Yellow Ḍākinī, and Ḍākinī of Infinite Qualities—then spent three years on the summit of Mount Malaya, which is heaped with precious gems, cataloging the teachings in words and letters. Once they had perfectly arranged all writings, including those of the spontaneously self-manifesting Nirmāṇakāya, they placed them inside a cave called the Actual Source of Ḍākinīs.

On another occasion, Garab Dorje traveled to the great charnel ground known as Śītavana, on the northeastern border of Bodhgayā, which has a large stūpa at its center and is inhabited by a multitude of hostile Ḍākinīs and vicious animals. He remained there teaching the Dharma to Ḍākinī Sūryakiraṇā and uncountable others.

At the time, Mañjuśrīmitra received a prophecy from Ārya Mañjuśrī, and accordingly, Mañjuśrīmitra bowed at Garab Dorje's feet and stayed with him for seventy-five years. When finally Garab Dorje vanished in a mass of light at the head of the Danatika River, Mañjuśrīmitra cried out three times in grief, and a volume of scripture containing Garab Dorje's last testament, *Three Words That Strike the Essence*, fell into his hand. Merely by seeing it, Mañjuśrīmitra's wisdom realization became equal to his master's.

Mañjuśrīmitra divided the 6,400,000 verses of the Great Perfection into three categories: Mind, Expanse, and Upadeśa.[162] Of these, he divided the *Heart Essence* [*Nyingtik*] cycle into two: the explanatory tantras and the aural tantras. He annotated the aural tantras, and not finding an immediate recipient to whom to disseminate the explanatory tantras, he concealed them as treasure in Bodhgayā. He then stayed in the great Sosadvipa charnel ground, where Śrī Siṃha came, bowed at his feet, and received the instructions in their entirety. When at last Mañjuśrīmitra departed in a mass of light, Śrī Siṃha lamented with grief, and a tiny container holding Mañjuśrīmitra's last testament, *Six Meditation Experiences*, fell into his hand.

One hundred and twenty-five years later, Mañjuśrīmitra the Younger was miraculously reborn from the bud of a lotus. He taught Ācārya Āryadeva the *Heart Essence* instructions of the Great Perfection and as a result, Āryadeva vanished in a stainless Body of Light. Mañjuśrīmitra revealed the meaning of the *Oral Instructions of Mañjuśrī*, which abides as the essence of the Great Perfection teachings, to Buddhajñānapada as well.

At last, after Ācārya Mañjuśrīmitra had vanished, Śrī Siṃha revealed the explanatory tantric texts in Bodhgayā. He divided the Sole Essence Upadeśa class of the Great Perfection into four sections: outer, inner, secret, and supremely secret. He again concealed the first three of these sections as treasure. The fourth, in accordance with a prophecy from the Ḍākinīs, he sealed inside a pillar in the Auspicious Myriad Gate temple. Śrī Siṃha then resided in the Siljin charnel ground as chief of the Ḍākas and Ḍākinīs.

Vimalamitra and Jñānasūtra both received teachings from this master. The former received the outer, inner, and secret Upadeśa. In addition to all of that, Jñānasūtra received the oral instructions, along with the books, and gradually he received all the empowerments. When at last Ācārya Śrī Siṃha vanished into a stainless Body of Light, Jñānasūtra prayed to him, and his last testament, *Seven Pith Instructions*, fell into Jñānasūtra's hand. At the Guru's command, he brought forth the supremely secret Upadeśa from inside the pillar of the Auspicious Myriad Gate temple and traveled to the Bhasing charnel ground.

At that time, Vimalamitra, urged on by Ḍākinīs' prophecies, became a disciple of Jñānasūtra, who conferred upon him all the empowerments. When Ācārya Jñānasūtra departed in the body of Great Transference, Vimalamitra prayed to him in despair, and Jñānasūtra's last testament, *Four Modes of Placement*, dropped into his hand. He then gained the inner confidence of realization.

Along with these, the history of the profound Treasure teachings will be briefly explained. Generally speaking, if anything is examined from the perspective of the true nature of Dharmatā, all elaborations are transcended. However, if the way in which things appear is considered, the entire premise of the profound Treasures might seem separate from the meaning of the Buddha's Speech, or the content of the Buddha's Speech might seem separate from the essence of the Treasures. But this is not the case. As Jamgön Kongtrul Lodrö Taye Rinpoche explains in *A Brief Account of Profound Treasures and Accomplished Treasure Revealers Called "Garland of Lapis Lazuli,"* a teaching from the first volume of the *Great Treasury of Precious Termas*:

> In terms of the absolute meaning, the teachings of the Buddha's Three Kāyas all come from the Wisdom Mind Lineage of the Victorious Ones, the Gesture Lineage of the Vidyādharas, and the Personally Heard Teachings Given by Voice. Therefore, they are not beyond or other than the treasures. Also, after the councils were successively held to compile the teachings of our shared Supreme Nirmāṇakāya,[163] the Lord of Sages [Buddha Śākyamuni], a large number of the collected teachings, mainly those of the Mahāyāna, disappeared from the human realm and were

> spread in the various realms of gods, nāgas, and other beings. As for the tantras, the Vidyādharas and Ḍākinīs compiled them and concealed them in Oḍḍiyāna Dharmagañja[164] and elsewhere, keeping them safe until a future time. When the right time came, the Mahāyāna sūtras were retrieved by followers of the Cittamātra school from Bodhisattvas such as Sarvanīvaraṇaviṣkambin. There are many examples of Treasure teachings, such as the *Prajñāpāramitā in One Hundred Thousand Lines*, which was brought from the realm of the nāgas by Nāgārjuna. A series of Mahāsiddhas who attained supreme accomplishment, such as Saraha, Hayagrīva, Sakara, Lūyipa, and Tsilupa, then appeared and revealed tantras, principally the *Guhyasamāja*, *Cakrasaṃvara*, *Hevajra*, and *Kālacakra*, and these were none other than profound treasures. Therefore, it is important to understand that aside from geographical differences between India and Tibet and the fact that individuals manifested in earlier or later time periods, the meaning of the teachings is the same in every way.

Our Teacher also taught how and why sūtras such as the *Sūtra of Revealing the Five Skandhas* and *Dhāraṇī of Secret Relics* abide as treasures, as well as the benefits of these sūtras, to whomever requested their teaching. In the *Sūtra of the Wise and the Foolish* as well, there is a story about a ritual text on the eight precepts of lay ordination[165] that emerges from a pillar in a householder's home. As this and other stories make clear, the ways in which the various kinds of treasure developed throughout Indian history, from different places and time periods, is inconceivable. And not only that, it is certain that treasures exist inconceivably throughout other world systems as well.

Therefore, a Buddha's enlightened activity has three distinctive qualities of greatness: it is not the case that a Buddha who acted to benefit beings in the past no longer does so in the present, so it is constant; it is not the case that a Buddha who acts in the east does not also act in the west, so it is pervasive; and it is not the case that effort and struggle are necessary, so it is spontaneously accomplished. Moreover, it is explained [in many sūtras] that Buddhas perform their deeds through every aspect of enlightened body, every aspect of enlightened speech, and every aspect of enlightened mind, which is likewise described in the *Sūtra of the Dialogue with the Nāga King*:

> There are four great treasures: the inexhaustible great treasure of the unbroken lineage of the Three Jewels; the inexhaustible great treasure of the boundless, supreme realization of the Dharma; the inexhaustible great treasure of satisfying sentient beings; and the inexhaustible great treasure that is equal to space.

Buddhas have no concept of effort, yet they constantly benefit sentient beings by having the perfectly pure ten powers,[166] with the promise to manifest any teachings according to beings' wishes. This gives evidence of the actual essence or nature of the Treasure teachings. Similarly, the *Sūtra of the Samādhi That Gathers All Merit* says:

> O Vimalatejas, for great, heroic Bodhisattvas who long for the Dharma, Dharma treasures have been placed into mountains, ravines, and trees. Dhāraṇīs and infinite entrances to the Dharma will also come forth.

Also:

> For those with perfect intention, even if no Buddha is present, teachings will emerge from the midst of the sky, and from walls. . . .

And:

> O Vimalatejas, for those great, heroic Bodhisattvas who have perfect aspiration and veneration, even if they live in a different world system, the Bhagavān Buddha will reveal his face and cause them to hear the Dharma.

The sūtras say:

> Mañjuśrī, the source of all elements is the treasury of space. Likewise, the source of all Dharmas is the treasury of Buddha's wisdom mind, so partake of the meaning of the treasures!

In the *Sūtra of the River's Play*, it says:

The teachings that I have revealed
From my heart, conceal as treasures in your hearts,
Or hide them in the essence of the earth.
Otherwise, tīrthikas will rise up
And corrupt their true meaning,
So do not stop the flow of the river.

In these and other references, Buddha gives an explicit presentation of treasure locations, the various types of treasures—such as earth treasures, mind treasures, pure visions,[167] and so on—and their purpose and reason to exist. Such passages occur extensively in other sūtras and tantras as well.

That being so, one might wonder what special features are ascribed to this profound Treasure tradition. In addition to the Wisdom Mind Lineage of the Victorious Ones, the Gesture Lineage of the Vidyādharas, and the Personally Heard Teachings Given by Voice described above, the Treasure tradition has three special lineages: the Lineage Empowered by Prayer, in which karmically destined individuals are empowered through prayer to reveal particular treasures entrusted to them; the Lineage of Wisdom Prophecies, in which prophesied treasure revealers, or tertöns, are told to benefit beings in the future through specific profound treasures; and the Lineage of Sealed Treasures from Guru Rinpoche Entrusted to Ḍākinīs, in which mamos and Ḍākinīs who are keepers of teachings and treasure guardians are entrusted with treasures and commanded to give them to future treasure revealers with specific family lineage and identifying traits, in specific locations, at specific times, and under specific circumstances.

If one wonders whether one can trust that treasure revealers do not need to rely on other lineages of teachings in their lifetimes, which is explained as characteristic of "close lineages," they are indeed supremely trustworthy. Why is this? As described above in the profound sūtra quotations, the Buddhas have promised to bless individuals who have perfect aspiration, as evidenced by the Great Ācārya Padmasambhava and the other great regents of the Three-Kāya [Trikāya] Buddha, who granted their blessings to karmically destined disciples through the Wisdom Mind Lineage like fathers passing on their inheritance. That way, since there is no adulteration by ordinary persons, samaya breakers, beguiling demons, and others, the blessings for attaining accomplishments are extremely potent. If this is not accepted, what has just been explained about the transmission of profound sūtras and tantras will be of no benefit. Why? Because the places from which the great charioteers[168] have extracted these teachings, and the Buddhas and Bodhisattvas from whom they have received them, are beyond the scope of childish, self-absorbed minds. If exalted beings are thought to be spiritually superior and therefore different, there is no doubt the same applies here. Besides, the Buddha said, "Aside from me and those like me, no one can judge others."

Moreover, as the *Avataṃsaka Sūtra* says:

> Those who wish to enter the domain of the Victorious Ones
> Must train until their minds are like the sky.
> Eliminating clinging to thoughts, thought patterns, and
> conceptions,
> Enter this domain with a skylike mind.

If the meaning of this is mindfully embraced, one will have the good fortune to quell one's mind, wasted by miserable passions, with the amṛta of the profound Dharma.

Thus, as explained above, the profound teachings that derive from the Wisdom Mind Lineage of the Victorious Ones, the Gesture Lineage of the Vidyādharas, and the Personally Heard Teachings Given by Voice—namely, Tantra of the development stage, Mahāyoga; the transmission of the completion-stage Anuyoga; and Upadeśa of the Great Perfection, Atiyoga, known as the three inner Yogatantras—are unique to our Early Translation tradition. Mahāyoga has both a Tantra Section and a Sādhana Section, with the Sādhana Section further divided into Buddha's Speech and the Treasure teachings. Anuyoga as well is divided into sūtras and śāstras, and Atiyoga is divided into the three classes of Mind, Expanse, and Upadeśa. These are also further subdivided into innumerable main and branch sections, and due to the kindness of the Early Translation translators and scholars, all of them flourished in the snowy land of Tibet.

In the beginning, the Land of Snows was an island with a large lake. There Avalokiteśvara and Ārya Tārā emanated as an old Bodhisattva monkey and a rock ogress, and from their union came the first seeds of the Tibetan race. Gradually the island evolved into a human land. For a time it was left in the hands of various classes of demonic ruling spirits, such as the masang and the triad of cha, mu, and tsuk.[169] Then, King Nyatri Tsenpo of the Śākya Licchavi race descended to the earth on a celestial rope and took control of the land of Tibet. His royal succession included seven heavenly kings called

Tri, six earthly kings called Lek, eight middle kings called Dey, five linking kings called Tsen, and so on. Bönpos governed the kingdom by means of legends and cryptic riddles. The Bön population of that era was made up of priests of the cha gods, who emphasized divination; priests of magic power, who emphasized astrology; priests of existence, who brought happiness to ghosts of the dead and places of the living; priests of the mundane world, who used various exorcism rites; and so on. Their doctrines spread and flourished, making Bön the earliest of all religious systems in Tibet.

Later, during the reign of Lha Totori Nyenshel, who was an emanation of Bodhisattva Samantabhadra, a rain of precious items—including a gold stūpa, a bowl engraved with the Wish-Fulfilling Jewel Dhāraṇī of Avalokiteśvara, and the *Sūtra of the Ritual for Amending Breaches*—fell onto the roof of the Yumbu Lagang Palace. This marked the earliest arrival of the precious Dharma in Tibet.

During the reign of Dharma King Songtsen Gampo, who was an emanation of Ārya Avalokiteśvara, the Holy Dharma minister Gar used miraculous means to invite the Nepalese princess Tritsun Bhṛkuṭi Devi and the Chinese princess Wencheng Kongjo to Tibet. They brought with them two Jowo Śākyamuni statues as supports of worship for Tibet. The king dispatched Tönmi Sambhota to India, where the latter studied the five sciences, and especially the science of grammar, under Devavidyāsiṃha and the Brahmin Lipikāra. Tönmi achieved perfect mastery of all of them. He then introduced an alphabet to Tibet, where there had previously been none, and translated twenty-one Avalokiteśvara sūtras and tantras into Tibetan. The Dharma King and his consorts built the temples of Rasa Trulnang, Ramoche, and Tradruk, and many temples for subduing and re-subduing borders.[170] The king gave his retinue and subjects much advice related to the meditation and recitation of Avalokiteśvara, and many excellent yogins emerged. King Songtsen Gampo was the first to establish the tradition of the Holy Dharma in Tibet.

Then Ārya Mañjughoṣa came to the land of Tibet in the guise of a ruling king, King Trisong Detsen.[171] When His Majesty turned twelve years old, he happened upon an inscription[172] composed by his royal ancestor, and a strong wish to propagate the Buddhist teachings arose in his mind.

In order that opposition to his Buddhist activities should not arise among his ministers and subjects, who delighted in evil, King Trisong Detsen skillfully presented them with various options, and eventually the king and his ministers agreed on building a temple as a support for spiritual practice.

The king invited the Great Abbot Śāntarakṣita from Sahor to give Dharma teachings on the ten virtues, the eighteen elements,[173] the twelve links of interdependence,[174] and so on. When they began construction of the temple, pernicious gods and demons in mental bodies plotted to harm them through a fantastic display of malicious attacks. But as it is said:

Once the strength of a Bodhisattva is gained,
Untamable beings are exceedingly rare.

Thus, ultimately speaking, there is no one at all whom the great heroic Bodhisattvas, permeated by compassionate emptiness, cannot subdue. So it was not as if Abbot Śāntarakṣita was incapable of subduing beings. However, while all of the 1,000 Buddhas of this fortunate eon share the same essential qualities, without increasing or decreasing, and without good or bad, their individual manifestations are unique, owing to the diverse nature of their Bodhisattva vows and aspirations, and their enlightened activity is displayed in response to their students' specific dispositions, capacities, and wishes. Likewise, Abbot Śāntarakṣita, Ācārya Padmasambhava, and Dharma King Trisong Detsen all manifested uniquely when their previous aspirations for enlightened activity ripened. This is explained in the *Noble Shoulder Tantra* as follows:

Buddha, even though your nature is naturally free from attachment and aversion,
You manifest desirable qualities for those who have desire,
And you manifest wrath for those who are wrathful.
By skillful means, you always guide beings. I bow to you.[175]

In harmony with this, the king dispatched messengers bearing gifts of gold to invite the Great Ācārya Padmasambhava, King of the Holders of Vidya Mantras, with mastery over the four kinds of sublime activity.[176] Through his clairvoyance, the Great Ācārya was already aware of this and instantly traveled to Mangyul.[177] From there, in a display of miraculous power, Padmasambhava gradually set foot upon each and every region of Tibet. He brought every last major god and demon, such as the twelve Tenma sisters,[178] the thirteen great gods,[179] and the twenty-one genyen,[180] under his control using the brilliant power of mudrā and made them his faithful subjects. Master and patron [Padmasambhava and King Trisong

Detsen] met in the tamarisk grove at Dragmar and traveled together to Samye. There the Great Abbot Śāntarakṣita examined the suitability of the land. The Great Ācārya Padmasambhava went to the top of Hepo Mountain and bound the gods and spirits under oath. He performed a vajra dance in the sky to consecrate the land, and wherever his shadow appeared on the ground, lines were drawn, and the foundation was laid upon them. Through the power of his meditative focus, the master compelled the local gods and spirits to help, and whatever was built of the Unchanging Spontaneously Accomplished Temple of Samye during the day by humans was exceeded by nonhumans at night. Outside, the temple resembled Mount Meru, with its four continents,[181] subcontinents, sun, moon, and iron perimeter. Inside were placed masterful representations of the Great Enlightened Buddha and other sacred images of maṇḍalas and deities. To invite all the Buddhas abiding as manifestations of infinite Kāyas and wisdoms, as numerous as the countless tiny particles on each particle, a consecration was performed with samādhi and the four seals, making them inseparable from the samaya representations and ensuring that they remain there firmly. As the consecration flowers were tossed, auspicious omens and signs appeared in the ten directions and throughout the beginning, middle, and end of the ceremony. These wondrous, virtuous phenomena, which were supremely beautiful to behold, became obvious to all the gods and humans of Tibet.

Then the sovereign king decided to establish the main body of the Buddha's teachings to allow the light of the Dharma of study and realization to dawn anew in the land of Tibet, a realm of darkness. A large group of the brightest youths was gathered, led by Vairotsana,[182] a living embodiment of Buddha Vairocana, and they were trained in the art of translation. Realizing that the establishment of the Dharma required a foundation of ordained Saṅgha, the king invited the twelve monks of the Sarvāstivāda order and others from India. Here again, it was not as if the Great Ācārya Padmasambhava, who was inseparable from the perfect Buddha, whose pure five aggregates wafted the sweet fragrance of morality, was incapable of acting as preceptor to give ordination. To entrust future disciples with an authentic origin through the pure example of a sublime being who would show how not to stray from the rules of the Vinaya, our sole crown jewel, the Great Abbot Śāntarakṣita, a saffron-robed Buddhist monk and master of the three trainings, was asked to assume the empowering role of preceptor. He then ordained the "seven men to be tested."[183] From there, numerous others, such as the Zhang minister named Dama, gradually took Buddhist ordination.

Then both groups of the revered Saṅgha—the group of ordained monks and the group of white-clad, braided-haired yogins—were established. Vimalamitra, who was prophesied and praised as Chakgya Gyachen in a direct pronouncement by Samantabhadra, was foremost among the many Indian paṇḍitas who were then invited to Tibet.

Most notably, Vairotsana underwent fifty-seven major hardships and innumerable minor hardships in order to bow at the feet of Śrī Siṃha and other scholars and siddhas in the holy land of India. He received all the common and uncommon oral instructions, primarily those of the Great Perfection. Graced with these inconceivable and supremely auspicious Dharma gifts, Vairotsana returned to Tibet.

The patron was not an ordinary person but a genuine emanation of Ārya Mañjuśrī in the form of the Dharma King Trisong Detsen. This was the "greatness of the inviting patron."[184]

The places where the translations of the teachings were done were not ordinary towns, cities, or crossroads either, but holy places such as Lhasa, Tradruk, and Samye, which had been walked upon and blessed by sublime beings. This was the "greatness of the place of translation." To be sure, great beings have unanimously praised Vairotsana, saying, "Although he is called a translator, he is in fact a paṇḍita." Vairotsana, who was an emanation of Buddha Vairocana, was expert not only in the words of ordinary languages, but also in the words and meanings of many special languages, especially Sanskrit and Tibetan. In an effort to repay his kindness, which is more difficult to measure than the far reaches of space, his life story will be briefly given here.

Vairotsana's family name was Pagor. There are two theories as to his birthplace mentioned in the two different versions of Vairotsana's biography: according to the *Crystal Cave Chronicles*, he was born in Nyemo, but Vairotsana's autobiography, the *Great Image*, clearly states that he was born at the junction of the Nyang and Tsang rivers, near the present-day town of Zangkar, where the river turns its course eastward by the great palace of Samdrubtse. Apparently, in that holy place there are even footprints clearly visible in the rocks, left by the great translator as a child. Most say that his father was Pagor Dorje Gyalpo and Pagor Hedö was his paternal uncle, though it is stated in the *Crystal Cave Chronicles* that the latter was his father. His mother was Drenka Za Drönkyi. As a young boy, Vairotsana used to fly between the craggy mountains and come and go by miraculous means. He was ordained by Abbot Śāntarakṣita as one of the "seven men to be tested" and given the name Vairotsanarakṣita, meaning "Vairotsana

Guardian." He became supremely versed in the art of translation, and to this day no one in the Cool Land Blanketed by Sprouts, Tibet, has been able to match his level of mastery.

At King Trisong Detsen's command, Vairotsana traveled to India with Tsangben Legdrub. He met twenty-five great paṇḍitas, including Śrī Siṃha, and received many profound teachings on the Secret Mantra. From Śrī Siṃha in particular, Vairotsana received all the oral instructions for the mind, expanse, and especially the Upadeśa classes of the Great Perfection, which he put into practice until his wisdom mind became indivisible with his Guru's. Afterward, using the power of swift walking, he sped easily back to Tibet.

When Vairotsana accepted King Trisong Detsen as his disciple, the wicked ministers treated Vairotsana with hostility. Vairotsana then departed for Gyalmo Tsawarong, in accordance with his past aspirations to travel there. In that region, he caused the sun of the Buddha's teachings to dawn. In particular, he accepted Legdrub's immediate reincarnation, Yudra Nyingpo, as his disciple, and Yudra Nyingpo became Vairotsana's supreme heart-son. Then Vairotsana returned to Central Tibet [U and Tsang] and worked extensively for the Dharma. When he received the empowerments for the Eight Sādhana Teachings from Guru Rinpoche, his flower fell upon Wrathful Mantra Incantations, and he received the special transmission for the Haughty One.[185] He compiled a large collection of teachings such as the *Eight Commands: Gathering of the Sugatas* and so on. Vairotsana is praised as having realization equal to that of the Ācārya Padmasambhava himself. He had a vision of the Black Powerful One[186] and attained the accomplishment called "having wisdom eyes." With wrathful mantra incantations, Vairotsana liberated the enemies of the Buddhist teachings. This great translator, whose knowledge was equal to the far reaches of space, was the heart-son of Guru Rinpoche. In the renowned phrase "king, subject, and friend," the king is Sovereign King Trisong Detsen, the subject is Vairotsana, and the friend is Yeshe Tsogyal. Owing to the fact that he became the sole heart-son of Guru Rinpoche, Vairotsana received special transmissions for almost all the profound teachings of Guru Rinpoche. As a result, he took infinite rebirths as treasure revealers, some of whom were renowned throughout the central and outlying regions of Tibet, and others who were less well known. Among his body emanations were Terchen Dorje Lingpa, Kunkyong Lingpa, Chogden Do Ngak Lingpa, and Trengpo Sherab Özer; among his speech emanations was Rigdzin Terdak Lingpa; and among his mind emanations was Rongtön Dechen Lingpa. Through these emanations, Vairotsana brought inconceivable benefit to the Dharma and beings.

Among the renowned Ka Chok Zhang Trio, *Ka* stands for the great Dharma translator Kawa Paltsek. He was born in Kawa in the Central Tibetan region of Penpo. His father was Kawa Loden, and his mother was Droza Dzema. The Great Master Padmasambhava recognized him as the rebirth of an Indian mahāpaṇḍita, who had purposely reincarnated as a Dharma translator, and as such, Kawa Peltsek became supremely adept at Dharma translation. He was ordained by the Great Abbot Śāntarakṣita and was one of the "seven men to be tested." By receiving Secret Mantra teachings from Guru Rinpoche, extraordinary clairvoyance dawned boundlessly within him, and he attained the siddhi of effortlessly knowing others' minds. He is the forefather of all Tibetan calligraphers, and his instruction tradition, which flourishes in both Kham and Central Tibet, remains undiminished to this day. He also composed numerous commentaries, such as *Discourse on the Precious Scriptures*. Among his descendants as well there were many great illuminators of the Buddhist teachings, as we see in the case of the emanated treasure revealer Drapa Ngönshe,[187] and others.

Thus, Vairotsana, the Ka Chok Zhang Trio, Nyagchen Yeshe Zhönu, and others were all reincarnated masters who returned as great Dharma translators, and this was the "greatness of the Dharma translators who did the translations."

Those who taught the Dharma were not mere ordinary individuals, but beings like the Great Abbot Bodhisattva Śāntarakṣita, Vimalamitra, the Great Ācārya Padmasambhava, Ācārya Buddhaguhya, and so on, all of whom were actual Buddhas and emanations. This was the "greatness of the paṇḍitas who guided the translation of the teachings."

The material offerings were not merely a few gold coins, but rather offering maṇḍalas consisting of many rows of deerskin sacks filled with gold coins and gold dust, and this was the "greatness of the offering flowers."

The Buddha's teachings, which consist primarily of the common vehicle [Hīnayāna], the uncommon Great Vehicle [Mahāyāna], and the four and six special classes of tantra,[188] along with the śāstras that clarify their meaning, were all translated in their entirety, without error. This was the "greatness of the translated teachings."

It was through these six perfect aspects of greatness that the Dharma was established and translated, and it was due to the infinitely kind aspirations of these translators, paṇḍitas, patrons, and masters that the Early

Translation Vajrayāna teachings famously first came to Nyak, then to Nub, and finally to Zur.

Nyak Jñānakumāra was from Shelpa or Chö in Yarlung. He was born to Tagdra Lhanang and Suza Drönkyi of the Nyak clan, from which his name derives. His throat bore a mole shaped like a crossed vajra, and he was given the name Gyalwe Lodrö, "Victorious Intelligence." He received novice and full ordination from the Abbot Bodhisattva Śāntarakṣita, and his courageous eloquence in translating numerous Sūtra and Mantra teachings was inconceivable. Nyak Jñānakumāra combined the "four rivers of transmission" that flowed from the Great Ācārya Padmasambhava, Vimalamitra, Vairotsana, and Yudra Nyingpo into one: the river of general text interpretations, along with commentaries and summaries; the river of whispered lineage instructions, along with essential instruction and guidance that nakedly explains the teaching; the river of blessings and empowerment, including the way they are bestowed and introduced; and the river of traditional practices for accomplishing enlightened activity, with protector practices and wrathful mantras.

After the Great Ācārya Padmasambhava ripened him in the maṇḍala of Amṛta Quality,[189] Nyak Jñānakumāra made miraculous water come from dry rocks in the Crystal Cave in Yarlung Valley. Although the *Magical Infinity* must also have come through the Nyak lineage, it was mainly through the practice of Vajrakīlaya that Nyak Jñānakumāra attained clear signs of realization.

Following King Trisong Detsen's death, the hostile Queen Tsepongza demoted most of the translators and paṇḍitas and drove them from the court. While Nyak Jñānakumāra was staying in Yardrok, his own brother, Nyak Getön, turned on him and spread slander about him, claiming that he practiced the black magic of heretics. Realizing that his brother had all sorts of plans to harm him, Nyak Jñānakumāra fled.

When he reached the foothills of Chimyul in Kongpo, he saw seven she-goats wandering through a desolate valley. He told his attendant, Lelmik Ogtsen, to drive them away. "But what if they have an owner? What will he say?" the attendant protested.

"How can goats wandering in a desolate valley have an owner? Now drive them away!" Nyak ordered.

When their owner, Chim Jarok, the "Raven of Chim," discovered this, he charged them with stealing. "You need to repay me sevenfold!" the goatherd demanded. But when Nyak handed over the sevenfold compensation,

Chim was still not satisfied and chased them with an iron hammer. Nyak ran away and locked himself inside a temple. The goatherd forced open the door, slammed the threshold with his hammer, and almost hit the head of a young monk, it is said.

Nyak was not allowed to remain there either. He set out for Central Tibet, but when he arrived, he encountered a man named Drose Chung, who was chasing a deer. The man's horse shied at the sight of Nyak, and the deer escaped. He grew enraged and tried to murder Nyak. Fearing for his life, Nyak managed to slip out of sight and escape.

At around this time, Queen Margyen poisoned the crown prince, Mune Tsenpo. Ācārya Vimalamitra came from China by miraculous means to lead the funeral assembly, where Nyak met with him and offered a large sack of gold dust to him. Vimalamitra asked, "Translator, are you and your attendants well and safe?"

Nyak replied:

> We tried to do well in the hills of Yardrok,
> But Getön would not allow it.
> We tried to do well at the base of Chimyul,
> But the hellish Jarok would not allow it.
> We tried to do well in Central Tibet,
> But Drose Chung would not allow it.

Reflecting that the maltreatment of translators would be disastrous for the Buddhist teachings, Vimalamitra brought forth from his heart the *Perfect Practice of Vajrakīlaya* and the *Blue-Skirted Vajrakīlaya Cycle* and taught these to Nyak.

The paṇḍita and translator practiced together inside the Na Cave in Lhodrak Kharchu, using twenty-one ritual daggers [kīla] made of acacia wood. Their practice was so potent that the ritual daggers began spontaneously hitting against each other. At that moment, while he was in meditation, Nyak raised his ritual dagger and said, "This is for the Raven!" and all ravens in the sky flocked together. Again, he rolled the ritual dagger and said, "This is for the Raven of Chim!" and in flew a pair of ravens from Chim. Nyak grew angry and threateningly waved his ritual dagger at one of the ravens, and it died at that moment.

At that, Vimalamitra said, "The power of your fierce tantric practice has enabled you to kill. Now let's see if you can bring back to life by the power of Dharmatā! Revive it!" But Nyak was unable to resurrect the raven, unlike Ācārya Jālandharipa and his disciple Kṛṣṇācārya, who were able to do so. Vimalamitra sprinkled some sand on it, and instantly the raven came to life and flew away.

Vimalamitra explained: "If you are unable to liberate your own ego through your realization, then even if the wrathful ritual you undertake is successful, it will be a terrible offense." Vimalamitra then performed the ritual for guiding the dead to the purelands.

After that, the local guardian deity of Chim appeared in the guise of a white yak, and Nyak liberated him straightaway. Then, by the power of brandishing his ritual dagger, Nyak liberated Chim Jarok, along with his major, middling, and minor life-supporting wolf spirits,[190] his servants and slaves, horses and watchdogs, friends, acquaintances, and relations, thus eradicating his family line.

Nyak then tried to attack his own brother, Nyak Getön, but such ferocious sorcery greatly depends upon the interdependent circumstance of enduring hatred, and due to the benevolence of Ācārya Vimalamitra, Nyak was overcome with great compassion. His mind naturally turned to Dharmatā, and his efforts to perform the ritual failed. Ācārya Vimalamitra said, "If you find an assistant with all the signs of a sorcerer, you will succeed." So Nyak set out in search.

Back then, blacksmiths were called sogpos. Nyak happened upon an angry-looking blacksmith named Sogpo Betse and noted that the man had all the physical signs and indications, such as knotted hair and a triangular lower body. Nyak came down from behind him and offered his assistance by using the bellows. Meanwhile, he gave teachings on the causal vehicles, but the blacksmith paid him no heed. Then Nyak expounded the Kriyā, Upa, and Yogatantras, and the blacksmith listened occasionally, but mostly he just heard the clanging and banging of his hammer. Then, while he was teaching the three inner tantras, Nyak swallowed some hot iron rods from the forge. The blacksmith was shocked. "How did you get such miraculous powers?" he gasped.

"I learned it by practicing the teachings I just taught you," Nyak replied.

The blacksmith was filled with faith, offered Nyak all his smith tools, and became his disciple. His name was changed to Lha Palgyi Yeshe.

Odren Palgyi Zhönu was also recognized as having the proper marks of a Vajrakīlaya practitioner, so the three of them, master and disciples, practiced together. When Getön caught wind of this, he began scheming to murder them. People tried to dissuade him, saying that it was not right to mistreat a monk, but Getön did not listen. The night before his departure, Getön dreamed that many women had gathered around him and chopped off his head. When he told his wife, she begged him not to go. Ignoring her, Getön leaped on his horse and galloped off.

A huge bird swooped down and startled his horse. Getön was reduced to bits of flesh and drops of blood. It is known that it was a guardian deity who came and liberated him. Sogpo Palgyi Yeshe then removed Getön's heart and offered it to his master, who said:

> Commit not a single negative act.
> Perform abundant virtuous deeds.
> Subdue your own mind well.
> May all beings be happy!

In fact, Nyak's guardian deity had transformed into a hawk and liberated Getön, as well as Getön's life-supporting wolf spirits, servants and slaves, horses and watchdogs, and all his friends and relations, thus eradicating his family line.

Nyak dealt the same fate to Drose Chung, summoning his consciousness from the grasslands where he was grazing his horses and annihilating him through ritual stabbing with his dagger. He turned the Dro clan guardian deity into a blue wolf and then completely obliterated everyone as before, wolf spirits, servants, slaves, and all.

Furthermore, by apprenticing himself to learned and accomplished masters who were like the actual Buddha, the great translator Nyak became immensely well versed in grammar, logic, dialectics, and all aspects of outer and inner Mantra. He became a great translator and translated many holy teachings into Tibetan. Nyak became a lineage holder of Sūtra [Anuyoga], *Magical Infinity* [Mahāyoga], and Mind [Mind Class of Atiyoga],[191] and through his teachings, he produced many extraordinary disciples, so his kindness is beyond conception.

In the end, Nyak Jñānakumāra attained supreme accomplishment through the *Whispered Lineage Vajra Bridge* and the class of upadeśa, and he departed in a mass of empty luminous light.

Nyak Jñānakumāra led his main disciples to become the "eight glorious Vajrakīla masters." Sogpo Palgi Yeshe, Odren Palgyi Zhönu, Nyenchen Palyang, and Tagzang Palgyi Dorje were his four earlier disciples, and Lamchok

Palgyi Dorje, Darje Palgyi Dragpa, Dra Palgyi Nyingpo, and Lhalung Palgyi Dorje were his four later ones, making eight glorious sons in all. His nephews, Upa Dosal, Gyepak Sherab, and Busuku Chok, also performed vast enlightened activity.

It is said that the Early Translation Vajrayāna teachings fell to Nub in the middle period.[192] Nubchen Sangye Yeshe's father was Salwa Wangchuk of the Nub clan, and his mother was Chimo Tashi Tso. Nubchen was born in the first spring month of the Male Water Rat year, in the foothills of Drak in Central Tibet. A sandalwood tree sprouted up at the ancestral burial ground in Drak Riwoche, and a Chinese monk who examined it determined that it was a sign a Nirmāṇakāya emanation would be born. He taught them the way to nurture and care for the tree, and in time his prophecy was realized.

Nub's layman name was Dorje Tritsuk, his Dharma name was Sangye Yeshe, and his secret name was Dorje Yangwang Ter. When Nub was seven years old, he entered the retinue of Odren Palgyi Zhönu and trained in all the sciences. When he received the empowerment of the Eight Heruka Sādhanas from the Great Ācārya Padmasambhava, his flower landed on the body maṇḍala of Mañjuśrī, and with the practice of this maṇḍala, signs of accomplishment manifested. After that, in the Five-Pronged Vajra Cave on the border of India and Nepal, Nub received many tantras and upadeśa from Guru Padmasambhava. Also, he studied and mastered all the sūtras and inner and outer tantras of the Mantrayāna, along with their upadeśa, under the guidance of masters such as Śrī Siṃha, Vimalamitra, Kamalaśīla, Dhanadhala, Tragtung Nagpo, Śāntigarbha, Dhanasaṃskṛita, Sokyadeva, Dhanarakṣita, the Brahmin Prakaśalaṃkara, Dharmabodhi, Dharmarāja, Tsuglak Palge, Vasudhara, Chetsen Kye, and other translators and paṇḍitas from India, Nepal, and Drusha.[193] He also studied under the learned Tibetan translator Nyak Jñānakumāra and all eight of his glorious disciples, particularly Sogpo Palgyi Yeshe and Zhang Gyalwe Yönten, who was a disciple of the two masters Nyak and Ma Rinchen Chok. Nub traveled to India and Nepal seven times and translated numerous tantras, upadeśa, rituals, and protector prayers.

In Vārāṇasī, Nub met Ācārya Prakāśālaṃkāra and received many teachings. In particular, he received the complete empowerment for the Anuyoga sūtras and the oral instructions for the *Embodiment of Wisdom Mind.*

As for the way in which Nub attained accomplishment, during the nine months he spent in Zhugi Dorje Gombu, his mind was liberated, and he recognized the abiding nature of Dharmatā. In Bodhgayā and in Yungdrung Rinchen Terne, Vajrapāṇi, the Lord of Secrets, actually appeared before him, and his vajra landed in Nub's hand. Vajrapāṇi bestowed on Nub the name empowerment.

In Ölmo Tsel, the child of a gandharva gave Nub the name Sangye. Nub was venerated by a yakṣa in Gangzang and by three young nāga brothers on the shore of Nine Island Lake. In the Lhe charnel ground, the child of a preta bowed at his feet. In Öme Tsel, Yamāntaka appeared before him and granted empowerment and accomplishment. Once Nub had brought the gods and demons under his power, he was empowered as a master of Secret Mantra, and the lords of the Ḍākinīs[194] who protect the Mātaraḥ and Yamāntaka cycles were given to him as his guardians. In accordance with a prophecy from Mañjuśrī, Ekajaṭī granted him accomplishment substances in the Sanglung Nagpo charnel ground in India, and with this, his pure wisdom dawned from basic space and the realization of the great bhūmi[195] was actualized. He had visions of the complete maṇḍalas of Pema Garwang and Yamāntaka and received their empowerments and accomplishments. Furthermore, he possessed unobstructed clairvoyance and other supernatural powers. His wondrous life story is simply inconceivable, filled with accounts of his ability to walk on water, pass freely through mountains of solid rock, and perform other miracles.

Nubchen Sangye Yeshe established his main practice place at the sacred site of Yangzong in Drak, Central Tibet. In general, this period in history was marked by the collapse of imperial law following Langdarma's reign and the rise of sectarian infighting. Nubchen and his disciples experienced great hardship as a result, and two of Nub's own sons were killed during three consecutive uprisings waged by the locals. In Nub's own words:

> Turbulence arose in Central Tibet;
> The people robbed my food for survival.

And:

> Although I am but an inferior monk of Nub,
> I truly aspired to accomplish the Dharma.
> Enemies full of hate have not allowed it.
> To protect the Buddha's teaching,
> I emanated wrath right away.

Intending to demonstrate the power of goodness,
I learned various black magic liturgies.

Nub then brought forth the wrathful mantras of the oceanic Yamāntaka cycle he had learned in India and Nepal. When he was sixty-one years of age, a rebellion broke out in Drak, and Nub demolished many towns with the sharp wrathful mantras of Yamāntaka. Nub fled to Yulrong, but again, he was not allowed to stay there, so he took over the Je Fortress in Nyemo. There he was encircled by bandits with weapons and almost lost his life. From atop the fortress, Nub called on the fearsome gods and demons to bear him witness, and he invoked the truth in verse. He then flapped his Dharma robe, and the oath-bound Dharma Protectors clearly appeared and said, "With our power and strength, we can reduce Mount Meru to dust, strike the sun and moon together like cymbals, or flip the sky and earth upside down. Up until now, however, because your karmic debts from previous lifetimes rose up, we were not able to help you. Now we shall obey your command!"

Nub drew forth his acacia wood ritual dagger from the hem of his Dharma robe and summoned the vital-essence syllable of the oath-bound deities. He rolled the ritual dagger between his palms and aimed it at the hillside where the armed men were camped. A huge fire sprang up on the mountain, and all the men were burned to ashes. For three years after defeating his enemies, Nub was poor and destitute.

During the reign of King Ralpachen, Nub had traveled frequently between India and Tibet. When King Langdarma came to power and tried to destroy the Buddha's teaching, he asked Nub, "What powers do you have?"

"Watch what I can do merely by reciting a mantra," Nub replied, pointing the threatening mudrā at the sky. Above his mudrā, there appeared nine black iron scorpions the size of yaks stacked on top of each other.

When the king saw this, he was terrified and said, "I swear I shall not harm this Buddhist yogin! Please practice the Dharma!"

"And now watch this!" Nub persisted, and he shot a bolt of lightning from his index finger that struck the rock face of the mountain opposite them and split it asunder.

At that, the king was quite terrified and promised, "I shall do nothing to harm you or your retinue!"

It is therefore due to Nubchen Sangye Yeshe's kindness that the holders of mantra who wear white clothes and long braided hair remained unharmed during Langdarma's persecution.

But Nub, unable to bear the destruction of the Buddha's teaching at the hands of Langdarma, carefully compiled all the razorlike wrathful mantras and prepared to put an end to him through wrathful compassion. Once the evil king had been put to death by Lhalung Palgyi Dorje, Nub hid the wrathful mantras as treasure, concerned they might be misused.

Śāstras composed by Nubchen Sangye Yeshe include *Armor Against Darkness: Extensive Commentary on the "Embodiment of Wisdom Mind"*; *Weapon of Speech That Cuts Through Difficulty*; *Commentary on the Clear Realization of the "Eighty-Chapter Magical Infinity"*; and *Lamp for the Eye of Samādhi: Upadeśa of the Great Perfection*. Through the enlightened activities of teaching and practice, Nubchen Sangye Yeshe spread the teachings of the three development and completion stages[196] throughout the world. Although he had many disciples, five were especially sublime: his four heart-sons and his one supreme son. As expressed in one of Nub's spiritual hymns:

In the Nub monk Yangwangter's
Forest of perfect sublime knowledge,
A tree of precious qualities grew,
And I placed it inside five supreme vessels.
One took the roots—
That was Lönchen Phagpa.
One took the leaves—
That was Legpe Drönme.
One took the flowers—
That was Dengyi Yönten Chok.
One took the fruit—
That was Yeshe Wangchuk.
And one took the whole tree—
That was Yönten Gyatso.

So the four heart-sons were Pagor Lönchen Phagpa, who was learned in the tantras, which are the "roots"; Sutönpa Legpe Drönme, who was learned in the *Eight Volumes of Amṛta*, which are the "leaves"; Dengyi Yönten Chok, who was learned in rebuttals, which are the "flowers"; and

So Yeshe Wangchuk, who was learned in the key point of the View, which is the "fruit." Nub's one supreme son, who was learned in all four of these, was Khulung Yönten Gyatso.

Also, the historical account of the empowerment of the *Embodiment of Wisdom Mind* states:

> The special transmission for the empowerment, tantra, and precious instructions was given to Khulungpa Yönten Gyatso. The special transmission for the four rivers of empowerment[197] was given to Sutön Legpe Drönme.

If a careful calculation is made according to the chronology found in the widely known *Kālacakra Tantra*, Nubchen appeared in our world exactly 1,712 years after the Buddha's parinirvāṇa. This is based upon the fact that the Buddha departed in the year of the Iron Dragon [881 BCE]. Twenty-eight years after Buddha's parinirvāṇa, in the Earth Monkey year [853 BCE], the Secret Mantra texts fell upon the roof of King Ja's palace. Nubchen was born 1,684 years later, in the Water Rat year [832 CE]. That same year, King Trisong Detsen, who was born in the Iron Horse year [790], turned forty-three, and six years had passed since the Fire Sheep year [827] when the "seven men tested" were ordained. King Trisong Detsen passed away in the Earth Tiger year [858], when Nubchen was twenty-seven years old. Nubchen passed away eighty-five years later, in the Water Tiger year [943], which indicates that he lived for thirty-seven years after the persecution of the Buddhist teaching by Langdarma. Nub lived in the human realm for 111 years. Ultimately, through the path of the Natural Great Perfection, he passed beyond suffering in a spontaneous Body of Light.

As it is said, "In the end, the Nyingma tradition fell to Zur." Here, this refers to the three Zur family lineages during the later spread of Buddhism. Deshek Zurpoche Shakya Jungne planted the roots of the Nyingma school teachings; Zurchungpa Sherab Dragpa extended its branches; and Zur Shakya Senge made its leaves and fruit flourish.

Zurpoche Shakya Jungne [1002–1062] came to the world as a manifest emanation of Yangdak Heruka. He was born in an area of Dokham called Yardzong, or Sarmo, as the son of the patroness Dewacham. When he first entered his mother's womb, his father had several dreams, such as a thousand-spoked golden wheel appearing in his hand and Ārya

Avalokiteśvara dissolving into his wife's form. Knowing that his son was a Nirmāṇakāya emanation, he named him Shakya Jungne.

Zurpoche's father taught him to read and write, and Zurpoche went on to receive the cycle of the *Magical Infinity* and the minor upadeśa. Over time, he received the three stages of ordination[198] from Lachen Gongpa Rabsal. Because he was a Nirmāṇakāya emanation, Lachen explained, it was not necessary for his name to be changed. With his grandfather Rinchen Gyatso, Zurpoche studied and mastered the three Vehicles of Characteristics,[199] the Kriyātantra, *Vajravidāraṇa*, *Vairocana*,[200] the *Magical Infinity*, and the *Glorious Paramādya*, as well as the Secret Mantra's inner upadeśa and path of skillful means.

As Zurpoche said, "Riding the horse of the subtle channels and winds, wearing the robe of yogic inner heat [tummo], accompanied by the precious instructions as my comforting friend, and guided by faith, I crossed the region of Dokham and approached the direction of Dam [in Central Tibet]." When Zurpoche was on the way from Kham to Dam, two devaputras appeared from among the clouds and showed him the way, and he arrived in Central Tibet.

When Zurpoche was practicing the Kriyātantra in Yarlung Namolung, his unsurpassed Secret Mantra Mahāyāna nature was awakened. "This arduous path of accepting and rejecting is the cause of being bound. May I find the path of the unsurpassed Secret Mantra, which has less hardship and is easier to practice," he thought.

That very night, Zurpoche heard a voice saying to go to meditate at a forested mountain. So he set off for Tsang, following the path of the Tsangpo River. "Who here is learned and accomplished in the teachings of the Secret Mantra?" he asked.

"There is someone in the Triple Forest," he was told. Hearing that, he recalled his previous dream, and he headed there. Zurpoche met Cheshak Chok of Gegong, from whom he received teachings on the sādhana for making amṛta medicine, and others.

Zurpoche had many gurus, but it was especially from Nyang Yeshe Jungne of Chölung that he received teachings of the Magical Infinity and the Mind Class of the Great Perfection, on which his flower had fallen. First, from Namkha De, Zurpoche studied the *Embodiment of Wisdom Mind* and the *Parkhab Commentary on the "Guhyagarbha Tantra,"* along with the Upadeśa of the Great Perfection. From Nyenak Wangdrak of Yulzer and Che Shakya Gyaltsen, Zurpoche received the secret empowerment and the path of skillful means. From Trochung of Upper Nyang, he received teachings on primordially pure great emptiness and self-accomplishing clear light, as well as *Stages of the Path of Magical Infinity*. From Rok Shakya Jungne of Chimpu and Sherab Tsultrim of Denma, he received *Yangdak Heruka*. From Zhutön Sönam Shakya, he received the entire *Embodiment of Wisdom Mind*. Also, from Tongtsab Jangchub, Gyatön Lodrö, and Kadö Yeshe Nyingpo, he received the reading transmission, empowerment and sādhana, tantric commentary, and ritual activities for the *Embodiment of Wisdom Mind*. Zurpoche only pleased his gurus, presenting all of them with elaborate gifts, including horses, and offerings made free of the three dualistic concepts of subject, object, and action.

It was in this manner that Zurpoche received the upadeśa of many learned masters. Their wisdom was contained in his experience, and he became learned and adept in all the tenets of the Tripiṭaka and Tantrapiṭaka. He then combined root tantras with explanatory tantras, root texts with commentaries, tantras with sādhanas, sādhanas with ritual arrangements, and so on, and became skilled in their applications. In a mountainous forest, he applied himself one-pointedly in the practice of glorious Yangdak Heruka, so he developed the strength of great confidence in the three stages of development, completion, and Great Perfection. The knots in the subtle channels of his throat cakra—the cakra of enjoyment—were released, and his perfect sublime knowledge expanded limitlessly. To the large assembly of disciples who gathered around him, he taught the *Embodiment of Wisdom Mind* and the *Tantra of the Magical Infinity*.

Zurpoche always completely avoided all distracting activities. He was never arrogant, and he shunned the bustle of worldly affairs. He did not entertain hopes of attaining enlightenment at some future time but focused with fierce diligence on directly experiencing enlightenment right now, in the present moment, within the continuity of his own mind.

Once a man who appeared to be a yogin came to partake of torma offerings. The yogin was given a small amount, but he got the whole torma. As the man was rounding the wall to leave, he said, "This Zurpoche is famous and knowledgeable, but his torma offerings certainly are not even close to the daily torma of Rok Shakya Jungne."

An attendant overheard him and told the Guru, who said, "Call him here!" The attendant set off to call the man and found him inside a cave, eating tsampa from a skull cup. "Please come," urged the attendant, but the yogin declined, saying, "Rok Shakya Jungne is in Chimpu, where he has already attained mastery over his life span. Tell Zurpoche to send someone to receive teachings from Rok Shakya Jungne." Then the yogin left without touching his feet to the ground.

Zurpoche sent Zangom Sherab Gyalpo with offerings carried on a mule to request the teaching. When Zangom arrived in Samye and asked around, no one could tell him the Guru's whereabouts. Finally, an old woman said, "He used to live here on the mountain of Chimpu." Then a herdsman said, "I think he is here on this mountain, because sometimes I can hear his drum and the sound of his rulu mantra."[201] So Zangom turned his mule out in a patch of green grass and prayed with faith and devotion. There was a loud sound, and suddenly he saw the door of a cave. With his powerful devotion, Zangom was able to pass right through it. Eighteen secret protector-gings swarmed around him and shouted, "Kill him!"

But Rok Shakya Jungne replied, "He is karmically destined, so that would be wrong."

Zangom relayed his story, whereby Rok replied, "How auspicious that I, Rok Shakya Jungne, should have a disciple named Zur Shakya Jungne, with Sherab Gyalpo serving as our link." Then Rok gave Zangom the empowerments of sixty-two maṇḍalas, such as Buddhasamāyoga, the twelve self-and-other maṇḍalas of Yangdak Heruka, and Yangdak combined with Vajrakīla. When Zangom had received all the texts, reading transmissions, and subsequent oral instructions, he came back down to Samye, where he found a young boy seated on his mule wearing a silk turban. Zangom went back and asked Rok who the boy was. "That is Brahmā Crowned with Conch Shells,"[202] Rok explained, and he gave Zangom an offering text[203] for this protector. Later, Zangom offered the instructions to Lama Zurpoche in secrecy.

The master and his disciples all meditated for many years, and by sustaining teaching and studying, Zurpoche greatly benefitted beings. However, Zurpoche was focused only on being in solitude. "All these virtuous deeds are a distraction for me," he said. "I am going to Ngadak Drak in Bodong."

No sooner had he settled into solitary meditation than his disciples arrived, having followed him there. "If your purpose in coming to stay with me is to attain enlightenment, then meditation practice is the only thing that will help you. Nothing else. Cast away all worldly distractions and devote yourselves to practice. I also will do nothing but practice." Master and disciples then engaged in individual practice.

After a time, Zurpoche received a prophecy from the Ḍākinīs, urging him to go down to the lowlands to benefit beings. He traveled to Tanak and settled into an east-facing cave with an owl's nest inside. There, through engaging in the practice of the Yangdak Heruka nine-deity maṇḍala, he had a clear vision of the great glorious Yangdak Heruka. Thereafter, owing to the name of the place where he lived, he became renowned as Lama Ugpa Lungpa, "Guru of Owl Valley."

Sometime later, after continuously perceiving the five Buddhas on the southern mountain of Wensermo, Zurpoche announced that he needed to build a temple there. He covered a spring, where the nāga Dungkyong lived, with a sheet of copper, and on top of that he built the outer support of the temple, with an upper shrine supported by four pillars, an upper court with eight pillars, a lower court with twenty pillars, and so on. The upper shrine contained images of the peaceful deities, with the magical manifestation of Vairocana in the center. The eight-pillared upper court held the two gatekeepers, Wrathful Hayagrīva and Swirling Amṛta. In the north and south wings, he placed the Great Mother Prajñāpāramitā and Dīpaṃkara, each surrounded by four offering goddesses. In the protector shrine, he placed relief images of Legden, Palden Lhamo, Brahmā, and Indra. Frescoes of the lineage masters were painted on the walls of the eight-pillared upper court, and the surrounding walls depicted the twenty-one maṇḍalas, such as the Hundred-Petaled Lotus. On the walls of the twenty-pillared lower court, there were frescoes of the Thousand Buddhas, the Buddhas of the ten directions, Amitāyus surrounded by the Eight Close Sons,[204] the seven Buddhas of the past,[205] the twelve deeds of a Buddha, Bodhisattva Dharmodgata, Tārā Who Protects from the Eight Fears,[206] the Lords of the Three Families,[207] the Malaya Pureland, the Wheel of Life,[208] and so on. Furthermore, Zurpoche manifested himself as the splendid and dazzling form of the great glorious Yangdak Heruka, and using him as a model, sculptors crafted a statue of the deity.

On another occasion, a patron named Drotönpa offered to Zurpoche a place called Dropuk, where Zurpoche built a temple devoted to the Buddhas of the three times.[209] It had eight shrines of various sizes, an upper court supported by twenty pillars, and a lower court with sixty pillars. Zurpoche established a great Dharma college there as well, where he was able to build an inconceivable number of supports of Buddha's enlightened body, speech, and mind, which served as fields for gathering the two accumulations for all beings, and specifically for those of that region.

At the age of sixty-one, after sustaining his teaching, practice, and enlightened activities in an inconceivable way, this holy being, an undisputed Nirmāṇakāya emanation who had perfected the precious qualities of the five paths[210] and reached the state of spontaneously accomplished Vidyādhara, focused his wisdom mind toward transforming his physical body into light. He requested that [his disciple] Zurchungpa be summoned from Drak Gyawo.

When Zurchungpa arrived, the master said, "I am entrusting this place to you, Zurchungpa. You must look after my disciples and give them teachings according to their abilities. Care for them as I have done. Disciples, you should know that Zurchungpa has attained the spiritual accomplishments of the Great Glorious Heruka's enlightened body, speech, and mind, so he is greater than I am. View everything he does as excellent. Do not disobey him. Do not tread upon his shadow, his footsteps, or his clothing. He will care for you as I have done, so approach him with perfect devotion."

Zurpoche then departed for his hermitage in Sampa. One day, he said to his attendant, "Tomorrow morning, bring me my breakfast early." Just as the sun was rising, the attendant went before the master and found him seated on his bed, donning his most elegant robes. "Where are you going in those fancy robes?" the attendant asked.

I am going to the Pureland of Great Bliss.
I am inseparable from the Great Glorious Heruka,
So pray to the Yidam deity!

With that, Zurpoche picked up his vajra and rang his bell. As the ringing sound filled the room, Zurpoche's body transformed into the nature of pure light, and he dissolved into the heart of the Great Glorious Heruka.

Lhaje Zurpoche had an inconceivable number of direct and indirect disciples. Foremost among them were his "four pinnacles": Zurchung Sherab Dragpa [known as Zurchungpa], who reached the pinnacle of view and realization; Minyak Khyungdrak, who reached the pinnacle of *Magical Infinity* explanation; Zhang Göchung, who reached the pinnacle of profound knowledge; and Zangom Sherab Gyalpo, who reached the pinnacle of accomplishment in meditation. There were also the "eight hidden pinnacles," the "hundred and eight great meditators," and so on, and many others who were famous for displaying miracles, such as flying through the sky. Of the "four pinnacles," the one who was like the king of elephants was Deshek

Gyawopa, otherwise known as Zurchungpa Sherab Dragpa [1014–1074]. He was the principal successor to the Owl Valley mantra holder [Zurpoche]. Zurchungpa's father was Tagpa Gomchen, who sometimes lived as a mendicant, and his mother was Majo Sherab Kyi. He was born in Yeru, one of the regions of Tsang, in the Male Wood Tiger year [1014], amid wondrous auspicious signs. He learned to read and write when he was seven, and by age nine he could chant the sādhana of the peaceful and wrathful deities. One day when he was thirteen, he was in bed reading a text, and his consort ran into the room, saying, "The fields are flooding! How can you just lie there?"

Zurchungpa headed out across the floodwaters wearing his new lower garment. As he was shoveling a trench to divert the water, his consort shouted, "Hey! You did not even change out of that new robe I worked so hard to make for you! Now you've gone and ruined it!"

"If you care more about this garment than you do about me, then take it!" he said, and he threw it at her.

"You've insulted me!" she cried angrily, and she ran off to her village.

Zurchungpa was filled with sadness about life in saṃsāra. He took her spindle from the rafters and shouted after her. She stood waiting, hoping that he would call her back to him. He held up the spindle and said, "Male wealth is for males, and female wealth is for females. So here, take your spindle." Disappointed and depressed, she left for her village.

Then, without conferring with his father or requesting supplies from his mother or worrying about what his friends would think, Zurchungpa took his wolfskin coat and set off to meet Zurpoche. Along the way, he met two nomads from Tanak, who were carrying turquoise and copper, and a man from Zhang, who was bringing armor, and they traveled together. On arriving, Zurchungpa had only his wolfskin coat to offer. When the others had made their offerings, Lama Zurpoche said to his attendants, "Let's see if they have renounced saṃsāra or not. Bring them some beer gruel and vegetable soup." The two nomads declined to partake, the man from Zhang ate a small portion, and Zurchungpa ate everything without leaving anything. The Guru said, "We will keep the wolfskin coat and the armor. Give the turquoise and copper back to their owners."

The nomads were unhappy. "Returning our offerings is a sign that he will not teach us," they said, and they left.

Then the Guru asked Zurchungpa, "What is your clan?"

Fearing that it might seem competitive if he revealed that his clan was the same as the Guru's, Zurchungpa said, "I am from a small Zur clan [Zurchung]." Just by his saying this, Zurchung became his name. Recognizing that Zurchungpa was karmically destined, the Guru permitted him to study, and Zurchungpa developed outstanding intellectual prowess.

In the beginning Zurchungpa was extremely poor, and he sustained himself by picking up tormas cast out by the Guru and using them to make beer gruel. The other monks complained, "His breath reeks of sour beer. But he hasn't offered any to his guru or his Dharma brothers."

The Guru said, "Today, Zurchungpa, go collect wood." After Zurchungpa had left, the attendants searched his hut, but they found only a skull cup of beer gruel underneath a patched quilt. The Guru then said, "Zurchungpa, if you have run out of food, come join us in our kitchen."

"I would ruin the offerings made to the Guru," Zurchungpa said, and he patiently endured constant hardship.

One day, the Guru brought a rosewood bowl, big enough to hold nine handfuls of food, to Zurchungpa's room and asked, "Zurchungpa, do you have something for me to drink?" Zurchungpa filled his guru's bowl with beer gruel, and the Guru drank it down. "I'd like some more," he said, and he drank another bowlful. Then he asked, "Is there any more left now?"

"There is about a quart left," Zurchungpa replied.

"Now you do not have much left. If you did, your merit would become as vast as all of Tibet. However, due to the auspicious circumstance of your service to me, great merit will come to you." The Guru gave him three sacks of barley and said, "When this is gone, supplies will come to you without obstacle."

Regardless of what he studied or meditated upon, Zurchungpa exerted himself day and night without stopping. Because he was a Nirmāṇakāya emanation, knowledge and wisdom spontaneously welled forth from within him. Although inconceivable visionary experience and realization had dawned in him, he could not even afford paper and pen. Lhaje Zurpoche said to him, "There is a wealthy female meditator named Jomo Yungmo who lives with her daughter in a place called Pengyi Khangngön. Go live with her."

"I do not wish to be a householder," Zurchungpa protested.

"Do not be small-minded," the Guru replied. "I am aware of the dividing line between what the Buddha allowed and prohibited. When you accept their resources, you will be able to request empowerments, write texts, and receive the Dharma in its entirety. This will complete their meritorious accumulations, and it will enable you to achieve your goals as well. Indeed, this is best."

Zurchungpa followed his guru's command, and so all his wishes were fulfilled.

Then one day, the Guru said, "Do not stay there any longer. Bring your books and supplies and come here."

"Is it appropriate to do that? These two have been so kind to me," said Zurchungpa.

"Do not be narrow-minded," the Guru said. "You will soon be capable of benefitting beings. In these degenerate times, you must spread the Buddha's teachings and work for the welfare of many beings. That is also the best way to repay the kindness of Jomo Yungmo and her daughter. If you hide yourself away there, you will accomplish neither your own aim nor the aim of others."

Zurchungpa did just as he was told and perfectly fulfilled his guru's wishes.

At one point, Zurchungpa received a prophecy about a sacred place. The prophecy came to him in three stages. Initially, because he was a yogin who had realized emptiness, he disregarded it as just delusion. Eventually, five sixteen-year-old girls appeared before him, adorned with bone ornaments, dancing and ringing skull drums. They said, "Dear brother, if you meditate on the nine mountains, you will accomplish the two aims." They pointed toward Drak Gyawo.

Zurchungpa realized that the nine mountains, nine springs, and nine alpine meadows were symbolic of the nine successive yānas[211] in their completeness. He said to himself, "Drak Gyawo looks like the Bhagavān Great Glorious Heruka surrounded by the eight Gaurī[212] goddesses, so practicing there will bring accomplishment quickly and great blessing. Anyway, saṃsāra is nothing but suffering, so I really must give up all worldly entanglements. The bustle of everyday affairs, profit, and power will not help me in future lifetimes. Trying to please and flatter people with pretense is not only difficult in the short term, it is utterly meaningless in the long term. I will go to meditate alone."

Zurchungpa entrusted his monks to the three "useless men," ordering them to uphold the teaching of exposition and study, and left for Drak Gyawo. There he dedicated himself solely to practice, and the local guardian deity caused a great obstacle with magical upheavals and disruptions. However, to such a supreme one among siddhas, dreams and waking appearances are all perceived as equally false. One night in a dream, on the peak of Drak Gyawo, a dark man appeared and snatched him by his two feet, twirled him around up high, and threw him. He dreamed that he landed in a wide plain in the Tak River valley. When he awoke, he found that he was actually in the midst of that plain, and he had to ascend the mountain again. But he remained undeterred by these great shows of magic.

Another time, his hermitage filled up with young goat-sized scorpions, and Zurchungpa, with his realization of going beyond the cause and result of karma, grabbed each scorpion by the claws and ripped it in half, saying, "I confess each nonvirtuous misdeed!" With these puns,[213] he teased those who rely on words rather than on meaning.[214] Then he threw the scorpions away, and they all transformed into Buddha Vairocana and disappeared into the sky.

Another time, an army of ants appeared, and Zurchungpa told his attendant to bring him a mallet. He used the mallet to smash all the ants, and the attendant gasped in horror, "Think what a terrible thing you've just done!"

"If that didn't arouse your faith, then how's this?" Zurchungpa put the ants in his mouth and blew out, and all the ants transformed into Vajrasattva and rose straight up in the sky. At that, the attendant was filled with immense faith. With his miraculous power beyond imagination to kill and restore to life, Zurchungpa bound three local deities, all of them siblings, under oath. They actually appeared before him and bowed at his feet.

A spring that welled forth when Zurchungpa thrust his ritual dagger into a boulder still flows today. It was there that he engaged in the practice of mudrā samādhi[215] from the *Secret Magical Infinity* and saw the face of Vajrasattva. The valley of Tak became completely filled with Vajrasattvas. Zurchungpa attained the sense sources of the exhaustion of appearances, so that he could transform his body into fire, water, wind, and dust, and everything spontaneously appeared as the luminous nature of Vajrasattva, radiant and clear. The power of his noble thoughts grew stronger and stronger, but he realized that they were not truly reliable. After that, appearances, mind, and Dharmatā merged into one taste, and Zurchungpa reached the level of wisdom mind, where all phenomena are exhausted. He gained control of the five elements, so that he could pass unimpeded through earth, rocks, and boulders and soar through the sky like a bird.

After that, Lama Zurchungpa resolved to remain in retreat in Drak Gyawo for twenty-four years in one long, continuous practice session, with his mind focused on attaining the Rainbow Body. During this period, two events forced him out of retreat, so in all, he remained there for thirteen straight years plus one additional year, making a total of fourteen years. For a long time, he would not even allow his attendants to visit him. After some time, there was not even any smoke or sounds that emerged from his hermitage. Concerned that his guru might have fallen ill, his attendant went to check on him, and he found that the Guru's mouth and nose were covered with cobwebs. Thinking that the Guru had died, the attendant burst into tears. This dispersed the Guru's meditation, and the Guru said, "If you had only let me remain in this state, my head would have been unburdened from bearing this skull. Now I will have to take one more rebirth." This rebirth was said to be Sakya Lochen. It seems that as a sign of accomplishment on the path, all of Zurchungpa's phenomena were about to be exhausted in the expanse of Dharmatā with his skandhas disappearing into emptiness.

One reason he had to interrupt his retreat was that the three "useless men" were unable to uphold the Buddhist teachings. Gojatsa went to see Gö Khugpa, claiming that he needed the mother tantras in preparation for the path of skillful means. Mikchung Wangseng went to see Sumpa Yebar, claiming that he needed the Yogatantras in preparation for projecting the maṇḍala. Gochung Wange went to see Pangka Darchungwa, claiming that he needed to study logic in preparation for the philosophy of the basis and path.

The *Guhyagarbha: The Root Tantra* contains both the path of skillful means and the path of liberation, so Gojatsa failed to discern the defining characteristics of the mother tantra. The maṇḍala emerges from its own natural state, so Mikchung Wangseng's realization was askew. Logic is a verbal philosophy, therefore it cannot be applied to the basis and path, which Gochung Wange failed to understand. It was for these reasons that the three "useless men" were unable to uphold the center for higher learning,[216] and Zurchungpa was forced to break his retreat.

Another reason was that since the victorious Zurpoche, his master, had decided to attain the state of union in that lifetime, without leaving his body, before completing the construction and consecration of the Dropuk Temple, Zurchungpa had been called from retreat by Zurpoche, who had said, "You should preserve my legacy."

Zurchungpa's miraculous abilities were truly extraordinary. He was known for traveling on sunrays. He could give a teaching in the morning in Owl Valley, a teaching at noon in Dropuk, and a teaching at night in Drak Gyawo. The distances between these three places were vast, yet each day he could deliver teachings in each one of them. Likewise, when he beheld Ḍākinīs dancing in Lhazermo, he commissioned them to build a shrine with nine supports: seven pillars and two lofty columns. This became known as the Ḍākinī Temple. Images of the forty-two peaceful deities and the Dharma Guardian Legden Degu were made, and frescoes of both the extensive and brief maṇḍalas of the Magical Infinity were painted on the walls. When the consecration was performed, Zurchungpa struck the statue of Legden with his sleeve and asked, "Are you going to guard the Buddha's teachings?" The statue bowed its head in reply. "Will you esteem the eminence of the Triple Gems?" And the statue's lips moved up and down.

Similarly, when Zurchungpa beheld the Great Glorious Heruka in a vision, he built a Yangdak Heruka temple on the very site where the left foot of the deity was placed. His disciple Matok Jangbar completed the temple with the wood of a sacred tree, trickling with sap, which he cut down and offered. When the first cut of wood was presented to the Guru, the local protector deity, Trengwa, retrieved a tamarisk pillar that had been left behind and sent it down the Tsangpo River. It sank at a place called Camel Passage and stayed underwater for five days. Zurchungpa sent two of his disciples there, saying, "Stack these white tormas on the rock, throw this red torma into the water, and get him to send me my wood right away!" The water deity was frightened by this threatening order and instantly sent up the pillar. This is but one of many examples in which deities and spirits obeyed Zurchungpa's commands.

When the time drew near for Lhaje Zurchungpa, adorned as he was with such wondrous precious qualities, to enter enlightenment, his disciples entreated him to have a son. With the samādhi of the five enlightenments,[217] Zurchungpa invited the Lord of Secrets, Vajrapāṇi, into his consort's womb. Vajrapāṇi revealed himself as Zur Dropukpa Shakya Senge, born with wondrous marks and signs.

Then, at the age of sixty-one, in the year of the Male Wood Tiger [1074], Zurchungpa imparted his final testament, known as the *Eighty Chapters of Personal Advice*, which begins:

> Be a child of the mountains,
> Wear ragged clothing,

Eat plain food,
Let your enemies have their way,
Leave your land uncultivated,
Resolve to practice the Dharma. . . .

Amid lights and earth tremors, Zurchungpa departed for Akaniṣṭha, the Citadel of the Vajra Array.

Lama Zurchungpa had numerous disciples, such as the "four pillars," the "eight beams," the "sixteen galleries," the "thirty-two rafters," the "three useless men," the "two great female meditators," the "two runners," the "two from Tagur," and the "boastful one." They brought inconceivable benefit to the Dharma and beings.

Zurchungpa's son, the great Lord of Secrets of Dropuk, Zur Shakya Senge [1074–1134], became like the fountainhead of the *Guhyagarbha* explanatory teachings here in Tibet. One of Zurchungpa's female disciples, named Jo Semo Damo Tsugtorjam, seemed to Zurchungpa capable of bringing forth a Nirmāṇakāya emanation. He approached her brother, Datik Chöshak, one of the "four pillars," and asked, "Could I have your sister?"

"As you wish," Datik replied. He placed a vajra and bell in his sister's hands and said, "Take these and offer them personally to the Guru. Do not let anyone else do it for you." He thereby set up a very auspicious connection.

But because she was not taken in as the Guru's wife, the monastic community reviled her and sought to banish her. Kyotön Shakye intervened and said, "I had a dream in which a great Buddhist master was sitting upon her ring finger. If he turns out to be a Dharma heir of some sort, he may well benefit the teachings. Let's let her stay."

Likewise, the other "pillars" dreamed of Buddha statues, golden vajras, and other items dissolving into the noble lady's body, so she was allowed to stay. In the year of the Male Wood Tiger [1074], when the great translator of Ngok [Loden Sherab] turned sixteen, Dropukpa was born. The Guru said, "When my son first entered her womb, I had the impression that Vajrapāṇi had dissolved into her. He will come to benefit beings." He named the boy Shakya Senge.

When the father, Zurchungpa, gave up all of his belongings as an offering, the family was left with almost nothing. The mother said, "You knew well ahead that we were giving birth to a child. Why didn't you keep even a dab of butter paste?"[218]

"If he has merit, butter paste will come to him even if I don't provide it," Zurchungpa replied. "If he does not, providing for him will do no good anyway." No sooner had Zurchungpa taken a seat on his upper terrace than a wealthy nun appeared and offered them many sacks of barley and a large amount of butter. Zurchungpa rejoiced by saying, "Offerings from Dokham have arrived and the butter paste has come. Merit will come to the child and he will benefit beings."

When the child was eight months old, his father passed away. His mother and maternal uncle looked after him, and he lived in Dapu until he was fifteen. Then he traveled to Chubar to meet Len Shakya Zangpo, from whom he received the *Secret Magical Infinity*. He also went to Kyonglung and received teachings from Lama Yangkheng. When Dropukpa was nineteen, he had his formal enthronement ceremony, and he became inundated with duties and responsibilities and distracted from his studies. At one point, Dropukpa found an opportunity to spend one year with Gongbur Kyo, but after that his activities increased greatly once again and he had no chance to go anywhere. Instead, he invited a host of learned and accomplished gurus to come to him and was thus able to complete his studies.

From the "four pillars," Dropukpa received all of his father's teachings on the trilogy of Sūtra, Magical Infinity, and Mind, along with their tantras, upadeśa, activity rituals, sādhanas, practice instructions, and empowerments in their entirety. In particular, from his uncle Datik he received detailed teachings on the Sūtra cycle; from Len Shakya Jangchub, he received the tradition of the Great Perfection cycles;[219] from Lhaje Shangnak, he received the final Great Perfection transmission lineage; and so on. In brief, by studying and contemplating with many gurus, he successfully resolved all his uncertainties and doubts.

On one occasion, Dropukpa and four of his students went to meet Padampa Sangye, who was residing in Tingri. On the day they were set to arrive, Padampa Sangye said to his disciples, "An emanation of Vajrapāṇi is coming today. You must go out to welcome him."

They prepared silk scarves, a ceremonial parasol, and other items, but it was not until the sun was beginning to set that five mantra holders appeared, a master and his disciples. "There's no one else around," Padampa's disciples told him.

"They are the ones you must welcome," Padampa said.

Meanwhile, Lhaje Dropukpa said, "Now, let's see if Padampa Sangye is clairvoyant or not." He sent one of his disciples ahead, disguised as himself, and he followed behind, posing as the attendant.

Padampa noted the goiter in Dropukpa's neck and said:

> With respect, the goitered one should lead,
> For it is best if master and disciple are not reversed.

This filled Dropukpa with devotion, and he received the nectar of Padampa's teachings. Padampa affirmed and encouraged him, saying, "You will become a great glorious master of the Buddhist teachings!"

Another time, when instructing an artist on how to paint a Vajrapāṇi image, Dropukpa actually revealed himself as Vajrapāṇi and told the artist to paint the image just like that.

These are just some of the many reasons why Dropukpa was widely known as the glorious Lord of Secrets, having come to spread the teachings of the Secret Mantra in the northern land of Tibet.

Overall, Dropukpa's gathering of students was unfathomably large. Specifically, he had 1,000 disciples who emerged as great spiritual mentors graced with Dharma parasols, each of whom oversaw a monastic center[220] and upheld and protected the Buddhist teachings. So even in the long term, Dropukpa's activity was inconceivably vast.

Once, while teaching at Dropuk, Dropukpa was sitting on a throne with no back, and monks surrounded him on all sides. From every direction it appeared that he was facing the audience, and people became convinced that he was the actual manifestation of the lord of the maṇḍala of the *Mirror of All the Vajrasattva Magical Infinity Tantras*. He was indisputably renowned as a Nirmāṇakāya emanation.

Dropukpa's summer and winter teachings were regularly attended by about 500 aspiring scholars, and his spring and fall teachings were attended by about 300. All told, there were well over 10,000 students in attendance, so it became common practice for people to pay a gold coin to get a good seat in the teaching yard. With his perfect qualities of knowledge, love, and power, and his total mastery of the meaning of the *Glorious Guhyagarbha: The Tantra That Ascertains the Absolute Nature Just As It Is*, Dropukpa attained the "eye of Dharma."[221] Because of that, there is a Dropukpa tradition for studying the *Guhyagarbha* that is as famous as the sun and moon and is much talked about even today.

When the time came for the great Lord of Secrets Dropukpa to display his final deed, he said to his four disciples named Tön, "Bring supplies for a feast offering.[222] I shall gather some as well." The four Töns did as they were told, and they ascended to the peak of Taglha Ridong Mountain in Dropuk, where they performed an abundant feast offering. Afterward, Dropukpa gave numerous instructions on his secret teachings and said, "You must not be sad without me. I am now going to depart for the realm of the Vidyādharas without leaving my body behind. After I go, you will enjoy auspiciousness. Your lineages and the Buddhist teachings will flourish." The four Töns were stricken with grief and felt as if their hearts had been torn from their chests. They wailed and lamented, writhing back and forth on the ground and calling his name. Finally, he returned, alighting like a bird on the earth, and said, "I asked you not to behave like this. I gave you plenty of good advice before."

The following year, in the year of the Male Wood Tiger, when he was sixty-one, Dropukpa departed for the citadel of Akaniṣṭha, the Gathering Place of the Great Assembly. During the cremation, a handsome young mantra holder appeared and offered a beautiful horse with a wondrous saddle of naturally curving conch. No one knew where he had come from or where he had gone, so they concluded that a deity had brought the offering. Similarly, offerings were made by tsen spirits, mamos, and nāgas, so that four kinds of wealth unknown to humankind appeared.

Dropukpa had twelve heart-disciples: four disciples named Nak, four disciples named Tön, and four disciples known as Mepo. The four named Nak were Chetön Gyanak, Zurnak Khorlo, Nyangnak Dowo, and Danak Tsugtor Wangchuk. The four named Tön were Nyetön Chöseng, Gyatön Dorje Gönpo, Zhangtön, and Gyatön. The four Mepo were Tsangpa Chitön, Yutön Horpo, Bangtön Chakyu, and Upa Chöseng. This lineage listing is known as the Upper Zur tradition of Central Tibet; the Lower tradition of Kham lists a different lineage.

It is due to the kindness of great Dharma charioteers such as these, who were Bodhisattvas of the higher bhūmis, that the teachings of the Early Translation school continue without interruption even now, at the very end of the era.

Buddha says in the *Mahāparinirvāṇa Sūtra*:

> Twelve years after my parinirvāṇa,
> On a wondrous lotus island,
> One known as Padmasambhava
> Will come as Lord of the Secret Mantra teachings.

As well, it says in the *Magical Infinity of Mañjuśrī*:

> The glorious Buddha born from a lotus,
> Is an omniscient treasure holder of wisdom,
> King of various magical manifestations,
> Great Buddha, lineage holder of Vajrayana.[223]

Likewise, other sūtras and tantras, such as the *Holy Golden Light Sūtra* and the *Tantra of the Perfect Embodiment of the Unexcelled Nature*, contain the Buddha's prophetic praises of the Great Ācārya Padmasambhava. From the perspective of absolute truth, Padmasambhava was completely inseparable from the wisdom mind of the Three-Kāya Buddhas. Because he mastered the enlightened activity of all Buddhas throughout the ten directions, his outer, inner, and secret biographies are said to be beyond the reach of even those who dwell on the sublime tenth Bodhisattva bhūmi.[224] He manifested as 100 teachers of Sūtra and Mantra in the billionfold Sahā world system,[225] and in our world alone, his single form emanated eight manifestations, which further emanated twenty manifestations, and so forth. Through them, Padmasambhava benefitted beings in inconceivable ways. As it is said:

> I have written and concealed one thousand nine hundred
> autobiographies
> For the benefit of future disciples with pure samaya.

As described earlier, the translators, paṇḍitas, patrons, and court gurus held a council in the land of Tibet. They established a Buddhist college for the study of the Vehicle of Characteristics and a meditation center for the practice of the resultant Vehicle of Mantra. In particular, in Dregu Geur in Chimpu, the Great Ācārya Padmasambhava granted entry into the maṇḍalas of the Eight Heruka Sādhanas, which are the vital heart essence of the eight Vidyādharas of India, to the Sovereign King Trisong Detsen, along with the nine karmically destined heart-sons and others, and he gave the empowerments. He then had them each practice the Yidam deity of their karmic connection according to the particular Buddha family upon which each of their flowers landed, and he brought them to fruition, complete with wondrous signs of accomplishment.

In addition, Padmasambhava made fortunate an unfathomably huge entourage of pure, karmically destined disciples, including the twenty-five Mahāsiddhas of Chimpu, the thirty mantra holders of Sheldrak, the fifty-five realized yogins of Yangzong, the hundred Mahāsiddhas of Yerpa and Chuwori, and so on. In short, he caused the dazzling radiance of the Buddha's teachings to spread throughout the entire country of Tibet. As he himself said:

> In the dark age of degeneration, treasures will safeguard the teachings in the final period. ༔

And just as Padmasambhava promised, with his words of powerful love for beings of future generations, countless treasures were concealed in the five common locations for profound treasures: the earth, lakes, rocks, trees, and temples; and the five uncommon treasure locations: east, west, south, north, and center. He concealed 108 treasures, the main ones being his five great heart treasures, which include astrological sciences that set forth the points of good, bad, right, and wrong; riches that repair the deterioration of the outer universe; medicine to dispel the compounded disturbances of animate beings; the class of enlightened activity practices such as fierce mantras to guard the Buddha's teachings; and the profound oral instructions that confer the level of perfect omniscience, which are the upadeśa of the development and completion stages, and in particular the Trio of Ka Gong Pur, which is the Eight Heruka Sādhanas [*Ka*], the Guru Yoga treasure cycles [*Gong*], and the practice of Vajrakīlaya [*Pur*]. In addition, he concealed countless other treasures, with and without names, such as the 72,000 minor treasures. He prophesied the individuals endowed with ten qualities of greatness[226] who would reveal the treasures, their disciples with ten qualities of purity[227] who would be the holders of Treasure teachings, and the times when the treasures would be revealed. To ensure that places would give blessings to the people who lived in them in the future, Guru Padmasambhava walked the length and breadth of Tibet, setting foot upon every mountain, rock, and snowy range, most notably the five lands,[228] the three main valleys,[229] the single island,[230] the twenty snowy mountains,[231] and the very remote eight great caves,[232] and blessed them as sacred places for practice.

To the king and his ministers, subjects, patrons, monks, yogins, yoginīs, and so on, Padmasambhava gave oral instruction and advice according to their individual karma. Then he sang:

I am leaving, going to the Glorious Copper-Colored Mountain. ༔
I am going to introduce the Dharma to the rakṣasas . . . ༔

Then he departed for the southwestern continent of Cāmara, land of the rakṣasas.[233] But in fact, as he himself pronounced, Padmasambhava looks after the benefit of all beings, throughout all times and in all directions, until saṃsāra is emptied:

For men and women who have faith in me, ༔
I, the Lotus-Born, have gone nowhere; I sleep by their door. ༔

Furthermore, the prophetic treasure text revealed by Chögyal Ratna Lingpa reads as follows [giving words spoken by Khandro Yeshe Tsogyal]:

Because Tibetans, in general, are so interested in things that are new ༔
And because of my special love and affection for beings of degenerate times, ༔
I have filled all of Tibet with treasures, ༔
The exceedingly profound, ultimate quintessential teachings, ༔
And made aspirations that they meet with karmically destined heirs. ༔
In future times, superficial intellectuals
And meditators with haughty sectarian bias ༔
Will puff themselves up with arrogance and criticize the Treasure tradition, ༔
Yet most degenerate-age practitioners will be guided by treasures. ༔
They are profound, complete, unobscured, and extensive, ༔
And even one tiny piece of instruction will certainly liberate beings. ༔
Thus, fortunate and learned ones with awakened karma, ༔
While aware of impermanence, practice the Treasure teachings. ༔
You will find the path to liberation within one lifetime, O followers. ༔
All you fortunate ones in the degenerate age with devotion to the treasures, ༔
I pray that you behold the Guru's face right now. ༔
Since all of you have great merit, be joyful. ༔
These words of mine are rarer than the finest gold. ༔

During the period when Guru Rinpoche lived in Tibet, the queen of Ḍākinīs, supreme consort abiding in Dharmakāya, Yeshe Tsogyal, who was the actual Goddess Sarasvatī, appeared in the body of a woman in order to benefit beings. She was one of the Guru's five supreme consorts,[234] and she recorded all of his unwritten tantras, scriptures, and upadeśa. She remained in the Land of Snows for over a century after Guru Rinpoche departed for the land of rakṣasas, during which time she compiled all his teachings, perfectly retained within her infallible memory. She wrote them down in the symbolic script of the Dharmadhātu Ḍākinīs on five kinds of yellow scrolls[235] and placed them in various treasure caskets, which she concealed in inconceivable numbers throughout Tibet. She locked them each with a seal.

Also famous for concealing numerous treasures were masters such as the great paṇḍita Vimalamitra, the Dharma King Trisong Detsen and his sons, the Enlightened Translator Vairotsana, Nubchen Sangye Yeshe, Namkhe Nyingpo, Nyagchen Yeshe Zhönu, Nanam Dorje Dudjom, and Nyangben Tingdzin Zangpo.

Then, when the prophesied time came, when the karmic power of aspiration was awakened, when a guru, deity, or doctrine-holding Dharma Guardian requested directly or indirectly, and when all the other causes, conditions, and auspicious connections ripened at the right time, the major and minor treasure revealers of Tibet, beginning with the illustrious early eleventh-century Ācārya Sangye Lama, appeared, both in succession and at random. Among them, Nyangral Nyima Özer, Guru Chökyi Wangchuk [known as Guru Chöwang], and Rigdzin Gökyi Demtruchen [known as Rigdzin Gödem] are called the "three supreme Nirmāṇakāyas." When Dorje Lingpa, Pema Lingpa, and the holder of the seven transmissions, Pema Ösel Do Ngak Lingpa [tertön name of Jamyang Khyentse Wangpo], are added to the first two, they are known as the "five tertön kings." Then there are the "eight Lingpas," such as Terdak Lingpa, and the "eleven faultless Lingpas," such as Orgyen Lingpa.[236] There have been numerous other treasure revealers, namely the "hundred and eight major tertöns," such as Trime Özer, Trime Kunga, and Trime Lhunpo, known collectively as the "three Trimes," the "thousand minor tertöns," and so on, each of whom has brought forth inconceivable treasures—Dharma teachings, wealth, sacred substances, and so on—from their respective treasure locations, in accordance with their special gifts. Then, by way of the six kinds of liberation[237] inherent in treasures, these masters brought inconceivable benefit to sentient beings.

Dharma King Trisong Detsen had three sons with noble family lineage and Dharma knowledge: Mune Tsenpo, Murub Tsenpo, and Mutik Tsenpo. During their reigns, they did much to uphold and serve the teachings of their father and forefathers. Mutik Tsenpo had five sons; the second, Tri Ralpachen, was an emanation of the Lord of Secrets, Vajrapāṇi. Tri Ralpachen constructed 1,000 Buddhist temples, the temple of Önchangdo Tashi Gepel foremost among them, and assigned the monks to seven local families who ensured that their needs were met. In an effort to make the archaic translations rendered by his forefathers easier to understand, Tri Ralpachen instituted a new, more refined translation system. His extraordinary efforts to sustain the Buddhist teachings make him the third of the "three ancestral Dharma kings"—Songtsen Gampo, Trisong Detsen, and Tri Ralpachen—who are revered as supremely wondrous and kind. These three kings caused the brilliance of the Victorious One's teachings to spread throughout the length and breadth of Tibet, the Land of Snows.

As it says in the *Former Lives of the Buddha*:

> When one finds the excellent path of enlightenment,
> At that time, all demons become jealous,
> Just as when one finds many priceless jewels,
> All robbers are taking aim toward one.[238]

As this describes, a period followed when evil ministers became displeased and conspired to destroy Buddhist law. They killed King Tri Ralpachen and enthroned his younger brother, Langdarma Udum Tsenpo, who exiled the eldest brother, Lhase Tsangma, to the borderlands. Langdarma demoted monastics, armed them with bows and arrows, and forced them to become hunters. Among the many cruel and oppressive deeds enacted during his four-year regime, many translators, including Ma Rinchen Chok, were stabbed to death, and Dharma translation was halted.

During that period, lay mantra holders who lived as householders in their own homes or in solitude in the mountains, secretly sustaining the continuity of the transmission of the profound traditions of the development and completion stage teaching and practice, were neglected and ignored. It was due to this lucky circumstance that the special lineal traditions of the Early Translation school remain undiminished.

Then, in accordance with Palden Lhamo's prophecy, Lhalung Palgyi Dorje assassinated Langdarma. While Mar Śākyamuni, Yo Gejung, and

Tsang Rabsal were meditating in Chuwori, they saw a monk out hunting. When they asked about the reason for this, he relayed the whole story. Terrified, they loaded the Vinaya texts onto a mule and fled, first to Ngari, then to Garlok, and finally to Amdo. Later, through the full ordination lineage passed from Lachen Gongpa Rabsal to ten men from Central Tibet and Tsang, including Lume, the dying embers of the holy Vinaya teachings were reignited from Amdo, the eastern region of Tibet.

Langdarma's son, Namde Ösung, had two sons, Tashi Tsegpa Pal and Kyide Nyima Gön. The latter was banished to Ngari, where he had three sons, Palgyi Gön, Detsuk Gön, and Tashi Gön. Their small dominion, like a "hat," was in the western region of Tibet. Tashi Tsegpa Pal resided in Kham, where he had three sons, named Palde, Öde, and Kyide. They controlled the government of U-Tsang, and their dominion, like a "boot," was in the region of Central Tibet. Tashi Gön had a son named Ökyi Gyaltsen, who had two sons, Songe and Kore. Songe built the Toding Temple in Guge and sent a group of twenty-one Tibetan youths of varying intellectual acuity to Kashmir to study the Dharma. Songe himself took full monastic vows and was given the name Yeshe Ö. His younger brother's son, Lhade, had three sons, of whom Lhatsun Jangchub Ö was most highly regarded.

Of those students who were sent to India to study the Dharma, only Rinchen Zangpo and Legpe Sherab survived. The other nineteen died in Dribten in Kashmir. Rinchen Zangpo studied with numerous paṇḍitas at Vikramaśīla University, among whom his main teacher was Dīpaṃkarabhadra. Under their guidance, Rinchen Zangpo clarified his understanding of the four classes of tantra [Kriyā, Caryā, Yoga, and Anuttarayoga] and returned to Tibet to translate Buddhist texts.

Later, there were a great number of precept lineages known as the Vinaya lineages of Upper Tibet, such as the lineage that was passed mainly from Paṇḍita Dharmapāla and the "three Pālas" [Sadhupāla, Guṇapāla, and Prajñāpāla] to Gyalwe Jungne of Zhang Zhung, and the lineage that was passed from the great Kashmiri paṇḍita Śākyaśrībhadra to the "three disciples named Pal," including Sakya Paṇḍita Kunga Gyaltsen Pal Zangpo.[239]

Briefly, the royal lamas Yeshe Ö and Jangchub Ö, the translator Rinchen Zangpo, and others underwent hundreds of hardships to invite the great paṇḍita Lord Atiśa from the eastern Indian state of Bengal and translate numerous teachings from the sūtras and tantras, thereby reestablishing the traditions of teaching and study. They were well known for reviving the dying embers of Buddhism from the west of Tibet, whereas Dromtön

Gyalwe Jungne, who invited Lord Atiśa to Central Tibet and excellently upheld the teachings in the wake of the latter's three turnings of the Dharma Wheel, is well known for causing the dying embers of Buddhism to blaze from the center of Tibet.

During the early spread of Buddhism in Tibet [7th–9th c.], Vairotsana, Kawa Paltsek, Chokro Lui Gyaltsen, Ma Rinchen Chok, Nyak Jñānakumāra, and others translated numerous sūtras and tantras from the words of the Buddha and their commentaries, and upheld the doctrinal systems of teaching and practice. Those who hold to their views and commentaries are known as followers of the Nyingma tradition, the Ancient School of the Early Translations. Later, a fresh wave of translators, beginning with the great translator Rinchen Zangpo [958–1055] and including masters such as Drogmi Lotsawa Shakya Yeshe [992–1072?], Gö Lotsawa Zhönu Pal [1392–1481], and Marpa Lotsawa [1012–1097], prepared new translations of the tantric scriptures and upheld the doctrinal systems of teaching and study. Those who adhere to the views and teachings of this period are known as followers of the Sarma tradition, the Later Translations of Secret Mantra.

In general, different religious traditions have come to exist as teachings have been passed along from their origins depending on what was suitable to various places, times, and beings' natures and capacities, and have been named after various monasteries and holy places. Several Buddhist schools emerged for these reasons, each with its own philosophical system and transmission style. They occurred as follows.

In the eastern Indian state of Bengal, in the Palace of Golden Victory Banners, the glorious Lord Atiśa [982–1054] was born as the son of King Kalyāṇa Śrī. Atiśa relied on numerous masters, including the great paṇḍita Nāropa [1016–1041], who expounded the view; the Mahāsiddha Ḍombipa, who blessed his mindstream; Jowo Serlingpa, who bestowed the stages of mind training; and others who revealed activity practices and upadeśa, displayed miraculous powers, gave Vajravārāhī blessings, bestowed Nāgārjuna's oral instructions, stabilized Atiśa's bodhicitta, and gave elaborate explanations of words and meanings, so that he sat on a high throne of a learned and accomplished master. Atiśa served as the principal disciplinarian of Vikramaśīla University. Fifty-one paṇḍitas entrusted to him the keys to 108 temples and enthroned him as Lord of the Teachings, and he perfectly guarded the teachings.

Lord Atiśa then traveled to Tibet and gave teachings according to the supreme, middling, or inferior capacities of beings. His teachings exhibited four aspects of greatness: since they included all Dharma teachings, from the Vinaya all the way to the unsurpassed Vajrayāna *Guhyasamāja Tantra*, in an effort to establish the requisite circumstances for an individual to attain full enlightenment, this was the greatness of unerring realization of the entire Buddhist doctrine. These teachings are, in essence, meant to subdue one's mind. This was the greatness of all the Buddha's teachings being internalized as precious oral instructions. Because they emphasized the power of altruistic bodhicitta and the true view, this was the greatness of easily realizing the wisdom mind of the Victorious One. Since they are based on renouncing saṃsāra and pure morality, this was the greatness of naturally stopping all wrongdoing.

In short, Lord Atiśa's body was adorned with Buddha Śākyamuni, Avalokiteśvara, Acalā, and Ārya Tārā; his speech was adorned with the teaching and study of the three piṭakas: Vinaya, Sūtra, and Abhidharma; and his mind was adorned with the three trainings: morality, samādhi, and sublime knowledge. His many disciples, including Dromtön Gyalwe Jungne, the three Geshe brothers, and others, were trained by means of the seven Kadam deities and teachings.[240] The holders of this lineage caused the teachings of Sūtra and Mantra to spread and flourish. They were known as Kadampas, followers of the Kadam tradition.

According to the needs of his most limited students, Mahāsiddha Tilopa [988–1069] relied on the masters of the four special transmissions.[241] For his middling students, Tilopa manifested as the Nirmāṇakāya son of Yoginī Cinto,[242] received tantric teachings from Vajrapāṇi, and attained accomplishment. For his superior students, Tilopa took the aspect of Pañcapaṇi, the brother of Determa, "She Who Grants Bliss," and with that, he arrived at Dharmagañja in Oḍḍiyāna, where he met a Dharmakāya wisdom Ḍākinī. When she revealed the symbolic signs of the three mudrās,[243] he supplicated her thus:

> From the tsakli[244] treasury of wisdom body,
> Please grant me the wish-fulfilling lineage.
> From the seed-syllable treasury of wisdom speech,
> Please grant me wish-fulfilling dreams.
> From the ritual-object treasury of wisdom mind,
> Please grant me the wish-fulfilling path of liberation.

The Conqueress replied:

Conqueror who shall be my consort,
Cakrasaṃvara, Lord of Supreme Bliss,
Buddha Tilopa, Protector of Beings,
I shall offer you the three wish-fulfilling jewels.

Along with an offering of the desireless desire of great exaltation, she offered him all the precious instructions of the aural lineage. A lineage of fortunate disciples, led by the great Indian paṇḍita Nāropa and the Tibetans Marpa, Milarepa, and Dagpo Lhaje ["Physician of Dagpo," Gampopa], evoked the power of the Mahāsiddha Tilopa's aural lineage instructions and became holders of his special transmission lineage. They were known as Kagyupas, followers of the Kagyu tradition. Könchok Gyalpo [1034–1102] was a direct descendant of Ācārya Padmasambhava's disciple Lui Wangpo of Khön. Könchok Gyalpo's teacher was Drogmi Lotsawa Shakya Yeshe, who received all the precious oral instructions from Mahāsiddha Virūpa, who had received the empowerment of the fifteen goddesses of Nairātmyā[245] directly from the wisdom deity herself. From Drogmi, Könchok Gyalpo received the main practice of the *Path of Secret Mantra and Its Fruit*. For the continuity of the cause, ālaya,[246] he established the view of the indivisibility of saṃsāra and enlightenment. For the continuity of the method, or path, he meditated upon the path of the development and completion stages connected with the four empowerments.[247] For the continuity of the ultimate result, he was empowered with the five Kāyas—the Three Kāyas and the Svabhāvikakāya and the Jñānadharmakāya—and the five wisdoms—the wisdom of Dharmadhātu, mirrorlike wisdom, the wisdom of evenness, the wisdom of discernment, and all-accomplishing wisdom. He relied on many learned and accomplished masters, primarily receiving teachings on the three tantras.

Könchok Gyalpo happened upon a place in Wönpori where the earth was white and rich and a river flowed by on the right.[248] The geomancy was excellent, so he established a Dharma center there. Over time, a succession of many learned and accomplished saintly masters came, the five Sakya patriarchs principal among them.[249] They taught Sūtra and Mantra in general, and in particular they focused on the scholarly textual tradition of the eighteen renowned philosophical scriptures: the *Prātimokṣa Sūtra*, *Vinaya Sūtra*, *Abhisamaya Alaṃkāra*, *Sūtra Alaṃkāra*, *Uttara Tantra*, *Madhyantha Vibhaṅga*, *Dharma Dharmatā Vibhānga*, *Bodhicarya Avatāra*, *Mūlamadhyamaka Prajñā*, *Catuḥśataka*, *Madhyamaka Avatāra*,

Abhidharma Samucchaya, *Abhidharma Kośa*, *Pramāṇa Samucchaya*, *Pramāṇa Vārttika*, *Pramāṇa Viniścaya*, *Pramāṇa Yuktinidhi*, and *Trisaṃvara Pravedha*. Whatever teachings they gave possessed the four measures of an authentic aural lineage: they had the scriptural authority of oral transmission, the transmissions had upadeśa, the upadeśa had a lineage, and the lineage had blessings. Through their efforts, the doctrine of the Path and Its Fruit[250] spread and flourished widely.

Particularly noteworthy is the fact that the Mongol emperor Sechen Khan [Kublai Khan] conquered Tibet and later offered it to Drogön Chögyal Phagpa. Although Drogön Chögyal Phagpa's dominion extended throughout the length and breadth of the Land of Snows, he followed the example set by previous sublime masters, who understood that all Buddhist teachings exist without contradiction, and he granted permission for all religious systems to be practiced according to their own unique traditions. Therefore, the Sakyas have an exceedingly great legacy of serving the Buddha's teachings in general. These are the Sakyapas, followers of the glorious Sakya tradition.

Padampa Sangye [11th c.?] was born the son of a sea captain, Vīryavarman, in the South Indian region of Beta, in a province known as Carasiṃha.[251] In his youth, Padampa entered Vikramaśīla University and engaged in study and contemplation. Over thirteen sky-activity gurus accepted him as their disciple, and in total he received the complete oral instructions of fifty-four different male and female siddhas. He practiced for over seventy years and acquired mastery of the two kinds of siddhis.

Padampa Sangye traveled to Tibet and mainly taught his *Threefold Lamps That Pacify Suffering*, along with *Mahāmudrā*, *Upadeśa for Seeing with Naked Awareness*, and *Precious Advice for Bringing Realization onto the Path*. He accepted the Ma So Kam trio,[252] the four yogins, and the twenty-four yoginīs, among others, as his disciples, and by relying upon the mantras that perfectly pacify all suffering, he pacified the temporary and ultimate sufferings of living beings. This tradition is known as Zhije, "Pacifying Suffering." The Great Mother Prajñāpāramitā, Perfection of Wisdom, emanated in female form as Machik Labdrön [1055–1149] in order to benefit beings. Machik met Padampa Sangye, and from Kyotön Sönam Lama she received oral instructions on the Sacred Dharma of Chö, "cutting through" demons. She practiced these over a long period in various sacred practice caves, and especially her cave in Zangri Kharmar, the Copper-Mountain Red Citadel. She said:

> My Dharma tradition is called Mahāmudrā Chö. It is the practice of the outer meaning of the *Prajñāpāramitā Sūtra* and the inner meaning of the unsurpassed Secret Mantra rolled into one. This is what is known as Mahāmudrā Chö.

As this explains, Machik Labdrön founded a system that combines all the Bodhisattva practices of the pāramitās, called the "sphere of activity of Bodhisattvas," or "advice for cutting right through the conceit of all four demons."[253] She passed the tradition down through two lineages: her blood lineage, led by her son, Nyingpo Drupa, and her disciple lineage, led by Khugom Chökyi Senge. These lineages spread and multiplied greatly. By relying upon the skillful means of casting one's body out as food, they benefitted innumerable human and nonhuman beings endangered by disease, evil spirits, and destitution. Followers of this tradition are known as Chöpas, practitioners of Chö.

The illustrious Khyungpo Naljor [11th–12th c.] was born in Nyemo Ramang in the region of Rutsam in Eastern Tsang. He made seven journeys to India, where he attended four root gurus, foremost among them being Maitripa, thirteen gurus who were deeply kind, and 150 gurus who were learned and accomplished. From them, Khyungpo Naljor received the Dharma in its entirety. In particular, from Niguma [Nāropa's sister], who received teachings directly from Vajradhara, he received the *Six Dharmas of Niguma*. Ḍākinī Sukhasiddhi accepted him as her disciple and promised that she would bless him and his lineage with her actual presence.

When Khyungpo Naljor returned to Tibet, he built 108 Buddhist monastic centers, including the Zhong Zhong[254] Temple in Zhang, in the span of three years. He brought inconceivable benefit to beings, including overcoming enemies in battle with his emanated army. He had many students, including four ultimate disciples, foremost among them being Latöpa Könchok Khar, one foreign heir, and the "seven jewels of the Zhangpa lineage."[255] The Dharma lineage was then passed to Khedrub Tsangma Shangtön, who founded the Jagpa Kagyu lineage, and Khetsun Zhönu Drub, who founded Samding Monastery[256] in Panam county. These two branches, Jagpa and Samding, form what is known as the Zhangpa Kagyu.

In addition, Jonang Kunpang Tugje Tsöndru, Kunkhyen Dolpo Sherab Gyaltsen, Bodong Chokle Namgyal, and others appeared, each with his own unique view, and illuminated the Buddha's teachings on Sūtra and Mantra. Furthermore, as explained above, the ways in which these teaching lineages were transmitted and monastic centers arose were based on place, time, circumstances, and so on, and these in turn branched into numerous subdivisions. For example, the Kadam school has both Old Kadam and New Kadam; the Kagyu school has four major lineages and eight minor lineages; the Sakya school has the Sakya tradition proper, the Ngor tradition, and the Tsarpa tradition; and the Chö school has the Father lineage of Chö and the Mother lineage of Chö, showing how numerous distinct philosophical schools and traditions, each with their own special features, can arise from a single basis. Yet all of these are contained within the four major Tibetan Buddhist schools—Sakya, Geluk, Kagyu, and Nyingma—and the ultimate, essential goal of each is the same: to attain the level of perfect omniscience. Further details can be known by referring to their specific religious histories.

This concludes the first section, briefly describing how the Buddha's teachings came to exist in our world.

A Brief History of the Successive Rebirths of Kyabje Dudjom Rinpoche

Now there will be a brief explanation about each verse of the prayer to the successive rebirths of the Great Treasure Revealer, Dharma King Dudjom Rinpoche, which are impossible to fully describe.

1

In the sky of unchanging Dharmadhātu, the bliss and emptiness of Samantabhadrī,
You gather wisdom clouds of boundless omniscience and love
And skillfully shower us with a compassionate rain of virtue and goodness.
Supreme Lord Guru, to you I pray.

Flawless great **bliss** and unborn **emptiness**, the union of emptiness and interdependent origination, arise as the great uncompounded Dharmakāya, **Samantabhadrī**, supreme in all aspects. **In the** stainless **sky of unchanging Dharmadhātu, you gather** infinite **wisdom clouds of boundless omniscience and love**, the skillful means of sacred appearance, the miraculous manifestations of wisdom Kāyas and purelands of the five Sambhogakāya Buddha families. Root **Guru, Supreme Lord** of the hundred Buddha families, who **skillfully showers** beings exactly according to our needs with the **compassionate rain of** Dharma, which establishes **us** temporarily in the positive phenomena of **virtue** and **goodness** in the higher rebirths of humans and gods, and ultimately in the pure phenomena of the forever excellent, constantly blissful state of Buddha, **to you I pray**.

Nuden Dorje Chang

2

Here in this illumined realm in what is known as the fortunate eon,
You are the crown of all thousand Buddhas.
Manifesting in the form of a supreme powerful yogin,
Nuden Dorje Chang, to you I pray.

In general, a "fortunate eon" refers to any place and time in which Buddhas appear and their teachings spread. That is what is meant by "fortunate eon." At a time when human life spans lasted 40,000 years, Buddha Krakucchaṃda appeared and turned the Wheel of Dharma. When human life spans lasted 30,000 years, Buddha Kanakamuni appeared and turned the Wheel of Dharma. When human life spans lasted 20,000 years, Buddha Kāśyapa appeared and turned the Wheel of Dharma. When human life spans lasted 100 years, Buddha Śākyamuni appeared and turned the Wheel of Dharma. In the future, Buddha Maitreya will appear and turn the Wheel of Dharma. After that, the other Buddhas will come one by one and turn the Wheel of Dharma. The very last Buddha to appear will be Buddha Vairocana, or Sugata Adhimukta [Buddha Möpa Taye], whose life span, sphere of activity, and duration of teachings will equal that of all the other Buddhas combined, and he will turn the Wheel of Dharma. The gods on the side of virtuous goodness proclaimed, "A la la![257] This is a fortunate eon!"

Long ago, a gathering of 1,000 Bodhisattvas engaged in enlightened activities and made aspirations to attain enlightenment. This is why there is an exact number of 1,000 Buddhas in this fortunate eon. As for the way that they developed bodhicitta, according to the Hīnayāna tradition, our Buddha Śākyamuni, in his previous life before this one, was born as King Prabhāta, who practiced generosity, made aspiration prayers, and resolved to attain enlightenment.

According to the Mahāyāna, long ago, there lived a universal monarch named Arenemin, the ruler of all four continents. His principal priest, a Brahmin named Sagarānu, had a son, Sagaragarbha, who attained fully enlightened Buddhahood and became known as the Victorious Ratnagarbha. King Arenemin and his thousand sons served this Buddha, and each one gave rise to bodhicitta, resolving to attain supreme enlightenment for the sake of all beings.

In another account, when the Buddha was reborn in hell as a wagon puller, he was overcome with compassion for a fellow wagon puller and said to one of the hell guards, "Please let my friend go. I will pull this wagon myself." The hell guard grew angry and killed him by piercing his head with a trident. He was reborn in a god realm. This is considered the first time the Buddha developed bodhicitta.

Also, it says in the *Sūtra of the Three Heaps*:

> When our Teacher was born as a merchant's son named Manifest Joy, he attended the Sugata named Great Beauty and made the aspiration to attain supreme enlightenment.

Also, it says in the *Play in Full Sūtra*:

> At the beginning, you offered Amoghadarśin a sal flower[258] . . .

As this says, it was in the presence of Sugata Amoghadarśin that Buddha first developed bodhicitta.

As such, there are distinct differences between the views of the Mahāyāna and Hīnayāna on how the Buddha first developed bodhicitta. Even within the Mahāyāna, many differences occur among the sūtras. All the various assertions appear to be due to circumstantial variations in what is intended and what is needed, adapted to particular times or mentalities of disciples as well as categorical differences between aspirational bodhicitta, applied bodhicitta, and ultimate bodhicitta,[259] and so on. Therefore, asserting with one-sided bias that "this alone was when the Buddha first developed bodhicitta" and arranging events in chronological order is pointless. This is what the great masters of the past have said.

In any case, many eons ago, before this **illumined realm in what is known as the fortunate eon**, there was a world system called Richly Adorned. There, in the Palace of Perfect Purity, lived a universal monarch named King Dhṛtarāṣṭra, along with his seven precious royal emblems,[260] his 700,000 queens, and his 1,000 sons. One day, King Dhṛtarāṣṭra went to a remote location and came before the great tantric yogin Nuden Dorje Chang. The king prostrated before the master and knelt down with his palms joined at his heart. "All my young sons have entered the unsurpassed Dharma," the king explained. "Who among them will be the first to reach the level of Buddhahood? Great holy yogin, please grant me a prophecy!"

Nuden Dorje Chang wrote the names of the young princes in melted, refined gold on sheets of lapis lazuli and placed them inside a vase made of the seven precious materials.[261] He sealed the top of the vase with silk cloths in five colors and placed it on a lotus flower. He arranged an inconceivable array of offerings, including various kinds of flowers, incense, perfumed salves, sweet-sounding bells and musical instruments, small and large drums, food offerings and edibles such as celestial food, beverages such as tea and fruit juices, the three whites,[262] the three sweets,[263] and various kinds of fruits. Then he opened[264] the Maṇḍala That Encompasses All of Buddha's Words and undertook seven days of worship. At the end, he bestowed the twenty-five general empowerments, the ten specific empowerments, and the four special empowerments.[265] When he had completed these, he took the princes' names from the vase one by one. The first was Youthful Pure Wisdom. As soon as his name was spoken, the earth quaked strongly and music spontaneously resounded from the instruments. Youthful Pure Wisdom was prophesied to become Buddha Krakucchaṃda, "Destroyer of Saṃsāra." Following that, the name of Youthful All-Victorious was drawn, and he was prophesied to become Buddha Kanakamuni, "Golden Sage." Following that, the name of Youthful Peaceful Lord was drawn, and he was prophesied to become Buddha Kāśyapa, "Guardian of Light." Following that, the name of Youthful All-Accomplishing One was drawn, and he was prophesied to become Buddha Śākyamuni. Following that, the name of Youthful Belt-Wearer was drawn, and he was prophesied to become Buddha Maitreya, "Loving-Kindness." The prophecies continued until the final name was drawn, that of the youngest prince, Youthful Boundless Intelligence, who was prophesied to become Buddha Adhimukta, "Boundless Dedication."

Queen Supreme and Queen Incomparable[266] were bathing in Joyous Pool, when two sons bearing all the signs and marks of perfection miraculously appeared upon their laps. Queen Supreme's son, Dharma Mind, was prophesied and empowered to become Vajrapāṇi, who would compile the teachings of his thousand brothers. Queen Incomparable's son Youthful Dharma Intelligence was prophesied and empowered to become Lord Brahmā, Wish-Fulfilling Jewel, who would request his thousand brothers to turn the Wheel of Dharma.

Thus, **the crown of all thousand Buddhas**, the primordial protector Samantabhadra, **manifesting in the form of a supreme powerful yogin**, gave empowerment to the 1,002 youthful princes, and prophesied the Buddhas of the past, the Buddhas of the future, and the Buddhas of the present. This is the Powerful Vajradhara, **Nuden Dorje Chang; to you I pray.**

Śāriputra

3

When the beings of this age of strife, abandoned by other Buddhas,
Were embraced by the Kin of the Sun, Buddha Śākyamuni,
You appeared with supreme sublime knowledge, no different from Buddha himself.
Noble Śāriputra, to you I pray.

Possessing unconditional great compassion, the Buddhas constantly look upon all sentient beings throughout every direction and time with impartial compassion. However, long ago, when the Bodhisattvas, heirs to the Victorious Ones, first developed the mind of bodhicitta and made aspirations particular to the karma of ordinary disciples, our Teacher, the Conqueror Buddha Śākyamuni, thought of the **abandoned beings of this age of strife**, when the five degenerations[267] would run rampant, and when the time would not yet have come for sentient beings to be tamed by **other Buddhas**. With deep and powerful love for them, he made 500 great aspirations. Accordingly, at that time, it is said that Lord Buddha, the "**Kin of the Sun**,"[268] Teacher to those of us who cling dearly to ordinary existence, **embraced** the beings of the fivefold degenerate era and vowed to enact his enlightened activity to benefit them, without relying on other Buddhas.

Regarding this, the name "Kin of the Sun" refers to a Buddha, for a Buddha is a kin of the sun. Just as there is only a single sun, there are just one or two Buddhas, so the metaphor "Kin of the Sun" is used to illustrate that extreme rarity.

Śāriputra, who appeared as Buddha's follower in the perception of ordinary disciples, was not, in fact, an ordinary individual. He was an emanation who **appeared** as an Arhat, **supreme** among those **with sublime knowledge**, with precious qualities of renunciation and realization **no different from Buddha himself. Noble Śāriputra, to you I pray.**

Moreover, Ārya Śāriputra, supreme among those with sublime knowledge, and Maudgalyāyana, supreme among those with miraculous abilities, are known together as the "two supreme disciples." So here the story of Śāriputra is told together with that of Maudgalyāyana.[269]

Long ago, during the reign of King Bimbisāra, there lived a Brahmin named Tiṣya, who was learned in the Vedas and their branches. He united with a woman named Śārikā, and afterward she dreamed that a man holding a lamp in his hand made an opening in her hip and entered her body. She had other auspicious dreams, such as climbing to the summit of a great mountain, flying through the sky, and many people paying homage to her. Śāriputra transmigrated from the god realms and entered Śārikā's womb for his last incarnation in saṃsāra.

When the baby boy was born, he had a perfect body, he was lovely to behold, he was beautiful and luminous, his skin shone like gold, his hair twirled like a parasol, his fingers were long, his forehead was broad, his eyebrows were joined, and his nose was high-bridged. Tiṣya's father thought to himself, "This is Tiṣya's son, so we should call him Upatiṣya, 'Nearby Tiṣya'"; and that is the name he chose.

"His grandfather named him after me, but I would rather my son be named after his mother," Tiṣya thought. So he announced, "This is my wife Śārikā's son, so I will name him Śāriputra, 'Son of Śārikā.'" He assigned eight nursemaids to his son's care, and by the time the boy was fully grown, he was versed in the Brahmin code of conduct and the four Vedas, along with their branches, and he could defeat anyone in debate.

At the same time, in the City of Wooden Palisades,[270] there lived a Brahmin named Potalaka, who was a royal minister, and whose dominion and prosperity rivaled those of the son of Vaiśravaṇa,[271] God of Wealth, yet he was childless. Wishing for a son, he learned that if he supplicated and made offerings to Umā, Varuṇa, Brahmā, and so on, he would beget a son. He did as instructed, yet his wife did not conceive, and he was besieged with grief. Then Potalaka recalled hearing that a baby is born when three circumstances are present: the father and mother unite in desire, the mother is ovulating, and a consciousness about to take another birth wishes to enter her womb. Accordingly, before long, life entered her womb, and it was a being entering its final birth.

A wise woman possesses five distinct attributes: she knows when a man is desirous and when he is not; she knows the timing and phases of her menstrual cycle; she knows when she is pregnant; she knows the baby's previous birth; and she knows whether the baby will be a boy or a girl. If it is a boy, it will be carried on the right side, and if it is a girl, it will be carried on the left side. Knowing that she had conceived a boy, Potalaka's wife said to her husband, "My lord, your son has entered my womb! I am pregnant with a boy! Please be glad and joyful!"

Her husband was overjoyed. "May I behold the face of my beloved son, whom I have awaited for so long! May our lineage endure for a long time! Wherever he is born and wherever he goes, may I also follow him inseparably." Saying this, he dedicated offerings for the child. Then, in nine months' time, a baby boy with a perfect body was born. For twenty-one days, a great celebratory feast was held in honor of his birth.

"This baby boy was lifted from the lap of the gods and given to us, so we will name him Kolita, the 'Lap-Born,'" his father announced. "And since he belongs to the Maudgal clan, we will name him Maudgalyāyana, 'Son of the Maudgals.'" Eight nursemaids were assigned to care for Kolita. As the boy grew older, he learned to read and write and so forth, and became versed in the Vedas.

When Upatiṣya [Śāriputra] and Kolita [Maudgalyāyana] were fully grown, the mere mention of each other's names made their hearts leap for joy. Upatiṣya approached his father and said, "Father, I am going to the City of Wooden Palisades."

"Why are you going there?" his father asked.

"I am going to see Kolita, son of Potalaka," replied Upatiṣya.

"Is he more intelligent than you are?" asked his father.

"No, but he is much richer."

"If Kolita comes here, we will need to share our knowledge with him. You should not go there," his father warned.

On the same day, Kolita approached his own father and said, "Father, I am going to the city of Nālandā."

"Why are you going there?" his father asked.

"I am going to see Upatiṣya, son of Tiṣya," he replied.

"Is he richer than you are?" his father asked.

"No, but he is very intelligent," said the Lap-Born.

"If he comes here, we will need to share our wealth with him. You should not go there," Kolita's father warned.

Kolita begged and pleaded, until at last his father permitted him to go. He rushed off to the place where Upatiṣya lived.

As soon as Upatiṣya caught sight of Kolita, he shouted, "Friend, come here! We need to renounce the world!"

Kolita replied, "Why would I want to perform worship, make fire offerings, and undertake ascetic practices when I already have everything I need, including attendants, in the palm of my hand? I have been born into the class of elephants,[272] so why would I renounce the world?"

Upatiṣya replied:

When the fruit tree falls,
What use are its branches and leaves?
Likewise, when a person dies,
What use is clinging to things?
Come, friend, let us renounce the world.

"We must ask our parents," Kolita said. He went before his parents and said, "Father and mother, please listen. I am going to renounce the world."

"Why do you want to renounce the world?" his parents asked.

Kolita replied:

To wear bark and grasses,
To eat roots and fruits,
And live among beautiful wild animals,
The forest life is indeed superior!

Killing, imprisoning, and beating others
In order to rule a kingdom,
Which destroys the happiness of future lives,
Would never be done by the wise.

"You are our beloved only son! We could never bear to part with you!" his parents said.

"Mother and Father, if you give me permission, that will be excellent. If you do not, I will refuse to eat from now on. Nor will I show you respect," Kolita told them.

"Don't even think of such things!" his parents replied. They did not grant their permission.

Kolita fell into despair, and for six days he refused to eat.

"Kolita, you are young and have not experienced suffering. Leading the life of a monk is difficult. Living in total seclusion is difficult. Stay here and you can make offerings and perform meritorious deeds," said his parents.

Kolita was silent. Then his parents called their relatives together, and they all repeated his parents' wishes three times, but still Kolita said nothing. Then his parents asked Kolita's friends to persuade him, and his friends also tried three times, but just as before, he made no reply. Then his friends went and spoke to Kolita's parents: "Parents of Kolita, please listen. Why let him die? Becoming a monk is praised by the wise. Even if Kolita were to become extremely happy as a monk, at least you would still be able to see him alive. If he does not like being a monk, later on he can reverse his ordination as some sages have done. Your son has no other home than yours, so taking ordination would be excellent!"

At that point, his parents realized that the time had come for their son to become a monk, and they gave their permission.

Kolita was overjoyed and rushed to see Upatiṣya. "My parents gave me permission to renounce the world!" he cried.

Upatiṣya went before his own parents and said, "Father and Mother, my faith lies only with what is true and pure, and I request your permission to renounce the world and become homeless."

"Son, would renouncing the world bring you joy?" his parents asked.

"Oh yes, it would bring me great joy!" he cried.

"Well, then, go forth and take ordination," his parents replied, granting their permission.

After that, the lifelong friends Upatiṣya and Kolita made their final decision and renounced their worldly lives. At last, they departed for the city of Rājagṛha. First they went to listen to the teachings of each of the "six tīrthika teachers": Maskari Gosaliputra, Sañjayī Vairaṭīputra, Ajita Keśakambala, Kakuda Kātyāyana, Pūrṇa Kāśyapa, and Nirgrantha Jñātiputra. But they heard not one word that pleased them.

At the time, the Blessed One had attained fully enlightened Buddhahood, and he had made his way gradually to the Bamboo Grove, where he was residing. The time had come for Upatiṣya and Kolita to be trained, and the Teacher asked himself, "Should they be trained by me or by the Arhats?" And he answered himself, "The Arhats will train them." Then he thought, "Should they be trained by miraculous means or through the path of conduct? They will be trained through the path of conduct." Moreover, he concluded that the Living One Assaji,[273] who was able to subdue the minds of gods and humans alike, should be the one to train them.

The Blessed One instructed Assaji, "Direct your mind toward Upatiṣya and Kolita."

Assaji, who was exceptional at fulfilling the Blessed One's commands, prostrated at the Blessed One's feet and took his leave. Early the next morning, Assaji dressed himself immaculately in his lower monastic robe, his monastic upper garment, and his outer Dharma robe,[274] and, carrying his begging bowl, he set off for the city of Rājagṛha to beg for alms.

Upatiṣya caught sight of Assaji from a distance and thought, "I have never seen a monk with such a noble demeanor!" Upatiṣya approached him and asked, "Who is your teacher? For what purpose have you renounced the world? Whose teachings do you prefer?"

Assaji replied, "My teacher is the one who went forth from the Śākya clan and attained Buddhahood. It is for this purpose that I renounced the world. It is his teachings that I prefer."

Upatiṣya replied, "Venerable Monk, please tell us what he teaches!"

Assaji said, "I am young and have just recently renounced the world. I am not able to explain the vastness of his teachings; I can only tell you the meaning."

"Venerable Monk," Upatiṣya continued, "it is the meaning that I seek. It can be long or short, but please tell me!"

Then Assaji began:

> All phenomena arise from a cause,
> And also their cause and their cessation
> Are explained by the Tathāgata.
> Such is the speech of the Great Renunciate.

When Upatiṣya heard this, he developed clear and stainless Dharma eyes and perfectly understood the nature of phenomena. "Where is the Blessed One residing now?" he asked.

"In the Bamboo Grove in Rājagṛha," Assaji replied.

Upatiṣya was overjoyed. He prostrated before Assaji and circumambulated him. Then he went to Kolita, who saw him approaching and said, "Your eyes are bright, and your complexion is perfectly clear! Your skin is pure white! Have you found the amṛta of the Dharma?"

"Yes," replied Upatiṣya, "I have."

Kolita said, "Please teach me this Dharma!"

Upatiṣya recited the verse Assaji had told him, and Kolita asked him to repeat it once more. Upatiṣya recited it again, and Kolita, too, realized the truth and recited it once again.

"Where is the Blessed One residing now?" Kolita asked.

"In the Bamboo Grove," replied Upatiṣya.

"Then let us go practice monastic discipline in his presence," Kolita decided, and the two set off for the Bamboo Grove.

They saw Assaji seated at the base of a tree, and Upatiṣya asked Kolita, "Should we prostrate first to the Blessed One, or to the one who first taught us the Dharma?"

"We must prostrate to the one who first taught us the Dharma," Kolita replied.

They went before Assaji and offered prostrations in the same way that a Brahmin who worshipped the moon would prostrate to the moon. For as the Blessed One has said:

> Whenever one learns the Dharma from someone,
> Whether old or young,
> Respect and pay homage to that one,
> Just as a pure Brahmin worships a fire.

The two friends then approached the Blessed One, who saw them coming and said to his disciples, "Monks, do you see these two?"

"Yes, we do, Revered One," they answered.

"Of these two, one will be supreme among the disciples with sublime knowledge, and the other will be supreme among the disciples with miraculous powers."

The two friends went before the Blessed One and prostrated themselves at his feet. "Revered One," they began, "if you grant us entry into the excellent teachings of the Vinaya and give us the vows of full ordination, we will practice monastic discipline in the Blessed One's presence."

The Blessed One replied: "Monks, come forth and practice monastic discipline."

They shaved their heads and beards, and after only a week had passed, when they took up their begging bowls and water flasks, their conduct resembled that of monks who had been ordained for 100 years.

The other monks asked the Blessed One, "What kind of past karma has Śāriputra accrued that has given him such keen, profound, and discerning intelligence?"

The Blessed One addressed the monks:

Long ago, a Brahmin living on a rocky mountain married a woman of the same caste, and they made love and gave birth to a son, whom they named Śūrpaka. After a time, they made love again and gave birth to a daughter, whom they named Śūrpaṇakhā. Eventually the parents died, and Śūrpaka, being fond of the wilderness, led his sister into the forest. When Śūrpaṇakhā matured, she began to feel restless with desire.

"I cannot live a secluded life like you," she said. "Come, let's head for the city."

On the outskirts of the city, the two siblings approached a house to beg for alms. The Brahmin who lived there heard them outside and came to the door. "What have we here?" he exclaimed. "An ascetic wandering around with his wife?"

"She's not my wife; she is my sister," replied Śūrpaka.

"Have you already promised her to someone, then?" asked the Brahmin.

"No, I have not promised her to anyone," said Śūrpaka.

"Well, then, give her to me! I'll make her my wife," said the Brahmin.

"She has renounced sensual pleasures," protested Śūrpaka.

Śūrpaṇakhā, who was desirous to the point of suffering, quickly interjected that she was eager to marry.

"All right, then," Śūrpaka said. "I'll let you two decide."

At that, the Brahmin received her as his bride.

"Brother, come and live with us," Śūrpaṇakhā said.

"I have no interest in pursuing desire," Śūrpaka explained. "I will remain in solitude."

"In that case, when you have obtained a gathering of qualities, please come back and teach me," said Śūrpaṇakhā.

Śūrpaka then went to a secluded place and in time attained enlightenment as a Pratyekabuddha. Out of heartfelt love for his sister, he flew through the sky like a great swan[275] with outstretched wings. Since ordinary beings swiftly entrust their minds to those who exhibit miracles, Śūrpaṇakhā reverently touched his feet and asked, "Did you obtain the gathering of qualities you were seeking?"

"Yes, I did," answered Śūrpaka.

"Noble One, you accept alms, and I seek merit, so you should stay here. I will provide your alms," Śūrpaṇakhā said.

"Sister, you must ask your husband," Śūrpaka replied.

She asked her husband, who responded, "Of course! I have had to give alms unwillingly to those who were not even renunciates, so why would I not offer alms to someone like this, a renunciate who has practiced fearless conduct and become a great being? Give him alms!"

For three months, they provided alms to the Pratyekabuddha. They dressed him in a suitable cotton cloth and even offered him a knife, a needle, and thread. He took them, and sharpened the knife in front of them.

At this, Śūrpaṇakhā prayed, "I wish for my sublime knowledge to be as sharp as that knife."

The Pratyekabuddha took the needle and pierced the cloth deeply. Śūrpaṇakhā prayed, "By the root of this virtue, may I develop profound sublime knowledge just like this deeply piercing needle!"

The Pratyekabuddha pulled on the thread, and it moved unhindered. "By the root of this virtue, may I become endowed with discerning intelligence!" Śūrpaṇakhā prayed.

Śūrpaṇakhā was later reborn as Śāriputra, and because she had made offerings to a Pratyekabuddha and made aspiration prayers, she was reborn with sharp, profound, and discerning intelligence.

Saraha

4

Completely intoxicated with indestructible, flawless youth,
With the wisdom arrow of all appearances arising as great exaltation,
You sealed the life force[276] of all beings of the three realms.
Brahmin Saraha, to you I pray.

Since sentient beings do not abandon habits they have had from the beginningless beginning, passions arise, such as attachment to what is positive and aversion to what is negative. From that they accumulate all sorts of karma and continuously fall into saṃsāra, where they experience the delusion of happiness and suffering.

Completely beyond all that, there is **indestructible** great inconceivability,[277] the primordially pure mind of enlightenment, the great emptiness of the formless Dharmakāya. This basic space has the quality of arising in the aspects of Rupakāya, and when this occurs, these wisdom forms are unsullied by even one iota of karmic or emotional obscuration, arising purely as **flawless** wisdom-body appearances, free of aging and infirmity, **completely intoxicated with** the vitality of **youth. With the wisdom arrow of all appearances** of samsaric and transcendent thoughts **arising as** the unobstructed power of **great exaltation, you** shot at the target of sentient beings' belief in ego. These **beings** are the animate life that clings and grasps onto the inanimate vessel of **the three realms**—the desire realm, the form realm, and the formless realm. They never experience a moment's peace, as if living in a den of venomous snakes.

Saraha introduced sentient beings to their minds as basis Mahāmudrā, the source of all precious qualities of existence and peace, and directly set forth path Mahāmudrā by gradually explaining the path of the four yogas—one-pointedness, simplicity, one taste, and nonmeditation—to those with superior faculties, or by giving upadeśa for incisively revealing Mahāmudrā to those of the very highest faculty. They were easily enthroned in the kingdom of Vajradhara, fruition Mahāmudrā, completely uprooting the cause and result of the suffering of saṃsāra, thus having **sealed** their **life force. Brahmin Saraha, to you I pray!**

Here some short stories have been included. From the *White Lotus of Compassion Sūtra*:

> After my nirvāṇa, in the city called Suvarṇimadroṇa, there will be two Brahmin monks named Bhikṣupaṇḍita and Sañjayī. They will be known for their great miraculous abilities, great power, and great might. They will be bright, disciplined, fearless, and well educated; they will be holders of the Sūtras, holders of the Vinaya, and holders of the Abhidharma; and they will perfectly teach this [*White Lotus of Compassion*] sūtra to many beings, allow others to perfectly hold this teaching, perfectly encourage them, and perfectly delight them. These two, likewise, will be endowed with morality and miraculous abil-

ities, and through those, they will spread this teaching ever further.

In the *Dohākośa* and elsewhere, it is said that Saraha came to this world 300 years after the parinirvāṇa of the Buddha. This dating is problematic because it is too late, since Saraha was said to be the student of Rāhula [Buddha's son]. According to the oral tradition of Bodhgayā, in the city of Suvarṇimadroṇa, in the central district of Vārāṇasī, Śaṃkarapati [Saraha], known as Bhikṣupaṇḍita, and [his younger brother] Śaṅkara Swāmi, also known as Truly Victorious, were born into the caste of Brahmins, who delight in the six practices.[278] After becoming accomplished in all the śāstras, they reflected, "Here at home, we venerate Maheśvara, but the teachings of the Victorious Buddha are truly amazing. We must certainly investigate which one is the most eminent: our Maheśvara or the Victorious Buddha."

The two Brahmin brothers had heard that Maheśvara and Umā[279] actually abided at Mount Kailash, so they decided to go and ask their questions. With great difficulty, they started their journey, but the gods helped them and they arrived swiftly. There they saw the mount of the Great God [Maheśvara], a young king bull as white as a cloud, freely roaming about and grazing. The sight of him filled them with immense joy.

Immediately after that, they saw Goddess Umā inside the forest picking fruit, and filled with devotion, they prostrated. They had heard that their Lord dwelled in a grove of blooming flowers, so they went closer and saw the Great God surrounded by a retinue of 1,000.

Lord Gaṇeśa [son of Maheśvara and Umā] took them by the hand and led them before Maheśvara, where they made prostrations with reverence.

"Where have you two come from?" Maheśvara asked.

They recounted their story. When the time came for the monks to have their meal, 500 Arhats arrived from their dwelling place at Lake Manasarovar. The divine couple [Maheśvara and Umā], along with their retinue, served the Arhats their meal, and when the Arhats had finished eating, the divine couple and retinue listened to their teachings. Then the Arhats returned home.

Maheśvara then turned to the two Brahmin brothers and said:

Joyfully worshipping Buddha's disciples daily will grace us with holy qualities.
When worshipping Buddha—the universally renowned Supreme

One with marks of great qualities who dispels the faults of the world—with an extremely joyful mind,
There will be an experience similar to nirvāṇa.
This Unexcelled One of the three worlds,[280] Buddha with peerless qualities, will be worshipped by the wise.

Maheśvara thus said, "You two must worship Buddha and his excellent teachings." The two Brahmin brothers requested supreme accomplishment, and Maheśvara granted them longevity equal to that of the sun and moon. Then the two returned home, and they cast out the Vedic teachings like straw and gave away everything in their home. The elder brother established Nālandā University at the birthplace of Śāriputra, and the younger brother built the Mahābodhi Temple of Bodhgayā, the Vajra Seat. Then the two brothers received monastic ordination from Rāhula. The elder brother was given the name Rāhulabhadra, and the younger brother [Śaṅkara Swāmi] was named Vīryabhadra, and they became holders of the Tripiṭaka.

As they sought something far superior to the Vehicle of Characteristics, their preceptor Rāhula emanated the maṇḍala of Guhyasamāja for the elder brother and conferred the empowerment, taught the tantra, and imparted the upadeśa. He gave many other Secret Mantra teachings as well.

The two brothers then resided at their respective temples. Outwardly, they perfectly upheld the teachings of the Śrāvakas, and inwardly, they familiarized themselves with the yogas of the Vajrayāna. They lived for nearly 500 years.

Rāhulabhadra [later known as Saraha] gave monastic ordination to Nāgārjuna and granted him all the precious oral instructions. Rāhulabhadra composed, among other things, the *Commentary on the Difficult Points of the "Buddhakapāla Tantra" Called "Jñānavatī."* He entrusted Nālandā University to Nāgārjuna and began living with an outcaste yoginī, an arrowmaker's daughter from the lineage of nāgas, who had accepted him as her disciple.

Everyone criticized this, saying, "He has fallen from the Brahmin caste and the deportment of a great monastic regent!" Saraha responded to this with three songs, known as his *Dohā Trilogy* [*Dohākośa*], sung successively to the people, the queen, and the king, in the manner of a straight arrow. According to legend, he then departed for Śrī Parvata.

Saraha's main disciple was Ācārya Nāgārjuna, who, according to tantric tradition, was said to have attained the accomplishment of supreme Mahāmudrā. Nāgārjuna granted the precious oral instructions of his teachings of Guhyasamāja and so on to his four supreme disciples, Śākya Kalyāṇamitra, Āryadeva, Candrakīrti, and Nāgabodhi.

Kṛṣṇadhara

5

Adorned with the garland of the fortunate sole king
Indrabhūti's command,
You served as an honest minister, enacting the king's laws
To bring about benefit and happiness.
Buddhist minister Kṛṣṇadhara, to you I pray.

To the west of India, in the region known as Glorious Oḍḍiyāna, there was a city called Radiant Jewels, in which there was a lapis lazuli palace adorned with various precious gems. Inside the palace, upon a grand and magnificent throne made with many kinds of jewels, sat the great Dharma Guardian **King Indrabhūti,** who was the fortunate sole king due to the accumulated merit of many lifetimes. Although the king had 108 queens, he had no son to carry on his royal lineage.

On special auspicious days, such as the fifteenth day of each lunar month when the moon was full, as well as days marking the time when previous Buddhas came into the world or turned the Wheel of Dharma, the king assembled all his court monks and commanded them to recite the *Cloud of Dharma Sūtra*. He made offerings to the Three Jewels above, gave charitable gifts to the lowly and poor below, and performed all sorts of virtuous deeds in hopes of having a son.

King Indrabhūti had very nearly emptied his entire royal treasury, yet the stream of beggars was endless. The king became depressed and thought to himself, "If only my outer and inner ministers[281] could bring me a wish-fulfilling jewel from an ocean isle to fulfill everyone's needs and wishes! They could add it to my royal treasury, and from its power I would be granted a son, and I could protect my subjects from poverty and suffering!" He convened a council.

His minister was delighted to be given the king's vitally important command, which was like a precious rosary or **garland** that **adorned** his neck. Having given up all self-serving craftiness and deceit, he abided perfectly according to **the king's laws** and ensured that his subjects did the same. The minister knew in his heart whatever the king was thinking, and he accomplished whatever actions he was commanded to do. All his actions brought benefit and happiness to the king and his subjects. The **minister** was learned and **honest**.

Long ago, in India and countries like Oḍḍiyāna, each king was served by an external minister, called a "confidant magistrate," whose purpose it was to guard the kingdom and who performed the Vedic rites of the ṛṣhis. Each king was also served by an intimate "internal minister," or "counselor," whom he consulted about political matters. During this period, among all the inner, outer, and intermediate ministers, one in particular stood out as supreme: the Dharma minister Kṛṣṇadhara. In precise accord with the command issued by the Great King [Indrabhūti], he boarded a ship along with its captain and sailed out to an island in the sea. There he retrieved a precious jewel, and on his way back to the palace, he beheld Prince Padmasambhava born in the form of a young boy in the heart of a lotus flower. He invited the boy to be the destined son of the king, thereby fulfilling all the hopes in the king's heart. The king was overjoyed. Through the power of the jewel, all the king's subjects were relieved of their poverty, and the kingdom of Oḍḍiyāna became fortunate and virtuous in every way. **Buddhist minister Kṛṣṇadhara, to you I pray.**

Hūṃkāra

6

With the magical, blissful dance of the Glorious Heruka,
You manifested unchanging supreme wisdom.
Awareness Holder of Viśuddha Mind,[282]
Ācārya Hūṃkāra, to you I pray.

It says in the *Heruka Galpo Tantra*:

Yangdak Heruka alone
Embodies the great exaltation of all the Buddhas.
This profound yoga perfects the Three Kāyas;
The magical Ḍākinī is supreme bliss.

As this reveals, the **Glorious Heruka** who liberates all phenomena of saṃsāra and enlightenment—arising in the form of suffering and happiness—into immaculate basic space, the expanse of perfect evenness, is the Great Blood-Drinker [Yangdak Heruka]. He is characterized as follows: His **magical dance** of naturally luminous blissful wisdom, completely free of all obscuration by the impermanent, flawed happiness of the three realms, is sublime in every way and has the capacity to transform into anything within the sphere of existence and peace.[283] The essence of the magical dance is the wisdom of emptiness, sealed within the boundless space of great sole inconceivability, so it is forever **unchanging, supreme wisdom**, never hidden within the confines of temporary defilements, its outer clarity arising as the **manifest** Kāyas and purelands. The Great Ācārya **Hūṃkāra, holder** of the **awareness** within the **mind**s of all the Buddhas, gained mastery of the oceanlike Dharmadhātu of completely pure[284] stainless wisdom, unaffected by even one speck of obscuration from dualistic perception or its habit, naturally existing as completely perfect from the beginning without having been sought. **To you, I pray**!

The story of this master, Ācārya Hūṃkāra, was discussed earlier in the context of the brief histories of the Eight Heruka Sādhanas, and he is mentioned in the section on the sādhana teaching of Viśuddha Mind.

Drogben Khyeuchung Lotsawa

7

In the presence of the Lotus-Born Second Buddha,[285]
You gained tantric accomplishment, with wisdom realization equal to his.
Your mere gaze drew birds from the sky.
Drogben Khyeuchung Lotsawa,[286] **to you I pray.**

When the Buddha thought about passing into nirvāṇa, he lovingly addressed Ānanda and the general assembly of disciples:

Do not be sad, Ānanda.
Do not cry and weep, Ānanda.
After I have vanished from this place,
On an island in Lake Dhanakośa,
The one called Padmasambhava, the Lotus-Born,
Who is greater than myself, will appear.

As described earlier, in accordance with this prophecy, on an island in Lake Dhanakośa, Guru Padmasambhava took birth from the heart of a lotus flower, in the manner of spontaneously arising awareness. He looked after the kingdom of Oḍḍiyāna in harmony with the Dharma, practiced fearless conduct in the eight great charnel grounds, and so on, sustaining his enlightened activity for the benefit of beings, taming each according to his or her individual needs.

Padmasambhava then traveled to Tibet and taught the resultant teachings of the Secret Mantra Vajrayāna to an assembly of extraordinary disciples. This nonattached, self-arisen **Second Buddha**, **the Lotus-Born** Padmakāra, established beings in the kingdom of Dharmakāya Samantabhadra within one body and lifetime. **In** his **presence**, Drogben Khyeuchung Lotsawa [8th c.], along with an assembly of pure disciples with fortunate karma, received the empowerments and precious oral instructions for the Oceanlike Collection of Teachings, like a vase being filled to the very brim. By devoting himself one-pointedly to practice, Drogben's **wisdom** became equal to that of the Great Ācārya himself, the very embodiment of the uncommon, supreme spiritual accomplishment of the Four Kāyas[287] and the five wisdoms. In the perception of his fortunate disciples, he displayed the manner of **attaining** secret, profound **tantric accomplishment**, so that by his **mere gaze**, he unobstructedly **drew birds from the sky**. Great master among translators,[288] Drogben Khyeuchung Lotsawa, to you I pray!

This particular Dharma translator was from the Drogmi clan. Right from his youth he was able to translate; hence his name, which means "Boy Translator, Dharma Practitioner of the Drogmi Clan." In the presence of Guru Rinpoche, he mastered all the teachings of the Secret Mantra. His ordination was that of a lay householder, and he wore the white robes and long hair of a mantra holder.

Smṛtijñāna

8

Guided by the actual presence of Mañjuśrī, Lion of Speech,
You saw all phenomena exactly as they are
And you liberated beings through skillful means, O Brave Heart.
Lord Smṛtijñāna, to you I pray.

Heretical teachers, who have fallen into the dualistic extremes of eternalism and nihilism and who, like savage beasts, babble baseless teachings that have no connection with the path of liberation, are conquered by the splendor and brilliance of the **Lion of Speech** [Bodhisattva Mañjuśrī], who is the wisdom form of all the Buddhas' sublime knowledge. Mañjuśrī **actually** showed his face to Ācārya Smṛtijñāna [892–975], blessed him, and **guided** him, so that Ācārya Smṛtijñāna **saw** with vivid clarity and precision **all** relative **phenomena exactly as they are** through the spontaneous power of discerning wisdom. Ācārya Smṛtijñāna then performed the enlightened activity of a Bodhisattva with **skillful means** to subdue beings according to their individual needs, and he taught the Dharma that **liberates** miserable **beings** from the torments of saṃsāra. **O brave-hearted** master, **Lord Smṛtijñāna, to you I pray.**

Ācārya Smṛtijñāna attended many spiritual teachers, including Paṇḍita Nāropa, who was versed in all Buddhist and non-Buddhist scriptural traditions and supreme among debaters. Smṛtijñāna possessed clairvoyance and traveled to Tibet for the sake of his mother. In Khab Gungtang,[289] he took on the guise of a cowherd. The reason for this was that his mother had been reborn as a scorpion inside the three-legged stove of one of the villagers, so he had disguised himself in order to rescue her.

At the time, the translator Chal Lotsawa had just come from India, and everyone was flocking to him with great faith. Not realizing that Smṛtijñāna was an Ācārya, people disregarded him. In reply, Smṛtijñāna wrote a verse in Sanskrit above the main gate into Gungtang:

> The hare-marked moon,[290] garlanded with planets and stars,
> Moves across the sky at night, yet rejecting this,
> You claim that the moon's reflection in a clear pool is in fact the moon!
> Grasping onto form as true is the work of a child's mind.

When the translator saw it, he said, "Who wrote this?"

"A yogi who takes care of the livestock wrote it," the people told him.

"Where is he?" the translator asked.

"Out in the pasture," they replied.

"When will he be back?" asked the translator.

"When the sun goes down."

"It must be Smṛti," the translator thought, having recognized his exquisite Lantsa script.[291] He sat down to wait, but no one came.

The translator returned early the next morning, and after many attempts to meet Smṛtijñāna, the master at last allowed it.

The two had previously been master and disciple, and the translator began to weep. "You are enduring such hardship!" he said.

"It is for my mother that I am doing this," Smṛtijñāna replied.

"Where is she?" the translator asked.

"She is here."

At that, the translator used his money to purchase the three-legged stove [in which Smṛtijñāna's mother had been reborn as a scorpion]. With the wages Smṛtijñāna had collected from tending cattle, he guided his mother to the higher realms by means of a ritual for cleansing the lower realms. The translator was not able to persuade Smṛtijñāna to stay, and the latter set off for Kham. Later, Smṛtijñāna performed some small enlightened activities in Tibet. The translator said, "This master is extremely learned. Tīrthika practitioners were so scared that he would destroy their teachings that they expelled him from India."

Rongzom Chökyi Zangpo

9

Through your mastery of all ten sciences,
The sun of the Buddha's teachings shone with glory.
Great Paṇḍita of Tibet, Land of Sal Trees,
Rongzom Chökyi Zangpo, to you I pray.

As it says in Gö Lotsawa Zhönu Pal's *Blue Annals*, which bears the name of the color of precious lapis lazuli:

> We in the Land of Snows have a single crown jewel and two earrings. The single crown jewel is the Great Ācārya Padmasambhava. The two earrings are Rongzom Paṇḍita Chökyi Zangpo [11th c.] and the Lord of Yogins, Milarepa [1052–1135].

As this rapturous praise expresses, Omniscient Rongzompa gained a thorough knowledge and perfect **mastery of the ten sciences,**[292] namely the five major sciences—art, medicine, language, logic and philosophy, and inner awareness—as well as the subdivisions of poetry, semantics, composition, performing arts, and astrology, which are all within the science of language.

The science of art includes the sublime arts of sculpting, painting, or otherwise creating sacred representations of the Victorious One's enlightened body, speech, and mind, to affirm the deeds of the Buddha and accomplish the welfare of sentient beings. These artistic traditions developed and flourished long ago in excellent places such as India, China, Nepal, and Tibet, where the Buddha's teachings were once widespread. This science also includes ordinary crafts, such as architecture, culinary arts, textile arts, furnishings, and the production of other goods needed for beings to live in this world.

The science of healing and medicine is used to dispel diseases caused by imbalances in the body's four elements: earth, the element of flesh; water, the element of blood; fire, the element of warmth; and wind, the element of breath. Many different illnesses arise from the secondary conditions of wind, bile, and phlegm, which result from the primary cause of the three poisons.[293]

The science of language is the complete elucidation of the parts of speech used to convey subject matter, fully elaborated within Tönmi Sambhota's śāstras, called *Root Grammar in Thirty Verses* and *Grammar of Morphology*,[294] which are based upon śāstras on Sanskrit linguistic conventions.

The science of logic and reasoning is the unmistaken ascertainment of perceived objects or phenomena by means of a subjective, unmistaken cognition that relies upon the three kinds of valid cognition: direct perception, inference, and relying on scriptural quotations.

The science of inner awareness is the classification of the view, meditation, and conduct of each of the nine Buddhist vehicles that carry one along the path to omniscience.

The arrangement of essential names, words, and syllables into verse, prose, or a combination of the two to illustrate and express desired meanings constitutes the body of poetry. Just as a naturally beautiful person might adorn his or her body with ornaments, various common and uncommon descriptive words—literal, figurative, and so on—are used to enhance and adorn. By utilizing the excellent body and ornaments of poetry, the feelings of pleasure and pain commonly experienced by human beings can be brought forth in lyrical and melodious ways, either orally or in writing. Poetry is used to compose songs of praise in verse, prose, or some combination thereof, about sublime beings by relying upon the Buddha and his speech, the Holy Dharma. By adding vital essence to dry words, expressions become lyrical and melodious, and especially sublime meanings are revealed.

Phenomena that are related to each other are given names, and furthermore, many words can share the same meaning, or one word can have many different meanings. This is composition.

Semantics is an art in which either metered verse derived from Vedic Sanskrit or prose is used to elucidate concise accounts, to summarize extensive presentations, to keep proper sequences unmuddled, and to ensure the proper compositional structure of both common worldly works and those related to the Holy Dharma.

The performing arts include visual or physical theater, in which ornaments, costumes, and accoutrements are used in live performances of dramas. These are also called performing arts with form. In addition, there are performing arts that are mainly for listening, such as oral storytelling. Stories can take the form of tales from ancient times about different countries' gods and goddesses, ghosts and harmful spirits,[295] kings and queens, boys and girls, married couples, servants, and so forth, through which various karmic experiences of happiness and suffering, which arise based on the characters' respective karmic perceptions, are recounted to the audience. Storytelling can also take the form of elaborate narratives that describe how sublime beings came into our world. Such wondrous accounts of the life stories of Buddhas and Bodhisattvas have inconceivable purposes and benefits, such as humbling beings when they are elated, uplifting them when they are sad, and ultimately establishing them at the level of Buddhahood. Examples include the *Wish-Granting Tree* by the Kashmiri poet Kṣemendra, a poetic retelling of stories of the former lives of Buddha Śākyamuni, and the sacred biographies of Bodhisattvas such as the Eight Close Sons, the Mahāsiddhas of India such as the Great Ācārya Padmasambhava, and the past realized masters of Tibet.

Astrology is used to predict how the movement of planets and stars in the sky will affect seasonal shifts on Earth; to reveal the significance of lunar phases; to accurately set forth time periods, such as years, months, and days, based on the seasonal movement of the sun toward the south or north; to explain feelings of happiness and suffering in the elements of the body, speech, and mind experienced by beings who dwell in and move about the Earth based on the positive and negative conjunctions between stars and planets that dwell in and move about in the sky; and to present clear methods and rituals to dispel accumulations of bad circumstances and increase accumulations of good ones. Particularly, there is the detailed classification of the world system, including Mount Meru, the four continents, the eight subcontinents,[296] and the stars and planets according to the "Outer Kālacakra"; the detailed classification of the vajra body found in the "Inner Kālacakra," which unfolds from [the "Outer Kālacakra"]; and the "Other Kālacakra,"[297] with a view defined by the four branches of approach and accomplishment.[298] Through the practice of emphasizing the essences of the four vajras,[299] one can cleanse the four states—waking, dreaming, deep sleep, and samādhi—and unite with the state of the Great Heruka, the all-pervasive embodiment of the result of purification, which is the Four Kāyas. The Great Heruka is endowed with the most supreme quality, which is the union of bliss and emptiness.

In summary, Rongzom Chökyi Zangpo **mastered all ten sciences**: the five major sciences, including art, medicine, language, logic and philosophy, and inner awareness, and the five minor sciences, including poetry, semantics, composition, dance and drama [performing arts], and astrology. He then continued the work of the translators and paṇḍitas of the past, who, in their great kindness, had brought about the dawn of the **Buddha's** holy **teachings**, which enabled beings to be completely victorious in the battle against the four māras, in the land of Tibet. Like the glorious **sun** that brilliantly illuminates everything, he **shone** with the **glory of** realization of the Dharmakāya for oneself, and with the compassionate Rupakāya for others. Just as a **sal tree** towers above all the many hundreds of trees in the forest, the Buddhist **land of** Tibet stands out among many hundreds of countries as uniquely sublime, and among Tibet's many hundreds of scholars, the **Great Paṇḍita Rongzom Chökyi Zangpo** was unrivaled. **To you, I pray!**

Now, to elaborate a bit upon this story, Dharma Lord Mipham Rinpoche [1846–1912], who was actually Mañjuśrī, wrote about Rongzompa as follows:

> At the point when the designations "Secret Mantra of the Early Translations" and "Secret Mantra of the Later Translations" were beginning to be used, Mañjuśrī came in human form as the great paṇḍita Rongzom, whose scholarship was unrivaled throughout the three times here in the Land of Snows. He was born into an extraordinary lineage of Secret Mantra siddhas as the son of

Rongben Rinchen Tsultrim, in a place called Narlungrong in the lower Rulak region of Tsang. Right from the moment of his birth, he was spontaneously endowed with the precious qualities of exalted knowledge, holy conduct, and unobscured clarity. For these reasons, some people, including his father, claimed that he was the immediate rebirth of Paṇḍita Smṛtijñāna. Others claimed that he was the rebirth of Paṇḍita Sukṣmadirga, who had come to Tibet with Smṛtijñāna. Even as a young child in his mother's lap, Rongzompa spoke Sanskrit and gave all sorts of Dharma discourses. His mother swaddled him in her arms and set off with her relatives to see the great Jowo [Atiśa] Dīpaṃkara, whom they met near the hot springs of Rong.

"From the moment this child was born," they began, "he has been speaking the language of India and giving Dharma discourses. What does it mean? Jowo, please give him a teaching!"

The Jowo held the child on his lap. Smiling, he asked him in the language of India, "*Kina ho?*"[300] The child answered this and several other questions without difficulty.

"This child is the immediate rebirth of the Great Ācārya Kṛṣṇācārya," the Jowo informed them. "How could I possibly presume to give him a teaching?"

The Jowo praised him and expressed great devotion, and the child became renowned as an undisputed Nirmāṇakāya emanation.

At the time, some claimed that Kṛṣṇācārya had reached Buddhahood in the bardo[301] and certainly would not have taken rebirth. Others claimed that while it was indeed said that Kṛṣṇācārya attained supreme accomplishment in the bardo, even if he was a Buddha, there would be no reason why he could not return as any of the Nirmāṇakāya emanations—creations, births, and great enlightenment.[302]

As a child, Rongzompa was overjoyed whenever he saw an Indian Ācārya, and he was able to communicate in a natural manner with them. At a young age, while he was studying with Gartön Tsultrim Zangpo, Rongzompa used Dharma speech to playfully debate him, and everyone gathered there was overwhelmed by his quick-witted brilliance. Once, when his father came to bring him provisions, the other Dharma students said,

"This little son of yours is foolish and overly talkative! We are all tired of listening to him, so it would be best if you could take him away."

The father went to speak to the master and ask if he should remove his son, but the master said, "Do not speak of it. It is because he has already perfectly understood the entire Buddhist doctrine, not because he is pointlessly annoying."

At age twelve, Rongzompa trained in philosophy and the methods of logic. During pauses in his studies, he would repeat every word his teacher had said, just like a recording, even while in the children's play area. He had only to hear a teaching once to gain perfect mastery, not mistaking a single word, and Rongzompa soon became known as an emanation of Mañjuśrī.

At age thirteen, Rongzompa's studies and contemplation were complete, and it seemed that no one could offer anything new to improve his education. Even without training, he was able to effortlessly understand a volume of Vivarta script merely by glancing over it.[303] He was famous for his natural ability to understand Sanskrit and many other languages, and he even understood the languages and sounds of animals. Right from his youth, he composed numerous śāstras, including his *Commentary on the "Doorway to Speech like a Sword."* Rongzompa brought immeasurable benefit to those with devotion to Dharma, and particularly those who had entered the door of the Secret Mantra, with his many instructions for accomplishing activities[304] and siddhis. He not only knew all the famous major texts of India and Tibet on the outer and inner sciences, the Piṭakas, the Vedas, the śāstras on logic or reasoning, the central works on verse and poetry, and so on, which goes without saying, but his knowledge was not merely superficial; he spontaneously knew the infinitely vast categories of the textual traditions by heart, thereby embodying the attributes of a great noble one who possesses the four perfectly pure discernments.[305] He had only to peruse the profound Indian root texts of the sūtras, tantras, and śāstras once, or at most twice, to understand all the words and meanings, and he was known for having the power of unforgetting memory; he never needed to consult the texts again.

The master himself said, "My studies were not limited, as there was no Dharma text in Tibet that I did not study. Nor was I unable to swiftly grasp what I learned, for I had only to read a text once."

While it might appear that Rongzompa was speaking from an ordinary perspective about the method of study and reflection, in fact it was his attainment of the samādhi of the dharma stream that enabled him to retain countless teachings every instant.

Rongzompa's ability to relate the Sanskrit and Tibetan languages and show how grammatical conventions are used to produce specific meanings was unparalleled. Due to the power of his stainless sublime knowledge, with which he nakedly revealed the ultimate meaning of all knowable things through the path of reasoning, and his peerless eloquence, which was profound, vast, and swift, he was considered worthy of public praise by many scholars as the fivefold embodiment of the sublime knowledge of Dignāga, the analytical refutation of Dharmakīrti, the learning of Vasubandhu, the eloquence of Candragomin, and the compositional skill of Aśvaghoṣa. His scholarly contemporaries also lauded him by saying, "There is no one in Tibet or even in India who surpasses him when it comes to the major texts on grammar and philosophy."

Furthermore, the people living during that era said:

> Murwa Tsurtön[306] is learned in writing,
> Drangi Medrak is learned in ritual arrangement,
> Gö Lotsawa Khugpa[307] is learned in grammar and logic;
> Only Rongzom Chözang has all these qualities.

This and many other verses became well-known reverential sayings.

This great paṇḍita, for whom every field of knowledge was unobscured, in his sole concern with benefitting others, composed an exceptionally large number of śāstras on the sūtras, tantras, sciences, and even on worldly matters such as agriculture, animal husbandry, and dairy production. Some historical sources suggest that his writings filled nearly sixty volumes; others state simply that his writings were numerous. It is said that Ḍākinīs came and took away the majority of the Secret Mantra upadeśa contained within his writings. Because Rongzompa possessed unimpeded clairvoyant knowledge of his disciples' minds and of the three times, and because he wrote with a mind of great compassion purely to bring benefit, whatever he composed became beneficial for his disciples. Yet even if his lineage disciples had not received the reading transmission of Rongzompa's precious Mantrayāna oral instructions, it was famously said that if those instructions were put into practice, there was no one who would not receive signs of his blessings. Even after Rongzompa passed away, some people reported that when they prayed to him, he actually came to them and clarified their confusion regarding his precious oral instructions. Such was the extraordinary blessing and beneficial nature of his writing. Whenever he was requested to write about any textual tradition, there was nothing he did not know, and his compositions poured forth unobstructedly, without his ever needing to consult any references.

Rongzompa's compositions are all genuine śāstras: the quotations he includes are worded perfectly, without a single mistake; his writings are beautifully expressed, have excellent meaning, and are logical, clear, and well written. All his words are impeccable, their meanings aligning with the Dharma from every angle, and the key points of intellectual understanding are thoroughly explained. For these reasons, all scholars accept them as consistent with the writings of Buddha.

Rongzompa studied with many Indian paṇḍitas, including the Indian teachers Mañjuśrīvarma, Mañjuśrījñāna, Upāyaśrīmitra, Buddhakārabhadra, Devakāracandra, Paramiśvara, and Aśokavajra. He then served as their translator and translated the Speech of Buddha and its commentaries [śāstras], such as the *Vajrabhairava Tantra*, *Three-Chapter Tantra*, *Archenemy Yamāntaka Tantra*, *Guhya Mañjuśrī*, *Cakrasaṃvara Root Tantra*, and *Complete Vajra Analysis of the Meaning of the Yamāntaka Mantra*. His translations were so superb that they became the standard of excellence for the New Translation period [10th–15th c.]. All the Indian paṇḍitas said, "Dharmabhadra,[308] you must compose many Dharma texts and protect living beings. We have seen our people in India writing books without even a third of your knowledge on grammar and logic, let alone the rest of your knowledge, so why are you not writing?"

Once, when he was a young child studying the teachings of the Early Translation school under Dotön Senge, Rongzompa dreamed that he was eating barley dough made of the *Guhyagarbha Tantra* and a vegetable dish made of the *Sarvabuddhasamāyoga Tantra*.

He told his teacher, who said, "This is a sign that you have fully understood these teachings. You should write a commentary on them."

To fulfill his teacher's command, Rongzompa wrote three upadeśa texts based on the three tantric trainings: the *Extensive Sūtra of Samayas*, which defines the meaning of the higher training in morality; the *Four Modes and Fifteen Branches Commentary*, which explains the higher training in samādhi; and the *Three Upadeśa on the View and Meditation of the Great Perfection*, which explains the higher training in sublime knowledge. In addition, he wrote *Commentary on the "Buddhasamāyoga Tantra,"* various commentaries and upadeśa on the Yamāntaka cycle, including his *Commentary on the "Lower Realms Purification Tantra"* and *Commentary on the "Bhairava Tantra,"* and an enormous number of śāstras, such as *Entering the Way of the Great Vehicle*.

Among the many scholars living in the four provinces[309] of Tibet at that time, some eagerly and humbly accepted Rongzompa and acclaimed him as an emanation of the Buddha himself. Others, though, wondered how someone born in Tibet could compose even more śāstras than the scholars of India, and many of these [doubting Tibetan scholars]—including Yangkhye Lama of Shab, Marpa Dowa, Uyukpa Dawa Samten, Dö Khyungpo Hungnying, Setrom Gyatso Bar, Tsamtön Gocha, Ngakha Darchung, Gö Lhetse, and Gya Gyeltsul—went before the great master to see if they could discredit him, debating like king bulls trying to tear at him with their horns. But when they arrived before the great noble Lion of Speech[310] himself, who sat with perfect regal poise, merely hearing the thunderous roar of his melodious voice proclaim the complete presentation of scripture, reasoning, grammar, and meaning was enough to crush their mountainous pride, and they all bowed their heads at his lotus feet and became his disciples.

Gorub Lotsawa Gelong Chökyi Sherab, a monk translator from Gorub, who was known for his learning and perfect memory, also slandered Rongzompa at first. Later, when he saw Rongzompa's *Entering the Way of the Great Vehicle*, he was filled with great devotion. In the end, he venerated him by making many material offerings, confessed his earlier wrongs, and requested to be accepted as a disciple. Gorub Lotsawa received many teachings, including the *Secret Tantra of the All-Victorious Wrathful Mañjuśrī*. While he was studying the *Secret Tantra*, the Great Rongzom Paṇḍita said, "If we had the Sanskrit manuscript, it would read like this."

Gorub Lotsawa memorized what Rongzompa said. Sometime later, he acquired the Sanskrit manuscript from a paṇḍita named Jowo Kṛṣṇa, and when Gorub Lotsawa saw it and listened to it being read, he discovered that it was exactly as the great Rongzom had said it would be. Gorub Lotsawa was filled with tremendous devotion and offered the Sanskrit manuscript to Rongzompa, who revised it and taught it to him once more.

These stories are also included in Ngorchen Kunga Zangpo's *Classification of Caryātantras*. Likewise, the many wondrous stories of Rongzompa also appear in the writings of translators during the New Translation period. All the Tibetan translators, such as Marpa Chökyi Wangchuk, and intelligent persons renowned for their learning bowed at his feet and acclaimed his undisputed scholarship. Even today, there is no denying that whoever lays eyes upon his śāstras, whether lengthy or brief, will be convinced that he is unmatched. For these reasons, he was acclaimed by the great Gö Lotsawa and others who said, "There has never been a scholar in Tibet who equaled him."

Although Rongzompa reached the state of an unrivaled great Lord of Speech, he never had even the slightest inclination to praise himself or belittle others. He always took the lowest seat and behaved in a mild and disciplined manner, abiding in the way Ācārya Śāntideva did. Because this great being felt no malice or disdain toward anyone and possessed the power of tremendous love and compassion, he freely granted the Dharma to those he set upon the Buddhist path, and to ordinary beings he gifted all sorts of material goods without the slightest trace of miserliness.

In his great compassion, Rongzompa made sure that none of his students were ever forsaken. He protected his vows and samayas like a precious jewel or his own life force, and he brought others to that same state.

In all of these ways, Rongzompa effortlessly and naturally manifested the sacred histories of holy masters. He flew up sheer, mirrorlike rock faces just like a bird, inserted ritual daggers into boulders, flew through the sky, knew the abodes and behaviors of Tibet's gods and demons, read the minds of his disciples, and so on. His endless signs of accomplishment struck wonder in the minds of ordinary people, and his fame spread throughout the people of his day. However, these minor signs of realization are nothing special for such a great, sublime master, who had attained the four perfectly pure discernments.

In order to spread the teachings of the Secret Mantra throughout the snowy land of Tibet, this great being appeared as a great Vajradhara tantrika and reached the age of 119 years, passing away without any signs of illness. His lineage sons continued to endure, and they were all accomplished Vajrakilaya practitioners without exception.

Rongzompa's disciple lineage consisted of seventeen translators, including Gorub Lotsawa, Marpa Dowa, and Gö Khugpa Lhetse; thirty-five Mahāsiddhas, including Yak Dorje Dzinpa; 180 great yogin meditators, including Je Gönpuwa, the brother of Machik Zhama; and a large number of disciples, such as 500 lamas who were worthy of being honored with parasols,[311] and including the layman Dorje Wangchuk of Yolchak and Yangkhye Lama.

The teachings of the Early Translation school constituted the principal practice of the Great Rongzom. In particular, all the Secret Mantra teachings of the Early Translation school—the instructions given by Padmasambhava, Vimalamitra, Vairotsana, and others—were contained within and transmitted to Rongzompa. His main practice was the Nyingma teachings. He mastered the approach and accomplishment of Mātaraḥ, Yamarāja, and Vajrakīla, and with this power he subjugated all the gods and demons of the eight classes[312] throughout Tibet, who offered him their life essence. Rongzompa wrote various instructions on the life essences and favorable substances of Tibet's gods and demons.

At the end of his life, he gave many of his own teachings in Sanskrit to his daughter, a wisdom Ḍākinī in the guise of a human girl, who spoke exclusively in Sanskrit. When the girl turned sixteen years old, the master, seated on a stone throne adorned with a brocade back, was giving her an explanation of the tantras when she flew off into the sky and went to Kecara.[313] A drop of her secret blood fell in front of the teaching throne, and from it grew a medicinal rose bush bearing flowers of the five colors,[314] left as an object of devotion. Although [previously] there were two elderly people who used to see flowers of the five colors, now [at the time of Ngorchen Kunga Zangpo, who lived in the fifteenth century] only white and yellow are visible. This is explained in the Central Tibetan edition of Rongzompa's biography, called *Four Branches and Leaves*.

In brief, this master [Rongzompa] was a peerless being who resided at the level of the truly great Noble Ones, and indeed his entire sacred life story of scholarship and realization is beyond the scope of ordinary minds. For the sake of ordinary beings, only the well-known and undisputed part of the sacred biography of this paṇḍita who unlocked the eight great treasures of sublime confidence[315] is told here [by Mipham Rinpoche], based on the writings of Dorje Wangchuk, the layman of Yolchak, who was a direct disciple of the master. These writings are found in the great Gö Lotsawa's *Blue Annals*, adorned with a few small extracts from the writings of [other] Tibetan scholars of the past.

Let the hundred-petaled lotus of devotion unfurl with these words of Ju Mipham Rinpoche.

Katok Dampa Deshek

10

From the Supreme Conqueror Padmasambhava's ocean of compassion,
You arose radiant with the thousandfold light of sublime activity.

Sun of the Nyingma teachings, founder of Katok,[316]
Dampa Deshek, at your feet I pray.

From the Supreme Conqueror Padmasambhava's ocean of unceasing **compassion, the sun of the Nyingma teachings,** Victorious **Katokpa, arose** from the shoulder of the Eastern Mountain, **radiant with the thousandfold light of** supremely **sublime activity**—peaceful, increasing, powerful, and wrathful. This was the merit of glorious good fortune of the beings living in the land of Tibet. He was not an ordinary source of refuge who taught the means for achieving temporary, fleeting, worldly happiness. He was a great Bliss-Gone Buddha [**Deshek**], who reached the heart of enlightenment, just as the Tathāgatas of the past had done, without any hardship whatsoever. This was for establishing all beings throughout the vast reaches of space without exception in the state of temporary benefit and ultimate happiness, through the path of the holy [**Dampa**] Dharma. Katokpa Dampa Deshek, **at your feet, I pray**.

The renowned Victorious Katokpa Deshek Sherab Senge [1122–1192], also known as Lama Pobpa Taye, was born in a place called Belmo, known today as Serkhang, in the Drizagang district of the Four Rivers and Six Ranges region of Greater Tibet.[317] It is located near the Serden River to the right and the Terlung Pöchu River on the left, in the snowy Treshö mountain range.

Sherab Senge's father was a tantric yogi named Tsangpa Paldrak, and his mother was Tsangmo Rinchen Gyen. They had four sons and one daughter, the eldest of whom was Je Phagmo Drupa Dorje Gyalpo. The second son was Victorious Katokpa Dampa Deshek Sherab Senge himself, who was born in the Male Water Tiger year of the second rabjung, or sixty-year calendrical cycle, amid wondrous signs and indications. His father named him Gewa Pel, "Glorious Virtue."

From his early youth, Sherab Senge had a handsome face and physique, an articulate tongue, and a mind turned away from saṃsāra. He rejected meat and alcohol and kept his daily conduct pure. His mind was disciplined, and he had great compassion. He had a devoted interest in the subjects of study, reflection, and meditation, and his holy conduct was impeccable.

Between the ages of six and nine, Sherab Senge studied reading and writing, painting and sculpting deities, statue proportions, ancient and modern healing arts, Indian and Chinese astrology, Tibetan grammar and orthography, śāstras on secular traditions, and the legal system of the monarchy. He memorized the *Prajñāpāramitā Sūtra in Eight Thousand Lines* and made that his daily recitation. He received the lay vows of upāsaka from Lama Paldzin.

When he turned nine, Sherab Senge became weary of saṃsāra and, at his father's command, he entered the local monastery, known as Palgyi Chökhor. With his brother Je Phagmo Drupa, he studied the Vinaya, the Sūtra section, the *Prajñāpāramitā*, and various tantras and śāstras. He took the Bodhisattva vows and studied the *King of Samādhi Sūtra*, the *Sūtra That Elucidates Wisdom Mind*, the *Laṅkāvatāra Sūtra*, and the *Prajñāpāramitā Sūtra in Eight Thousand Lines*. His oral examinations delighted his teacher.

When Sherab Senge received the empowerments and instructions for Vajracaṇḍikā and Cakrasaṃvara, an extraordinary realization was born in him. When he received the life force empowerment of Palden Lhamo, even without performing the practice he actually saw Palden Lhamo. He undertook wrathful subjugating practice with Lama Phagmo Drupa and succeeded in directly annihilating the anti-Buddhist Minyak Gyalpo [king of Minyak].[318]

At the age of sixteen, Sherab Senge went to a place called Kampo, where he met Geshe Jampa Namdak and received many commentaries on major texts, explanations of the tantras, empowerments, and oral instructions. His studies delighted the lama. At age nineteen, he traveled to U and Tsang. There, from Geshe Dotok Telpa Gyaltsen, Geshe Gyamarwa, and others, Sherab Senge received numerous teachings on Buddha's words and its śāstras, as well as tantric explanations and empowerments for the *Kālacakra Tantra* and so forth. At age twenty-one, from the Kadampa scholar Senge Zangpo at the glorious Reting Monastery, Sherab Senge received Atiśa's *Lamp for the Path to Enlightenment*, explanations of the transcendent perfections, the Madhyamaka philosophy, and elaborate tantric teachings, empowerments, and guidance.

From the Sakya teachers Sönam Tsemo, Kunga Legpa, and others, Sherab Senge received the *Hevajra Tantra*, the Path and Its Fruit, the *Vajra Tent*, the Sakya Vajrakīlaya, and so on. He also received numerous empowerments, reading transmissions, and instructional guidance for Yamāntaka according to the Gö, Ngok, and Nub traditions. Particularly, Sherab Senge actually went to Tuṣita Heaven and received teachings directly from Maitreya, so that all his uncertainty was cleared away and arose as pure perception.

From Kam Lotsawa, a disciple of Ra Lotsawa Dorje Dragpa [also known as Ralo], Sherab Senge received Cakrasaṃvara; from Chogro Lotsawa, he received Vajravārāhī; from Bari Lotsawa [also known as Rinchen Drak], he received miraculous script, as well as numerous empowerments and instructions. At age twenty-two, from Lobpön Ratna Senge, Sherab Senge received the empowerments and explanations of Cakrasaṃvara and Catuḥpīṭha. Relying on extracted essences,[319] he undertook austerities.

At age twenty-four [in 1145], in Penyul Gyal, Sherab Senge received monastic ordination from Jangchub Senge, and it was at this time that he was given the name Sherab Senge. From this teacher, he received numerous teachings from the Nyingma Secret Mantra tradition. He gained mastery of development-stage meditation and the yoga of channels and winds. He clearly perceived his own body in deity form without any obscuration. During this period, Sherab Senge reached the pinnacle of scholarship, set forth the assertions of debate, displayed the signs of accomplishment, saw deities in meditation, and completely perfected all the precious qualities of realization. Delighted holy masters praised him, and word of his scholarship and accomplishment spread throughout all of Central Tibet.

At age twenty-five, in snowy Labchi, Sherab Senge met Jetsun Rechungpa [a primary disciple of Milarepa], from whom he received *Blue Cakrasaṃvara* and the *Nine Cycles of the Formless Ḍākinīs*. From Repa Zhiwa Ö, he received the teaching cycle of yogic inner heat.

In the shedra[320] of the glorious Nartang Monastery, from Depa Nagyi Khenchen, Sherab Senge received the vows of full monastic ordination in the Lume tradition. He maintained pure conduct just like that of Upāli,[321] the great patriarch of the Vinaya. From Depa Nagyi Khenchen he received numerous Kama and Terma teachings.

In particular, from Dzamtön Chenpo Drowe Gonpo, who was a direct disciple of Zur Shakya Senge of the Zur lineage trio,[322] Sherab Senge received the empowerments and tantric explanations of the *Magical Infinity* and the four root sūtras of Anuyoga.[323] He also received all the profound key points of the Mind, Expanse, and Upadeśa classes of the Great Perfection in their entirety.

When Sherab Senge was twenty-nine years old, Lama Dzamtönpa prophesied, "If you practice in Kampo, you will attain the Rainbow Body. If you go to Katok in Kham, after twenty-five days Guru Padmasambhava will bless you. Since it is a holy practice place of Vairotsana, the teachings will prevail there for a thousand years."

Sherab Senge journeyed to Zangri Kharmar and received many precious instructions on Zhije and Chö[324] from Machik Labdrön's son Tönyön Samdrub, the Crazy Yogin Dönden, and others. Then he traveled to Khok in

Dagpo and met the peerless Dagpo Lhaje, from whom he received many empowerments and instructions from the Kagyu tradition, such as Coemergent Mahāmudrā. He practiced for four months in Tsari, where signs of accomplishment appeared and realization arose.

Heeding the call to "come see your old father," Sherab Senge went back to Dagpo and offered his experience and realization. His channels became capable receptacles of wisdom winds and fluids, the sound of the six-syllable mantra [OṂ MAṆI PADME HŪṂ] and rainbow light emanated from him, and other extraordinary and wondrous signs and indications occurred. The Guru gave him clothing and blessed objects, and he recited a prophecy as Dzamtönpa had spoken earlier.

In accordance with the joint command of Lama Dzamtönpa and Dagpo Lhaje Rinpoche, Sherab Senge decided that the long-term endurance of the Buddha's teachings was more important than the personal goal of dissolving his body into light. In search of Katok, he gradually journeyed east in the direction of Kham.

Along the way, Sherab Senge met the first Karmapa, Dusum Khyenpa Chökyi Dragpa [1110–1193]. They compared their realizations, and their minds merged as one. Consequently, Sherab Senge requested many empowerments and instructions, and he became the Karmapa's main disciple, among a thousand disciples honored with parasols. Thus, Sherab Senge attended over one hundred authentic masters all over Kham and Central Tibet and received and mastered all Buddhist vehicles.

Between the ages of thirty-three and thirty-five, Sherab Senge traveled to the regions of Minyak, Jang, and Ling,[325] acting as court guru for their respective kings. He ordained about 900 monks and gave extensive empowerments, reading transmissions, and explanatory guidance according to the wishes of disciples from all traditions.

At age thirty-six, Sherab Senge returned to his homeland and stayed in retreat. When the local protector deity of Sharkampo came to welcome him, Sherab Senge granted him a Dharma connection, but due to unfavorable circumstances he sent the protector deity away.

Then, taking his personal attendants, Tsultrim Rinchen and Dorje Gyaltsen, along as his traveling companions, Sherab Senge set out in search of Katok. When they arrived at Pema Yungdrung Tangmar, a Bön monastery in Horpo, the protector deity Lhamo Rangjung Gyalmo appeared before Sherab Senge on the roof of the temple. Pointing, she said, "Go up that slope, and I will offer you my assistance."

At first, Sherab Senge arrived at Katil. There he encountered thirteen children herding animals and asked them, "Where is Katok?"

"Up there," they pointed.

Sherab Senge went up that way, and above a lion-shaped boulder and a glittering turquoise lake he discovered the naturally formed syllables ĀḤ and KA TOK. He practiced inside a cave where Vairotsana had practiced and experienced excellent signs and indications. Beside the upper hermitage, a spring of longevity water gushed forth.

Horpo district was home to approximately 4,000 inhabitants. When their local chieftain, named Gelu, witnessed the precious Dharma master's display of signs and miraculous powers, Gelu showed little interest, because the chieftains of that region were all Bönpo. Gradually, however, as the time approached for karma and aspirations to ripen and auspicious circumstances came into alignment, Gelu became Sherab Senge's patron. One hundred Horpo youth were ordained, and the number of disciples requesting Dharma teachings increased with each passing day. Chieftain Gelu celebrated the master's activities and conduct, and with new intense faith, Gelu helped construct the monastery. Gelu humbly requested that the precious Dharma master make Katok his principal seat.

At the age of thirty-eight, in the Earth Hare year of the third calendrical cycle [1159], the perfect auspicious circumstances for beginning construction of the glorious Katok Monastery were present. When the local Bön protector deity, a rock nyen spirit[326] who was under a Bönpo oath, began creating harmful obstacles during the construction, the precious Dharma master taught the *Cakrasaṃvara Root Tantra*. A light snow fell, and taking Gelong Dingpo and Dorje Gyaltsen Sherab along with him, the master chased the local protector away. They watched as the lord of the rock nyen spirits and damsi demons dissolved into a boulder.

After piercing a hole in the boulder, Sherab Senge made his two disciples carry it. As the master slapped the boulder with his hand, the disciples hauled it to a spring beside the monastery. The rock nyen spirit promised he would do whatever the master asked.

The thousand or so disciples who had come for teachings constructed the temple by day and received teachings by night. From time to time, together with teachings, the purification of obscurations was also practiced. With all the framers, stone masons, sculptors, and artisans working together, the outer monastery, shrine hall, courtyard, entryways, and library were all beautifully completed. Inside, the precious Dharma master oversaw the construction of statues of the Eight Close Sons, the Gatekeepers,[327] and the Dharmapālas. He filled the statues with extraordinary blessed items, such as scriptures of Padmasambhava and Vimalamitra originating from Samye Monastery, Sanskrit texts of all five sections of the *Magical Infinity Tantra*, Dropukpa Shakya Senge's Dharma robe, a tooth of Zurchenpa [Zur Shakya Jungne], Jowo Atiśa's paṇḍita hat, Nubchen Sangye Yeshe's waist dagger, and relics of Buddha Śākyamuni. He also installed over 3,000 volumes of the Kangyur and Tengyur, including the Kangyur printed in gold, and twenty-five sets of the *Prajñāpāramitā* printed in gold as well as ten sets in silver.

When the consecration was finally held, a tent of rainbows filled the clear blue sky, a rain of flowers fell, melodious sounds of formless instruments resounded, and clear signs of the wisdom deities actually entering the statues occurred. Everyone was enthralled.

Nearly 4,000 monks from places such as Minyak, Ling Tsang, southern Kham, Tsongka, Jang, and Jitan received the vows of novice ordination. Katok Dampa Deshek [as he was now known] established many sādhana rituals,[328] such as those of the *Mahāsamaya Sūtra*, *Magical Infinity*, *Cakrasaṃvara*, *Kālacakra*, and *Hevajra*.

Dampa Deshek then traveled to the place where the king of Ling, Dralha Dargye, had passed away. He was offered a suit of armor, a Yazi sword,[329] and other items that belonged to Gyatsa [the older half brother of Gesar of Ling]. At the time, eight Bön priests were filled with unbearable passion and aggression, and they performed black magic against Dampa Deshek inside a wooden shed. Palden Lhamo knocked it down, and the precious Dharma master used boulders to draw a vajra cross on top of it. Nowadays, this place is known as Pawang Gyeleb, "Site of Eight Boulders."

Thus, in the two years that elapsed between the Female Earth Hare and the Male Iron Dragon, Katok Monastery [founded 1159] was fully completed.

At age forty, Dampa Deshek established a shedra on the shady slope and a retreat center on the sunny slope. He gave full ordination to nearly 1,000 monks and held an extremely secret *Mahāsamaya Sūtra* great accomplishment ceremony.[330] During the summer rains retreat, 900 fully ordained monks and 200 novices were recorded on the Saṅgha counting stick.[331] During the summertime, he gave explanatory teachings on numerous major Sūtra and Mantra texts to the students of the shedra, and during the wintertime he gave empowerments, guidance, and precious instructions to the retreatants.

Over a three-year period, Dampa Deshek turned the Wheel of Dharma according to the individual capacities of his students, teaching them the outer sciences, including language, logic and philosophy, art, medicine, astrology, and orthography; the Vehicle of Characteristics, including the Vinaya, Prajñāpāramitā, Madhyamaka, and Abhidharma; the empowerments, guidance, and reading transmissions of the tantras and sādhanas of the Sarma tradition, including the *Stages of the Path to Enlightenment*; the *Hevajra Tantra*; the Path and Its Fruit; the *Six Yogas of Nāropa*; Mahāmudrā, Zhije, and Chö; the *Kālacakra Tantra*; and the empowerments, instructional guidance, and upadeśa for the trilogy of Sūtra, Magical Infinity, and Mind; the three sections of Mind, Expanse, and Upadeśa, and other teachings of the Nyingma tradition. At times, he had to teach thirteen classes in a single day.

Many noblemen throughout Kham, U, and Tsang, including Gelu, the chieftain of Horpu; Tadzin of Minyak; the King of Jang; Dralha Dargye, the king of Ling; Kalewa of Kongpo; and the leaders of eastern Tsongkha, Gyalmorong, and other places came to pay their deep respects and offer their service. During this period, Lama Dzamtönpa reached 100 years of age, and signs occurred that he had attained the Rainbow Body. Dampa Deshek established a memorial offering day to commemorate the Guru.

Among Katok Dampa Deshek's fortunate disciples, who were as numerous as stars in the sky, Tsangtön Dorje Gyaltsen and Khenpo Drakye were as exalted as the sun and moon. Dampa Deshek had five disciples who attained the Body of Light: Lama Bumtön in Vairotsana's cave, Lama Göngyal in Tsari, Yönten Bum of U, Jamyang Yönten of Minyak, and Gelong Sherab of Ling. Others included the "three fine monks" of Gyalmorong, the "ten supreme and close ones," the "three who mastered patience," and the "hundred who were honored with parasols."

During that period, the congregation was made up of nearly 80,000 monks. More than sixty of them were found guilty of immoral monastic conduct, and Dampa Deshek expelled them from the monastery to the sound of a gandi[332] in accordance with the practice of the Vinaya.

All the monks in residence had become free of their homes and relinquished their attachment to this life. They relied upon alms for their sustenance. Outwardly, they conducted themselves according to the Vinaya. Inwardly, their hearts were filled with the great compassion of bodhicitta. Secretly, they had mastered the view and conduct of the Secret Mantra. They devoted their entire lives to the practice of Dharma. Therefore, here in the Land of Snows, Katok Dorje Den Monastery, the source of hundreds of thousands of scholars and siddhas, became an adornment that beautified the Buddha's teachings, and the banner of its renown waved throughout the three planes of existence.

This Buddhist master, Katok Dampa Deshek, composed the following works: *Analysis of Haribhadra's "Clear Meaning Commentary on the 'Prajñāpāramitā'"*; *White Silver Mirror: A Commentary on the "Prātimokṣa Sūtra" of Bhikṣu Monasticism*; *Treasury of Gems: General Analysis of the "Abhidharma Kośa"*; *Commentarial Notes on the "Mūlamadhyamaka Kārikā"*; *Precious Lamp: An Outline of the "Bodhicarya Avatāra" and Its Condensed Meaning*; *Rituals for Cultivating Bodhicitta*; *Summary of Training*; *Commentary on "Stages of the Path"*; *Notes on "Revealing the Names of Mañjuśrī"*; *Sprouts of Gold: Summary of Mahāmudrā Guidance*; *Notes on the "Parkhab Commentary on the 'Guhyagarbha Tantra'"*; *Notes on "Stages of the Path" and Its Condensed Meaning*; *Notes on the "Ocean of Magical Manifestations"*; *Summary of Upadeśa on the Lasso of Skillful Means*; *Main Sādhana Practice* [of the *Lasso of Skillful Means*]; *Extensive Twenty-Five-Chapter Commentary on the "Embodiment of Wisdom Mind"*; *General Commentary on the "Embodiment of Wisdom Mind"*; *Structural Analysis of the "Embodiment of Wisdom Mind" Called "Sunshine of Excellent Speech"*; *Condensed Meaning of the "Embodiment of Wisdom Mind" Called the "Garland of the White Lotus"*; *Parkhab Commentary of the Wisdom Mind of Samantabhadra*: *Notes on All-Inclusive Awareness, the Vajra Adornment*; *Outline of the Path of the Great Perfection; Extensive, Middling, and Concise General Commentaries on the "Lamp for the Eye of Samādhi"*; *Summary of the "Stages and Paths"*; *Summary of a Venomous Snake*; *Summary of the Sword*; *Extensive, Middling, and Concise Classifications of the Tantras*; *Summary of Empowerments*; *Extensive Commentary on the "Tantra of the All-Doing Great King"*; *Vajra Quitch Grass: Determining Self-Awareness*; and *General Outline of Vehicles: The Flower Ornament of General Chö*.

In addition to these and other commentaries on major Buddhist texts, Dampa Deshek composed guidance manuals, sādhanas, works on pure perception, practical instructions, and songs of realization.[333] His compositions filled more than nineteen volumes, but most of these have been lost and are no longer extant.

From a young age, this master was inseparable from the Glorious Bernakchen Mahākāla, Śrī Devi Rangjung Gyalmo, and other protector deities. Local deities and Dharmapālas manifested the signs of having fulfilled his enlightened wishes, and he saw the complete maṇḍalas of the Three Noble Protectors [Mañjuśrī, Vajrapāṇi, and Avalokiteśvara], Maitreya, Vārāhī, Tārā, Māyājāla [Magical Infinity], Tsokchen Dupa, Cakrasaṃvara, Yangdak Heruka, and Vajrakīlaya. He spoke face to face with Saraha, Virūpa, Indrabodhi,[334] Bharadvāja, and others. In particular, he constantly saw the palaces and deities of the purelands of Guru Rinpoche and Amitābha, and received prophecies from them.

As for signs of accomplishments, Katok Dampa Deshek's body had no shadow; he passed unimpeded through stone and rammed-earth walls; he wrote Maṇi mantras and other letters in stone; he left handprints and footprints in stone; his ritual amṛta boiled spontaneously; the sounds of dancing and symbolic songs resounded from Ḍākinī gatherings; rainbow light shone forth; a rain of flowers fell; the spontaneous sounds of the six-syllable mantra [OṂ MAṆI PADME HŪṂ] and AMI DEWA were heard by all; and with his unobscured knowing, he could distinctly see throughout the three times. These and other indications were clearly observed by everyone.

At the age of seventy years [in 1191], Katok Dampa Deshek granted the bodhicitta ritual and empowerments to over 70,000 people. He gave oral instructions to his disciples and presented a paṇḍita hat and old Dharma cloak to his heart-son, Tsangtön Dorje Gyaltsen, signifying his appointment as Dampa Deshek's regent.

"Khenpo Yegyal must look after the shedra, and Khenpo Kongpo Lama Buchu must look after the retreat center. Dorje Gyaltsen, give teachings to both of them," he said, conferring his authority.

The Dharma Lord Tsangtönpa then received teachings from Omniscient Dampa Deshek Rinpoche on the tantras, sādhanas, and practical applications of the three inner tantras, passed down through the lineage of the glorious Zurpa father and son.[335] This lineage tradition has been passed down systematically without decline, and even today it flourishes throughout Kham and Central Tibet.

At age seventy-one, Dampa Deshek said to his main heart-disciples, "Lama Dagpo Chöje [Gampopa] showed me the dirt encrusted on his back from the hardship he endured and said, 'This is it!' No matter how high your realization, the essence of the Buddha's teachings is subduing the mind, so you must pay close attention to your actions. No matter how articulate you are, words are just a shell; it is their meaning that must be practiced and meditated on. Then you must look to see whether this reaches the essence. Whether you are practicing the Mahāyāna or the Hīnayāna, there is no more crucial purpose than subduing your own mind. Be humble and focus one-pointedly on practice. The gurus of my lineage have dissolved into light in an unbroken succession, and this is thanks to practice. Indeed, if I had gone to Kampo, from the perspective of others, I would have dissolved into light. However, hoping to benefit the Buddhist teachings, I chose instead to foster a community of disciples and engage in teaching, debate, and so on. For my own phenomena, there is no difference. I have perfectly accomplished my ultimate goal."

Dampa Deshek then gave them many oral instructions, and said, "Whatever you do, never forget that you must turn your minds away from saṃsāra, direct your gaze inward, and meditate on bodhicitta, the mind of enlightenment." He gave this advice again and again.

Dampa Deshek then performed a vast feast offering, and when his students implored him to remain, he sang a song of realization that began:

> Now that my true purpose is fulfilled, in the Pureland of Great Bliss,[336]
> I will go before the Buddha of Boundless Light.

On the full-moon day of the fourth Tibetan month, in the Water Rat year of the third calendrical cycle, as Dampa Deshek was reciting words of truth and prayers of aspiration, such as "May the Buddha's teachings endure forever," he directed his gaze to the west, relaxed into the nature of mind, and passed into peace.

Lingje Repa

11

Heart-son of Deshek Phagmo Drupa,
You perfected your realization through the inner path.
Supreme Heruka of the saints of Snowland,
Glorious Lingje Repa, to you I pray.

In the snowy land of Tibet, the Secret Mantra, which is the essence of the Buddha's teachings, spread through both the Nyingma and Sarma schools according to specific places, times, and the capacities and aspirations of disciples. Among these schools, the tradition of the New Tantras, a section of the eight chariots of the practice lineage,[337] was upheld in part by a direct disciple of Dagpo Lhaje, Deshek Phagmo Drupa Dorje Gyalpo, the life force of the Kagyu teachings. Deshek Phagmo Drupa had an inconceivable lineage of disciples, among whom Taklung Tarpa Tashipal had perfect devotion, Parbuwa Lodrö Senge had perfect sublime knowledge, Chenbu Gyare had perfect ability, and so on. But Deshek Phagmo Drupa's inner heart-son, who had ultimate realization, was Napuwa Lingje Repa Pema Dorje [1128–1188].

In general, "sons" refer to supreme beings who possess exalted noble qualities. Specific descriptions are used to identify those who are foremost at a given time, such as "Son of the Body, Rāhula," or "Sons Born of Speech, Śrāvakas and Pratyekabuddhas," or "Heart-Son Bodhisattvas." Furthermore, in some cases, a sole sublime being will become the son of all three secrets,[338] so not all of these beings can be identified with certainty.

In this case, **Deshek Phagmo Drupa**'s **heart-son** was not merely versed in the outer disciplines of body and speech. **Through the path** of the four **inner** yogas, the basic nature of Mahāmudrā was not left dormant, and his **realization** of unobscured great wisdom was **perfected**. This **supreme saint of Snowland** who attained ultimate accomplishment in that very lifetime released his dualistic conceptual thoughts into the space of selfless evenness. He was inseparable from the maṇḍala of the glorious **Heruka** Cakrasaṃvara. **Glorious Lingje Repa, to you I pray.**

Lingje Repa was born in the Upper Nyang region of Tsang, in Langpona, in the year of the Earth Monkey. His father, who was learned in medicine and Tantra, was Gyalpo Drubpe of the Lingme tribe, and his mother was Tummo Darkyi. Lingje Repa studied medicine and Tantra, and he received monastic ordination from Oma Tangwa. He trained with masters such as Zhang Lotsawa and Ra Lotsawa Dorje Dragpa. Together with a noblewoman named Menmo, he practiced in the manner of a yogin.

It was after reading a story in the *Ratnakūṭa Sūtra* that Lingje Repa realized that his relationship with Menmo was the result of karmic residue. Long ago, sixty monks had chastised two Bodhisattvas for teaching the Dharma to an assembly of women, and also accused the Bodhisattvas of breaking their ordination vows by engaging in sexual intercourse. As a karmic consequence of this slander, which resulted in loss of faith in the two Bodhisattvas, the sixty monks suffered incessant rebirths in lower realms and other rebirths with unfavorable conditions. Finally, when they were reborn in human form, they all went before Buddha Śākyamuni, promised to keep their vows, and became Bodhisattvas. When Lingje Repa read the story, he understood that in a former rebirth he had been Vīryaprabha, one of the sixty monks. This explained why in the present life he had broken his monastic vows in joining with Menmo.

Lingje Repa and Menmo requested instructions from Gyalwa Khyungtsangpa Yeshe Lama. When Khyungtsangpa told many stories about how he had actually met Rechungpa, Lingje Repa lost faith in him, and after that, Lingje Repa's realization lost some of its warmth.

Next the pair traveled to Loro and requested empowerments from Ācārya Lo. From Rechungpa's disciple Sumpa Repa, Lingje Repa received all the instructions in their entirety. In a dream, a luminous man appeared to him and said: "Five and a half years from now, you will achieve your goal."

When he was thirty-eight, in the winter of the Wood Bird year [1165], Lingje Repa traveled to see Phagmo Drupa Dorje Gyalpo, and spontaneous faith arose in him. Phagmo Drupa was known reverently as Je Drogön, Lord Protector of Beings, and indeed it occurred to Lingje Repa that all the birds and wild animals around him were the master's emanations. Although the master disapproved of yogins and householders, he nonetheless took an immense interest in Lingje Repa.

Lingje Repa vowed to remain in meditation retreat for seven years and seven months, but after three days, an unimpeded realization arose in him. He [left his retreat and] returned to the assembly. He shared his experience as follows:

> Master, you asked me to meditate upon the original meaning,
> And I have done so.
> Now the object and subject of meditation are lost and gone,
> And there is no longer anything to practice in retreat.

Drogön Phagmo Drupa was delighted, and word of Lingje Repa's high realization spread as far as the Ganges River. Drogön held an auspicious celebration and sent the lady named Menmo away.

Taking nothing whatsoever with him, Lingje Repa journeyed to Kham and went to meet with the gurus of Loro.

After that, he went back to Phagmodru, where the holy remains [of Phagmo Drupa] had already been cremated. Lingje Repa sang an elegy, which began:

Like the city of Kuśinagarī,[339]
The deep forest of glorious Phagmodru . . .

Lingje Repa stayed in Drak Yangzong and many other places in U-Tsang. He was invited to Napu by the king of Napu and established a monastery there. At Samye, a woman gave him a single volume of scripture, which he swallowed, and from then on, there were no teachings that he did not know.

Lingje Repa began writing a commentary on the Tantra, as commanded by the Ḍākinī. As soon as he began, he was criticized by people who said, "You are teaching others without first studying yourself!" He then discontinued his writing and sang a hymn begging the Ḍākinī for her forgiveness.

His final teaching, which he tucked between the pages of a book, reads:

The actual glorious Heruka came and benefitted beings.
Do not think that I am not here! Look within your own mind.
When you see your mind's nature, you will meet me.

While Lingje Repa was giving a brief Dharma teaching, two samaya-breakers came into his presence, and he passed away. During the cremation, there was not a trace of smoke, a wonderful fragrance emerged, and the flames danced in various patterns.

Lingje Repa had many disciples, including Tsangpa Gyare, the one who was capable of everything.

Drogön Chögyal Phagpa

12
By the thousandfold light of your sublime wisdom and love shining,
The lotus grove of benefit and happiness bloomed instantly in the cool land of Tibet.
Mañjuśrī in the form of a divine human king,
Drogön Chögyal Phagpa, to you I pray.

Mañjuśrī, lord of the sublime knowledge of all the Buddhas, took **the form of a human king,** who was the true **divine** savior and protector of beings, Drogön Chögyal Phagpa. When the **light** of his Buddha activity of wondrously **sublime** omniscient **wisdom** and **loving** compassion, indivisibly united, **shone** in **thousandfold** light like the countless rays of the sun, **the lotus grove of benefit and happiness**—which is the temporary attainment of the higher realms of gods and humans and the ultimate placement of beings at the level of omniscience—**bloomed instantly in the cool land of Tibet**, ringed by snowy mountains, without needing to open gradually over time. **Drogön Chögyal Phagpa, to you I pray!**

Drogön Chögyal Phagpa Lodrö Gyaltsen Rinpoche [1235–1280] had the good fortune to be born as the son of Zangtsa Sönam Gyaltsen. He was a Bodhisattva abiding on the higher bhūmis[340] who intentionally took rebirth in the human realm. As a result, from the beginning his nature, love, and Bodhisattva conduct were exceptional, and he was adorned with the title Phagpa.[341] The inexhaustible treasury of his intelligence and liberating confidence burst open and overflowed. He performed miraculous activities, such as slicing off his head and four limbs with a sharp blade and transforming them into the arrangement of the five Buddha families. This and his perfect deeds of enlightened body, speech, and mind caused unswerving faith to be born in the hostile Mongolian king [Kublai Khan], who went on to receive empowerment from him on three occasions.

In appreciation for the first empowerment, the king made Chögyal Phagpa an offering of temporal authority over the thirteen myriarchies of Central Tibet.[342] For the second empowerment, the king offered the three provinces of Tibet.[343] For the final empowerment, the king offered the Chinese kingdom of Khotan.[344] Unsurpassed happiness, well-being, and spiritual sustenance ensued.

As it says in the *Mañjuśrī Root Tantra*, the syllable DHĪ[345] is a synonym for "intelligence," which reveals the first part of Chögyal Phagpa's name.[346] In keeping with prophecies, assuming the form of an ordained king, he manifested as an ordained monk and illuminated the Buddha's teachings. He dwelled evenly in the wisdom realization of noble beings, having exhausted all conceptions of attachment and aversion, and sustained the doctrine impartially. He clarified the complete teachings of theory and practice and caused the sun of well-being and happiness to shine upon the Land of Snows. Even the supremely learned Chomden Rigpe Raldri of Nartang Monastery was powerlessly overcome with faith when he encountered Chögyal Phagpa's accomplished qualities.

Chögyal Phagpa's liberated life story is truly inconceivable. He had many disciples who upheld his lineage, including the Shar, Nub, and Gung Trio,[347] Lama Dragpa Özer, and Lama Tashipal. Chögyal Phagpa also composed *Letter of Praise to the Dharma King of the Three Realms*, renowned in the three worlds.[348]

Kharnakpa of Drum

13

Seeing Dharmatā just as it is, free from elaboration, supreme ultimate truth,
You were liberated from the chain of existence
And attained the kingdom of unwavering Dharmakāya.
Kharnakpa of Drum, to you I pray.

Seeing Dharmatā just as it is, supreme ultimate truth, without obstruction, **free from** all conceptual **elaboration** of ordinary mind's dualistic perception of phenomena, with the sublime mind of nondual wisdom, all **the chains of existence** naturally dissolve and are **liberated** just as particles can never cling to the stainless sky. He **attained the kingdom of** Samantabhadra, the **Dharmakāya, unwavering** from the nature of the three states of being[349] throughout the three times. Tertön **Kharnakpa of Drum, to you I pray!**

The following passage was jointly revealed by Tertön Drum and his patron-disciple from Paro, named Nagpo Khar:

The religious tradition of Tibet is ridiculous. ༔
Each ordinary householder spouts his own spiritual jargon, ༔
Boldly claiming there isn't any difference [between their claims and true Dharma]. ༔
Those with wind disease are told it comes from demons and are treated with coolness.[350] ༔
Unashamed, they hover over the sick, ༔
Each of them carrying his own version of an astrological chart.[351] ༔
This horde of fools unites and ousts the wise. ༔
When these signs occur, ༔
Without ignoring them, the time to reveal this treasure hidden in Paro, Bhutan, has come. ༔
A treasure revealer named Kharnakpa of Drum will appear. ༔

The scriptural transmission of Rāhu Razor's Wrathful Mantras, renowned as the *Triangular Fire Pit of Space*, was extracted from inside a leather amulet in the beak of a brown garuḍa in the Khyerchu Temple in Paro. The scriptural transmission of this teaching appears to still exist even today. It is said this teaching is Vidyādhara Kumāraja's[352] terrifying black magic of Rāhula, so it is held to be from a very early time.

Hepa Chöjung

14

Through vast, fearless wisdom activity and fulfilled
aspiration prayers,
You have the power of the one who wielded the Yogurt
Drinker's vajra[353]
To dash the brains of the unruly and vicious.
Hepa Chöjung, at your feet I pray.

Long ago, the Bodhisattva Vajrapāṇi made aspiration prayers to protect Buddha's teachings. In the same way, Hepa Chöjung gathered **vast** amounts of the two accumulations of merit and wisdom over many eons, completing his former conduct and entering unobstructedly into **fearless wisdom activity**, perfectly **fulfilling** the power of his **aspiration prayers** to subdue beings according to their individual needs. In the case of **unruly and vicious** beings who harmed sentient beings or scorned the Buddha's teachings, those so wicked that it was difficult to subdue them through peaceful activities, he **dashed** their **brains** and annihilated them, just as was done by Indra, the king of the gods, **the one who wielded the Yogurt Drinker's vajra** and swiftly vanquished the asuras in battle with his matchless **power**. You are known as **Hepa Chöjung; at your feet I pray**!

Hepa Chöjung was born in a place called Drakar, in the Sangen region. From Kongpo Gyarawa Namkha Chökyi Gyatso, he received the empowerments and reading transmissions of the *Peaceful and Wrathful Deities* of Pema Lingpa. He composed numerous ritual arrangements, appendixes, and other works on the peaceful and wrathful deities. He was the principal successor of the holder of the Dharma lineage of Victorious Katokpa Dampa Deshek. He acquired mastery of both the supreme and common spiritual accomplishments, and his wrathful activity of annihilation and protection was unobstructed.

Tragtung Dudul Dorje

15

Great master of marvelous holy places and hundreds of treasures,
Including hidden lands, teachings, wealth, samaya substances, and others,
Lord of the ten bhūmis, sovereign among saints,
Tragtung Dudul Dorje,[354] to you I pray.

The Omniscient One of Oḍḍiyāna, as well as oceans of Vidyādharas, Ḍākinīs, and siddhas, prophesied many **hidden lands**,[355] which are particular purelands of the five inexhaustible wheels of ornaments—wisdom body, speech, mind, qualities, and activities—in order to benefit future karmically destined practitioners. Tertön Dudul Dorje [1615–1672] visited all these hidden lands, delighted the Victorious Ones by practicing with diligence, and scattered flowers of consecration.[356] He opened doorways to certain holy places so that the right time to subdue fortunate disciples would not pass. He brought forth whatever hidden-treasure **teaching** cycles were suitable, with each cycle including the Three Roots;[357] Dharmapālas; the vast ocean of peaceful and wrathful deities; the triad of Guru Rinpoche, the Great Perfection, and Avalokiteśvara; upadeśa; and activity practices. He revealed skillful methods for attaining a long life, which is the basis of comfort and happiness, as well as **wealth** treasures to protect ordinary, worldly beings from the suffering of poverty and lack of material goods and resources. For those yearning for extraordinary liberation, Dudul Dorje revealed teachings on the indispensable seven riches.[358] For those with dull faculties who struggle with hearing, contemplation, and meditation, he brought forth **samaya substances**[359] endowed with the four types of liberation,[360] mainly the thousandfold liberation through tasting, whereby a substance liberates simply by being tasted; **and others**. In brief, he was a great being who, without relying on others, had absolute mastery of sublime **wondrous holy places** and **hundreds of treasures**, including the eighteen kinds of treasure,[361] all of which are beyond the scope of ordinary beings. This **lord of the ten bhūmis**, supreme among Vidyādharas, **sovereign among saints, Drinks** the **Blood [Tragtung]** of saṃsāra's three realms of existence, marked by attachment and clinging to magical, nonexistent appearances as actually real, through liberation within the natural state of selflessness, saṃsāra's great enemy, and revels in the state of evenness. **Indestructible** [**Dorje**] great emptiness Dharmakāya wisdom that **subdues** the four **demons [Dudul**] in the space of the Four Kāyas, **Tragtung Dudul Dorje, to you I pray!**

Specifically, "lord of the ten bhūmis" refers to an individual who has reached the tenth level, known as Clouds of Dharma, the ultimate Mahāyāna Bodhisattva path, and who predominantly engages in the perfection of wisdom. Such a being is rich with the power and ability to benefit various sentient beings with the rain of teachings of various spiritual vehicles. "**Sovereign among saints**" can be associated with the Mahāmudrā Vidyādhara or the Completely Accomplished Vidyādhara according to the path of Mantra. Regardless of how this expression is related to the path of Sūtra or the path of Mantra, it should be understood as a manifestation appearing for the benefit of beings, and ultimately a manifestation of the Second Buddha, Guru Padmasambhava.

Furthermore, this great Vidyādhara treasure revealer Dudul Dorje, who was an incarnation of Drogben Khyeuchung Lotsawa, was very clearly prophesied in thirteen different ancient treasure texts. In accordance with these, he took birth in the Female Wood Hare year [1615] on the shady side of the valley known as Ngulpunang, near the country of the Great Dharma King of Derge in Dokham.[362] His father was a learned physician of the Ling clan named Lukyab, and his mother was named Boluma. He learned to read and write from his father, who also trained him in healing therapies and other skills. From the age of six, Dudul Dorje had many pure visions. In his early childhood, he entered the glorious Lhundrub Teng Dharma school. During a refuge ceremony, he offered a snippet of his hair from the crown of his head to the siddha Kunga Gyatso of Derge, who was an emanation of the treasure revealer Rigdzin Gödemchen, and he received the name Kunga Sönam Chöpak. He once left a footprint in a boulder, and even now it is still behind the eastern door of the great assembly hall.

While Dudul Dorje was engaged in studying and training himself in various major texts of the glorious Sakya school, he searched for the meaning of the essential wisdom like a thirsty man craving water. He journeyed to the sacred practice place of Muksang and received many profound teachings, including the Great Perfection, with his guiding guru, Könchok Gyaltsen. He practiced these teachings, and the expanse of realization overflowed. Then he traveled to Central Tibet and met the great siddha of Nyangpo, Tashi Tseten, from whom he received much advice on ripening and liberating instructions. At Drakar Lhachung, he gave up eating solid food. By relying solely on extracted essences, Dudul Dorje was able to master the profound yogic path of the subtle channels, winds, and sole essence. From auspicious connections made when he first entered the door of Dharma, he was able to travel to Sakya and Ngor in Tsang,[363] where he received the *Great Collection of Teachings on the Path and Its Fruit* and other teachings. Later, during his return journey, he touched his head to the feet of the great Vidyādhara Jatsön Nyingpo at Bangri[364] in Kongpo and received empowerments, guidance, and upadeśa in their entirety.

In particular, during this period Dudul Dorje received a prophecy indicating that he was destined to reveal an earth treasure. Accordingly, he traveled to Puwo and diligently practiced Ratna Lingpa's *Quintessential Secret and Unsurpassed Vajrakīlaya* at the Turquoise Lake Palace in Tsari. As he did so, he dreamed that Ḍākinīs invited him to the Copper-Colored Mountain, where he stayed for twenty-eight days. There he received complete ripening empowerments and liberating instructions from Guru Rinpoche and was granted prophecies about hidden treasures. These are clearly described in Dudul Dorje's own writings, called *Powerful King of Pure Vision*. When he went to meet the glorious Orgyen Tendzin, the master pondered the dream with enormous delight, and with deep reverence he enthroned Dudul Dorje as a vajra master. Dudul Dorje lived in the manner of a great tantric Vajra Holder.

Dudul Dorje's first profound treasure came according to the treasure guide[365] he had received. At the age of twenty-nine, relying upon the noble woman Pema Kyi as his activity consort,[366] Dudul Dorje brought out a treasure guide from Yutso Rinchen Drak, and from the Secret Great Exaltation Cave at Puwo Dongchu,[367] he revealed the cycles of the *Complete Gathering of the Holy Dharma's Wisdom*. These were his main profound treasures, and all his later revelations were their supplements, he said.

In succession, Dudul Dorje brought forth the following Treasure teachings: from Tsawa Drodrak, he brought out the *Holy Teachings of the Heart Essence of the Nirmāṇakāya*, including the practice of Kṣetrapāla; from Puri Dagdzong Cave, he brought out the *Cycle of the Profound Meaning of the Secret Heart Essence*, including *Glorious Cakrasaṃvara* and the *Four-Armed Protector*; from Puri Shelgyi Yangdrom, he brought out the cycle of the *Heart Essence Triad of Amitāyus, Yangdak Heruka, and Vajrakīlaya*, including their combined and individual sādhanas, and also those of the

Protectors Ekajaṭī and Rangjung Gyalmo; from the northern rock face of the Dongchu River in Puwo, he brought out the *Guide to the Hidden Land of Pemakö*; and from Tromzil Tromkaryak in Derge, Kham province, he brought out the cycle of the *Three Yidam Deities: Red Yamāri, Black Yamāri, and Bhairava*. He wrote down the cycle of the *Peaceful Practice of Mañjuśrī*, but he does not appear to have put these other treasures in writing.[368] From Jab Chagpurchen, he retrieved the cycle of the *Glorious Four-Faced Protector* and the cycle of the *Sādhana of Mahādeva*; from the upper shrine in Samye's central temple, he retrieved the *Guru Embodiment of Vidyādharas*, the *Sunlight Heat Longevity Sādhana*, and the *Cycle of the Dharma Guardians Zhanglön and Pomra*; and from the upper shrine of the Rasa Trulnang Temple,[369] he retrieved the *Cycles of the Wish-Fulfilling Crown Jewel of the Aural Lineage*, but it is clear that he did not decipher them.

Dudul Dorje retrieved the *Cycle of the Peaceful and Wrathful Deities of the Magical Infinity and of the Eight Heruka Sādhanas, Including Their Protectors*, from Mount Duri Namchak Barwa in Puwo; and from the Stone Stūpa of Ratsak, the yogin wearing a conch rosary brought out the *Cycle of the Glorious Tiger-Riding Protector* and offered it to Dudul Dorje. In addition, it is clearly stated in Dudul Dorje's *History of Treasures* that over the course of his life, he brought out numerous profound treasures from places such as Shinje Dongkha in Yutso, Rigdzin Sangpuk, Serachok, Nabun Dzong, and Tashö Kyilkhor Tang. He opened up numerous great holy places in Central Tibet and the border regions, principal among them being the hidden land of Pemakö.[370] Along with the abovementioned Treasure teachings, Dudul Dorje revealed an inconceivable number of holy statues, ritual implements, and sacred substances. In brief, he revealed the vast majority of a hundred Treasure teachings in sacred power places, a thousand substances that liberate upon tasting, and so on, all of which he was prophesied to inherit.

At the age of forty-two, Dudul Dorje received an invitation from Lama Jampa Puntsok of Derge and his nephew. At the monastic school where he had previously resided, Dudul Dorje constructed the famous Dudul Lhakang, thereby fulfilling a prophecy that he would benefit both the Buddha's teachings and the temporal world. He visited all the great Early Translation Nyingma monasteries, traveling as far as Katok Dorje Den, and accepted many fortunate students as his disciples. The dwelling where he stayed for a long time while engaged in spiritual practice at Nobkyi Putak Pudrak, near Dzing Namgyal, exists even today.

Dudul Dorje then traveled to Ling Tsang, where he established an auspicious connection of priest and patron with the king of Ling. While Dudul Dorje was performing the ritual of the vase consecration of Avalokiteśvara, King of Space, inconceivably wondrous signs and omens occurred. The transmission of this ritual practice is still extant today.

Over time, Dudul Dorje received invitations to travel to Markham county, Gatö, Barma Lhatong, Riwoche, and elsewhere, which he accepted. He brought infinite benefit to the teachings and beings. Notably, in Por Shedrak, Dudul Dorje met Namchö Mingyur Dorje, with whom he exchanged teachings and established an excellent auspicious connection. Their meeting had been arranged by Mahāsiddha Karma Chagme, who scattered flowers of praise on Dudul Dorje.

Of his countless disciples, Dudul Dorje's main Dharma holders were the great Lhatsun Namkha Jigme, Rigdzin Longsal Nyingpo, Bhakha Tulku Chökyi Gyatso, Dzogchen Pema Rigdzin, Kunzang Khyabdal Lhundrub, Drubchen Pema Norbu, and the many Vajra Holders in the vicinity of Tawu. In particular, Dudul Dorje's own descendant lineage, beginning with Gyalse Norbu Yongdrak, continued in succession and achieved inconceivable enlightened activity.

After completing his work, and after illuminating the gateway to the sacred hidden land of Pemakö, Dudul Dorje departed for the great Palace of Lotus Light in the Male Water Rat year [1672] at the age of fifty-eight. As he did so, measureless wondrous miracles occurred, such as sounds, lights, and a rain of flowers. Most notably, he dissolved almost completely into light, leaving only a one-cubit-high physical form, which revealed numerous major and minor relics following its cremation.

Gyalse Sönam Detsen

16

The actual emanation of Pema Dragpo is Longsal Nyingpo.
As his descendant and lineage holder of his teachings,
You illuminated the tradition of the essence of the absolute meaning.
Gyalse Sönam Detsen, to you I pray.

The quality of the Dharmakāya, great emptiness beyond phenomena that arise, abide, and cease, is that it never falls into the category of appearances, even at the level of subtle particles. Yet the quality of this space is the unobstructed vajra speech of all Buddhas, which instantly subdues and pacifies through extremely wrathful expressions that easily subdue angry, malicious beings who cannot be subdued through peaceful means. **Pema Dragpo emanated** in human form as Longsal Nyingpo. From the expanse [**long**] of wisdom of primordially pure great emptiness arises unobstructed compassion, which is the self-radiance of the spontaneously present nature of luminous [**sal**] wisdom. This unobstructed compassion appears outwardly as various forms of the Nirmānakāya, the great flaming ones.[371] The principal or **essence** [**nyingpo**] of these [wrathful manifestations] is Longsal Nyingpo. Their enlightened speech appears as signs, is heard as messages, and becomes symbols. Gyalse Sönam Detsen was the **lineage holder of** the **teachings** given in response to students' devoted wishes and the **descendant** of the lineage of Nirmāṇakāya emanations who held those teachings. Thus, Gyalse Sönam Detsen **illuminated the tradition** of the Kama and Terma teachings, the **quintessence** of the teachings on the **absolute meaning**. Wearing the mighty armor of the bodhicitta of previous compassionate heirs [**se**] of the Victorious Ones [**gyal**], he unmistakably planted the fertile seeds of liberation in the minds of whomever he saw as objects of his compassion. **Gyalse Sönam Detsen, to you I pray**!

The precious Gyalse Sönam Detsen [1679–1728] was the immediate reincarnation of the Great Treasure Revealer Rigdzin Dudul Dorje. He was born in the Wood Hare year of the eleventh calendrical cycle. He studied with numerous learned and accomplished masters, including his father, Je Terchen Lama Longsal Nyingpo, as well as Khyabdal Lhundrub, Terchen Tagsham Dorje, the eighth Shamar Rinpoche, and Dzogchen Pema Rigdzin. He received the elixir of their teachings until he was satisfied. He stayed at Katok Monastery and looked after its Saṅgha for many years. At the age of forty-nine, his wisdom mind dissolved in the Dharmadhātu.

Dudul Rolpa Tsal

17

Cared for and blessed by your Yidam deity,
You held the Ḍākinīs' secret treasury through the power of
your previous fortunate karma
And led all those connected to you to the pureland of Lotus Light.
Dudul Rolpa Tsal, to you I pray.

Generally, the term "god" or "deity" [lha] is used in historical accounts of the world to describe kings who ruled over many lands. Such leaders or kings were called "gods" because they were said to belong to a class of powerful human beings who were descended from celestial gods. Furthermore, followers of eternalist doctrines use "god" to refer to extraordinary beings, such as Brahmā, Indra, Śiva, and Viṣṇu, who are regarded as creators of the universe. There are also the six kinds of gods of desire,[372] of the seventeen levels of the form realm, and the four extremes of the sense sources of the formless realm.[373] These beings of the higher realms enjoy physical and mental bliss and happiness and are called gods.

Far more sublime than any of these are the "supreme deities"[374] beyond worldliness: the Three Jewels or, according to Mantra, the Three Roots, and so on. **Cared for by** his **Yidam deity**, Dudul Rolpa Tsal was **blessed**, so that phenomena, sounds, and thoughts became the nature of vajra body, speech, and mind. **By the power of** his **previous fortunate karma** resulting from accumulating vast amounts of merit and wisdom many eons earlier, Dudul Rolpa Tsal **held the secret treasury** of the **Ḍākinīs** of wisdom space, who enjoy all phenomena of saṃsāra and enlightenment in flawless great exaltation. Dudul Rolpa Tsal **led all those connected to** him, either positively or negatively, **to the pureland of Lotus Light**.[375] He was the immediate rebirth of Gyalse Sönam Detsen, and he delighted in the display of great heroic activity to subdue the four demons in unborn space. **Dudul Rolpa Tsal, to you I pray.**

In the Four Rivers and Six Ranges region of Dokham, there is an area of Dome called Duzhi, or Four Knots, and at one of these [knots], called Rekhe, Terchen Dudul Dorje and Rigdzin Longsal Nyingpo both discovered profound treasures. Dechen Lingpa, Rigdzin Tsewang Norbu, and numerous other holy masters have praised Rekhe as a vajra holy place. Dudul Rolpa Tsal [18th c.] was born in a place called Ajam, a part of the Sangen Rekhe district, which is safely guarded by the Iron Being, a Dharma Protector of Vajrakīlaya activity. His father, Katok Dudul Gyalse Pema Namgyal, hailed from the paternal lineage of Dudul Nuden Dorje, who was one of the twenty-one regents of Guru Rinpoche bearing the name Nuden and holding the powers of Vidyādharas. Katok Dudul Gyalse Pema Namgyal had his seat in the region of Sertang in Dokham. He possessed clairvoyance and could see the past, present, and future unobstructedly. His son, Dudul Rolpa Tsal—whose full name was Serpa Tergen Dudul Rolpa Tsal Nuden

Namkhe Naljor—was unrivaled in the precious qualities of knowledge, love, and power.

Dudul Rolpa Tsal gained mastery over his life span and lived for nearly 180 years. He also discovered numerous profound treasures, including *Red Garuḍa with Wings of Fire*. In his later years, he traveled gradually through the areas of Dragyab and Sangen. He mastered the enlightened activities of annihilation and protection, and used his wrathful power to annihilate and bring under his power all vicious and obstructive humans and nonhumans. He was enthroned as the head of all the monasteries from the great monastic center of Katok Dorje Den to the area of Sangen, and accordingly, he visited them and made them his monastic seats.

Garwang Dudjom Pawo (Dudjom Lingpa)

18

Having received the father's gift from self-appearing nonhuman spiritual teachers,
The treasures of Samantabhadra's wisdom mind overflowed from your expanse.
Yogin of space, you are truly the crazed King of Wrath,
Garwang Dudjom Pawo,[376] to you I pray.

As said in the *Guhyagarbha*, "The Tathāgata himself expressly spoke to the Tathāgata himself"; similarly, Dudjom Lingpa did not rely only on spiritual teachers who appear in human form as in the phenomena of those with conditioned mind. By the power of the manifestation of awareness from perfectly pure Dharmatā, the self-**phenomena** of Dudjom Lingpa arose as **self-appearing nonhuman spiritual teachers,** just like the sun reveling in its own rays, and he **received** the **gift** of the uninterrupted blessings of the Wisdom Mind Lineage of his sole **father**, the original protector Samantabhadra. The treasury of **Samantabhadra's wisdom mind** is entirely free of anything to be accepted or rejected, and in all three times, saṃsāra and enlightenment are evenly pure. It is a Dharma **treasure** of the inexhaustible, all-encompassing purity of appearance and existence, which **overflowed from** the **expanse** of this infinite wisdom mind without relying on diligent training. Freed from the binding noose of the two-stage path of characteristics,[377] Dudjom Lingpa never wavered from the wisdom realization of the

yoga of space, the nondual Great Perfection, even as the self-radiance of his spontaneously present nature appeared in the form of the compassionate emanation Trowo Tumdrak Barwa, "Wrathful Fierce Flaming One," the great demon of demons. He was **truly the crazed King of Wrath**, Guru [Pema] Dragpo, emanating as **Garwang,** Lord of the Dance in the realms of existence. Through his formidably powerful and wrathful activities, he vanquished [**jom**] the hordes of demons [**dud**] of wrong view. Tragtung Dudjom **Pawo**, "Blood-Drinking Demon-Vanquishing Hero," **to you I pray!**

Tragtung Dudjom Lingpa [1835–1904] was prophesied in Tertön Sangye Lama's treasure prophecy:

> After five hundred years, in a treasure prophecy of Kham ༔
> Dudjom Dorje will open the profound treasure door. ༔

Also, Tertön Rashakpa's treasure prophecy says:

> In the region of Kham, an emanation of Drogmi[378] will appear ༔
> At his heart center, he will have a dark brown triangular birthmark. ༔

Bönpo Lhabum's treasure prophecy says:

> Tertön Dudjom Dorje Drolö[379] will ༔
> Open the profound treasure door and guard the Nyingtik teachings. ༔

Drubtop Kharnakpa's treasure prophecy says:

> At the very end of the degenerate era, your reincarnation ༔
> Dudjom Pawo will teach the Khandro Nyingtik. ༔

Sangye Lingpa's treasure prophecy says:

> The father will have the form of a tantric yogin ༔
> Who is short-tempered, weary of saṃsāra, diligent in Dharma practice, ༔
> And bears the name Madman. He will be accomplished in practice. ༔

Rangrung Menpa's treasure prophecy says:

> In the future, at the very end of the harsh eon ༔ [380]
> I, Padmasambhava, will incarnate as Dudjom Dorje. ༔

Orgyen Lingpa's treasure prophecy says:

> A treasure revealer named Dorje Drolö will appear . . . ༔

And Dudul Dorje's treasure prophecy says:

> One bearing the celestial name Garwang, with fearless conduct ༔
> Who has a mole shaped like a jewel in his right armpit . . . ༔

Yakchar Ngönmo's treasure prophecy says:

> In the degenerate age, Padmasambhava Dorje Drolö ༔
> Will take on the guise of a human being and care for students. ༔

And the second Dudul [Dudul Rolpa Tsal] uttered these words:

> In the Water Snake year, I will pass into space. ༔
> In the Female Wood Sheep year, in Serlung in Kham, ༔
> I will be called Dudjom Dorje. ༔
> On my body, a triangular mole will appear at my heart center. ༔
> On the back of my right ear, a lion-face birthmark will appear. ༔
> I will open the door to the two kinds of profound treasure ༔[381]
> And lead anyone connected to me to the southwest Palace of Lotus Light. ༔
> My mother will be a supreme emanation of a flesh-eating Ḍākinī ༔
> Bearing the name Puṇḍā and behaving like a madwoman. ༔

Sangye Lingpa's treasure prophecy says:

> Belonging to the class of charnel ground Ḍākinīs, ༔
> His mother will be a fierce and wrathful one bearing the name Gyen. ༔

In the words of Dudul Dorje:

Sovereign of Ḍākinīs, Princess Trompa Gyen, ༔
Bearing the name Buddha, offering great exaltation, ༔
Emanation of the Nepalese subject,[382] with a name ending in Drön, ༔
Beloved consort who gives rise to the wisdom of bliss and emptiness. ༔
Her son as well will appear along with the incarnations of Dharma King Trisong Detsen, Prince Mutik Tsenpo, and Ācārya Yeshe Yang, ༔
As well as Yarlung Bami. ༔ [383]
At that time, sixteen emanations of the king and his subjects will gather. ༔

Jigme Trinle Özer[384] said:

In Lower Go, a sprout of iron will appear. ༔

According to Mingyur Namkha Dorje:[385]

Riding a yellow-striped tigress, ༔
The supreme emanation of the Three Roots, Dorje Drowolö, from the east ༔
Will go west, in the direction of Varuṇa. ༔
Blazing with a hundred rays of light, the hare-marked moon will rise. ༔

Again, the Guru Rinpoche treasure prophecy says:

In the future final period, ༔
My emanation, who is none other than myself ༔
In the form of a wild hidden yogin ༔
Will clearly behold the truth of Dharmatā ༔
And the expanse of all dharmas will burst open, revealing the three treasures. ༔[386]
This magical emanation, Vidyādhara of spontaneous presence, ༔
Tragtung Dorje Drowolö, ༔

Will appear as the lord of Padmasambhava's secret treasury. ༔
Of those with the vital auspicious connection to meet him, ༔
One thousand fortunate disciples will attain the level of Vidyādhara, ༔
And there will be a meeting of the King and the subjects. ༔

The prophecy continues:

Do not doubt these profound teachings, ༔
Thus validated by sublime prophecies. ༔
The time to tame beings has not quite come. ༔
When the perfect time arrives, beings will be benefitted. ༔
Right now, if all of you teachers and students are faithful and diligent, ༔
And strive to attain siddhi with certainty, ༔
Then one billion disciples will be led to the state of purity. ༔

Again, the prophecy says:

From the magical manifestations of Dharmatā, ༔
The *Infinity of Pure Wisdom Phenomena* arises. ༔

Accordingly, Mañjuśrī, Lion of Speech, actually appeared to Dudjom Lingpa and handed him an egg-sized gold box, the color of coral, and he received the special transmission for the *Infinity of Pure Wisdom Phenomena* cycle of teachings.

Also, the prophecy continues:

From the manifestation of clear light great exaltation, ༔
Profound teaching overflows from the expanse of wisdom mind. ༔

Accordingly, Noble Avalokiteśvara appeared before Dudjom Lingpa and bestowed a thumb-sized crystal box, on the surface of which the five-colored syllables OṂ, HŪṂ, TRAṂ, HRĪ, and ĀḤ appeared like reflections in a mirror, whereby the *Profound Teaching Overflowing from the Expanse of Wisdom Mind* arrived, along with Avalokiteśvara's empowerment, reading transmission, and sādhana.

Also, the prophecy continues:

> From the great, vast expanse of wisdom mind ༔
> The *Vast Space Treasury of Dharmatā* will overflow. ༔

As said, the great, glorious Lord of Secrets appeared before Dudjom Lingpa and bestowed a thumb-sized turquoise stūpa, within which the images of the vowels, consonants, and Essence of Interdependence mantra appeared, and the *Vast Space Treasury of Dharmatā* overflowed, along with the sādhanas of the Lord of Secrets, the Dark-Red Yakṣa,[387] Dza[388] and Tsen,[389] Dorje Legpa,[390] and others, with the complete empowerments and transmissions, and the complete empowerments, transmissions, and sādhanas of Lhachen Mahādeva.

From another treasure prophecy of Padmasambhava, the Great Master of Oḍḍiyāna [revealed to Dudjom Lingpa]:

> From Dodrak Martak in Kham province, ༔
> He will reveal the *Profound Secret Heart Essence of the Ḍākinī.* ༔

And:

> In the center of Ngala Tagtse ༔
> Is the deeply profound *Vajra Essence.* ༔

And:

> For the countless beings of the five-hundred-year period, ༔
> I, Padmasambhava, and those like me, ༔
> Through essential loving compassion, ༔
> Have concealed one thousand and four treasures ༔
> In places all over the Earth. ༔
> Now, in this age of the worst degeneration, ༔
> The minds of sentient beings who commit cruel and evil actions ༔
> Are indeed difficult to tame. ༔
> However, in order to protect the remaining students ༔
> Who are karmically connected through aspiration, ༔
> I appoint you as master of enlightened activity. ༔

These extremely clear prophecies are found in about ten different ancient treasures from the past. Similarly, the *Historical Account of the Origin of the Teaching of Vajrakīlaya Namchak Pudri* says:

> In Lower Dokham, in the eastern Minyak Rab Range of the Six Ranges region, in a place called Wazhab Senge Drakar or Dra Chakhung, Dudjom Lingpa was born to a father named Ahten of the Nub family line and a mother named Mutsa Bodzok on the full-moon day of the first lunar month, the Miracle Month, of the Female Wood Sheep year [1835]. When he was born, snowflakes shaped like flowers fell, a canopy of rainbows arched over their yak hair tent, and many other wondrous signs occurred.
>
> From Dudjom Lingpa's birth until the age of three, gatherings of Ḍākas and Ḍākinīs guarded and kept watch over him. At times, malicious male and female demons, damsi spirits, and other types of obstructors appeared to him in visions. One time, a Ḍākinī came in the form of his mother and led him to the northern pureland of Lapis Lazuli Radiance. There he met the Medicine Buddha, named Victorious Unequivocal King, who granted him empowerments and blessings and crowned him as his regent. As a result of this experience, Dudjom Lingpa's habits from previous lives were awakened, and he recalled numerous deities, mantras, and samādhis. Through their power, he was victorious over a great many obstacles.
>
> While at play, he displayed startling miracles, such as effortlessly crossing a wide river roiling with powerful waves or piercing straight through a great mountain. In all his dreams, he was given prophecies about what was to come. As a result, his parents cherished him intensely, and because of his extreme wildness, they were obliged to watch over him constantly.
>
> At the outset of his tenth year, his maternal uncle took the boy to his own home, where he was to stay for a while. The uncle made him do all sorts of chores, such as looking after the livestock, and because he disliked this, the boy used a wooden arrow to jam holes in all the bronze cauldrons, iron pots, and vessels. All he did was smash and break things. His uncle and aunt said, "This boy is possessed by an evil spirit. If he learns to read, he might become a

Buddhist practitioner. Otherwise, if he remains a layman, he will definitely bring ruin upon himself and others." They prepared to send him to study Dharma.

Then, according to a prophecy from a Ḍākinī, Dudjom Lingpa bowed his head at the feet of a guru bearing the name Mañjuśrī, renowned as the rebirth of Bodhisattva Dripa Namsal,[391] who was karmically connected to him from previous lifetimes. Thus, he entered the door of the Dharma. As for reading and writing and the like, he had only to be shown symbols and he knew it all effortlessly. Over time, he received guidance on the preliminary practices, as well as empowerments and transmissions for the treasure cycle of his previous emanation, Rigdzin Dudul Dorje. He engaged in the practice of Dorje Drolö and received signs of accomplishment. Guru Rinpoche actually appeared to him, introduced him to the view of the Great Perfection, and gave him numerous prophecies and instructions.

Furthermore, without his relying even slightly upon the hardship of diligent training in this lifetime, his fortunate karma from training in previous lifetimes was gradually awakened. On various occasions, the Great Wrathful Mother Tröma, Saraha, the eight Vidyādharas, the twenty-five disciples of Guru Rinpoche,[392] Longchen Rabjam [Longchenpa], and others appeared to him in magical wisdom form and graciously took him under their care, and through that, the power of his sublime knowledge of all aspects of the profound and extensive Dharma blazed without limit. On the path of primordial purity and spontaneous presence,[393] he practiced the samādhi of the flowing river of nonmeditation, and his realization became boundlessly vast. He directly beheld the truth of Dharmatā and reached the pinnacle of awareness. Through this power, he became thoroughly immersed in pure visions, so at any moment, he could see infinite miraculous Buddha manifestations in countless purelands.

The Lords of the Three Families granted empowerment with the seals of their wisdom body, speech, and mind, and from the auspicious transfer of their blessings of ultimate lineage, the symbolic signs of the sky treasury of Dharmatā were naturally released. The treasury of his wisdom mind overflowed from the expanse. In response to repeated requests from the Guru and Consort, as well as many Ḍākinīs, who prophesied that the time had come, on the tenth day of the sixth month of the Female Earth Sheep year [1859], at the age of twenty-five, Dudjom Lingpa retrieved his treasure from a rocky mountain in Bate in Mar. It contained a statue of Tārā made of clay and wormwood, Saraha's prayer beads, and a treasure guide. Furthermore, from a rocky mountain called Ngulgö, he revealed a supplementary guide, *A Mirror That Reflects the Treasure Guide of the "Profound Secret Heart Essence of the Ḍakinī."* The guide clearly revealed that on the morning of the tenth day of the waxing gibbous moon in the eleventh month, Dudjom Lingpa should retrieve a profound treasure from Shadrak Dorjechen on the right side of Ngaröl Taktse in the Lower Ser. When he did so, the Ḍākinī guarding the treasure appeared before him and sang a song, which was heard by his treasure companion, Dechen, and others as well. On the face of the rock cliff, which was extremely steep and smooth like the surface of a mirror, a staircase of rainbow light appeared, and he went up unhindered to a height of about five fathoms [thirty feet]. There a semicircular crack opened in the rock, and from inside this treasure door, Dudjom Lingpa retrieved seven treasure boxes containing the cycle of instructions on the Three Roots, primarily the *Secret Sealed Mind Sādhana of Dudjom Vajrakīlaya Namchak Pudri*, along with protector practices. In their place, he inserted a treasure replacement[394] and resealed the treasure door.

That time, the treasure guide read:

Radiant rainbow light is a sign that your lineage holders
  will reach liberation. ༔
A rain of flowers is a sign of increasing merit. ༔
The wafting of sweet fragrances is a sign that the blessing
  will not fade. ༔
If the sun's light blazes, it is a sign that these teachings
  will spread throughout the world. ༔
If you can save your life, you will dispel the suffering of
  beings. ༔

If these five purposes come together, you will possess qualities of excellence. ༔
When all auspicious circumstances assemble, you will be victorious in all directions. ༔

All the signs and indications described here occurred in everyone's shared perception. At the time, a local leader and some lay and ordained people confronted him: "Seeing as these northern plains, mountains, and valleys alike have been completely filled with rainbows in the middle of this winter month, it would seem that something malicious has been done to our local protector deity. If you do not hand over whatever treasures you have taken, we will turn our troops on you!"

Dudjom Lingpa then quoted the Great Ācārya of Oḍḍiyāna:

When a destined individual encounters my treasures, ༔
The ferocious gods and demons of China and Tibet all assemble. ༔
Even though they present themselves as good, they wreak all sorts of harm, ༔
Screaming their war cry—*Ki!*—they snatch and grab! ༔

"What he said is indeed true," Dudjom Lingpa replied. "You all can go ahead and lead your army to attack me! I have my own excellent ways and means to deal with that." He then abided free of conception, and in the end, the enemy and the disputes simply faded away.

For a period, the Ghili family acted as his patrons, and he stayed with them and was nicknamed "Ghili Tertön."

At this time when he was young, Dudjom Lingpa lived as a wild hidden yogin; his parents were quite poor, so some people scorned him. In particular, many northern Mongol nomads, bandits, and raiders from the border regions attacked him and his patrons and disciples, causing them much harm. "If I sit here quietly doing nothing, this will never end," he thought to himself, and he invoked the Dharma Protectors Great Wild Shen and Rāhula the Demon,[395] whose invocation prayer is called *Poison Razor*. Some of the harm-doers went blind, some went mad, and most of them vomited their own blood and died. Their homes, retinues, family members, and livestock were all obliterated and vanished without a trace. From then on, people would say, "Don't bother the Ghili Tertön or he'll curse you!" Word of his magical power spread throughout the region.

Gradually, Dudjom Lingpa traveled to Mardo Tashi Gakhyil and Dropuk Khandro Duling, where he established his spiritual seat. One time, in a vision, Ḍākinīs led him to the Copper-Colored Mountain, where he spent twelve years. There he received the ripening empowerments and liberating instructions of the oceanlike Sūtra, Mantra, and Tantra from Guru Rinpoche and was appointed as his regent. He also visited many earthly and celestial purelands in countless pure visions, such as the naturally occurring land of Oḍḍiyāna, Cool Grove [Śītavana in India], the Five-Peaked Mountain [Wutai Shan in China], the Sindhu Kingdom [in modern Pakistan], Potala [pureland of Avalokiteśvara], Land of Dreadlocks [Changlochen, the pureland of Vajrapāṇi and Vaiśravaṇa], and Arrayed in Turquoise Petals [Yulokö, the pureland of Tārā], where he received teachings from Vidyādharas and Ḍākinīs and enjoyed gaṇacakra feasts with gatherings of Ḍākas and Ḍākinīs.

Then, according to his treasure guide, in the Female Earth Ox year, the seal of secrecy on his profound treasures was released. At the urging of the assembly of Ḍākinīs guarding the teachings, he first opened the Vajrakīlaya yellow scroll and deciphered its meaning. As he did so, the earth shook with a great roar, and a loud clap of thunder was heard. Snowflakes shaped like flowers fell, and a lattice of rainbows arced over the whole region. As soon as he had finished, a strong wind rushed through and carried off some of the loose-leaf sheets [on which the treasure was deciphered] in all directions. Many excellent auspicious signs occurred, indicating that the forces of negativity would be tamed, the lineage holders would attain good fortune and liberation, and this profound teaching would spread and flourish in all directions. From this very treasure site, Dudjom Lingpa simultaneously brought out the other cycles of instruction on the Three Roots and Dharma Protectors, and gradually put them in writing so that their meaning was understandable. At that time, numerous great beings from the region unanimously and indisputably praised Dudjom Lingpa and his teachings. Like the light-giving orb of the shining sun unobscured by clouds, his renown spread in all directions. Led by the main Dharma holders prophesied to receive specific transmissions, a constant stream of disciples surrounded him like honeybees swarming around a fragrant lotus. He devoted himself exclusively to teaching and propagating the amṛta of the ripening empowerments and liberating instructions. These he gave freely to everyone, regardless of status, without a trace of face-saving pretense, always maintaining the spontaneous conduct of simply relating to whatever arose. This made everyone afraid of him.

From his prophesied activity consorts, several young Bodhisattva emanations were born, and all of them nourished the teachings and beings. According to his treasure guide, Dudjom Lingpa knew there were various profound treasures destined for him in Dome Yungdrung Chagtse, Chagrichen, Amnye Dralkar, Mayul Orgyen Pezha, Drakar Treldzong, Dakrik Sangwa Nyenpo in Puwo, Pu Ridak Dzongpuk, Gyala Sengdam in Lower Kongpo, Lhari Tökar, the White Stūpa at Samye, and Chulung Dragmar in Tsang. However, he realized that if practitioners were able to practice, the instruction cycles of his principal profound treasures were enough to enable them to accomplish their goal, so he did not exert himself in retrieving those other destined treasures. In particular, the Guru and Consort [Padmasambhava and Yeshe Tsogyal] repeatedly praised him and urged him to open the door to the most secret power place of immortality in the hidden land of Pemakö. Although he wished to go there, the collective merit and karmic fortune of beings at that time temporarily prevented this auspicious circumstance from happening.

Among Dudjom Lingpa's heart-sons and disciples, there were ten treasure revealers who were lineage holders empowered to work for others' well-being, thirteen great beings who attained the indivisibility of Rainbow Body within a single lifetime, 100 Vidyādharas who attained accomplishment, and 1,000 who attained the common siddhis. The prophecies about Dudjom Lingpa's enlightened activities and the infinite flourishing of his profound teachings were truly realized.

With his present students in mind, Dudjom Lingpa addressed

his assembled heart-sons and disciples: "Now, as legions of barbaric foreign troops gradually surge into Central Tibet and our chances for happiness are few, the time has come for us to move to Guru Rinpoche's hidden land [Pemakö]. You all make your way there, supplicating that sacred place. I, too, will go there. In fact, this old man [Dudjom Lingpa] will make sure to get there before you do."

Dudjom Lingpa possessed the precious qualities of the ten powers, including power over his own rebirth. At the age of sixty-nine, on the eighth day of the eleventh month of the Water Hare year [1904], without any signs of illness, he departed for the great Palace of Lotus Light. There were countless amazing miracles at the time, such as sounds, lights, and a rain of flowers. In particular, his precious remains vanished into light, leaving a tiny form the size of an eight-year-old child, which became a heap of numerous major and minor five-colored relics during the cremation.

Here, a brief summary of Dudjom Lingpa's general biography has been given. The full story is told in the Great Treasure Revealer's autobiography, *Clear Mirror: Accounts of Secret Experiences, Visions of the Magical Display of Dharmatā*. His principal profound treasures were contained in three cycles: the *Profound Secret Heart Essence of the Ḍākinī* in the Earth Treasure cycle; the *Profound Teaching Overflowing from the Expanse of Wisdom Mind* in the Mind Treasure cycle; and the *Infinity of Pure Wisdom Phenomena* in the Pure Vision cycle.

This concludes the second section, written briefly about the rosary of previous lifetimes of the Great Treasure Revealer Dharma King Dudjom Rinpoche about which one could speak forever and never finish.

Jigdral Yeshe Dorje: A Brief Biography of the Great Treasure Revealer Dharma King

19

From the continent of Cāmara, the Guru and Consort
Bestowed on you the warmth of their wisdom, and from this confidence

You raised aloft the victory banner of the Great Secret
Vajrayāna teachings in all directions.
Jigdral Yeshe Dorje, to you I pray.

Having mastery of the purelands and Kāyas of the twenty-five characteristics of the result,[396] free of any partiality or bias, always in the three times and timelessness, the enlightened speech of all Buddhas, Lord of the Padma Family, Dharmakāya Buddha of Boundless Light, filled with love for the beings of the age of the rampant five degenerations, appeared as the magical Great **Guru** emanation, the basis or father of all tantrika emanations, the Great Ācārya of Oḍḍiyāna, Padmasambhava, from the Nirmāṇakāya emanation pureland, the **continent of Cāmara**, the Glorious Copper-Colored Mountain. Indivisible from his wisdom mind was the Great Mother **Consort** of the space of great emptiness, endowed with the most sublime of all aspects, the wisdom of great exaltation, as the Nirmāṇakāya emanation of Yeshe Tsogyal. These two indivisibly **bestowed** on Kyabje Dudjom Rinpoche **the warmth of their wisdom**, making him inseparable from them, and told him to benefit beings without delay. With **confidence** gained from their words, Kyabje Rinpoche elucidated the teachings of the extraordinary **Secret** Mantra Vajrayāna, which is more sublime than the common vehicles in four ways,[397] for fortunate students in this very world. Among an oceanic assembly of Vidyādharas and siddhas who appeared in this world, Kyabje Rinpoche was like the full moon amid all the planets and stars. At all times and **in all directions**, he **raised aloft the victory banner of the** exceedingly secret **Great Secret teachings** of the tantras, transmissions, and upadeśa—the tantras of development-stage Mahāyoga, the transmissions of completion-stage Anuyoga, and the upadeśa of Great Perfection Atiyoga—on the rooftop of the Mansion of Complete Victory of Buddha's Teachings.[398] For his own benefit, he became free of fear of the three realms of samsaric existence, and for others' benefit he became free [dral] of fear [jig] of clinging to the extreme of lesser peace and happiness. With nondual vajra wisdom [yeshe], he completely vanquished the enemy of dualistic perception and ordinary thought. Great hero of the absolute meaning, **Jigdral Yeshe Dorje, to you I pray!**

To begin, flowers of reverence are scattered with this offering verse:

Your three inconceivable secrets are well beyond the scope of
ordinary mind,

Yet out of great compassion for beings with thoughts, you reveal the dance of manifestations
In various conceivable aspects of playfulness according to beings' wishes.
To the glorious Three-Kāya Guru, I bow.

As it says in the *Ornament of the Mahāyāna Sūtras*:

Rebirth can occur by karma,
By the power of prayers to benefit others,
By the power of samādhi,
And by having the power over rebirth.
That is what the wise believe.

These four ways of taking birth are described based on the specific categories of Buddhas, Bodhisattvas, and sentient beings.[399] Here in this life story, rebirth must be seen as belonging to the last category, the power over rebirth. This is explained in the *Sūtra of Stainless Space*:

> Ānanda, the Tathāgatas are not apparent to all sentient beings, but the spiritual friend is fully apparent and so can teach the Dharma and plant the seed of liberation. For this reason, you should cherish the spiritual friend even more than the Tathāgatas.

Likewise, the *General Sūtra That Gathers All Wisdom* says:

Know that the Guru is even more sacred
Than the Buddhas of a thousand eons.
Why is this? Because all the Buddhas of a thousand eons
Became such by relying on a guru.
Long ago, before there were gurus,
The name "Buddha" did not even exist.

The Guru is similarly praised in other sūtras and tantras as well.

So then, what exactly does this mean? Vajra mind is completely free of all obscurations of the habits of the three appearances.[400] Vajra mind, which has never wavered, never wavers, and will never waver from the Dharmakāya, abides indivisibly with the seven branches of union[401] and the five certainties[402] of the Sambhogakāya, the essential source of the Kāyas and purelands of all the Buddhas of all directions and times. Then, just as the moon never departs from the sky, yet its reflection appears vividly in containers of water, likewise miraculous emanations appear everywhere in realms of beings to be subdued. This is the wondrous quality of the Buddhas' omnipresent enlightened activity. As it says in Orgyen Dechen Lingpa's *Treasure Prophecy*:

> In the future, to the east of Tibet's nine snowy peaks ༔
> In the secret pureland of the self-arisen Vārāhī, ༔
> From the lineage of kings, an emanation of Drogben ༔
> Bearing the name Jñāna will uphold the fearless conduct of Mantra. ༔
> With uncertain appearance and childlike behavior, endowed with sublime knowledge, ༔
> He will bring forth new treasures or uphold the teachings of old treasures. ༔
> All who make a connection will be led to Cāmara's Glorious Mountain. ༔

Just as this vajra prophecy proclaims, the great, all-victorious Vidyādhara, Jigdral Yeshe Dorje, lauded with flowers of praise by noble Bodhisattvas dwelling on the sublime levels, was a threefold magical wisdom emanation: a body emanation of Khyeuchung Lotsawa, one of the twenty-five disciples who were the distilled essence of Guru Rinpoche's enlightened mind; a speech emanation of the Queen of Space, Yeshe Tsogyal; and a mind emanation of Victorious Lord Padmasambhava. Kyabje Rinpoche was born in the east of the snowy land of Tibet, situated to the north of the Noble Land's Vajra Seat [Bodhgayā, India], in one of the three principal hidden lands, the holy place of Pemakö, "Perfect Lotus Ornament." Kyabje Rinpoche's father was Katok Tulku Norbu Tendzin, the son of the Gampo Pön family in the royal lineage of the Kanampas in Puwo, who were descended from Jatri Tsenpo.[403] Kyabje Rinpoche's mother, Namgyal Drolma, belonged to the pure and unbroken lineage of Yönpu Chöje in the southern land of Bhutan, who was descended from the Great Treasure Revealer Ratna Lingpa.

Jigdral Yeshe Dorje was born in the Male Wood Dragon year, known as Krodhin[404] [1904], amid wondrous signs, and the lotus flower of major and minor marks[405] unfurled. Not long afterward, just as the Vidyādharas of the past had foretold in their clear-eyed prophetic revelations, several of his predecessor's direct disciples and grand-disciples arrived in Pemakö, chief among them being the principal heart-son of both Jamyang Khyentse Wangpo [1820–1892] and Jamgön Kongtrul Lodrö Taye [1813–1899], as well as Vidyādhara Dudjom Lingpa's prophesied Dharma holder, Dza Pukung Tulku Rinpoche Gyurme Ngedön Wangpo, who was the Bliss-Gone Medicine Buddha himself, disguised as a saffron-clad Buddhist monk who appeared as a great friend to the Dharma and beings in this degenerate time, and Ling Lama Tubten Chöjor. Having ascertained the reincarnation of the Supreme Vidyādhara guru, they embraced him as the sole destined deity upon which their Buddha-family flower had fallen, and enthroned him upon a golden throne.

Right from his early youth, Kyabje Rinpoche's natural inclination for the Mahāyāna was awakened, and his mind was benevolent toward everyone. He had only perfectly pure perception toward deities and the Guru. Guru Rinpoche actually appeared before him, crowned him with the name Orgyen Drodul Lingpa, authorized him as his own regent, and gave him prophecies and encouragement. From Orgyen Chönjor Gyatso, Kyabje Rinpoche received refuge vows, and from Nyarong Khenchen Jampal Dewe Nyima, also known as Pende Özerchen, who was a disciple of Mipham Rinpoche, the actual Mañjuśrī, he received the complete vows of lay ordination. From Mindrolling Vajra Holder Namdrol Gyatso, Ngawang Palden Zangpo,[406] and others, he received the Bodhisattva vows that came from two traditions—the tradition of Profound View and the tradition of Vast Conduct. From Lama Könchok Rabten and others, he briefly studied reading and writing, and received explanatory guidance on grammar, poetry, Śāntideva's *Way of the Bodhisattva*, Nāgārjuna's *Letter to a Friend*, Ngari Panchen Pema Wangyi Gyalpo's *Perfect Conduct: Ascertaining the Three Vows*, and so on. From Lama Pema Tendzin, Kyabje Rinpoche learned Indian astrology and Chinese divination, and from Agye Gendun Rabgye, he received the *Four Medical Tantras*. From the Khenchen who bears the name Jampal, he received the oral transmission of the Early Translation tradition; many tantric commentaries, such as the Zur tradition of exegetical commentaries on the *Guhyagarbha* and the Khenchen's own commentary, *Hidden Meanings of the "Guyhagarbha Root Tantra" Called "Celebration of Awareness"*; the great empowerments of the *Eight Heruka Sādhanas*; Sangye Lingpa's *Embodiment of the Master's Realization*; and the *Four Heart Essences* of Omniscient Longchenpa, great charioteer of the Luminous Vajra

Essence Vehicle. From Togden Tenpa Rabgye, he received the stream of upadeśa of great guidance through experience, including the empowerments and transmissions of the *Four Heart Essences* from the lineage of Nyoshul Lungtok Tenpe Nyima. From Jedrung Trinle Jampa Jungne, also known as Dudjom Namkhe Dorje, of Kham Riwoche, Kyabje Rinpoche received the *Four Heart Essences*; the Seventeen Tantras of the Upadeśa Section of the Great Perfection, such as the *Penetration of Sound*, which is the root tantra, and its subsidiary, *Natural Liberation of Awareness*; Jamgön Kongtrul's *Treasury of Precious Instructions*; and the reading transmission for the entire Translated Speech of the Buddha [Kangyur]. He also received the complete reading transmission of the Translated Speech of the Buddha from both Jangsem Lodrö Gyaltsen and Dungkar Ngedön Gyatso. From Ngagtsun Gedun Gyatso, he received all thirteen Dharma cycles of the Great Treasure Revealer Pema Lingpa and Omniscient Longchenpa's *Seven Treasuries*. From the Mindrolling Vajra Holder Namdrol Gyatso, he learned the elaborate ritual songs, music, and dance associated with the sādhana practice of the oceans of the Great Secret tantric section from the tradition of Minling Terchen Gyurme Dorje, who was an emanation of Vairotsana, as well as many other profound teachings.

In accordance with Vimalamitra's promise to send an emanation of himself to Tibet once every hundred years, Vimalamitra actually appeared as the universally renowned Great Khenpo of Nyoshul, Ngawang Pal Zangpo. Kyabje Rinpoche studied with and exchanged the gift of supremely excellent profound teachings with the direct disciple of Ngawang Pal Zangpo, the renunciate yogin Chatral Sangye Dorje, as well as with Lama Orgyen Rigdzin, Katok Chagtsa Tulku, Chogtrul Gyurme Dorje, and Tulku Sangye of Putö Pulung Monastery, all of whom were exalted beings residing on the level of the great Noble Ones.[407]

Most notably, Pukung Tulku Rinpoche Gyurme Ngedön Wangpo and the Great Treasure Revealer Zilnön Namkhe Dorje introduced Kyabje Rinpoche directly to his own true nature, the basic state of the natural Great Perfection, and placed him upon the throne of the oceanic Kama and Terma teachings. These two masters served as unsurpassed empowering conditions, and he revered them as the Lords of the Buddha Families. In particular, he studied with Pukung Tulku Rinpoche Gyurme Ngedön Wangpo for sixteen years. He received from him the complete tantras, transmissions, and upadeśa for the *Secret Heart Essence*[408] from the lineages of Jamyang Khyentse Wangpo and Jamgön Kongtrul Lodrö Taye, Dharma Lord Mipham Rinpoche, and others, as well as Tragtung Dudjom Lingpa's complete treasure cycles, just as if the contents of a vase had been poured into another, filling it to the very brim. As it says in *Stages of the Path*:

> Being a guide, with a treasury of knowledge, with all rivers of empowerment complete,
> Eager, learned in Tantra, skilled in the activities,[409]
> Holder of upadeśa, with signs of accomplishment: these are the eight qualities.[410]

It was from great vajra masters such as these, holders of the threefold vows,[411] that Kyabje Rinpoche received permission-blessings and empowerments for the common outer tantric sections; the ripening empowerments, liberating guidance, and supporting transmissions for the oceanlike uncommon inner tantras, the tantric sections of the three yogas; Omniscient Longchenpa's *Seven Treasuries, Trilogy of Rest, Trilogy of Natural Liberation*, and *Trilogy of Dispelling Darkness* (commentaries on the *Guhyagarbha Tantra*); Omniscient Jigme Lingpa's *Treasury of Precious Qualities: Root Text and Autocommentary*; commentaries on the *Guhyagarbha* written by Minling Terchen Gyurme Dorje, his brother [Lochen Dharmaśrī], and his son Pema Gyurme Gyatso; the *Collected Works of Tsele Natsok Rangdrol*, by the great scholar from Kongpo; as well as the Dharma cycles of all the other major and minor treasure revealers. Kyabje Rinpoche listened to all the extant streams of Kama and Terma teachings with tremendous diligence and without the slightest concern about time, circumstances, or personal hardship.

Moreover, as the Lord of Sages said:

> Whenever one learns the Dharma from someone,
> Whether old or young,
> Respect and pay homage to that one,
> Just as a pure Brahmin worships a fire.

Just as his words explain, the defining characteristic of sublime beings is that they do not perpetually fall prey to the eight worldly concerns,[412] such as fear of losing their elevated status. So on various occasions, whether they appeared as famous high lamas, humble hidden yogis, or anything else, as long as they were sublime beings with a pure Dharma lineage, Kyabje Rinpoche strove to receive all the rare streams of Kama and Terma empowerments and transmissions, permission-blessings, reading transmissions, and even simple Dharma connections from them all, either inviting them to his own abode or meeting them at theirs, doing whatever was necessary according to time, place, situation, or the lamas' wishes and commands.

Indeed, some spiritual seekers rely on masters who are famous for their scholarship or meditative realization, or those who have high secular status. Such seekers brag about their gurus and publicize their studies to everyone. From lamas who appear to be ordinary, who live simply and seem pathetic from both worldly and religious vantage points, they receive teachings secretively, making sure no one else finds out. They shy away from attending such gurus, like someone who hopes to get the flesh of a "seven-birth Brahmin"[413] but fearful of touching his corpse as though he died of leprosy. Kyabje Rinpoche was not like that. He relied upon his gurus without ever straying from the meaning expressed by the Buddha:

> Follow the Guru closely with reverence and respect, do whatever he says, do not contradict his words, do not critique his deeds, do not analyze his face, and do not perceive him as faulty.

In brief, as Vilāsavajra explains in his *Clarification of Commitments*, Kyabje Rinpoche respectfully attended anyone who possessed the six aspects of a master,[414] using the three ways of pleasing the Guru,[415] without any confusion as to what was to be adopted and avoided, as explained in the sūtras and tantras using the four metaphors,[416] the five knowledges,[417] the six key points of sacred commitments,[418] and so forth. Kyabje Rinpoche has said: "As for myself, I have never once incurred a breach of commitment by even thinking about acting in a way that might be inappropriate, let alone actually doing something, even a tiny thing, that would displease my Gurus. This is my most important achievement."

Thus, on every occasion and in every place, as Kyabje Rinpoche listened to his spiritual teachers and reflected on their words, the music of his illustrious names and renown resounded as pure nectar in the ears of living beings. Or as the master himself wrote in his *Prayer with the Various Names of Dudjom Tulkus*:[419]

> When the faculties of your karmic body first awakened,
> Conditioned by habit from the beginningless beginning,

The tantric adept Lopön Ngagchang[420]
Named you Nyima Gyaltsen, "Victory Banner of the Sun." To you I pray.

To your holy lord father, Jampal Norbu, a royal descendant,
A Ḍākinī said, "A son greater than his father will appear."
As prophesied, your name was given before your birth.
To you, the one known as Yeshe Dorje, "Wisdom Vajra," I pray.

In the deathless, quintessential secret Godāvarī,[421]
The Lotus-Born's regent, the Yogin of Space [Jedrung Trinle Jampa Jungne],
Blessed and crowned you with the empowerment name, Jigdral Dechen Dorje Dragpo [Tsal],
"Wrathful Vajra Power of Fearless Great Exaltation." To you I pray.

When you trained in the conventional sciences
Under the supreme mahāpaṇḍita,[422] chief among the learned, virtuous, and kind,
He named you Dawa Sarpa, unprecedented youthful "New Moon" who delights the Lotus-Born.
To you I pray.

When your continuous mind was blessed with the lay prātimokṣa vows,
From the very embodiment of compassion, the one bearing the name of Mañjuśrī,[423]
You were known as the all-victorious Gyurme Gelek, "Unchanging Virtue and Excellence."
To you I pray.

When, under the great Bodhisattva Ngawang Palden Zangpo,
You donned the armor of resolve to attain supreme enlightenment,
You were named Gyalse Lodrö Trime Pende Da Özer Palbar,
"Bodhisattva Stainless Intelligence, Gloriously Blazing Light Rays of the Moon of Benefit and Happiness." To you I pray.

When the gracious Lord of the Family, Gyurme Ngedön Wangpo,
Granted you entry into the great maṇḍala of the Vajrayāna
And empowered you as his closest disciple,
You were known as Dorje Dutsal, "Powerful Indestructible Assembly." To you I pray.

When the Dharma Lord Trulshik Rinpoche [from Sikkim], king among the supreme guides,
Put you into the maṇḍala of the Unsurpassed Quintessential Secret Heart Essence,
You were named Yenpa Lode, "Carefree Wanderer."
To you I pray.

When Padma Tötreng with Consort, embodiment of all the Buddha families,
Confirmed you as charioteer of the path of the Great Secret,
With prophecies and aspirations, they conferred a grand empowerment
And praised you with the name Drodul Lingpa, "Great Treasure Revealer Subduer of Beings."
To you I pray.

Kyabje Rinpoche authored the first two lines of the above supplication—"When the faculties of your karmic body first awakened, conditioned by habit from the beginningless beginning"— as an expression of modesty. If we disciples completely regard our Root Guru, who is pure from the beginning with no habitual tendencies from karmic winds, as a Nirmāṇakāya emanation, rather than as someone who took birth in an ordinary body due to habitual tendencies, there is greater merit in thinking this way. Therefore, I think we would accumulate more merit if we recited the stanza like this:

As you have primordially developed bodhicitta and vowed to benefit beings,
When your maṇḍala of major and minor marks blossomed in this world,
The tantric adept Lopön Ngagchang
Named you Nyima Gyaltsen, "Victory Banner of the Sun." To you, I pray.

Similarly, in his record of teachings received, Kyabje Rinpoche describes his extraordinary Root Gurus as follows:

> Especially, Victorious Padmasambhava's successors, sovereign masters who revealed treasures
> And performed the enlightened activity of actual Buddhas to subdue me and other students in the degenerate era,
> Dudjom Namkhe Dorje Tsal and Dechen Zilnön Dorje,
> Two incomparable great treasure revealers, rest your indestructible lotus feet upon the pistil of my heart.
>
> After perfectly planting the fertile seeds of the marvelous three vows[424] in the soil of my mind,
> You showered down a rain of Dharma—empowerments, tantric teachings, and upadeśa—and ripened the excellent fruit of everlasting happiness.
> Gyurme Pende Özer and Gyurme Ngedön Wangpo,
> Two peerless masters, I worship your lotus feet as an adornment of my crown cakra of great exaltation.
>
> With the warm rays of the ripening empowerments and liberating instructions, you fully nourished the feeble lotus roots of my obscured intelligence
> And unfurled the petals of celebration of joyous good fortune.
> Venerable Gyurme Namdrol Gyatso and Orgyen Chönjor Gyatso,
> Two unrivaled teachers, I approach the dust beneath your feet as the glory of my crown.

From these holy masters, whom Kyabje Rinpoche praises so highly, he received the nectar of the profound and vast Holy Dharma in its entirety, like a vase being filled to the brim. Not only would it be impossible for me to describe everything here, but Kyabje Rinpoche himself has detailed everything very clearly in his *Record of Profound and Extensive Dharma Teachings Received Called "Precious Lamp."* Therefore, I will cut short my elaborations, which are like holding a lamp up to the sun.

Regarding his meditation practice, whenever Kyabje Rinpoche received teachings from his Gurus, he did not leave them as mere hearsay but instead, following his Root Gurus' instructions, put them into practice in remote mountain hermitages and meditation caves. He proceeded straight through the scriptures' four branches of approach and accomplishment in the sādhanas of the infinite supreme deities, focusing mainly on the Three Roots practices from the Tantra and Sādhana sections of Mahāyoga. Depending upon his availability and circumstances, he completed the recitations according to their requisite number, duration, or indications.[425] Signs and indications of successful practice emerged exactly as described in each scripture, either in actuality, in visions, or in dreams, and he gained mastery of the supreme and common spiritual accomplishments.

In Buddha Longevity Cave, Kyabje Rinpoche performed the practice of indestructible longevity.[426] He had a vision of Buddha Amitāyus, and the amṛta, the liquor of longevity, boiled. Since fully realized Noble Ones never involve themselves with the demon of self-righteousness or desire, Kyabje Rinpoche never overstepped the seal of the ten secrets[427] described in the tantras.

There were numerous profound treasures destined for Kyabje Rinpoche, including earth treasures, such as three elaborate, middling, and concise Three Roots sādhana cycles; sacred representations of Buddha body, speech, and mind; great sacred substances that liberate upon tasting; and so forth. But other than those teachings that belonged to the mind-treasure class—such as the Peaceful and Wrathful Guru cycles, including the *Heart Essence of the Lake-Born Vajra* and Dorje Drolö cycles; the Yidam deity cycles, including those of Hayagrīva and Vajrakīlaya; and the Peaceful and Wrathful Ḍākinī cycles—Kyabje Rinpoche did not attempt to reveal the others, as he was concerned mainly with the teachings of the Nyingma Kama and the previous treasures.[428]

As it says in the *Inscribed History of Prophecies*:

> On the edge of the red-faced[429] land of Tibet, ༔
> On the border between Khatra and Mön, ༔ [430]
> In the glorious cave at Paro Tagtsang, ༔
> In the Wish-Fulfilling Lion's Lair, ༔ [431]
> In order to subdue wrath with wrath, ༔
> I, Padma Tötreng Tsal, ༔
> Through the samādhi of vajra wrath, ༔
> Arose in the form of the Wild Subjugator ༔[432]
> And subdued the demons, obstacle makers, king spirits,[433] senmo spirits, and samaya corruptors ༔

Throughout the snowy land of Tibet and Mön. ༔
I subjugated and actually took the hearts and life force ༔
Of the hordes of haughty gods and demons ༔
And charged them with caring for this holy place and its treasures. ༔
My direct disciples will open the door. ༔
Through them, for the sake of the karmically destined of the future, ༔
In the manner of ripening, liberating, developing, completing, and oral instruction, ༔
Much will be revealed and separately concealed. ༔
The quintessence of them all ༔
Is the cycle of the *Three Roots Mind Sādhana*, ༔
Profound, vast, complete, and condensed. ༔
With love I transmitted it to Drogben Lotsawa. ༔
He will open it in four cycles, from elaborate to concise. ༔
The elaborate teaching, the cycle of the *Complete Gathering of the Sugatas*, ༔
A holy statue of Yizhin Palbar, ༔ [434]
And great-bliss pills that are liberating upon tasting ༔
I have placed in the cleft of the vajra lair, ༔
The throat of Mön's glorious Tagtsang Cave, ༔
Whose opening resembles a lion. ༔
The medium-length teaching, the cycle of the *Complete Gathering of Vidyādharas*, ༔
Upadeśa for happiness in the land of Tibet, ༔
And my own ritual objects and stūpa ༔
I have concealed on the face of Chim's Blazing Meteorite [435] rocky cliff, ༔
Which resembles a gong. ༔
The concise teaching, the cycle of the *Complete Gathering of Secrets*, ༔
The guidebook to Pemakö, ༔
And upadeśa for happiness in hidden lands ༔
I have concealed near Śrī Parvata Mountain in India ༔
In a boulder that resembles a treasure chest. ༔
The refined quintessence of all of these, ༔
The main teaching, the cycle of the *Quintessential Secret Gathering*, ༔
The pure essence of my mind's bindu, ༔
I cannot dare to leave hidden ༔
In an external material form as an earth treasure; ༔

I have concealed it in the repository of the expanse of the wisdom mind ༔
Of my manifestation, the magical being, ༔[436]
Filling his mind with dhāraṇī mantras of wisdom-awareness. ༔

All this occurred as described.

At the age of thirteen, Kyabje Rinpoche had the experience of seeing Guru Padmasambhava in a vision, and afterward, a group of girls handed him some golden scrolls inscribed with symbolic script. When he turned twenty-four as well, in Gawalung in Puwo, a golden scroll that measured three fingerbreadths across and about three handspans long, bearing symbolic Ḍākinī script, emerged from the spontaneously arisen Hayagrīva and Vajrayoginī's secret place of union and was placed directly into his hand. Likewise, at age thirty, while he was exerting himself in the approach and accomplishment practices of Vajrakīlaya, the supreme deity of enlightened activity, at Paro Tagtsang a golden scroll was placed in his hand. Although he was handed these and all sorts of other golden scrolls over the years, due to numerous outer and inner circumstances relating to place, time, companions, and such, the auspicious conditions were temporarily incomplete.

As for his mind-treasure cycles, I have heard Lama Könchok Rabten say that Kyabje Rinpoche received a mind treasure when he was five years old. At age thirteen, while he was practicing the approach and accomplishment phases of Rigdzin Dudul Dorje's Dorje Drolö treasure teaching, Kyabje Rinpoche's mind treasure—the development and completion stages of the *Sole Essence Sādhana of the Lotus-Born*—suddenly arose in the expanse of his wisdom mind. Later, when he turned twenty-four, as he was performing the approach and accomplishment practices of his predecessor Tragtung Dudjom Lingpa's *Dorje Drolö*, the secret Wrathful Guru sādhana, the *Sole Essence Sādhana of the Lotus-Born* once again suddenly and vividly arose in his wisdom mind, and he decoded it.

Likewise, in Paro Takstang in the southern land of Mön [Bhutan], while Kyabje Dudjom Rinpoche was practicing the sādhana of Vajrakīlaya, his Vajrakīlaya teaching cycle emerged. The manner of its transmission is described in the *Pudri Regpung* root text:

> When I, Jigdral Yeshe Dorje, was thirty-four years old, on the full-moon day in the twenty-fifth lunar mansion of the Fire Ox year, in the sixteenth sixty-year cycle [1937], I was engaging in

making blessed medicine using the Vajrakīlaya practice called *Namchak Pudri* [Meteoric Iron Razor That Vanquishes Māra], in the Lion's Lair cave of Paro Tagtsang in Mön. At one point, in a dream, a finely adorned girl who said she was Yeshe Tsogyal handed me an exquisite six-inch meteoric iron dagger. "This is the actual implement that Guru Rinpoche used here when he arose in the form of Dorje Drolö to bind the eight classes of gods and demons under oath and vanquish the noxious spirits. After that, when I saw him off to Gungtang,[437] he gave it to me. Now I am giving it to you. Keep it as your heart treasure," she said, tucking it inside the fold of my garment. Overjoyed, I grabbed it from her hand. First I need to take an empowerment, I thought, touching the dagger to my crown and throat. As soon as I touched it to my heart center, the dagger and my body merged inseparably. My upper body remained as it is now, but my lower body transformed into an iron dagger emitting fiery sparks. As the Vajrakīlaya mantra roared forth from my throat, I felt the whole earth shake.

At that, the girl said, "Oh, that is the real empowerment and blessing. That is the treasury of tantras, scriptural quotations, and upadeśa all rolled into one. It is very important that you do not ignore this or allow it to fade away. In ancient times you received these empowerments, precious oral instructions, and transmissions in their entirety from Guru Rinpoche—don't you remember?" She took my hand and drew me toward her, and I awoke.

Immediately, I was flooded with hazy memories from my distant past, and the teaching cycle of Vajrakīlaya in particular emerged with vivid clarity in my mind. If I had decoded the symbols that burst forth from the expanse of my awareness straightaway, this treasure teaching would have been even much more elaborate than the teaching cycles of my two treasure-revealer predecessors, and there would have been all sorts of upadeśa and activity-ritual sequences that were unprecedented. However, seeing how much energy it takes to reveal new treasures and how pointless it is nowadays, I let it be.

Later, when I was forty-five, on the tenth day of the Miracle Month of the Earth Rat year [1948], numerous outer and inner circumstances prompted me not to ignore my destined allotment

> of treasures, so in order to lay claim to my territory, I decoded the distilled quintessence, which was simply the root catalog. Oceanic assembly of Dharmapālas, Ḍākinīs, and oath-bound guardians, secure and protect it!

The holders of the teaching, as well, were prophesied thus:

> After the root text of the Vajrakīlaya *Pudri Regpung* had been decoded, in my deluded perception a lovely turquoise female dog[438] appeared before me and said joyfully:
>
> In the holy place where all those with samaya gather, ༔
> In a grove extremely secluded from those without samaya, ༔
> In the assembly hall of those under holy oath, ༔
> The holy symbolic words are thus: ༔
> From the timely ripening of former karma and aspirations, ༔
> The medicine that will benefit all future beings, ༔
> This supremely secret, essentialized treasury, ༔
> The essence of the wisdom mind of the three masters ༔[439]
> Is the development and completion stages and the Great Perfection, ༔
> Bound by the summaries of the nine yānas. ༔
> This concise writing with vast meaning, in the form of letters, ༔
> Arises like a rainbow in the sky. ༔
> This vital quintessence of the ever-noble three lineages of Samantabhadra, ༔
> Recognized as the extremely important teaching of this time, ༔
> Is to be taught to the beings bearing the names Jñāna Vajra, Karma Maṇi, ༔
> Puṇya, Padma, and Odi, ༔[440]
> And propagated in the Four Great Canyons and the Four Great Valleys, ༔
> Which will slightly revive the dying embers of the Buddhist teachings. ༔

In particular, one who rejoices in the essential meaning, ༔
A boy with naturally occurring auspicious marks, born in the Monkey year, ༔[441]
Will dissolve into the expanse of the Dharmakāya Samantabhadra, ༔
The self-occurring nature born of space. ༔
Like a tigress salivating over her prey, I, a female dog, ༔
Long ago, in Yangleshö Cave, ༔
Embraced the Great Guru's vajra decree. ༔
Proclaim this as a message to the supreme among the karmically destined! ༔
It has not deceived, does not deceive, and will not deceive! ༔
SAMAYA. ༔

Having said this, she vanished.

Regarding the qualities of Kyabje Rinpoche's wondrous body, generally speaking, in this world of karmic ripening, human beings of diverse races are born with bodies that largely reflect the outer elements, climatic conditions, and so on, of their particular countries of origin. The eyebrows, teeth, face shape, coloring, and other traits can make it possible to identify racial or ethnic heritage at a glance. For example, most Tibetans share traits such as flat or round faces and noses that are not very prominent.

It follows that Kyabje Rinpoche, who was born in Tibet, resembled the Tibetan people in countenance. However, the Lord Protector's skin was exceptionally soft and radiant, his eyes were vivid and clear, and his tongue was supremely agile and nimble, so that when he gave reading transmissions,[442] he could finish a whole volume in a flash. His hair was black and very thick, sleek, and untangled. These were but a few of the many auspicious marks and indications of physical perfection that he possessed, which were readily apparent to all. Notably, his nose was prominent with a slightly hooked tip. In fact, the maṇḍala of his face resembled the descriptions of the way Guru Rinpoche is to be visualized in the Guru Yoga sādhanas, where the Guru is in Nirmāṇakāya form—for example: "The Master is youthful with rosy-white complexion ༔"—so much so that his fortunate disciples did not need to struggle to visualize him as such. Simply seeing him was like meeting Guru Rinpoche himself, without any variance. One could gaze insatiably at his face, and this is true not just in his presence but also with photographs taken of him previously as well, in which the Master appeared in the manner of a tantrika; when one sees these images, faith and awe spontaneously arise. The subtle elements of his holy body had been fully refined into wisdom elements, so that even in the perception of ordinary individuals, he appeared youthful and charming, without any frailty, at a very advanced age.

Skillful means and wisdom,[443] the movement of the sun and moon, were purified in the space of luminous Dharmakāya in his central channel, so that the sound of his voice was extremely clear and melodious, free of any obstruction or defilement. Unlike the coarse filth uttered by ordinary people who are malicious and unruly, whenever Kyabje Rinpoche spoke to someone, his honeylike words touched their hearts. With his lotuslike tongue, he spoke flowerlike truthful words and expressed teachings with reverence, just the way our Guide, Buddha Śākyamuni, had taught.

Through the four ways of gathering disciples,[444] Kyabje Rinpoche fulfilled the individual wishes of all living beings, regardless of rank, and especially those who, due to previous karma, were poor, hungry, lacking clothing, or homeless. To them he offered encouragement, comfort, inspiration, and joy by granting Dharma teachings and providing material supplies and provisions. Kyabje Rinpoche was raised and nurtured by wisdom Ḍākinīs, and by the power of the brightly blazing qualities of his sprouting Buddha's lineage, worldly activity Ḍākinīs always made offerings to him.

As Śāntideva says:

> Whatever the Protector wishes,
> May sentient beings receive it.[445]

Aligned with this aspiration, this is the great, stainless, wisdom-body reflection of Kyabje Rinpoche inspiring fortunate, karmically destined disciples to exert themselves with confident faith, in order for the wisdom of realization—transmitted through blessing—to arise in the continuity of their minds, and for them to attain his state of enlightenment in a single lifetime.

As for the qualities of his sublime speech,[446] since Kyabje Rinpoche's speech arises as the cloud of the seed-syllable wheel, it no longer resembles that of ordinary authors, who can be skilled at commenting in verse but who have trouble when it comes to prose, or who are skilled at composing prose but who have trouble with verse, or who focus on the words yet lack essential meaning, and so on. Kyabje Rinpoche had a rich vocabulary in every respect, and his excellent, melodious, lyrical compositions deeply delighted the learned. Whether he spoke in poetry or prose, he expressed himself freely, and intellectuals could never refute his narratives and logical arguments, which had sound, authentic sources. In short, his writings were excellent in meaning and excellent in words, virtuous in the beginning, virtuous in the middle, and virtuous in the end, comprising all the characteristics of the Holy Dharma. Similarly, regardless of what he composed, whether about the development and completion stages, sādhana practice, or ritual arrangements, written in whatever style of the four links was needed—tantra linked to sādhana, sādhana linked to ritual arrangement, ritual arrangement linked to practical guidance, or practical guidance to the holy master's upadeśa—his writings have the ability to cause visionary experiences to arise, in which the jñānasattva of the deities can be actually summoned into the samayasattva.[447] His speech was indistinguishable from the writings of Minling Terchen Gyurme Dorje, who was the actual Vairotsana.

As Patrul Chökyi Wangpo [Patrul Rinpoche] says:

> Holy texts, meant only to benefit [beings] and inspire practice,
> Do not need to be taught in a structured, scholarly, poetic way.
> Common words and village words can perfectly explain the true path.
> This is the special quality of Bodhisattvas.

In this vein, for those sincerely seeking liberation, Kyabje Rinpoche granted upadeśa guidance based on students' experiences, which was attuned to their unique dispositions and faculties, using the tradition of guidance, using the tradition of direct introduction, or by "granting everything at once to the traveler crossing a mountain pass,"[448] and so on. Whatever teachings he gave were granted not as mere speculative ideas, like leaves of theoretical words covering the roots of meaning, but were put directly into one's mind, like an expert physician who applies moxibustion directly and unerringly to an acupuncture point. His speech, just like the speech of Longchenpa, could instantly liberate great meditators from the pain of dualistic mind's experiences. Whatever spontaneous songs or feast-offering melodies he wrote served as potent spurs to renunciation in the minds of disciples; all their habitual tendencies toward the deluded appearances of this life naturally ceased, and all appearances and thoughts arose as appearances of deities and the Guru. In these ways, Kyabje Rinpoche's speech was indistinguishable from that of Rigdzin Jigme Lingpa.

Kyabje Rinpoche spoke the following at a very young age:

> *Aho ye!* How wondrous!
> In Akaniṣṭha, at the center of the palace on the Glorious Copper-Colored Mountain,
> Vidyādharas, Ḍākas, and Ḍākinīs are gathered together,
> Delighting in a mesmerizing dance of great exaltation. Thinking of that,
> Deep in my heart, I recall my sole father, the Lake-Born Vajra.
>
> His dazzling body, with major and minor marks, overpowers the phenomenal world.
> His melodious voice, the great secret primordial sound, is sweet as a lute.
> His sublime mind has the nature of flawless luminous wisdom.
> What could rival the feast of gazing at the Guru's beaming face?
>
> Smiling, smiling, he makes joyful sidelong glances,
> Beautiful, beautiful, I listen to Ḍākinīs' secret words and mystic songs,
> Flashing, flashing, they sway and dance,
> Again, again, how unbearably I long to gaze at this wondrous scene.
>
> Yet the young eye-bubbles of this wretched child
> Are clouded by dense cataracts of dualistic thought;
> Alas, I lack the fortune to behold this sight!
> Overwhelmed with regret, I wail loudly: Lotus-Born! Do you hear me?
>
> If you hear me, take out your golden scalpel of wisdom and compassion,
> And remove the thick film of ignorance that obscures me.
> Come take me by the hand, your fingers laced in mine,
> And lead me, please, Sole Father, to your garden of joy.

If I lack the good fortune to be led there right away,
Send Vidyādharas, Ḍākas, and Ḍākinīs to console me,
So that I may happily enjoy the glorious festival of flawless great exaltation,
While I gradually make my way to you, Father.

Once this white eagle's youthful body of threefold faith[449]
Is fitted with a pair of soaring wings of View and Conduct,
And fully endowed with the sixfold power[450] of stainless samaya,
Then the citadel of Lotus Light is not so far away.

Assembly of gods and human companions, male and female, with a common karmic destiny,
Pray that we may join the ranks of the Vidyādharas.
In high, high spirits, laughing with joy and delight,
Let us go together, never parting, to the terrestrial pureland.[451]

This yearning melody, sung by a young cuckoo,
Bursts forth as the rapturous play of the throat's wheel of enjoyment,
As a messenger to invoke the Guru's wisdom mind:
Instantly send down the timely rain of your amṛta blessings.

This was spoken spontaneously by the fortunate child born in the land of Pemakö, Jigdral Yeshe Dorje, at the age of nineteen, on the tenth day of the eleventh lunar month of the Dundubhi year [1922].[452]

By reading this vajra song of yearning, you will understand.

Furthermore, some adherents of other philosophical schools, for no reason at all other than to increase their own fame, have discredited the contributions made to Buddhism by the Early Translation school's supremely gracious Vidyādhara lineage of authentic teachings and individuals. They do this under the pretext of "purifying" the Buddhist teachings. In order to compassionately care for such persons, Kyabje Rinpoche used scriptural citations and logical arguments to fully dispel all doubts.

But as Rigdzin Jigme Lingpa says:

Neither the experiences and practical knowledge of practitioners
Nor the authentic scriptural citations and reasonings of scholars
Can be used to subdue the jealous,
As we saw with Buddha Śākyamuni and Devadatta.[453]

Keeping these words in mind, if there is a great necessity to make any clarification, the sunshine of the scriptural citations and logical arguments of the great charioteers of the Early Translation school—past masters such as Rongzompa and Longchenpa and more recent masters such as Mipham Rinpoche—had already fully dispelled the darkness of ignorance and misunderstanding. Thus, Kyabje Rinpoche, seeing this effort at clarification as futile, chose not to create further contradiction, attachment, and aversion. He considered the ultimate life stories of Nāgārjuna and Lord Atiśa to be paramount.[454]

As it says in a book of advice:

This life is short, and there is so much to know;
Yet we do not know how long our lives will last.
Like a swan separating milk from water,[455]
Earnestly pursue your own aspirations.

For those of us who presume to be followers of the Buddha, if we can each perfect our learning and contemplation within a particular yāna that corresponds to our individual faculties and inclinations, with its own threefold system of basis, path, and result, then even though it may seem as if we have not served the Buddha's teachings in vast ways—as in the saying "destroying hundreds and moving thousands"—in fact, it is the most beneficial in not allowing the teachings of Buddha Śākyamuni to be contradicted or ruined from within.

As it says in Vasubandhu's *Well-Explained Reasoning*:

That which cures all enemy passions,
And protects beings from miserable existences,
Are the Buddhist śāstras, which serve to cure and protect;
These two qualities do not exist in other traditions.

The composition of śāstras, which expound the enlightened wisdom of the Buddha's words, is the work of learned scholars. The teachings speak of three distinguishing features of authors of Buddhist śāstras: at best, they should have seen the truth of Dharmatā; in middling cases, they should have had a vision of a Yidam deity or been given permission to compose śāstras, either directly or indirectly, by the deity and Guru; and at the very least, they should be learned in the five sciences.

Kyabje Rinpoche possessed not one but all three of these distinguishing features. In light of historical events that led to a general scarcity of sacred texts in both Buddhist and non-Buddhist traditions, Kyabje Rinpoche, with completely pure and selfless kindness, hoping to remedy the situation for holders of the Early Translation tradition, gathered scattered writings, brought forth hidden writings, condensed elaborate meanings, expanded condensed meanings, and organized texts that were in disarray, filling some twenty-five volumes, including the *Dharma History of the Early Translation School*, with his diverse collected writings on the most important śāstras. To preserve the Buddhist doctrine, Kyabje Rinpoche compiled the supportive teachings of the Nyingma Kama in more than fifty volumes and published them. For posterity, he brought hundreds of volumes of scripture to the holy land of India and combined the vital essence of the Nyingma Kama's scriptural stream with its stream of empowerments and transmissions.

The qualities of Kyabje Rinpoche's enlightened mind, which was utterly tranquil, disciplined, and stainless and spacious like the sky, can be illustrated by the words of the Glorious Protector Lui Wangpo [Nāgārjuna]:

> Though young, one enjoys the deep calm of an elderly person.
> Though learned, one has no pride about knowledge.
> Though radiant and majestic, one remains patient and gentle.
> Though ever loftier in accomplishment, one lacks any pride or
> arrogance.[456]

Just as this describes, even as a young child, Kyabje Rinpoche's disposition was naturally kind and disciplined. He was never threatening to anyone—his attendants and disciples, or anybody young, old, or middle-aged—not even in the way he looked at them or in his tone of voice. Not only that, but he showed humble respect to all—good, bad, and mediocre. He was never interested in earning glory by overwhelming everyone with his extensive knowledge of worldly virtues or his powerful mastery of the sublime Dharma.

Kyabje Rinpoche was a great charioteer of the Early Translation teachings, and his name was renowned throughout the world. Even when certain prominent teachers with sectarian views or greedy ambitions lacked faith in him and used him for their own selfish or political purposes, of course Kyabje Rinpoche never belittled the wishes of others nor tried to guard or fortify his own side. Instead:

> Answering harm with benefit
> Is the approach of holy beings.

As this verse says, Kyabje Rinpoche, without any contrivance, perfectly emulated the liberated life of Śāntideva. All conditioned, deluded thoughts, positive or negative, were of one taste, without distinction or exclusion, in the primordially pure expanse of Dharmatā, so that whatever anyone said to him, regardless of whether he had known them for a long time or had only just met them, or whether they were good or bad, or whether they said something that was or was not the case, he would simply say, "Oh yes, that is very true!" or "Yes, that's right!" or "How wonderful!" He would repeat people's words like an echo, without any clearly defined opinions or judgments. When that occurred, those who had understood, experienced, and realized the definitive truth of inconceivable Dharmatā were established at the level of irreversible faith. Ordinary, childish individuals saw that their conception of things as real, permanent, stable, and unchanging was utterly distorted and mistaken, and therefore untrustworthy and unreliable. As it says in the tantras:

> When phenomena reach the state of exhaustion,
> One's own beliefs fall apart as well.
> Without the limiting concepts of view, meditation, and conduct,
> The appearance of Dharmakāya does not exist.
> With the cessation of Kāyas and wisdoms,
> There are no Buddhas and no sentient beings.
> In brief, nothing abides,
> Nothing departs, and nothing arrives.

Kyabje Rinpoche never wavered from the meaning expressed here. The nature of his wisdom mind, utterly unfathomable to any sentient being of this world, including the gods, was as described by Omniscient Jigme Lingpa in the *Treasury of Precious Qualities*:

> Rich with every imaginable quality, the Guru
> Is the essence of all the Buddhas' wisdom and compassion,
> Appearing in human form in the perception of disciples.
> Unsurpassed source of all accomplishments,
> The Guru is in accord with everyone on the relative level,
> Yet contradicts everyone in all ways on the ultimate level.
> Endowed with wisdom realization, the Guru is more sublime than anyone.
> Skilled at cutting through doubts, the Guru patiently endures ingratitude and fatigue.
> The Guru is a great ship that delivers us from the ocean of saṃsāra,
> A true guide who prevents us from going astray on the supreme path,
> A rain of amṛta that quells the raging fires of karma and passions.
> The Guru dispels the darkness of ignorance like the sun and moon,
> Is a vehicle as enormous as the Earth,
> A wish-granting tree, the source of all benefit and happiness,
> An excellent vase containing the treasury of Dharma,
> Greater still than a perfect wish-fulfilling jewel,
> Impartial to all, like a father and mother,
> With compassion vast and swift, like a rushing river,
> Unchanging joy, like the King of Mountains,[457]
> And undisturbed evenness, like a rain cloud.
> Such a Guru is equal to all the Buddhas.
> Even if one harms the Guru, the Guru connects one to the path of happiness.
> Then, for noble persons who rely upon the Guru with sincere and genuine faith,
> The precious attainments of higher rebirths and sublime enlightenment will shower down like rain.

Kyabje Rinpoche fits this description by Omniscient Jigme Lingpa exactly.

As for Kyabje Rinpoche's awe-inspiring enlightened activities, which were always done with perfect timing, he founded Bejong Ewam Dechen Chökhor Monastery in Pemakö, king of hidden lands, and established a monastic community there. He restored Dechen Teng Temple, which is quite near the famous monastery Buchu Sergyi Lhakhang in Kongpo,[458] originally built during the reign of Dharma King Songtsen Gampo, who wished to propagate the Buddhist doctrine and guard against foreign invaders. Kyabje Rinpoche constructed Zangdok Palri Monastery [in Kongpo], complete with a tiered maṇḍala of Guru Rinpoche's Glorious Copper-Colored Mountain pureland filled with sacred statues and images. He established a ngagpa community called Lama Ling, built a retreat center called Sangchen Ösal Namdrol Chöling, and so on. In Rewalsar [also called Tso Pema], near the Indian city of Mandi, Himachal Pradesh state, he founded a retreat center and temple called Tso Pema Orgyen Heruka Nyingmapa Gompa, and in Kalimpong, West Bengal, he built [a second] Zangdok Palri Monastery. In Darjeeling, he built Tsechu Offering Center [Tsechu Gompa]. In the West, he established Yeshe Nyingpo[459] and Orgyen Chö Dzong[460] in the United States, and Dorje Nyingpo[461] and Orgyen Samye Chöling[462] in France. Befitting these occasions, he created empowering conditions and gave advice and instructions, laying many new foundations for the Buddhist teachings.

Patrul Rinpoche taught:

> Not engaging the mind improperly, not engaging the mind in self-interest,
> Not engaging the mind in thoughts with characteristics, not engaging the mind with anything,
> Here in the place of nonthought, the three vows coalesce, pure and engaged,
> Just as a river naturally becomes inseparable from the great ocean.

In like manner, Kyabje Rinpoche himself was completely beyond the web of conceptual fabrication of vows and non-vows. Nevertheless, keeping the collective positivity of others in mind, he requested that spiritual masters endowed with the qualities of steadfast discipline and scholarship act as the empowering condition of preceptor whenever he felt it was suitable, spurring on many bright young people who were free of the five certain conditions[463] and the four conflicting circumstances[464] [that pose obstacles to taking ordination]. By requesting them to take full monastic ordination in the unbroken precept lineage of Śāntarakṣita, Kyabje Rinpoche did everything possible to strengthen the foundation of Buddhism—the ordained

Saṅgha—by increasing the number of sublime individuals who uphold the victory banner of the saffron-clad.[465] For those who guarded the three bases of completely purifying the precepts,[466] Rinpoche provided provisions, supplies, and so on.

Thus, Kyabje Rinpoche never felt himself to be superior to anyone, tangibly or intangibly. As it is said:

> Though one may be adorned with ornaments, still one practices the Dharma,
> Is subdued and well disciplined, and upholds pure conduct,
> Abstaining from harming beings.
> That one is a monk, novice, and Brahmin as well.

Also, in *Letter to a Friend*, Nāgārjuna writes:

> Even householders with babies in their laps
> With knowledge can cross the river of the passions.

Some claim that liberation from saṃsāra can only be attained through monastic ordination, and that there is absolutely no other way to traverse the path to enlightenment. Or they claim that the path of Secret Mantra is the only way to swiftly accomplish the level of perfect omniscience, and that any other path one chooses is inferior. Persons who harbor such narrow-minded notions squander the roots of virtue and fail to embrace students' unique temperaments and faculties, and they are therefore unable to guide students on the path.

As it says in the *Avataṃsaka Sūtra*:

> Any skillful method that can be of benefit to all
> Is the supreme training of Bodhisattvas.
> A great rainfall from the clouds
> Brings a splendidly bountiful harvest.

Likewise, Kyabje Rinpoche revealed the path according to the individual predilections of his students.

His Root Guru, Puktrul Gyurme Ngedön Wangpo, said to him, "I have taught the *Great Treasury of Precious Termas* five different times. You will do so ten times." In accordance with this prophecy, Kyabje Rinpoche first gave the empowerments and transmissions of the *Great Treasury of Precious Termas* at an extremely young age, in Dragsum Tsodzong, Sangye Lingpa's sacred treasure place in Kongpo. On that occasion, at Druglha Rinchen Teng, a gentleman by the name of Kusho Kalzang-la, who was famous in that area for his vast knowledge, thought to himself, "How can it be that a child not yet twenty years old is conferring the *Great Treasury of Precious Termas*? This is simply unacceptable." Filled with doubt and seeking to disprove him, the man set out to test Kyabje Rinpoche by going to Dragsum Tsodzong to examine him. When he witnessed Kyabje Rinpoche performing the ritual traditions of the lineage in an extremely pure and authentic way, he was filled with shame and remorse and offered confession. Not long afterward, Kusho Kalzang-la brought his two sons, Kunzang and Gyurme-la, and the three of them went before Kyabje Rinpoche and humbly requested to be accepted as his students. Rinpoche accepted them, and in time they became his heart-disciples. Kusho Gyurme-la, in particular, honored and served Kyabje Rinpoche his entire life, using the three ways of pleasing the Guru right from his early childhood up through the time that Kyabje Rinpoche later moved to India and settled in Kalimpong, and he became one of Rinpoche's main heart-sons.

Kyabje Rinpoche boundlessly turned the Wheel of Dharma. In various sublime holy places, principal among them being the Unchanging Spontaneously Accomplished Temple of Glorious Samye, which is one of Tibet's three famous Dharma Wheels, the others being the Lhasa and Tradruk monasteries, Kyabje Rinpoche conferred the empowerments and transmissions of the *Great Treasury of Precious Termas* on ten separate occasions. He conferred the thirteen teaching cycles of Pema Lingpa three times, and the empowerments and transmissions of his predecessor Tragtung Dudjom Lingpa's Treasure teachings numerous times. Other principal teachings include the complete empowerments and transmissions of the Nyingma Kama, the precious Buddhist Canon, the reading transmission of the Nyingma Gyubum,[467] the great empowerments of the Eight Heruka Sādhanas, supportive teachings on Pema Lingpa's *Peaceful and Wrathful Deities*, and Jatsön Nyingpo's *Six-Volume Treasure Collection*.

Moreover, Kyabje Rinpoche's methodology was extremely detailed and refined, clean and swiftly performed. Therefore, whenever he taught, the complete path would be conferred in a single sitting, including ripening empowerments, liberating instruction, and supportive transmissions, given uninterruptedly with hardly any difficulties. This way, eager students traveling from distant lands experienced less hardship, and their goals were easily realized. Kyabje Rinpoche perfectly fulfilled everyone's hopes and wishes.

Needless to say, Kyabje Rinpoche performed many other enlightened activities for the benefit of beings. Using various kinds of medicine, primarily the countless universal panaceas such as refined precious pills and crystal amṛta, he completely dispelled the dense darkness of sickness for beings afflicted with physical imbalances.

Many beings become obsessed with endless spiritual and worldly pursuits, and sometimes they find themselves unable to correctly apply specific antidotes at the right time. They fall prey to the obstacle of entangled thought patterns and are unable to ease their minds. For those who suffer intensely from mental illness, Kyabje Rinpoche offered medicine to dispel their mental torment, either consumed by mouth or inhaled through the nose, freeing them from mental illness and setting their minds at ease.

The Great Ācārya of Oḍḍiyāna spoke thus about blessed medicine:

> It is the offering substance of every last Sugata,
> The elixir of all Gurus and Yidam deities combined,
> The heart blood of all the Ḍākinīs.
> If consumed, it has indescribable benefits:
> The qualities of the Five Buddha Kāyas will be obtained;
> Outwardly, it will conquer physical illness and evil spirits;
> Inwardly, it will purify the five toxic passions;
> All impaired and broken samaya will be amended;
> Secretly, spontaneously present wisdom will be realized.
> When Śrāvakas and Pratyekabuddhas consume this,
> They will traverse the ten Bodhisattva levels
> And become great Mahāyāna Bodhisattvas.
> If offered to the Guru, blessings will enter you.
> If offered to the Yidam deities, they will grant siddhis.
> If offered to the Sugatas, compassion will arise.
> If offered to the Ḍākinīs, they will reveal prophecies.
> If yogins or anyone else consumes it,
> Outwardly, illnesses, evil spirits, negativity, and obscuration will be cleansed;
> Inwardly, development-stage concentration will be clear;
> Secretly, the Dharmakāya of natural awareness will be realized;

All impairments, duplications, and omissions will be completely amended.
By wearing it next to the body, untimely death will be averted.
Even if one is maliciously poisoned, this medicine has the ability to neutralize the poison.
By rubbing it on one's body, all illnesses and evil spirits will be dispelled.
If it is burned, all malevolent forces and obstructors will be expelled.
And the place where this medicine is made
Will be equal to the Cool Grove charnel ground;
Ḍākas and Ḍākinīs will gather,
And the whole area will be blessed;
Timely rains will fall, and harvests and livestock will be excellent.
Whoever stays in the place where this medicine is made
Will experience samādhi.
Eventually, when one's life comes to an end,
Whether you are male or female, good or bad,
One will abide at the level of the Vidyādharas.
This is why it is the supreme samaya substance.

The praise uttered by the vajra tongue of Padmasambhava is echoed in the *Amṛta Tantra*:

The chief samaya substances are the five amṛtas,
The eight main ingredients, and the thousand branch ingredients.
Combine these samaya substances and vital elixirs into medicine.

As described, Kyabje Rinpoche collected the eight main ingredients and all the branch medicines, which are the thousand species of excellent, nontoxic medicinal plants growing in India, Nepal, Bhutan, Tibet, and throughout the Himalayan region. To these, he combined "all the vital medicinal elixirs of the phenomenal world into medicine," accomplishing the practical details exactly as described in the texts. When the circumstances of time and place were favorable and suitable, he mixed and blessed the medicine using the unelaborate practice of the sole hero[468] or the elaborate practice in a large gathering.[469] This enlightened activity is endowed with four kinds of liberation: liberation through seeing, through wearing, through tasting, and through touching. Kyabje Rinpoche's kindness in cultivating this alone is truly unrepayable.

Whatever activities Kyabje Rinpoche entrusted to the Dharma Protectors and Guardians, who were the spontaneous expression of his enlightened mind's nondual wisdom, they accomplished without delay. In particular, the great yakṣa Shenpa Marnak, "Dark-Red Butcher," was constantly with him and watched over him with unceasing vigilance. For instance, whenever sentient beings with evil karma attempted to injure Rinpoche's body, Shenpa Marnak would instantly banish them. Once, in the middle of the night, when Kyabje Rinpoche was a young man on pilgrimage in Central Tibet with his mother and attendants, as they were crossing Gampa Pass, they encountered a group of bandits. One of them seized the reins of Kyabje Rinpoche's horse, and they traveled with them for quite a distance. Suddenly, in front of them, a large number of young monks, with an aura of exceptional valor and courage, appeared out of nowhere and aroused tremendous fear in the thieves and bandits. They let go of Rinpoche's horse and fled, vanishing without a trace. The young monks seemed to chase after them, and then they, too, disappeared without a trace. Rinpoche was utterly unharmed. When his attendants were wondering and asking about the monastery the monks had come from, Rinpoche explained, "That was the yakṣa Shenpa Marnak. He came from the great charnel ground Play of Great Joy."

During Rinpoche's middle-age years, his lung condition appeared to worsen. His lungs wheezed persistently, and when his breathing difficulties became serious, his attendants implored him to see a specialist in Colorado in the United States. When he went for his appointment, the doctor was stunned. "How has this man stayed alive for so long? It appears that he has almost no lung function at all."

Afterward, Rinpoche continued traveling to other parts of the United States, Nepal, Hong Kong, France, and elsewhere, and he lived for several more years, working extensively for the benefit of the Dharma and beings. This was solely due to the strength derived from the enlightened quality of possessing the ten powers.

Finally, the time came for Kyabje Rinpoche to subdue students who were clinging to permanence, by means of the enlightened quality of the Guru's nonabiding Nirmāṇakāya. While it is certainly true that the conceptualized hierarchy of "good" and "bad" ways to die is completely irrelevant when it comes to the bodies of extraordinary Nirmāṇakāya Buddhas, in order to inspire others to enter the Buddhist teachings, Rinpoche displayed the truth of signs of accomplishment on the path. To indicate that his enlightened mind had dissolved into the stainless space of great wisdom realization of the Exhaustion of Phenomena Beyond Thought,[470] like space dissolving into space, his physical body shrank to a mere cubit in size. Kyabje Rinpoche left this body behind as an object of worship to support his followers' faith.

As explained in the Buddha's words and their commentaries, the sphere of the sun has no wax or wane: whether the sun revolves around the Earth or, as those living abroad claim, the Earth revolves around the sun, the sun's reflection, by virtue of the fact that it is no different from any other changing phenomenon, appears in many hundreds of millions of different bodies of water on the Earth, and these reflections appear to wax and wane. Likewise, the reflection of Kyabje Rinpoche's form, which was visible here in our world, has dissolved for a short while and merged into the heart of Buddha Radiant Lotus [Padmasambhava],[471] the basis of emanation[472] who abides forever in the Palace of Lotus Light, without wax or wane, as the embodiment of the seven branches of union.

It would be impossible for me to list all the names of Kyabje Rinpoche's host of heart-sons and disciples. This is because Rinpoche began giving teachings, empowerments, and transmissions at a very young age, and by the time he had reached the end of his life, he had turned the Wheel of Dharma an incalculable number of times in Tibet and Greater Tibet, Sikkim, Bhutan, Ladakh, Nepal, India, China, Europe, and the United States. On each of those occasions, many hundreds, thousands, and tens of thousands of close disciples gathered. Except for those rare individuals who possess infallible memories and can write everything down, people like me could never write it all down. As the saying goes, "Forgetful people have no knowledge." So I will leave it alone. In any case, as everyone can plainly see, Kyabje Rinpoche produced innumerable great masters graced with Dharma parasols, powerful leaders famed for their learning, accomplished yogins and yoginīs, and students who attained liberation solely through the power of their faith and devotion.

Now, to bring about temporary happiness and ultimate excellence, I will adorn the conclusion with Chatral Sangye Dorje's *Seed of the Three Faiths: A Supplication to* [Dudjom Rinpoche's] *Liberated Life*:

> Great Bliss Vajra, emptiness that is supreme in all aspects,
> Who projects and absorbs infinite oceans of emanations and
> purelands

Such as Drumbeat of Brahmā and Luminous Essence,[473]
Glorious, all-encompassing Lama, to you I pray.

Appearing as a Nirmāṇakāya Arhat when Buddha Śākyamuni was
teaching,
And as paṇḍitas, siddhas, Vidyādharas, hidden yogins, and more,
Revealing indefinite miraculous manifestations throughout the
three times,
One after another or all at once: to you, I pray.

Especially to you who were so clearly described
In the unerring prophecies of the Lotus-Born Guru and Dudjom
Lingpa,
Born in the pureland of Pemakö, king of hidden lands,
Into a lineage of Dharma kings, I pray.

Right from your youth, your noble propensities were awakened,
And you beheld the face of Guru Rinpoche, who empowered you
With the name Drodul Lingpa, and predicted and confirmed
You as a master of profound treasures; to you, I pray.

A wisdom Ḍākinī appeared before you to hand you treasure
inventories;
Dharma Protectors and Guardians watched over you like their child.
With mastery of the three blazes[474] and the three gatherings,[475]
You were worshipped upon everyone's crown; to you, I pray.

You attended numerous spiritual mentors,
Such as the supreme siddha, Gyurme Ngedön Wangpo,
Who filled your vase to the brim with ripening, liberating, and
supportive teachings.
By listening, reflecting, and meditating, your continuous mind was
fully enriched; to you, I pray.

Even at the end of the era, you aimed to preserve the Early
Translation teachings
And spread them in the ten directions; with this vast aspiration,

You founded Bejong Ewam Dechen Chöling
And other monastic centers. To you, I pray.

With vast objectives in mind, you let go of making an effort to reveal your own earth treasures,
In order to sustain the Ancient Teachings.
You raised aloft the victory banner of the teachings
Of the *Five Great Treasuries*, the confluence of all lineage traditions; to you, I pray.

With none of the exhausting hardship of provisional meaning,
You reached the highest level of accomplishment
Through the swift and easy secret path of unsurpassed Atiyoga;
To you who instantly blazed with the qualities of manifest realization, I pray.

Having clearly discerned the key points of the Causal and Resultant vehicles'[476] systems of view and meditation,
Without needing to consult or rely upon others,
Your inborn intelligence burst forth from the expanse;
To you who are praised as the peerless lord of scholars, I pray.

Without clinging to the inferior result of peace and happiness,
You used the six pāramitās and four magnetizing qualities[477]
To lead countless beings to higher rebirths and definitive excellence of enlightenment;
Great Bodhisattva, to you I pray.

As an offering shrine for beings in this degenerate age of strife,
You founded the Ngayab Pelri retreat center,
A complete maṇḍala temple with deities.
Supreme one who reversed the decline of the teachings, to you I pray.

Moreover, you produced numerous triple supports—statues, scriptures, and stūpas—
Perfectly exemplified by your original volumes;

To you who were dispatched as a messenger
By Padmasambhava, the sole friend and relative of Tibet's well-being,
I pray.

Traversing all of Bhutan, Nepal, Central Tibet, Amdo, Kham, India, and China
In their entirety, granting teachings, samaya substances, and so on,
You led everyone who met you, heard your voice, or even learned of you
To the Palace of Lotus Light; to you I pray.

Although great men, kings, ministers, and nobility
All bowed at your feet, you possessed no pride;
To you who simply sustained the fearless activity of an ordinary hidden yogin,
For whom the eight worldly concerns had equal taste, I pray.

You traveled to buddhafields, Lamas and deities accepted you as their disciple,
Ḍākinīs gave prophecies, and you had infinite pure visions.
Although that was so, you were glad to keep it secret;
To you who renounced vanity and self-righteousness, I pray.

When the time was right, you decoded your mind treasures, the Ḍākinīs' vital heart-blood,
Pithy, clear, quintessential teachings that cheered and satisfied all who encountered them,
And bequeathed them to your karmic heirs;
Dharma King of Treasure Revealers, to you I pray.

After organizing and bringing to light numerous ancient treasures,
Such as the Guru Sādhana, Great Perfection, and Avalokiteśvara trio, Eight Herukas,[478] Master's Realization, and Vajrakīlaya,
You elucidated the secret teachings with easy-to-practice
Ritual arrangements and upadeśa; to you I pray.

In sum, the blazing splendor of your knowledge, love, and skill
Made your Nirmāṇakāya emanation unrivaled and unequaled in the world;
Universally renowned, meaningful Protector,
Recalling the qualities of your three secrets, I pray.

In the future, after you have arisen as a noble king to vanquish the barbaric hordes
And propagate the fruition teachings,[479]
You will become the Buddha of Boundless Dedication [Möpa Taye],
Whose enlightened activity will equal that of a thousand Buddhas; to you I pray.

Supplicating through the power of recollecting
The sacred life story of this incomparable holy Lama,
May I be born again and again at your feet and attend you without separation.
May your realization of the ultimate meaning be transferred to my heart.

Once I have realized the view of original, boundless awareness-emptiness,[480]
Brought my "luminous enclosure"[481] meditation to fruition,
And made progress and gained confidence by practicing liberation upon arising,
May I attain Buddhahood on the level of Unsurpassed Wisdom[482] within a single lifetime.

At the insistent request of my sublime vajra brother, Rigzang Dorje, whom I could not refuse, the carefree, lazy beggar Sangye Dorje wrote this based upon all the qualities that I myself have witnessed in the Lama, and by consulting ancient and recent treasure prophecies for authentication; this is not the mere prattle of jesters. I composed this in Central Tibet, near the Rasa Trulnang Temple, at the seat of Mahāsiddha Tangtong Gyalpo, which is built on the slopes of the glorious Chagpori Mountain. May virtue and excellence increase! *Sarva maṅgalam.* May all beings be happy!

20

Furthermore, according to beings' natures, faculties, wishes,
And different fortunes,
You appear in whatever ways are necessary to subdue them.
To your infinite manifestations, I pray.

Kyabje Rinpoche's numerous wondrous and amazing Nirmāṇakāya emanations have appeared over time in the holy land of India and the snowy land of Tibet, in a succession of lifetimes that begins with the great lord of siddhas, Nuden Dorje Chang, a magical emanation of the Original Protector [Samantabhadra], who lived in a world system known as Richly Adorned, long before our current fortunate eon of illumination. He was followed by the emanated Arhat Śāriputra, who appeared in the holy land of India; the Great Brahmin Saraha, who appeared in the city of Sergyidre as a scholarly monk, who then entered into the fearless activity of a Mahāsiddha; the Great Ācārya Hūṃkāra, who appeared in the Kathmandu valley in Nepal; Jowo Smṛtijñāna, the Indian paṇḍita-siddha who traveled to the land of Tibet to lead his mother out of an ephemeral hell realm; the great Rongzom Paṇḍita Chökyi Zangpo, who appeared in Narlungrong in Tsangme, western Tibet; Katokpa Dampa Deshek, who appeared in the Drizagang region of Dokham; Glorious Lingje Repa, who appeared in the Upper Nyang region of Tsang; Drogön Chögyal Phagpa, master of the glorious Sakya teachings; Kharnakpa of Drum, who appeared in Paro in the southern land of Bhutan; Hepa Chöjung, who appeared in Drakar in the region of Sangngen in Dome; Rigdzin Dudul Dorje, who appeared in a place not far from the palace of the great Dharma King of Derge in Dokham; Gyalse Sönam Detsen, who was the immediate reincarnation of Rigdzin Dudul Dorje; Dudul Rolpa Tsal, who appeared in Bayul in Dokham; Tragtung Dudjom Lingpa, who appeared in the holy place of Wazhab Senge Drakar, also called Dra Chakhung, in the Minyak Rab Range in Dokham; Jigdral Yeshe Dorje, who appeared in the holy land of Pemakö, one of the three major hidden lands,[483] in the east of the snowy land of Tibet; the noble King Chakhorchen, who will appear in the northern kingdom of Shambhala, one of the six countries of Jambudvīpa;[484] the Buddha of Boundless Dedication [Möpa Taye], who will appear in the pure-realm world known as Richly Adorned in the beautifully illumined eon; and so on.

And that is not all. As it is said:

While it is possible that the waves of the great ocean,
Abode of sea monsters, may someday be late in coming,
For spiritual heirs to be subdued,
The Buddha is never late.

The **natures** of **beings** to be **subdued** are all subsumed within the desire realm, the form realm, and the formless realm. Taking birth in these three realms is the result of being motivated by the cause of the three poisons. There are the ruling faculties of the constantly disturbing passions of ordinary beings and the ruling **faculties** of complete purification contained in the minds of sublime beings. Sentient beings have their own diverse, individual **wishes**, and whether specific beings share a particular range of experiences or have unique environments, experiences, and so on, your manifestations of enlightened body, speech, and mind—distinct physical forms, teachings from your speech, and love from your mind—**appear according to beings' different fortunes, in whatever** skillful **ways are necessary to subdue them**. You appear **infinitely**, without any end or limit, and no one can say, "That's all there is." **To your** wondrous and amazing life story, which is beyond the conceptions of childish, ordinary people, **I pray**.

As it says in the *Treasury of Precious Qualities*:

From this, further emanations are indescribable,
As numerous as the many realms of the six classes of beings,[485] in
which
Brahmā, Indra, Maheśvara, and others subdue the gods,
Śrāvakas, Pratyekabuddhas, and Bodhisattvas turn the Wheel of
Dharma for humans,
And likewise Vemacitra for the asuras,
The Woodpecker[486] for birds,
Dṛḍhasamādhāna for animals, and so on;
In short, for hell beings, pretas, and everyone else,
Forms emanate in ways that resemble those they subdue,
And they never rest in their efforts to benefit sentient beings.

As such, in the realms of the six classes,
Due to the cause and effect of positive and negative actions and propensities,
Environments appear to be happy or sad, high or low,
And Buddhas benefit beings in harmony with individual perceptions.
The Dharma they teach is also indeterminate and accords with students' thought patterns.
As in a dream, one meets Buddha
And is also taught dreamlike emanated teachings.
One must understand this as essenceless and unreal,
As egoless, empty, and hollow, say the profound sūtras.

So, in a dreamlike display of saṃsāra and enlightenment,
Although the essential nature of the Buddhas that appear is pure,
They emanate so as to appear like their students.
Also, their seemingly impure manifestations of compassion
Will appear in an uninterrupted continuity for as long as saṃsāra exists.
The various emanations that appear in this way—
Either by occurring naturally or by being created
In carvings or drawn in pictures,
As temples, mansions, and gardens,
As magically emanated cities in the desert,
Lotuses, wish-granting trees, and wish-fulfilling jewels,
Boats, bridges, chariots, food, clothing, and
Other kinds of inanimate material objects,
And in living form, as a great fish during a famine,
A golden bee in a swamp of filth, and myriad other
Emanated forms—are the basis of every kind of happiness.
Without any conception or effort,
They always remain as the glory of great benefit.

Also, as it says in the third chapter of the *Way of the Bodhisattva*, called "Commitment to the Enlightened Mind":

If thinking of me
Brings thoughts of anger or faith to others,

May these always become the cause
For fulfilling all their wishes.

Whoever says anything bad about me,
Does harm to me,
And likewise insults me,
May they all have the fortune to be enlightened.

May I be a protector for those without protection,
A guide for those journeying on a path,
A boat, a ship, and a bridge
For those wishing to cross a river.

May I be an isle for those seeking an isle,
A lamp for those wishing for a lamp,
A home for those wishing for a home,
And a servant for all who want servants.

May I be a wish-fulfilling jewel, a perfect vase,
An accomplished holder of knowledge mantras, a great medicine,
A tree that grants all that is wished,
And one who bestows all that beings desire.

Like earth and the other great elements,
And also, always, like the sky,
For infinite beings, in many forms,
May I be a support for their lives to thrive.

Likewise, in all ways, for realms of beings
Reaching the limits of space,
Until they go beyond suffering,
May I also be a cause for their lives to flourish.

These passages perfectly describe the truth of his impeccable presence.

Dorje Nönpo

21

Eventually, when barbarians try to harm the Buddha's teachings,
You will be the one called Dorje Nönpo[487] **in Shambhala,**
Taking rebirth as the Kalkī king.[488]
To you who will defeat the enemy armies, I pray.

Eventually, beings' merit will diminish, and barbarians will **try to harm the** incomparable **Buddha's teachings**, the sole panacea for restoring well-being and happiness in the realms of conditioned existence. In general, these are demons and samaya corrupters who are born in border regions and who commit vicious actions and make perverse aspirations. They take human form, yet their temperaments are as stubborn and fierce as forest savages, and they refuse to obey the noble legal systems of civil and religious law. In particular, deep-seated habits formed by committing heinous crimes in previous lifetimes cause them to adhere with fanatical zeal to doctrines that promote violence, arrogantly claiming that their base actions, which terminate their own and others' lives, are great sacrificial acts of worship. **When** these **barbarians** who are followers of Muhammad rise up and inflict harm, the one who embodies the wisdom of the supreme knowledge of all Buddhas, Mañjuśrī, who is also **called Dorje Nönpo**, will **take rebirth** as Raudra Cakrin, the twenty-fifth **Kalkī king** in the line that originated with Dharmarāja Sucandra,[489] in **Shambhala**, the Dominion of the Source of Bliss. This is where our Teacher, Lord Buddha, turned the Dharma Wheel of the glorious nondual Kālacakra Tantra for Dharmarāja Sucandra, at the site of the Great Stūpa, which resembles a glorious mountain of white rice. Just as the warm rays of the sun naturally vanquish the frost, Raudra Cakrin will delight in battle with wrathful compassion, and he **will defeat the** encroaching **enemy armies** of bloodthirsty demons who enter the bodies of human beings born in wild and savage lands, not in central countries illumined by the lamp of Dharma. **To you, I pray!**

Of the renowned six countries of Jambudvīpa,[490] the northern one is Shambhala, or "Dominion of the Source of Bliss." In the exalted landscape of this country, tenth-level Bodhisattvas have appeared in a successive line of kings [known as Dharmarājas], the first of whom was an emanation of

Vajrapāṇi named Sucandra. Buddha Śākyamuni himself appeared to Sucandra in the form of Glorious Kālacakra and taught the 12,000 verses of the root tantra. After the reigns of seven kings had elapsed, at the time of the eighth reign, Noble Mañjuśrī himself came in the form of the Kalkī king Mañjuśrī Yaśas.[491] He granted unsurpassed Vajrayāna empowerments to all the adherents of various tantric disciplines of that country, such as Brahmin scholars of Vedic literature, uniting everyone in a single Mahāyāna caste. From him onward, the kings of Shambhala were given the title Kalkī, meaning "Holder of the Castes": as in Kalkī Puṇḍarīka, Kalkī Bhadra, Kalkī Vijaya, Kalkī Sumitra, Kalkī Raktapāni, Kalkī Viṣṇugupta, Kalkī Sūryakīrti, Kalkī Subhadra, Kalkī Samudra Vijaya, Kalkī Aja, Kalkī Sūrya, Kalkī Viśvarūpa, Kalkī Śaśiprabha, Kalkī Ananta, Kalkī Parthiva, Kalkī Śrīpāla, Kalkī Siṃha, Kalkī Vikranta, Kalkī Mahābala, Kalkī Aniruddha, Kalkī Narasiṃha, Kalkī Maheśvara, Kalkī Anantavijaya, and Kalkī Raudra Cakrin.

Our Teacher taught Kalkī Yaśas the *Abridged Kālacakra Tantra*, containing five chapters, with the condensed meaning of the *Kālacakra Root Tantra*. As it says in the great *Abridged Tantra*:

> The glorious Śākya clan had seven brilliant kings; the famous eighth
> was Glorious Mañjuśrī, to whom the highest gods bowed down;
> He was a Kalkī of the vajra caste who granted vajra empowerment
> and united all Buddhists in a single caste.
> Clearly ascending the sublime vehicle, frightening the asuras,
> Glorious Yaśas, with spear in hand,
> For the sake of sentient beings' liberation, fully elucidated the
> Kālacakra.

Also, as it says in the "Wisdom" chapter of the *Kālacakra Tantra*:

> Dharmarāja Yaśas told the Brahmin Sūryaratha:
> Thus, I, Lokeśvara, Protector of the World, dwell on the karmic
> bhūmis in the realms of the three planes of existence, O Sūrya!
> He who grants the path to sentient beings and removes the fear of
> hell is never any ordinary god!"[492]

The Brahmin Sūryaratha praised the Dharma king Yaśas thus:

> Being both an elder and a youth, you are the son of all Buddhas, and you are the Primordial Buddha.
> In union with women yet celibate, with your supreme compassion, you are a friend of the world and an enemy of the Lord of Death.
> You are peaceful, yet you are the Noble Vajra[493] who removes the fear of death and is always the demon of demons.
> Yaśas, you are liberated, yet you enter fully into this conditioned world to ripen beings.

King Mañjuśrī Yaśas's son was Kalkī King Puṇḍarika, an emanation of Avalokiteśvara. He composed a large commentary on the *Abridged Kālacakra Tantra* called *Stainless Light Commentary*. In the thirty-second reign if we count from King Sucandra, or the twenty-fifth reign if we count from King Yaśas, King Yaśas himself, who was actually Noble Mañjuśrī, will return in the form of Kalkī King Raudra Cakrin and defeat the barbarian faction.

As it says in the "World" [first] chapter of the *Abridged Kālacakra Tantra*:

> In the thirty-second and final reign, when the average human life span is 100 years, the enemy of the asuras, Cakra Bearer, will appear.

Also:

> In its center, in the final time after a total of twenty-five successive reigns,
> Within the Kalkī caste there will come a wrathful Kalkī king to whom the supreme gods, the kings of gods, bow in reverence.
> For holy ones, he will appear in peaceful form and be called "Bliss-Granter"; likewise, for the lineages of barbarians, he will appear as an annihilator.
> Mounted upon a stone horse, bearing a wheel, holding a spear to impale all enemies, brilliant as the sun!

This Kalkī king's vast and fierce armies will join forces with the twelve heavenly generals[494] and wage a powerful war in the entire southern region of Jambudvīpa. After defeating the entire barbarian faction, he will elucidate the Buddha's general teachings and the Vajrayāna. Once he has enthroned Brahmā as the king of the capital city [Kalāpa] of Shambhala and Indra as the king of the other parts of Jambudvīpa, he will propagate the Holy Dharma, and people's life spans and happiness will increase. This Kalkī king will go to the palace of Shambhala, and through the process of attaining the spiritual accomplishment of Mahāmudrā, his retinue and all those connected to him will go to a pureland of bliss.

Again, from the above-cited text:

> The army troops will all gather beneath him in battle to defeat the barbarians, and along with the powerful Viṣṇu,
> This Kalkī king will go to Mount Kailash, to the City of the Gods, the abode of the cakra bearers.
> At that time, all the castes of people on the Earth will have perfect Dharma, wealth, and fulfilled desires.
> Grains will grow in the wilderness, and trees will bow low with sturdy fruit. These things will come to pass.
> Having terminated the family lines of barbarians, along with beings encircling them,
> In fifty years, you will become an accomplished Kalkī who will depart for the lofty palace created by the gods, behind Mount Kailash.

This is but a small portion of a quite elaborate description.

Möpa Taye (Buddha Adhimukta)

22

In the future, as the final guide of this fortunate eon,
You will arise in the form of Sugata Möpa Taye.[495]
With the four limitless ways of subduing beings,
You will dredge the depths of the realms of beings—to you, I pray.

The first Perfect Guide of this fortunate eon was Buddha Krakucchaṃda, the second was Buddha Kanakamuni, and the third was Buddha Kāśyapa. These were the Buddhas of the past. The Buddha of the present is the fourth

Perfect Guide, King of the Śākyas, our refuge and protector of beings during the spread of the five degenerations. After the period of Buddha Śākyamuni's doctrine, Mipham Gönpo Gyalwa Jampa, "Invincible Protector, Victorious Loving One," also called the Future Buddha, Maitreya, and the rest [of the 1,000 Buddhas of this fortunate eon] will appear in succession, as prophesied in the *Fortunate Eon Sūtra*. **In the future,** [Kyabje Rinpoche will appear as] **the final guide of this fortunate eon**.

According to explanations found in the Mahāyāna scriptures, the mind of anyone who is classified as a sentient being is pervaded by Dharmakāya emptiness; the essential nature of sentient beings' minds, which is momentarily enveloped by the cocoon of temporary stains, is no different in nature, quality, rank, size, and so on, from the wisdom within the minds of Buddhas, who have purified the two obscurations; and sentient beings are all capable of becoming Buddhas. Through these three reasons, the cause of Buddha nature is established; and based on that, by exerting oneself exclusively in virtue, which is the path of accumulating merit and wisdom, one relies on the happy path of the Bodhisattva vehicle; and from this, the result is **Sugata**, "Gone to Bliss," going just as past Buddhas have gone from bliss to bliss. Previously, on the path of training, when they first generated the altruistic wish to attain supreme enlightenment, their aspiration was made according to their mind training in the four boundless wishes, with countless sentient beings as their object. Like a billion rivers swirling into one great ocean, the precious qualities of all the other Buddhas' life spans, enlightened deeds and activities, retinues, and pureland arrays will merge into the one who **will arise in the form of Sugata Möpa Taye**, who is from the pureland of Amitābha, "Boundless Light of Dedication," with the wisdom aspiration to shoulder the enormous burden single-handedly.

With the four limitless ways of subduing beings—subduing with wisdom body through vast merit, subduing with wisdom speech by granting spiritual instruction, subduing with wisdom mind through omniscient awareness, and subduing through inconceivable miraculous manifestations—he **will dredge the depths of the realms** of endless despair into which **beings** have plunged. Uplifting them, he will establish them in the supreme state of enlightenment, the place of eternal bliss. Buddha Adhimukta, **to you, I pray!**

As it says in the *Teaching on the Unfathomable Secrets of the Tathāgatas* from the *Heap of Jewels* sūtra collection:

To the right of the Transcendent Conqueror sat Vajrapāṇi wielding a vajra. Bodhisattva Śāntamati exhorted him, "Lord of Secrets, since you are seated beside the Tathāgata as his attendant, please reveal with your eloquent speech the secret topics of the Tathāgata, which are beyond the scope of Śrāvakas and Pratyekabuddhas, and of course that of ordinary sentient beings."

The Tathāgata, Sage of the Śākyas, also exhorted Vajrapāṇi with the same request, so the Lord of Secrets replied, "Long ago, from the time this Bhagāvan [Buddha Śākyamuni] was prophesied by Buddha Dīpaṃkara to become a Bodhisattva, I have constantly been his attendant. When I have explained to others a little of what secrets I have seen of the Bodhisattva's enlightened body, speech, and mind, describing it as being like this and like that, countless beings have benefitted."

At that time, some of the Bodhisattvas in the Tathāgata's retinue wondered, "How did the Lord of Secrets generate the merit to possess such eloquence? He has served and venerated all the Buddhas who have come. What sort of aspiration did he make to become like this?"

As they were thinking thus, the Transcendent Conqueror[496] spoke: "Long ago in times gone by, an inconceivable number of eons ago, during the beautifully illumined eon, there was a worldly realm called Perfectly Adorned, where a Tathāgata named King of Myriad Precious Boundless Qualities appeared. At that time, human life spans were 360 million years long. People did not experience untimely death, and the realm of the world was exceptionally prosperous and happy. Sentient beings had few passions, and everyone possessed the power to understand excellent teachings. In that worldly realm, there was a supremely prosperous, happy, and vast middle world[497] called Beautifully Illumined, with four continents. There, in the Palace of Perfect Purity, which was resplendent with vast riches, was a universal monarch named Dhṛtarāṣṭra, a nonreturner from unsurpassed enlightenment who wielded power over all four continents. He had a retinue of 700,000 queens, who were like precious gems, as well as 1,000 brave sons with marvelous physiques, all of whom entered the path to perfect enlightenment.

At that time, the Transcendent Conqueror, King of Myriad Precious Boundless Qualities, entered King Dhṛtarāṣṭra's Palace of Perfect Purity along with a Saṅgha of monks. King Dhṛtarāṣṭra reverently offered all his beautiful riches amassed over a full ten million years, listened attentively to the Conqueror's teachings, and gave rise to the five sublime states of perception.[498] Then, in order to venerate their father, Dhṛtarāṣṭra, the young princes built a mansion of rare and precious divine sandalwood. It was multistoried, vast, and spacious, with an area of ten square leagues, beautifully designed and richly adorned. Just half an ounce of this sandalwood was worth more than all of Jambudvīpa combined. King Dhṛtarāṣṭra, the princes, and their retinues of queens, servants, and companions entered the mansion, along with many offering substances, and the whole mansion magically rose up into space. Buddha King of Myriad Precious Boundless Qualities came there and placed the multistoried mansion back onto the ground, and everyone prostrated to the Tathāgata and listened to his teachings. The Tathāgata delighted and satisfied them with his Dharma discourse, and the king offered his entire kingdom to the Buddha.

Then, on one occasion during the full moon, when King Dhṛtarāṣṭra was enjoying music in his garden, his wives, Sadha and Anupama, were bathing upon a lion throne in a fine pool of lotuses. A beautiful, charming young prince seated in vajra posture miraculously appeared in each woman's lap. At that very moment, the gods cried down from the sky, "Hark! This one is Dharmacitta. That one is Dharmamati." And so the two boys received their names. As soon as the two boys appeared, they sat in indestructible vajra posture and uttered Dharma verses. They climbed down from their mothers' laps and prostrated before their father, who urged them to go before the Tathāgata. Father, mother, and princes all went before the Buddha and listened to teachings, with which they benefitted many sentient beings.

Then King Dhṛtarāṣṭra went into an isolated multistoried house and thought, "If all my young sons enter the path to perfect enlightenment, I wonder who will be the first to be enlightened?" He wrote down all of their names and placed them inside a vase made of seven precious materials. For seven days, he made offerings, and then, in front of his queens and sons, he drew the names out of the vase. The first name was that of Prince Viśuddhamati, and as soon as he retrieved it, the earth quaked violently and the spontaneous sound of crashing cymbals resounded. He would later become Tathāgata Krakucchaṃda. Similarly, the king drew forth the names of Vijayatisena, Santendriya, Sarvathasiddha, and Karagchen, who respectively became Buddha Kanakamuni, Buddha Kāśyapa, the present Buddha Śākyamuni, and the future Buddha Maitreya. Likewise, the king drew all thousand names, one by one, from Uttamamati to Chöpen Gyenpa, who would become the Tathāgatas Buddhasiṃha to Yönten Taye Dragpa, until he got to the very last one.

When King Dhṛtarāṣṭra drew the final name, that of the littlest prince, Lodrö Taye, all his brothers said, "We will have already matured all sentient beings. What will be left for you to do?"

The littlest prince replied, "The Buddha's teachings are like the sky, and sentient beings, too, will never end. So I will make the aspiration to have your combined life spans and other [qualities], and to perform deeds equal to all your deeds combined."

As soon as he had spoken, the voice of the gods rang out from space, "May it be so!"

Thus, the life span, number of virtuous followers, and deeds of Tathāgata Adhimukta, the last of the thousand Buddhas, will equal those of all the previous Tathāgatas of this fortunate eon combined.

Then the thousand princes said to Prince Dharmacitta and Prince Dharmamati, "Noble sons, what aspirations have you made?"

Sadha's son, Dharmacitta, replied, "Friends, I make the aspiration that I may enjoy your inner realization by becoming a wielder of the vajra, and without deviating from the secrets of the Tathāgathas, may I listen to, be inspired by, and realize all the outer and inner teachings of the Buddha."

Anupama's son, Dharmamati, replied, "I make the aspiration that I can request each of you to turn the Wheel of Dharma when you become Buddhas."

Thus, it is taught that King Dhṛtarāṣṭra became Buddha Dīpaṃkara, the thousand sons became the thousand Buddhas of this fortunate eon, the boy Dharmacitta became the Lord of Secrets, Vajrapāṇi, and the boy Dharmamati became Lord Brahmā.

Concluding Verses of Aspiration

23

By the power of praying with unshakable wholehearted devotion,
Throughout all my lifetimes, may I never be separate from you, Sovereign Protector.
By always worshipping you as my Crown Jewel,
May I have the good fortune to enjoy the amṛta of your wisdom speech.

These concluding prayers are written in twelve lines, symbolizing the level [of Buddhahood] called "lotus of nonattachment." Specifically, "**wholehearted**" means without any doubt or hesitation. [As it says in the Longchen Nyingtik Guru Yoga ngöndro prayer:]

I pray from the core of my heart,
Not merely mouthing the words.

The main organ that contains the body's vitality is the heart. From the depths of stainless mind, which is the source of the lamp of self-occurring prajñā that dwells within the lamp of the flesh heart [citta], come the three faiths—clear, enthusiastic, and confident.[499] With these, and without falling prey to pride and conceit, I pray with **devotion** of body, speech, and mind. **By the power of praying**, from now until I actualize the level of supreme enlightenment, **throughout all my lifetimes**, in as many rebirths as I require, in all times and directions, dwell as an adornment of my great-bliss crown cakra, as my refuge and **protector. By always worshipping you as my Crown Jewel, never separate from you, may I have the good fortune to** freely **enjoy the amṛta of** the teachings of **your wisdom speech**, which completely dispels the feverish torment of karma and passions.

24

By the power of your boundless great loving compassion,
You accepted me as a child of your heart.

May I awaken to my courageous and virtuous nature
So I can spread your enlightened activities in a hundred directions.

"**By the power of** all-pervading, **boundless great loving compassion—** the compassion of Nirmāṇakāya emanations—**you accepted me . . .**" is explained in a verse in the *Guhyagarbha Tantra*:

Supreme holy teacher and holy ones,
Bless me and think of me as your child and sibling.

As this expresses, you, Protector, accepted me **as your disciple, a child of your heart. May I awaken to my courageous and virtuous nature**, like Sudhana's,[500] **so I can spread your enlightened activities in a hundred directions.**

25

In the unexcelled Palace of Lotus Light,
In the one taste of the indivisible wisdom mind of the Guru and retinue,
May I attain fully manifest Buddhahood and become a Supreme Guide
For all infinite sentient beings throughout the far reaches of space.

In general, the places of sentient beings are determined by their various types of shared and specific karmic perceptions. They may dwell on the earth, above the earth, below the earth, and so on. Even in buddhafields, there are terrestrial realms and celestial realms. While it is indeed taught that buddhafields and places of sentient beings are inconceivably diverse, it is also said:

Ultimately, since there is no clinging to self,
There is no difference between places.

The sublime qualities encompassed by the state of Buddhahood are exceedingly superior to the qualities of worldly realms, so for this reason it is termed "**unexcelled.**" Likewise, the full array of qualities of the Kāyas and purelands of the five Buddha families throughout the infinite reaches of space is encompassed by the Lotus [Padma] family of enlightened speech, so in the realm of **Lotus Light**, which is made not of inanimate matter such as earth and stones but of light, we find Dharmakāya Amitābha, Sambhogakāya Avalokiteśvara, and Nirmāṇakāya Padmasambhava. This Trikāya teacher and retinue, whose enlightened bodies' major and minor marks are radiant with glorious majestic grandeur, whose unobscured enlightened speech is vividly resplendent, and whose unconfused enlightened mind is serenely clear, abide within an immeasurable and inconceivable **Palace**. Here, may the mind of my Vajra **Guru**, endowed with the three kindnesses,[501] and my own mind, so fortunately born as his **retinue** due to immeasurably vast merit accumulated in past lifetimes, become of **one taste**, an **indivisible wisdom mind**, like water being poured into water. Once having **attained fully manifest Buddhahood, may I become a Supreme Guide** who liberates **all infinite sentient beings throughout the far reaches of space**, and especially those with whom I have a connection, from saṃsāra's ocean of suffering.

Concluding Verses

Thus have I gathered mere flecks of Kyabje Rinpoche's oceanic activity,
Which are but a fraction of everything there is,
And with the thread of supremely pure intention
I have strung these gems into a necklace of liberated lifetimes,

To adorn the throats
Of supremely fortunate maidens
Who bloom with youth, faith, and diligence,
Nourished by the sublime food of previously accumulated merit.

To ensure that the pristine river of merit thus accumulated
Flows into the ocean of omniscience,
The billowing waves of aspiration surge,
Which are more than mere froth of flattery.

In particular, may all the leaders of humanity,
Reject the conduct of Indra's enemies,[502]
And follow respected holy leaders,
Governing with policies that benefit all.

May the mind of beings, like the rising orb of the moon,
Be unobscured by the sky's elephant[503] of wrong aspirations.
I pray that their virtues wax into fullness,
From light to the ultimate light.[504]

In the clear pool of the Three Piṭakas
Swim the guests with the threefold sublime knowing.[505]

May the swans[506] of the Supreme Assembly, the Saṅgha,
Pervade the full breadth of the ocean's raiments.[507]

May the Vidyādhara bees of the pinnacle vehicle's absolute meaning,[508]
Frolicking and hovering in the space of Dharmatā,
Hum the illuminating song of experience and realization,
And bedeck the lotus garden of the secret teachings.

First advancing the golden wheel with its thousand splendid spokes of the nine vehicles,
The four boundless wishes, like the branches of troops,[509] ended the battle of conditioned existence,
And the Great Secret teachings, the riches of the kingdom, satisfy fortunate beings.
May the feet of the universal monarch, our most kind Guru, be firmly planted in the essence of the five certainties.

The four streams of teachings of the Nyingma Early Translation school, endowed with the sixfold greatness,[510]
Were excellently drawn forth from the great cool lake of the bodhicitta of the charioteers[511] of the triple yogas.[512]
By the assembly of past translators and paṇḍitas of India and Tibet, who endured a hundred hardships,
May these never-dwindling streams swell to nourish the fields of fortunate beings.

In particular, the masters of hundreds of profound treasures, the earlier and later Vidyādharas [Dudjom Lingpa and Dudjom Jigdral Yeshe Dorje],
Brought back the king of wish-fulfilling jewels of profound instruction from the treasure island of the Three Kāyas.
Upon the fine robe of beings' merit, may these karmically destined ones, like gemstone traders,[513]
Always, in all ways, make offerings by turning the activity wheel of teaching and practice.

And may I, from now on, throughout my succession of lifetimes, never tumble off the cliff into the lower realms,

But rather, in the victorious palace of the Vajrayāna that arose upon the summit of the mountain of Buddha's teachings,
Where the Guru, Lord of the Buddha Family, offers a feast of supreme Dharma,
May I be inseparable from my Vajra family, nourished by the appearances of excellent good fortune.

May there be no talk of sickness for the countless beings resting in the lap of Jambudvīpa, our enchanting Mother Earth.
With timely scattering of cloud flowers, may we see young branches reveal their glistening beauty, and may medicinal herbs and crop spikes forever sway.
May all the warfare of the three fetters,[514] which are jealous of the glories of the four abundances,[515] be completely banished by the powerful weaponry of the ten virtues.[516]
By inviting the sun of a new golden age of peace and happiness as a guest in the sky of merit, may we enjoy the seven glorious qualities of higher rebirth.[517]

However densely the water ripples of the mirage of compounded samsaric phenomena form, may living beings, like keen-nosed deer, remain undeceived by them.
Wherever there is the amṛta of the Noble Eightfold Path[518] cascading down the mountainsides, clearing the suffering of thirst from conditioned existence, may we go there and enjoy it freely.
May we easily and instantly reach the holy medicinal land of ultimate goodness, rich with excellent qualities of exquisite tranquility, a pureland of glorious, perpetual joy,
The state where the wisdom realization of all infinite Buddhas inseparably merges, and forever become the same as them.

Formed within the auspicious endless knot at the heart center of Mahāhimasāgara,[519] in the world of forbearance that is our earthly sphere, in the lake where golden fish play,
Born from a wondrous, blazing lotus, the victory banner of your enlightened form bears the dazzling major and minor marks, and you hold the glorious, excellent vase of the treasure ocean of inexhaustible qualities;

With the wheel spokes of the four kinds of sublime activity, you destroy the passions of the three realms and fill the purelands of the threefold Buddha[520] with the sound of the conch of the supreme vehicle's Dharma;

In the lovely, cool shade of the compassion of a white umbrella, the one known as Tötreng Tsal, who twirls high above conditioned existence and the state of peace, may all our aspirations be fulfilled.[521]

This commentary on the supplication prayer to the successive rebirths of Kyabje Dudjom Rinpoche, called *The Ruby Rosary Joyfully Accepted by Vidyādharas and Ḍākinīs as the Ornament of a Necklace*, was written at the behest of the triply kind sovereign master and Great Treasure Revealer Dharma King Jigdral Yeshe Dorje's own direct disciple, Ngagchang Tsedrub Tharchin [Lama Tharchin Rinpoche], with whom I have shared an extremely loving friendship, right from the time we became playmates and Dharma brothers as young children, through to old age and senility. Over the years, he has plied me with gorgeous gifts, principally the five precious gems and metals and long silk offering scarves, and implored me to write this. Even though I am utterly destitute when it comes to the qualities of a scholar or the experience and realization of a practitioner and am unqualified to do so, in order to avoid confounding our auspicious connection, I closely consulted commentaries, annals, and Buddhist histories written by undisputed Buddhist scholars and combined them with my own understanding, taking care to prevent any shameless arrogance, pretension, or hypocrisy from arising in my mind. I completed this at my home, Kunzang Gatshal, in the north country bearing the sound of the unborn syllable ĀḤ,[522] on the twenty-fifth day of the eighth lunar month of the year of the Rabbit [1999], at the excellent, empowering time of night when cloud banks of offerings are set out in invitation to the hosts of Ḍākinīs of the Three Kāyas, in the middle of autumn, when the mountain forests and meadows are red, yellow, emerald, and turquoise, a splendid array of brightly colored leaves, and branches bow low with ripened fruits. My scribe was the Bhutanese Lama Phuntsok Gyaltsen. May this be the cause for the flourishing, propagation, and longevity of the Sūtra and Mantra teachings in general, and especially the teachings of the Great Secret Great Perfection!

Inspired by the drumstick of time and the six seasons,[523]
May living beings on the three planes of existence
Always hear the booming of the great Dharma drum of
Mahāsandhi,
The melodious roar of the primordial liberation of all existence.

Notes

1. Four seals: four teachings that apply to all phenomena: (1) All that is compounded is impermanent. (2) Anything that is flawed is suffering. (3) All phenomena are empty and selfless. (4) Nirvāṇa is peace.
2. The three planes (Tib. sa gsum) are below the earth, where nāgas dwell; on the earth, where humans and animals dwell; and above the earth, where devas (gods) dwell. A similar term, *'jig rten gsum*, is translated in this book as "three worlds."
3. Five inexhaustible wheels of ornaments (Tib. mi zad rgyan 'khor lnga): wheels of wisdom body, speech, mind, qualities, and activities.
4. Three faiths: clear faith, enthusiastic faith, and confident faith.
5. Selected words in this stanza are in bold type to indicate the names of Tragtung Dudjom Dorje [Dudjom Lingpa] and Jigdral Yeshe Dorje, to whom the homage is being made. *Tragtung* (Skt. Heruka) means "blood-drinking"; *dudjom* means "vanquisher of demons"; *dorje* means "vajra"; thus, *Tragtung Dudjom Dorje* means "Blood-Drinking Vajra, Vanquisher of Demons." *Jigdral* means "fearless" and *yeshe* means "wisdom"; thus, *Jigdral Yeshe Dorje* means "Fearless Wisdom Vajra."
6. Akaniṣṭha (Tib. 'og min): "the Beneathless Pureland That Is Above All" (Kyabje Thinley Norbu Rinpoche, *Cascading Waterfall of Nectar* [2009], p. 54).
7. Rupakāya (Tib. gzugs sku): "enlightened embodiment of form, which includes Sambhogakāya and Nirmāṇakāya" (*Cascading Waterfall of Nectar*, p. 4n5).
8. Dharmakaya pureland is just the basis of the arising of all the other purelands of the Sambhogakāya and Nirmāṇakāya, and should not be understood as something existing in reality.
9. The nine signs of a wisdom body of peaceful deities (Tib. zhi ba'i tshul dgu) are being delicate, flexible, intertwined, graceful, youthful, light, shining, glorious, and radiant (*Cascading Waterfall of Nectar*, p. 153). The nine expressions of the dance of wrathful deities (khro bo'i gar gyi nyams dgu) are the three aspects of wisdom body, which are captivating, heroic, and fierce; the three aspects of wisdom speech, which are attracting and laughing, harsh and threatening, and wrathful and thunderous; and the three aspects of wisdom mind, which are compassion, magnificent power, and tranquility (Kyabje Thinley Norbu Rinpoche, *The Small Golden Key*, pp. 83–84).

10. "Naturally fulfilled" here means self-accomplished. There is not anything to do; it is already complete.
11. Pure abodes (Skt. śuddhāvāsa): the five highest heavens of the gods of the form realms, where only Arhats abide. Of these five, the highest is Akaniṣṭha.
12. The Great Akaniṣṭha, or Great Ogmin ('og min), is a pureland of Buddha and not a worldly form realm.
13. The fulfilled male and female Bodhisattvas are in the form of Bodhisattvas, but they are already fully enlightened. See *Small Golden Key*, p. 9: "there are fulfilled Bodhisattvas whose wisdom minds are not different from that of the Buddha."
14. The common vehicles in this case refer to the Hīnayāna and the causal Mahāyāna.
15. The uṣṇīṣa (Tib. gtsug tor) is considered to be either the topknot of hair on Buddha's crown or a naturally elevated sign at the top of Buddha's head.
16. Silverstone (Tib. dobungwa; rdo bung ba): a type of medicinal mineral stone.
17. Svāstikas are a symbol of the quality of changelessness.
18. Lotus Mound or Great Bliss: Skt. Sukhāvatī, the pureland of Amitābha.
19. Highest Bodhisattva stage (Tib. sa bcu'i rgyun mtha'): the final stage of the stream of the tenth bhūmi, known as Clouds of Dharma (Skt. Dharmameghā). This is the pinnacle of the tenth bhūmi. At the very end of the stream of the tenth bhūmi, in the following instant, Buddhahood is attained.
20. Three Kāyas: the three "bodies" of Buddhahood. "The pure aspect of the essential nature is from the beginning the stainless Dharmakāya, completely pure formless form; the pure aspect of freedom from temporary obscuration, the immeasurable appearances of the qualities of Dharmakāya, is the Sambhogakāya, the immeasurable qualities of flawless inconceivable desireless exaltation form; and the manifestation of these Sambhogakāya appearances in the realms of sentient beings to guide them is the Nirmanakāya, unobstructed miraculous emanation form." Kyabje Thinley Norbu Rinpoche, *White Sail*, pp. 202–4, and *Cascading Waterfall of Nectar*, p. 53.
21. Luminous One: Skt. Prabhāsa.
22. Two accumulations: the accumulation of merit and the accumulation of wisdom.
23. The first seven bhūmis: (1) Supreme Joy (Skt. Pramuditā), (2) Stainlessness (Vimalā), (3) Radiance (Prabhākarī), (4) Shining Light (Arciṣmatī), (5) Purified Difficulties (Sudurjayā), (6) Undistorted Apparentness (Abhimukhī), (7) A Far Distance Away from the Hīnayāna (Dūraṅgamā).
24. "... he developed his accumulation of virtue from 77,000 Buddhas," i.e., from relying on 77,000 Buddhas.
25. The three pure Bodhisattva levels are the final three of the ten bhūmis: Unwavering (Acalā), Sublime Intelligence (Sādhumatī), and Clouds of Dharma (Dharmameghā).
26. Fourth Guide: Buddha Śākyamuni is considered to be the Fourth Guide of the 1,002 Buddhas of this fortunate eon.
27. Vehicle of Characteristics (Skt. Lakṣaṇayāna; Tib. rgyu mtshan nyid kyi theg

pa), also called the Vehicle of Cause or the Causal Vehicle: the yānas of the Śrāvakas, Pratyekabuddhas, and Bodhisattvas.

28. Three stages of enlightenment: the stages of enlightenment attained by an Arhat, a Pratyekabuddha, and a fully perfected Buddha.
29. Six Buddha Munis: the six supreme Nirmāṇakāya Buddhas who manifest in each of the six realms of existence: Indra (Kauśika) for the god realm; Vemacitra for the asura realm; Śākyamuni for the human realm; the king of lions, Dṛḍhasamādhāna, for the animal realm; Jvalamukhadeva for the preta realm; and Dharmarāja for the hell realm.
30. Five types of beings: gods, humans, animals, pretas, and hell beings. In this system, asuras are included in the category of gods.
31. Four ways of subduing beings: through the wisdom body of great merit, through teaching with wisdom speech, through pure awareness mind, and through inconceivable miraculous activities.
32. Ten directions: north, south, east, west, northwest, northeast, southeast, southwest, above, and below.
33. Six worlds: the realms of the six classes of beings.
34. To ripen beings means to bring the minds of sentient beings to a state of readiness for abandoning passions while simultaneously approaching enlightenment.
35. Two benefits: benefitting oneself (by attaining the Dharmakāya) and benefitting others (by attaining the Rupakāya).
36. Six clairvoyant realizations: the ability to see what is beyond ordinary sight, to hear what is beyond ordinary hearing, to know the minds of others, to know one's own and others' past lives, to perform miracles, and to know the exhaustion of the defilements.
37. Twelve deeds of a Buddha: descending from Tuṣita, entering the womb, taking birth, becoming skilled in the arts, enjoying the company of royal consorts, renouncing the world, practicing asceticism, proceeding to Bodhgayā, vanquishing hosts of demons, attaining perfect enlightenment, turning the Wheel of Dharma, and passing into parinirvāṇa.
38. Sublime knowledge: Skt. prajñā. Tib. shes rab.
39. Dīpaṃkara (Tib. mar me mdzad): Dīpaṃkara Buddha lived prior to the lifetime of Buddha Śākyamuni. In the time of Dīpaṃkara, the Buddha was incarnated as a hermit named Sumedha. In the *Vajra Sūtra* (or *Vajracchedika Sūtra*) the Buddha describes how Dīpaṃkara prophesied that Sumedha would become the future Buddha Śākyamuni.
40. Jambudvīpa: in Buddhist cosmology, the world in which we live.
41. Five visions: the place, Jampudvīpa; the time, when humans have 100-year life spans; the father, Śuddhodana; the mother, Māyādevī; and the caste, Ikṣvākus.
42. The full verse spoken by the Buddha at the time of his birth:

    I am supreme in this world.
    Eldest am I in the world,

Foremost am I in the world.
This is the last birth.
There is now no more coming to be.

43. Universal monarch (Skt. cakravartin; Tib. 'khor los bsgyur ba): A universal monarch is said to exist only during the times when human life spans are immeasureably long, up to 80,000 years. With golden, silver, copper, and iron wheels, the universal monarchs rule the four human continents: Pūrvavideha in the east, Jambudvīpa in the south, Aparagodānīya in the west, and Uttarakuru in the north.
44. Mahāprajāpatī Gautamī: Buddha's maternal aunt and adoptive mother. She was the first woman to request ordination from the Buddha and to join the Saṅgha.
45. Translation of this verse by Kyabje Thinley Norbu Rinpoche, *Sunlight Speech That Dispels the Darkness of Doubt*, p. 105.
46. Four great rivers of human suffering: birth, aging, sickness, and death.
47. Four Great Kings: the guardian deities of the four cardinal directions—Kubera in the north, Yama in the south, Indra in the east, and Varuṇa in the west.
48. Stūpa of Great Purity: Viśuddha Stūpa. According to Kyabje Dudjom Rinpoche, *Nyingma School of Tibetan Buddhism*, p. 30 of Notes for part 1, n400: "According to [E. Lamotte, *Histoire du Bouddhisme Indien*], p. 346, this incident occurred near Rāmagrāma, east of Kapilavastu. Khetsun Zangpo Rinpoche, however, informs us of a contemporary Indian view that the Sacred Stūpa (mchod-rten rnam-dag) was situated near Mankapur in Uttar Pradesh."
49. King Suprabuddha was Prince Siddhārtha's uncle (brother of Queen Māyā) and father-in-law (father of Yaśodharā).
50. Vajra Seat (Tib. rdo rje gdan): a reference to Bodhgayā.
51. Tenma: Tib. bstan ma. Skt. Sthāvarā.
52. Before Buddha's enlightenment had occurred, Māra cast doubt on it, demanding to know who would testify to Buddha's attainment. When the Earth Goddess Tenma bore witness to it, Māra was humiliated.
53. The four samādhis: see *Nyingma School of Tibetan Buddhism*, p. 61, where the four samādhis are translated as the "four concentrations."
54. Four Noble Truths: the truth of suffering, the truth of the cause of suffering, the truth of the cessation of suffering, and the truth of the path (the means to the end of suffering).
55. Rāhula and Ānanda: Rāhula was the Buddha's only son. According to the Mūlasarvāstivāda Vinaya, the tradition of monastic discipline followed in Tibetan Buddhism, Rāhula was conceived on the evening that Prince Siddhārtha left the palace and was born six years later, during the lunar eclipse on the day that the Buddha attained enlightenment. Ānanda was one of Buddha's closest disciples and his devoted attendant, renowned for his perfect remembrance of the Buddha's teachings.
56. The moon escaping from Rāhu is related to the lunar eclipse. *Rāhu* is a term for

a "planet" in Indo-Tibetan astrology, and is the name of an asura who seized the moon and the sun; the Buddha released them (*Samyutta Nikāya*). So the moon escaping from Rāhu is a metaphor for liberation.

57. Five noble ones: Buddha's first five disciples—Kauṇḍinya, Aśvajit, Bhadrika, Vāṣpa, and Mahānāma—who received the first teaching Buddha gave after his enlightenment, on the Four Noble Truths.
58. "Do not address the Tathāgata as 'Living One'": "Living One" is an expression for ordinary living people, so it is inappropriate to use it for the enlightened Buddha.
59. Twelve aspects: the three categories of the recognition of the essence, the practice of the action, and the realization of the result applied to each of the Four Noble Truths: what the essence of suffering is, suffering is to be understood, and suffering is understood; what the essence of the origin of suffering is, the origin of suffering is to be abandoned, the origin of suffering is abandoned; what the essence of cessation is, cessation is to be actualized, cessation is actualized; what the essence of the path is, the path is to be meditated on, the path has been meditated on.
60. Vulture Peak: Gṛdhakūṭa, a small mountain outside the city of Rajgir, India, the ancient capital of Magadha.
61. Anāthapiṇḍada: the chief male lay disciple of Lord Buddha and one of his wealthiest and most generous patrons.
62. Laywoman: Skt. and Pāli upāsikā (layman: upāsaka). Laypersons uphold the five vows of abstaining from killing, stealing, lying, sexual misconduct, and taking intoxicants.
63. Aggregates (Skt. skandha): form (rūpa), feeling (vedanā), perception (saṃjñā), intention (saṃskāra), and consciousness (vijñāna).
64. Flesh debts: karmic debts accrued from killing others that are later repaid by being killed.
65. Uḍumbara (Skt): Scriptures describe the uḍumbara flower as coming from heavenly realms and flowering only once every 3,000 years. It symbolizes the rebirth of the Buddha.
66. Heaven of the Thirty-Three: Skt. Trāyastriṃśa. Tib. sum cu rtsa gsum.
67. Three Jewels: Buddha, Dharma, Saṅgha.
68. Central land: a land where Dharma flourishes.
69. Ārya (Tib. 'phags pa), translated as "noble one" or "sublime being." Āryas are those who have directly realized emptiness and thus have risen above the state of an ordinary being.
70. Tripiṭaka: the three "baskets" of Buddhist teachings. These are Vinaya, teachings on discipline and behavior; Sūtra, teachings on meditation; and Abhidharma, teachings on sublime knowledge (Skt. prajña).
71. Ten points or transgressions: (1) After committing an act that goes against the Vinaya, clapping one's hands and saying *hulu hulu* purifies this downfall. (2) Rejoicing over those who act according to Dharma purifies one's own negative

deeds. (3) Everyone uses this earth, so even fully ordained monks can dig it. (4) If one is sick, one is allowed to sip alcohol from a pot with a hole in the way a leech does. (5) Sprinkling salt on a meal from an approved time allows one to enjoy it in the evening. (6) Traveling about two miles on a road is enough to allow one to eat again, and there is no need for traveling a half a league (about eight miles). (7) One is permitted to take an additional meal by touching it with one's two fingers. (8) One can have stirred milk and yogurt in the evening or at any unapproved time. (9) To make a new mat, it is permissible to use a patch measuring the length of the space between one's extended middle finger and thumb, taken from an old mat. It is not required for the patch to be as big as the space between Buddha's extended finger and thumb (which is said to be three times longer that those of ordinary people). (10) Receiving offerings, such as gold or silver, in a begging bowl adorned with a flower garland set on a small pedestal that is placed on a novice monk's head will allow a fully ordained monk to use these offerings. See also *Nyingma School of Tibetan Buddhism*, p. 32 of Notes, n429. Other versions of the ten points exist in other Buddhist traditions.

72. Profound View and Vast Conduct: the two main traditions of the Mahāyāna, founded by Nāgārjuna and Asaṅga, respectively.
73. Śāstra: a treatise or commentary on Buddha's words.
74. Pureland of Great Bliss: Sukhāvatī, the pureland of Buddha Amitābha.
75. Accomplishment: Skt. siddhi. Tib. dngos grub. Common accomplishment is thun mong gi dngos grub, and supreme accomplishment is chog gi dngos grub. In *White Sail*, p. 204, *siddhi* is defined as "accomplishment, including general [common] accomplishment within substantial existence and supreme accomplishment, which is enlightenment."
76. Five sciences: art, medicine, language, logic, and philosophy.
77. Eighth Bodhisattva level: Unwavering (Acalā).
78. Śrī Parvata: the abode of Saraha, a mountain in South India where Nāgārjuna spent his last days.
79. Tīrthika: heretical or non-Buddhist.
80. *Mahāyāna Samucchaya*: Tib. *theg pa chen po bsdus pa*. *Abhidharma Samucchaya*: Tib. *chos mngon pa kun las btus pa*.
81. Logic: Skt. pramāṇa.
82. Bliss-Gone Buddha: Skt. Sugata; Tib. Deshek; bde gshegs.
83. Wisdom permission (Tib. rjes su gnang ba): honorific term for granting permission with blessing.
84. Pañcalika: a kind of divine silk having a very special quality of being light, smooth, and precious.
85. Chalk scholar: Śiva ordered Viṣṇu to appear in the form of magical chalk to help provide Maticitra with written answers for debate.
86. Seven sections of Abhidharma: Tib. mngon pa sde bdun. Treatises compiled by seven Arhats.

87. Uṣṇīṣavijayā (Tib. gtsug tor rnam rgyal ma): a goddess who is one of the three long-life deities.
88. Greater Khecara (Tib. mkha' spyod chen po): *Khecara* means "enjoying the sky." Greater Khecara is an accomplishment with eight attainments: one's body becomes extremely (1) subtle, (2) light, (3) and pervasive throughout the three worlds; (4) one attains the qualities of Buddha, (5) one has clear wisdom phenomena, (6) wisdom phenomena are constant, and (7) one has power over all beings and (8) the ability to transform into whatever one wishes.
89. Threefold knowledge (Tib. gsum rig pa): knowledge of previous lifetimes, knowledge of future lifetimes, and knowledge of the cessation of defilements.
90. "The first of these": the first of the seven wondrous anecdotes just mentioned, the pleasing of the supreme Yidam deity. Each of these seven wondrous anecdotes is mentioned in the following life story of Śāntideva.
91. Spiritual friend (Skt. kalyānamitra; Tib. dge ba'i bshes gnyen): a Dharma teacher or Guru.
92. This is the thirty-fourth verse in the ninth ("Wisdom") chapter of the *Way of the Bodhisattva*. The translation is by Kyabje Thinley Norbu Rinpoche, in *Cascading Waterfall of Nectar*, p. 120.
93. The sword held by Mañjuśrī represents wisdom, cutting through ignorance and duality.
94. Upāsaka (Skt. and Pāli, masc.): a layman who upholds the five vows of abstaining from killing, stealing, lying, sexual misconduct, and taking intoxicants.
95. Four great praises: *Praise to Mañjuśrī with the Tilted Head*; *Praise to the Pointing Avalokiteśvara*; *Praise to the Tathāgata Who Surpasses Worldly Gods*; and *Praise to Tārā Who Holds a Flower Garland.*
96. The New Translation (Sarma) tradition includes the three newer schools: Kagyu, Sakya, and Geluk.
97. Shambhala: Skt. Śambhala.
98. Twelve masters renowned at Vikramaśīla University: Jñānapada, Dīpaṃkarabhadra, Laṅkajayabhadra, Śrīdhara, Bhavabhadra, Bhayakīrti, Vilāsavajra, Durjayacandra, Samayavajra, Tathāgatarakṣita, Bodhibhadra, and Kamalarakṣita.
99. Six Scholarly Gatekeepers: Śāntipa, Nāropa, Vagisvakīrti, Prajñākāragupta, Jñānaśrī, and Ratnavajra.
100. According to the Dro Kālacakra tradition, Kālacakrapada the Elder (early 11th c.) was the first Indian to receive the Kālacakra tradition. Kālacakrapada the Younger, also known as Śrībhadra, was the primary disciple of Kālacakrapada the Elder.
101. Wisdom Mind Lineage of the Victorious Ones, Gesture Lineage of the Vidyādharas, and Lineage of Personally Heard Teachings Given by Voice: This translation of the names of the three lineages follows that of Kyabje Thinley Norbu Rinpoche, in *Cascading Waterfall of Nectar*, pp. 167–68.
102. Sixth Buddha family: the embodiment of all the five Buddha families. "That

which is called the five Buddha families contains the inconceivable classes of all Buddhas synthesized into five families. Within each family, all the qualities of each of the other four families are perfectly complete and integrated. The distinction of the enlightened body, speech, mind, qualities, and activities of each family is called the Dharma of the result of twenty-five distinctions. Beyond that, there are hundreds, thousands, and millions of incalculable, inconceivable families and distinctions that are all praised as the appearance of all the aspects of enlightened qualities" (*Cascading Waterfall of Nectar*, p. 54).

103. Commentaries on the *Secret Essence Tantra*: Although a specific text is not identified, the quotation given here can be found in commentaries on the *Secret Essence* (*Guhyagarbha*) from the Zur tradition, such as the *Words of the Lord of Secrets* (*gsang bdag zhal lung*) by Lochen Dharmaśrī and the *Key to the Precious Treasury* (*rin chen mdzod kyi lde'u mig*) by Dodrub Tenpe Nyima.
104. Luminous Vajra Essence (Tib. 'od gsal rdo rje snying po): synonymous with the Great Perfection (Dzogchen) in general and the Upadeśa Section (man ngag gi sde) in particular.
105. Five Buddha families: Buddha, Vajra, Ratna (Jewel), Padma (Lotus), Karma (Action).
106. Resultant Bodhisattvas: fulfilled Bodhisattvas who have attained the result of fully enlightened Buddhahood.
107. Nāda: "dissolving in stainless sky, never permanently remaining in material, never permanently remaining in nothingness, in indivisible clarity and emptiness, to finally disappear in Dharmakāya's state. The nāda is not necessary to visualize; it is a demonstration or sign to abide in stainless, sole tig-le, immeasurable Dharmakāya. The ultimate phenomenon is the nāda" (*Cascading Waterfall of Nectar*, p. 155).
108. King of the great: Here, the king is Buddha, who is the principal Buddha of all Buddhas and therefore the king of the great.
109. Vajra mind: the mind of Buddha.
110. Sucandra, also known as King Sucandra and Dharmarāja Sucandra, was a contemporary of Buddha Śākyamuni who received the Kālacakra teachings from Buddha a year after Buddha attained enlightenment, and then passed away in the second year after receiving those teachings.
111. State of Vajradhara: enlightenment.
112. Three guiding vehicles: the Śrāvaka, Pratyeka, and Bodhisattva yānas.
113. The certain vehicle is Vajrayāna in this case. These are Secret Mantra teachings.
114. Five lineages: Śrāvakas, Pratyekabuddhas, Tathāgatas, Anyagotra (indeterminate lineage), and Agotraka (those without lineage).
115. Here, mamos are extraordinary treasure protectors and are positive, with eyes of wisdom.
116. There are many different categories of Ḍākinīs, and here they are Ḍākinīs who possess eyes of wisdom. Descriptions of different kinds of Ḍākinīs can be found in *Cascading Waterfall of Nectar*, e.g., pp. 272–73.

117. Three heavens: Akaniṣṭha (Tib. 'og min), Tuṣita (dga' ldan), and Trāyastriṃśa, or Heaven of the Thirty-Three (sum cu rtsa gsum).
118. Kyabje Thinley Norbu Rinpoche states here that the middle Indrabhūti is King Ja. This is also how Kyabje Dudjom Rinpoche identifies King Ja in *Nyingma School of Tibetan Buddhism*, p. 458.
119. Abandoning and accepting: abandoning previous worldly conduct and accepting the new, uncertain conduct of a yogin.
120. This explanation is based on the Zur tradition of classifying the eighteen great Mahāyoga tantras. There is also another way of classifying the eighteen tantras, into four sections, based on the explanation of Omniscient Longchenpa, not discussed in this book.
121. Five inner tantras: *Union of All Buddhas*; *Secret Moon Essence*; *Gathering of Secrets*; *Glorious Supreme Beginning*; and *Garland of Activity*.
122. Ācārya Vilāsavajra is also known as Līlāvajra and Gegpa Dorje (Tib. sgeg pa rdo rje) or Gegpe Dorje (sgeg pa'i rdo rje).
123. Ṣaṃṣara: Tib. Sham Sha ra.
124. Vajrakāya (Tib. rdo rje'i sku): "The main object of refuge is the pure aspect of the essential nature, which is from the beginning the stainless Dharmakāya; the pure aspect of freedom from temporary obscuration, the immeasurable appearances of the qualities of Dharmakāya, as the Sambhogakāya; and the manifestation of these Sambhogakāya appearances in the realms of sentient beings to guide them, the Nirmanakāya. These are the Three Kāyas. Although these Three Kāyas appear separately from the aspects of their qualities, they are actually indivisible as Svabhavikakāya, or Vajrakāya, which is the fourth Kāya" (*Cascading Waterfall of Nectar*, p. 53).
125. Vajradhātu maṇḍala: an important sādhana of Mahāyoga containing the forty-two peaceful deities.
126. "Tibet is deeply indebted to him": During his stay at Mount Kailash, Buddhaguhya gave teachings on the *Guhyagarbha* cycle to several prominent Tibetan disciples, including De Jampal and the translator Drenka Mukti.
127. Kama (Tib. bka' ma): the Buddha's Speech.
128. Three abodes: the abodes that are below the ground, on the ground, and above the ground. The Vīras and Ḍākinīs of the three abodes are in these three places.
129. Three obscurations: the obscurations of body, speech, and mind.
130. Eight Sādhana Teachings: the sādhana practices of the Eight Herukas, the ultimate Yidams of the Nyingma tradition.
131. Fully Ripened Vidyādhara (Tib. rnam par smin pa'i rig 'dzin): one of the four kinds of Vidyādhara, in which the mind has ripened as the enlightened body of wisdom deity.
132. Immortal Vidyādhara (Tib. tshe la dbang ba'i rig 'dzin): the Awareness Holder with the Power Over Life.
133. Irreversible stage: The "stage of no-return," so called because one will never return to saṃsāra.

134. Kula Dzogpa ("Perfected in Body"): one of the eight great charnel grounds that comprise the peaceful maṇḍala. It lies to the south.
135. Life force: Tib. srog. This term is contrasted with Tib. *zungs*, translated as "vitality."
136. Haughty spirits: Tib. dregs pa can.
137. ". . . a great bolt of lightning that liberated the tīrthika teachers": For the verb *sgrol ba* (to liberate) as it is used here: "The use of wrathful enlightened activity relying on a wrathful torma and using wrathful means, directed toward the defilements and bad karma of sentient beings in order to liberate them from suffering are special exceptions that are necessary and important during the lower activity of liberating enemies and obstructing forces, only for the benefit of others and never for one's own power. This activity is not to be carried out as a regular practice for any other reason. In order to clean one's own fear, paranoia, and any negativity, this method of transforming negative energy to positive comes from inner tantric teachings. It has nothing to do with anything in reality. Whoever practices this has to realize that all phenomena are like magic, like a magician who displays magic without believing it is true or that it exists in reality, in order to annihilate reality. It is the practice of transforming one's own previous reality paranoia and negative feeling into wisdom manifestation. New practitioners must understand this; otherwise, from thinking of reality, they can cause misconceptions about tantric teachings. Murders and killing can continuously be seen in reality, and people are interested in watching these on television without any point of view. These precious teachings are not like that, but are to transform negative habit into positive through many skillful means, with point of view, meditation, and activities" (*Cascading Waterfall of Nectar*, p. 254).
138. Three defilements: desire, existence, and ignorance.
139. Four classes of Tantra: Kriyā, Caryā, Yoga, and Anuttarayoga tantras.
140. State of indivisibility: the state of Vajradhara, which is the indivisibility of Dharmakāya and Rupakāya.
141. Transference: Tib. powa; 'pho ba.
142. Kama (Tib. bka' ma): "the spoken teachings, which come from Dorje Chang to one's present root guru in an unbroken lineage" (Kyabje Thinley Norbu Rinpoche, *Small Golden Key*, p. 22). Terma: treasures; "the precious sacred articles and Dharmas which were hidden until the time was appropriate for them to be revealed. These terma were hidden by Padmasambhava and other tertons, great saints having special marks or signs, in the ordinary places of the earth, lakes and oceans, rocks, trees, and the sky, and in the extraordinary places of the four directions and the center. At the times when the terma are of most benefit, the tertons uncover these sacred treasures." (*Small Golden Key*, p. 22).
143. There are four branches of the Vedas: *Ṛgveda*, *Yajurveda*, *Samaveda*, and *Atharvaveda*.
144. Activity emanations: emanations of the deity who appear in order to assist the

practitioner by enacting the four kinds of sublime activity (peaceful, increasing, powerful, and wrathful activities).

145. Four activity rituals: peaceful, increasing, powerful, and wrathful activities.
146. One widely known biography of Nāgārjuna is in *bka' babs bdun ldan gyi brgyud pa'i rnam thar* (The Liberating Biographies of the Lineage of Seven Transmissions) by Tāranātha.
147. Eight common accomplishments: the siddhis of making medicinal pills, making eye ointment for clairvoyance, power over realms underground, the sword of invincibility, swift feet, invisibility, deathlessness, and overcoming sickness.
148. Spending 200 years at Śrī Parvata: All told, it is said that Nāgārjuna lived for 600 years.
149. Viśuddha Mind: the practice of Yangdak Heruka, which is the practice of enlightened mind and is one of the Eight Sādhana Teachings of the Mahāyoga tantras. *Viśuddha* (Tib. yang dak) means "extremely pure."
150. His flower landed on the wrathful Hūṃkāra: This flower refers to the moment during an empowerment when the disciple tosses a flower of awareness (the flower representing the disciple's awareness) onto an image of the maṇḍala, which is divided into four quadrants in the four cardinal directions and the center, representing the five Buddha families. The place where the flower lands determines the disciple's Yidam deity.
151. Two stages: development stage and completion stage.
152. Great accomplishment stage: the fourth of the four stages of approach and accomplishment, which are approach, close approach, accomplishment, and great accomplishment. The short form of this term, *sgrub chen*, is used for a traditional elaborate ritual sādhana ceremony performed as a group practice that often lasts for ten days or more. The full term, *sgrub pa chen po*, is used for the stage of practice that is defined here in this note.
153. Thirty times six: thirty days times six, meaning six months.
154. Accomplishment of the sublime sovereign of all Buddha families: the state of Vajradhara, often described as the sixth Buddha family.
155. Hūṃkāra falls into the foremost: that is, the foremost of these time categories (six months).
156. Twelve Mātaraḥ: also known as the twelve Tenma sisters, female protector deities of Tibet, bound under oath by Guru Padmasambhava.
157. The Eight Sādhana Teachings were transmitted to the eight Vidyādharas and Padmasambhava by the Ḍākinī Lekyi Wangmoche (Mahākarmamendranī), who received the Vajrayāna teachings from Vajrasattva.
158. Eight Great Realized Masters: Mañjuśrīmitra, Nāgārjuna, Hūṃkāra, Vimalamitra, Prabhāhasti, Dhanasaṃskṛta, Rambuguhya, and Śāntigarbha.
159. Zi: a precious type of agate with special qualities, used as an amulet and as medicine.
160. Awareness: Tib. rigpa; rig pa.

161. Three realms (Tib. khams gsum): the desire realm, the form realm, and the formless realm.
162. Three categories of the Great Perfection: Tib. sems sde (Mind), klong sde (Expanse), and man ngag sde (Skt. Upadeśa).
163. "Our shared Supreme Nirmāṇakāya," Buddha Śākyamuni, appeared in this world and taught, so we have the shared phenomena of the manifestation of Buddha.
164. Dharmagañja (Skt.): "Treasury of Dharma," a palace where all the Secret Mantra tantras reside, located in Orgyen Khandro Ling, the Island of Ḍākinīs in Oḍḍiyāna.
165. Eight precepts of lay ordination: abstaining from killing; stealing; adultery; lying; taking intoxicants; using a high seat or bed; singing, dancing, and using perfume or ornaments; and having evening meals.
166. Ten powers: power over life, power of mind, power of resources, power of activities, power of birth, power of devotion, power of aspiration, power of miraculous abilities, power of Dharma, and power of wisdom.
167. The three types of treasures are Tib. sa gter (earth treasures), dgongs gter (mind treasures), and dag snang (pure visions).
168. Great charioteers: the guides, leaders, and founders of Buddhism, and specifically in this reference, the treasure revealers.
169. The masang (Tib. ma sangs) and the triad of cha (phywa), mu (dmu), and tsuk (gtsug) are various spirits and gods of the Bönpos of Tibet.
170. Temples for subduing and re-subduing borders were built to protect Tibet from negative forces beyond its borders.
171. Trisong Detsen: The lifetime dates 790– 858 are given for King Trisong Detsen by Kyabje Dudjom Rinpoche in *The Nyingma School of Tibetan Buddhism* and quoted by Kyabje Thinley Norbu Rinpoche.
172. The inscription, a prophecy written on a copper plate, said: "Five reigns from now, in the time of my descendant King De, the true doctrine will be propagated" (*Nyingma School of Tibetan Buddhism*, pp. 512–13).
173. Eighteen elements: the six senses, the six sense objects, and the six sense-consciousnesses.
174. Twelve links of interdependence: ignorance; intention; consciousness; name and form; sense sources; touch; sensation; craving; grasping; becoming; birth; and old age and death.
175. Translation by Kyabje Thinley Norbu Rinpoche in *Cascading Waterfall of Nectar*, p. 106.
176. Four kinds of sublime activity: peaceful, increasing, powerful, and wrathful.
177. Mangyul: the border area between Tibet and Nepal, sometimes called Mangyul Gungthang or Ngari Me (Lower Ngari), which was on an important route between the northern and southern Himalayas, through which Padmasambhava and Śāntarakṣita arrived in Tibet.

178. Twelve Tenma sisters: protector deities of Tibet who were bound under oath by Guru Rinpoche.
179. Thirteen great gods: mountain gods called on in songs of praise by the kings of Tibet, such as Songtsen Gampo and Trisong Detsen. They are said to be protectors of these kings.
180. Twenty-one genyen (Tib. dge bsnyen): a group of local spirits of Tibet who were sworn to be guardians of the Dharma after being subdued by Guru Rinpoche.
181. Four continents: Pūrvavideha (Noble Body) in the east; Jambudvīpa in the south (Land of Jambud Trees); Aparagodānīya (Bountiful Cow) in the west; and Uttarakuru (Ominous Sound) in the north.
182. Vairotsana: The name of this Tibetan translator is often spelled *Vairocana*, but here *Vairotsana* is given, the spelling used by Ani Jinba Palmo in her translation of his biography (*The Great Image* [Boston: Shambhala Publications, 2004]), in order to distinguish the historical translator from Buddha Vairocana and to align more closely with the Tibetan pronunciation, "Berotsana."
183. Seven men to be tested: the first seven monks to be ordained in Tibet by the Great Abbot Śāntarakṣita.
184. Greatness of the inviting patron: the first of the six perfect aspects of greatness of the Nyingma that follow in the text.
185. Haughty One: Here, a reference to the Black Powerful One.
186. The Black Powerful One: the main deity in the Wrathful Mantra Incantations sādhana teaching.
187. Drapa Ngönshe: the tertön who revealed the *Four Medical Tantras*, the root texts of the Tibetan medical tradition, in 1038 at Samye, where they had been concealed by Vairotsana.
188. Four and six special classes of tantra: The four classes of tantra are Kriyātantra, Upatantra, Yogatantra, and Anuttarayoga tantra. The six classes of tantra are the three outer tantras of Kriyātantra, Upatantra, and Yogatantra, and the three inner tantras of Mahāyoga, Anuyoga, and Atiyoga.
189. Amṛta Quality of the Ratna family: one of the Eight Herukas.
190. Life-supporting wolf spirits: In this history, the subtle life essence (Tib. bla) that circulates within the body was being held in the external support of wolf spirits, and whatever occurred to the external support would also occur to Chim Jarok, whose life essence was being held there.
191. Lineage holder of Sūtra, *Magical Infinity*, and Mind (Tib. mdo sgyu sems gsum): The word *mdo* refers to the *Embodiment of Wisdom Mind* and four other sūtras of Anuyoga; *sgyu* refers to *sgyu 'phrul drwa ba* (*Magical Infinity*), and particularly the *Guhyagarbha Tantra*, and the Tantra sections and Sādhana sections of Mahāyoga; and *sems* refers to the five sections of mother tantras translated by Vairotsana and the thirteen children sections translated by Vimalamitra and Yudra Nyingpo. Thus, this expression is used to refer to the holder of the main Kama teachings of the Nyingma tradition of Mahā, Anu, and Ati.

192. ". . . the Early Translation Vajrayāna teachings fell to Nub in the middle period": According to a common saying, the teachings "fell first to Nyak, fell to Nub during the intermediate period, and fell to Zur in the end" (*Nyingma School of Tibetan Buddhism*, p. 599).
193. Drusha: Gilgit, now in Xinjiang Uygur Autonomous Region.
194. Lords of the Ḍākinīs: Mātaraḥ and Yamāntaka.
195. Great bhūmi: the eighth, ninth, and tenth bhūmis.
196. Three development and completion stages: the stages of development, completion, and Great Perfection.
197. Four rivers of empowerment: the empowerment of the Yidam deity, the empowerment of the volumes of the tantras, the empowerment of the unobstructed power of self-awareness, and the empowerment of the spiritual teacher.
198. Three stages of ordination: lay ordination, novice ordination, and full ordination.
199. Three Vehicles of Characteristics: the yānas of the Śrāvakas, Pratyekabuddhas, and Bodhisattvas.
200. *Vairocana* refers here to the *Tantra of the Awakening of Great Vairocana*. See the entry *Vairocana* in the bibliography.
201. Rulu mantra: the mantra of Yangdak Heruka.
202. Brahmā Crowned with Conch Shells: one of the guardians of the ten directions. He guards the zenith.
203. Offering text: prayers of request for Dharmapālas.
204. Eight Close Sons: the Bodhisattvas Mañjuśrī, Vajrapāṇi, Avalokiteśvara, Kṣitigarbha, Sarvanīvaraṇavikṣambin, Ākāśagarbha, Maitreya, and Samantabhadrī.
205. Seven Buddhas of the past (also called the seven successive Buddhas): The first three Buddhas (Vipaśyin, Śikhin, and Viśvabhū) are from the previous eon, and the remaining four Buddhas (Krakucchaṃda, Kanakamuni, Kāśyapa, and Śākyamuni) are from this fortunate eon.
206. Eight fears: fear of lions, elephants, fire, snakes, rivers, captivity, thieves, and flesh-eating demons.
207. Lords of the Three Families: Avalokiteśvara, Mañjuśrī, and Vajrapāni.
208. Wheel of Life (Skt. bhāvacakra): symbolic image of saṃsāra, with its six realms of beings.
209. Three times: past, present, and future.
210. Five paths: the path of accumulation, the path of joining, the path of seeing, the path of meditation, and the path of no more learning.
211. Nine yānas: Śrāvakayāna, Pratyekabuddhayāna, Bodhisattvayāna, Kriyāyāna, Upayāna, Yogayāna, Mahāyāna, Anuyāna, and Atiyāna.
212. Eight Gaurī: blue Gaurī in the east, yellow Caurī in the south, red Pramohā in the west, black Vetālī in the north, orange Pukkasī in the southeast, dark yellow Ghasmarī in the southwest, dark blue Śmaśānī, in the northwest, and pale yellow Cāṇḍalī in the northeast.
213. Zurchungpa is playing with puns that are not possible to express in English

translation. The Tibetan *sdig pa* means both "misdeed" and "scorpion," and the word *bshags* means both "confess" and "cleave" or "split."

214. "... those who rely on words rather than on meaning": This is a reference to the "four reliances." They are as follows: Rely on the pure teachings of Buddha, not on a person with an ordinary mind full of passions; rely on the meaning, not on the words; rely on the absolute meaning, not on the relative meaning; rely on wisdom, not on ordinary consciousness (Kyabje Thinley Norbu Rinpoche, *The Dakini Letters*, forthcoming).

215. Mudrā samādhi: the meditation mudrās of the body, speech, and mind of the peaceful and wrathful deities.

216. Center for higher learning: Tib. shedra; bshad grwa.

217. Five enlightenments: enlightenment from the moon, enlightenment from the sun, enlightenment from a seed syllable, enlightenment from mudrā, and enlightenment from complete wisdom body, referring to the way of visualizing the form of wisdom deity through development stage practice.

218. Butter paste: a mixture of butter and roasted barley flour given to newborns to help them suckle.

219. Tradition of the Great Perfection cycles: the outer, inner, secret, and supremely secret cycles of the Upadeśa section of the Great Perfection.

220. Monastic center: Tib. drasa; drwa sa.

221. Eye of Dharma: one of the "five eyes." The others are the flesh eye, the divine eye, the prajñā eye, and the wisdom eye of Buddha.

222. Feast offering: "In general, the meaning of *tsok* is a gathering or heap of uncountable varieties of offerings of compounded substances, such as beautiful, splendid forms, pleasing sounds, delightful smells, delicious flavors, soothing feelings, and so on" (*Cascading Waterfall of Nectar*, p. 246).

223. Translation by Kyabje Thinley Norbu Rinpoche in *Cascading Waterfall of Nectar*, p. 173.

224. Tenth Bodhisattva bhūmi: Dharmameghā (Skt.), "Clouds of Dharma."

225. Saha world (Skt. sahāloka; Tib. mi mjed 'jig rten): the cosmos in which the present Buddha, Śākyamuni, has manifested.

226. Ten qualities of greatness: (1) the greatness of lineage, which is being born in a royal lineage; (2) the greatness of body, having the major and minor marks; (3) the greatness of qualities, having studied all fields of knowledge; (4) being learned, knowing all sūtras and tantras; (5) being thoughtful and considerate, so one does exactly as one promises to do; (6) having a highly realized view through meditation; (7) confidence, outshining others in brilliance; (8) the ability to debate, defeating opponents; (9) being capable of retaining teachings, distinguishing Dharma from non-Dharma; and (10) being forbearing and having a mind that is subdued.

227. Ten qualities of purity: (1) purity of lineage, being wealthy, youthful, and well educated; (2) purity of mind, being faithful, intelligent, and compassionate;

(3) purity of activity, being diligent and enduring hardship for Dharma; (4) purity of familiarity, with one's body, speech, and mind remaining in pure samaya under any circumstances; (5) purity of support, neither in disagreement with others nor under their influence; (6) purity of generosity, inspiring self and others through various skillful means; (7) purity of developing bodhicitta, not striving for the good of one's own body and life; (8) purity of material offering, not being stingy with one's treasured valuables; (9) purity of faculty, not disturbing others' minds; and (10) purity of nature, undeceiving in friendship and unbiased.

228. Five lands of Tibet: Zambulung of Shang in the center, Jönpalung of Kongpo in the east, Siptenlung of Mön in the south, Pakrilung of Og in the west, and Dromalung of Kyid in the north.
229. Three main valleys: the hidden lands of Dremo on the southwestern border of Tibet (modern-day Sikkim), Khenpa Jong in northwestern Tibet, and Lungsum Jong on the northeastern border of Tibet.
230. Single island: the hidden land of Pema Ling on the southeastern border of Tibet.
231. Twenty snowy mountains of Tibet: Mount Tanglha, Mount Makhar, Mount Kailash, Mount Bule, Mount Ode Gungyal, Mount Shampo, Mount Khari, Mount Lhagö, Mount Poma, Mount Dorje, Mount Jomo Kharag, Mount Hao Gangzang, Mount Tsedud, Mount Labchi, Mount Tsering, Mount Tridro, Mount Salje, Mount Lhari, Mount Tsari, and Mount Dala.
232. Eight great caves: Yangdzong Cave, Chimphu Cave, Kharchu Cave, Sheldrag Cave, Sengedzong Cave, Yerpa Cave, Yama Lung Cave, and Namkha Ding Cave at Chuwori.
233. Rakṣasas (Tib. srin po): one of the eight classes of gods and demons.
234. Five supreme consorts: Yeshe Tsogyal, Mandāravā, Śākyadevī, Kālasiddhī, and Tashi Kyidren.
235. Yellow scrolls: yellow scrolls of treasure revelations written in Ḍākinī script.
236. Eight Lingpas: Dorje Lingpa, Rinchen Lingpa, Pema Lingpa, Karma Lingpa, Samten Lingpa, Nyida Lingpa, Shikpo Lingpa, and Terdak Lingpa. Eleven faultless Lingpas: Rinchen Lingpa, Sangye Lingpa, Dorje Lingpa, Ratna Lingpa, Kunkyong Lingpa, Pema Lingpa, Tennyi Lingpa, Orgyen Lingpa, Karma Lingpa, Letro Lingpa (Jatsön Nyingpo), and Samten Lingpa.
237. Six kinds of liberation: liberation upon hearing, liberation upon wearing, liberation upon seeing, liberation upon remembering, liberation upon tasting, and liberation upon touching.
238. Translation by Kyabje Thinley Norbu Rinpoche, *The Dakini Letters* (forthcoming).
239. Three disciples named Pal: The other two disciples are Jangchub Pal and Dorje Pal.
240. Seven Kadam deities and teachings: Śākyamuni, Acalā, Avalokiteśvara, and Tārā are the deities, and the three Piṭakas are the teachings.

241. Four special transmissions: the yoga of illusory body and transference, the yoga of dreams, the yoga of luminosity, and the yoga of inner heat.
242. Yoginī Cinto: also known as Yoginī Cintā or Vilasyavajrā (Tib. sgeg mo rdo rje).
243. Three mudrās: the seals of wisdom body, wisdom speech, and wisdom mind.
244. Tsakli: small paintings of deities, ritual objects, and offerings that are used in empowerments.
245. Goddesses of Nairātmyā (Tib. bdag med ma): Goddesses with No Self.
246. Ālaya (Skt.): Tib. kun gzhi, the "basis of all."
247. Four empowerments: the vase, the secret, the wisdom (Skt. prajñājñāna), and the precious word empowerment.
248. A river flowed by on the right: i.e., on the right in relation to a place in Wonpori where Könchok Gyalpo later built a monastery.
249. Five Sakya patriarchs: Sachen Kunga Nyingpo, Sönam Tsemo, Jetsun Dragpa Gyaltsen, Sakya Paṇḍita, and Chögyal Phagpa.
250. The Path and Its Fruit: Tib. lamdre; lam 'bras.
251. Carasiṃha: likely the coastal region of modern-day Andhra Pradesh, India.
252. Ma So Kam trio: *Ma*göm Chökyi Sherab, *So* Gendun Bar, and *Kam*tön Yeshe Gyaltsen.
253. Four demons or māras: devaputramāra (the demon of the son of the gods), kleśamāra (the demon of the passions), skandhamāra (the demon of aggregates), and mṛtyamāra (the demon of the Lord of Death). Kyabje Thinley Norbu Rinpoche writes: "The demon of the passions causes all kinds of passions, including the passions of the three or five categories. Being very attached to desirable qualities causes the demon of the son of the gods, which causes beings to suffer by being lured. Although desirable qualities may sound pleasant, it is obvious that all sentient beings are suffering from attachment to desirable qualities, which is the demon of the skandhas. Since there are skandhas, there will be death and diminishment, which is the demon of death. From the beginning, these four demons are annihilated by Buddha. Buddhas have no passions, so passions are annihilated; therefore, they cannot be lured by the son of the gods, so there are no five skandhas, because the passions and the lure of attachment are purified. If there are no skandhas, there is no death, so from the beginning, death is annihilated." *Cascading Waterfall of Nectar*, pp. 92–93n133.
254. Zhong Zhong: Zhang Zhong and Shang Shong are alternative phonetic spellings.
255. Seven jewels of the Shangpa lineage: Ḍākinī Niguma instructed Khyungpo Naljor to keep his lineage secret by passing the teachings down to a single individual for the first seven generations. These seven lineage holders are known as the lineage of seven jewels: Buddha Vajradhara, Niguma, Khyungpo Naljor, Mochokpa Rinchen Tsöndru, Wontön Kyergangpa Chökyi Senge, Nyentön Rigung Chökyi Sherab, and Sangye Tönpa.
256. Samding Monastery: also known as Nyangme Samding Monastery.
257. A la la! (Tib.): Oh, joy!

258. Sal flower: the flower of a sal (Skt. śāla) tree, *Shorea robusta*, known for being offered when Buddha Śākyamuni developed bodhicitta for the first time.
259. Aspirational bodhicitta, applied bodhicitta, and ultimate bodhicitta: Aspirational bodhicitta is aspiring or wishing to attain enlightenment for the sake of all beings, like "wanting to go." Applied bodhicitta is engaging diligently in the trainings of the six pāramitās in order to attain fully enlightened Buddhahood, like "actually going." Ultimate bodhicitta is the realization of the wisdom of emptiness, free of all conceptions.
260. Seven precious royal emblems: precious golden wheel, precious wish-fulfilling jewel, precious queen, precious minister, precious elephant, precious horse, and precious general.
261. Seven precious materials: ruby, sapphire, lapis, emerald, diamond, pearl, and coral. Sometimes the list includes gold, silver, and crystal.
262. Three whites: yogurt, milk, and butter.
263. Three sweets: sugar, brown sugar, and honey.
264. To open a maṇḍala means to start practicing or accomplishing a maṇḍala.
265. The twenty-five general empowerments are the empowerments of the wisdom body of wisdom body, wisdom body of wisdom speech, wisdom body of wisdom mind, wisdom body of enlightened activities, and wisdom body of enlightened qualities. Likewise, there are five empowerments each for wisdom speech, wisdom mind, enlightened qualities, and enlightened activities, with a total of twenty-five. The ten specific empowerments in this case are those of longevity, mind, acquiring provisions, samādhi, birth, miracles, wishes, aspirations, and Dharma. "Four special empowerments" refers to the four rivers of empowerment, which are the empowerment of the Yidam deity, the empowerment of scriptures containing Buddha's words and tantras, the empowerment of the unobstructed power of self-awareness, and the empowerment of the spiritual teacher.
266. Queen Supreme and Queen Incomparable: wives of King Dhṛtarāṣṭra.
267. Five degenerations: degeneration of life span, degeneration of the passions, degeneration of sentient beings, degeneration of the times, and degeneration of views.
268. Kin of the Sun (Skt. Ādityabandhu): an epithet of Buddha Śākyamuni.
269. This account is found in the Vinaya section of the Derge Kangyur, in vols. 1, 4, and 6. It is mostly from vol. 1.
270. City of Wooden Palisades: Skt. Kāṣṭhavāṭa. Tib. grong khyer shing thag can. Many cities of ancient India were fortified by palisades contructed from wood.
271. Vaiśravaṇa: another name for Kubera, who is known as the God or Lord of Wealth and is one of the Four Great Kings, mentioned earlier in the text.
272. Class of elephants: the Brahmins, or priest class, the highest caste in ancient Indian society. Kolita believes that renunciates perform worship, make fire offerings, and undertake asceticism simply to attain more favorable circumstances, such as wealth, attendants, and rebirth into a high caste, all of which he already has.

273. Assaji: the Pāli equivalent of the Sanskrit name Aśvajit. "Living One" is an expression used by a teacher for a student.
274. Lower monastic robe: Skt. antarvāsas. Upper garment: saṅgati. Outer Dharma robe: uttarāsaṅga.
275. Great swan: symbol of the highest spiritual achievement of a renunciate. It is said that the swan can extract milk from water, symbolizing the ability to discern truth from illusion.
276. "You sealed the life force": *Seal* here is the translation of the Tibetan *rgyas' debs pa*, which means putting a seal on something, or making one thing inseparable from another, which is the archaic meaning. The arrow of great exaltation wisdom (of selflessness) is shot at the belief in ego, which is the life force of all beings of the three realms, annihilating ego along with all the suffering that results from it, and transforming it or making it inseparable (from wisdom), with the seal of great exaltation wisdom, by attaining the state of Vajradhara.
277. Inconceivability (Tib. thig le; Skt. bindu): This word has many different meanings that are variously translated by Kyabje Thinley Norbu Rinpoche as sole essence, sole oneness, all-pervasive soleness, great sole inconceivability, and inconceivability.
278. Six practices: teaching, studying, yajña (sacred fire offerings), officiating at yajña, giving gifts, and accepting gifts.
279. Umā: Pārvatī, the consort of Maheśvara.
280. The three worlds (Tib. 'jigs rten gsum) are the world of gods (devas) above the earth, the world of humans and animals on the earth, and the world of nāgas below the earth. A similar term, *sa gsum*, is translated in this book as "three planes."
281. Outer and inner ministers: In ancient times, outer ministers were those of lower rank who administered the external affairs of the kingdom, while inner ministers were higher in rank and closer to the king.
282. Here, Viśuddha Mind refers to the practice of Yangdak Heruka, one of the Eight Heruka deity practices that belongs to the mind category of all Buddhas.
283. Sphere of existence and peace: saṃsāra and nirvāṇa.
284. Completely pure: Tib. Yangdak; Skt. Viśuddha.
285. Lotus-Born Second Buddha: Padmasambhava. The expression "Second Buddha" is used for a number of beings who are equal in attainment and knowledge to Buddha Śākyamuni.
286. Drogben Khyeuchung Lotsawa: "Boy Translator of the Drogmi clan."
287. Four Kāyas: Dharmakāya, Sambhogakāya, Nirmānakāya, and Svabhāvikakāya.
288. Translators, in this case, means bilingual translators.
289. Khab Gungtang: literally, "Sky Plain Castle," an area on the border of Nepal and Tibet.
290. Hare-marked moon: In Asian cultures the moon is viewed as bearing the image of a hare (comparable to the West's "man in the moon").
291. Lantsa: Created during the 11th century, Lantsa script was based on the Nepalese

Rañjanā script and often used to write mantras and the Sanskrit titles of texts that were brought from India to Tibet.

292. Sciences: Skt. vidyā. Tib. rig pa.
293. Three poisons: attachment, aversion, and ignorance.
294. Tönmi Sambhota (7th c.), a minister of King Songtsen Gampo, created the forms of the Tibetan letters and composed eight treatises on Tibetan grammar. Only the two mentioned here are extant.
295. Harmful spirits: Tib. jungpo ('byung po), a kind of nojin (gngod sbyin).
296. Eight subcontinents: Deha and Videha surrounding Pūrvavideha; Cāmara and Aparacāmara surrounding Jambudvīpa; Śāthā and Uttaramantriṇa surrounding Aparagodānīya; and Kurava and Kaurava surrounding Uttarakuru.
297. The *Kālacakra Tantra* is divided into five chapters. The first, called the Outer Kālacakra, details the outer universe; the second, called the Inner Kālacakra, details the human body; and the final three, called the Other Kālacakra, detail the path and fruition (preparation, actual meditation practice, and enlightenment).
298. Four branches of approach and accomplishment: These four branches, which belong to development-stage meditation, form a sequence that includes approach, close approach, accomplishment, and great accomplishment.
299. Four vajras: body, speech, mind, and wisdom.
300. *Kina ho* may be an expression in the language of Nepal (which prior to 1923 was part of India), meaning something conversational like "How are you?" or "Where are you from?"
301. Here, *bardo* refers to the intermediate state after death.
302. Three types of Nirmāṇakāya emanations: creations, such as holy scriptures and statues; births taken in Nirmāṇakāya form in order to benefit others; and the supreme Nirmāṇakāya or the great enlightenment of Buddhas who benefit beings through the twelve deeds of a Buddha.
303. Vivarta was a written script invented by Tönmi Sambhota in the 7th century; it later fell out of use.
304. Activities: the four kinds of sublime activity.
305. Four perfectly pure discernments: the perfectly pure discernment of Dharma, of meaning, of the certainty of words, and of confidence.
306. Murwa Tsurtön: Tsurtön Wangyi Dorje (11th c.) was one of the four main disciples of Marpa Lotsawa and the principal recipient of Marpa's transmission of the *Guhyasamāja Tantra*.
307. Gö Lotsawa Khugpa (11th c.): an important translator of the Sarma period and one of the teachers of Khön Könchok Gyalpo.
308. *Dharmabhadra* is the Sanskrit translation of the name [Rongzom] Chökyi Zangpo.
309. Four provinces of Tibet: U-Tsang, Kham, Ngari, and Amdo.
310. Lion of Speech is an epithet for Mañjuśrī, and is also the name of one of the twelve manifestations of Guru Rinpoche, inseparable from Mañjuśrī. In this case, Rongzompa is being extolled with this name.

311. Honored with parasols: Holding a parasol overhead above a lama is a special gesture of honor reserved for lamas held in the highest esteem.
312. Eight classes of gods and demons: (1) Tib. du (bdud), Skt. māra; (2) mamo (ma mo), mātṛkā; (3) lu (klu), nāga; (4) ging (ging), kiṃkara; (5) drachen dzin (sgra gcan 'dzin), rāhula; (6) tsen (btsan), no Skt. equivalent; (7) sinpo (srin po), rakṣasa; (8) nöjin (gnod sbyin), yakṣa.
313. Kecara: the pureland of Vajravārāhī.
314. Five colors: red, blue, green, yellow, and white.
315. Eight great treasures of sublime confidence (Tib. spobs pa'i gter chen): recollection from being unforgetting, discerning intelligence, realization completely understanding the meaning of all sūtras, perfect memory from retaining whatever is learned, sublime confidence that satisfies all beings with perfect explanations, the protection of Dharma, bodhicitta without cutting the stream of the lineage of the Triple Gems, accomplishment by being able to accommodate higher teachings related to emptiness. These are the extraordinary qualities of beings who are extremely learned and realized.
316. Katok Monastery in Kham, oldest of the Nyingma monasteries; known as Katok Dorje Den.
317. Greater Tibet includes the three districts of Ngari, the four ranges of U-Tsang, and the six ranges of Dokham.
318. Minyak: located in present-day western Sichuan province.
319. Extracted essences: Extraction of essences from various substances such as the elements, minerals, or flowers, used as a method of lengthening life and developing physical strength.
320. Shedra (Tib. bshad grwa): center for higher learning.
321. Upāli (known as the Barber): one of the ten main disciples of the Buddha. He kept his precepts perfectly and was known for his preservation of the Vinaya.
322. Zur lineage trio: Zur Shakya Senge, Zurpoche Shakya Jungne, and Zurchung Sherab Dragpa.
323. The four root sūtras of Anuyoga are tantras titled *kun 'dus rig pa'i mdo*; *sangs rgyas thams cad dgongs pa 'dus pa*; *ye shes rngam glog*; and *gsang ba dur khrod khu byug rol pa*.
324. Zhije ("Pacifying Suffering") was the teaching tradition initiated by the Indian Buddhist adept Padampa Sangye, and Chö (*gcod*, "Cutting") was the teaching tradition of his Tibetan disciple Machik Labdrön.
325. *Ling* is the short form of *Ling Tsang*.
326. This nyen spirit was a local deity whose home was in a particular rock.
327. Gatekeepers: four female and four male wrathful deities.
328. Sādhana rituals: Tib. drubchö; sgrub mchod.
329. Yazi sword: Yazi is the seventh of the nine sons of the dragon, known for being part wolf and for fighting; his image was used on weapons.
330. Accomplishment ceremony: Tib. drubchen; sgrub chen.

331. Saṅgha counting stick: a stick of neem or tamarisk wood used for counting the number of participants when the prātimokṣa vow is given.
332. Gandi: a piece of wood that is beaten to invite monks for the Vinaya practice of confession.
333. Songs of realization: Skt. dohā. Tib. nyams mgur.
334. Indrabodhi: another name for Indrabhūti.
335. Lineage of the father and son: the lineage of the three Zurs—Zurpoche, Zurchungpa, and Zur Shakya Senge.
336. Pureland of Great Bliss: also translated as Pureland of Bliss or referred to as Skt. Sukhāvatī.
337. Eight chariots of the practice lineage: the eight independent schools of Buddhism that flourished in Tibet, namely the Nyingma, Kadam, Marpa Kagyu, Shangpa Kagyu, Sakya, Jordruk, Nyendrub, and Zhije and Chö. The "section of the eight chariots" mentioned here is the Marpa Kagyu.
338. Three secrets: enlightened body, speech, and mind.
339. Kuśinagarī: the city where the Buddha passed into parinirvāṇa.
340. Higher bhūmis: the three highest levels or stages of the ten-level Bodhisattva path.
341. Phagpa (Tib. 'phags pa, "Sublime"): Skt. Ārya.
342. Thirteen myriarchies: areas in the region of U-Tsang of approximately 10,000 households each, established during the rule of Drogön Chögyal Phagpa in consultation with Genghis Khan.
343. Three provinces of Tibet: U-Tsang, Kham, and Amdo.
344. Khotan, also known as Liyul: an ancient Buddhist kingdom on the Silk Road, now located in modern-day Xinjiang Province, China.
345. Syllable DHĪ (Skt.): often spelled DHĪḤ.
346. First part of Chögyal Phagpa's name: Chögyal Phagpa's name was Lodrö Gyaltsen. *Lodrö*, the first part of his name, is the Tibetan word for "intelligence."
347. Shar, Nub, and Gung Trio: the disciples of Chögyal Phagpa: Shar is Sharpa Yejung, Nub is Lopön Wuyukpa Sonam Senge, and Gung is Kyoton Trime.
348. Three worlds (Tib. 'jig rten gsum): the world of gods above the earth, the world of humans and animals on the earth, and the world of nāgas below the earth. In contrast, the three realms (Tib. khams gsum), in the epithet "Dharma King of the Three Realms," are the desire realm, form realm, and formless realm.
349. Here, the "three states of being" are being Samantabhadra, being Samantabhadrī, and being inseparable.
350. To treat wind disease with coolness is the opposite of normal wind disease treatments, which are not supposed to use anything that has a cooling nature. The usual treatment for wind disease is for a patient to be kept warm, wearing warm clothing particularly on the kidneys and feet, staying in warm and pleasant places, enjoying the company of warm people, and eating warm, nutritious, digestable food. In Tibetan medicine, external treatment for wind disease involves therapies using heat, massage, moxibustion, and herbal medicines that

are oily, buttery, heavy, and warm, and staying in warm places with amicable companions, so using anything with cooling properties will not treat wind disease. The example in the quotation given here shows that whatever is being done is incorrect and ineffective.

351. Those who are being discussed in this quotation have their own astrological charts with their own style of determining astrological calculations instead of using reliable astrological charts based on accurate astrological traditions, showing that they are not authentic.
352. Vidyādhara Kumāraja (1266–1343), also known as Rigdzin Kumārādza: the root lama of Omniscient Longchenpa.
353. "Yogurt Drinker" is the epithet of a sage (Skt. ṛṣi) named Ṛṣi Dadhīci, whose bones were used to make the powerful vajra or "thunderbolt" that became the chief weapon of Indra, king of the gods.
354. Tragtung Dudul Dorje: "Invincible Blood-Drinking Demon Tamer."
355. Hidden land: Tib. beyul; sbas yul. According to the Nyingma tradition, Beyuls are sacred hidden lands blessed by Guru Rinpoche for the benefit of future practitioners.
356. Scattered flowers of consecration: During Buddhist consecration rituals, flowers or rice that represents flowers are scattered by realized beings to represent blessings being conferred.
357. Three Roots: Skt. Guru, Deva, and Ḍākinī. Tib. Lama, Yidam, and Khandro.
358. Seven riches: faith, morality, generosity, knowledge, modesty, self-discipline, and wisdom.
359. Samaya substances: substances required for tantric practitioners in their ritual ceremonies. These include amṛta, rakta, balingta, and so on, as explained by Kyabje Thinley Norbu Rinpoche in *A Cascading Waterfall of Nectar*, pp. 250–61.
360. Four types of liberation: liberation through hearing, tasting, seeing, and touching.
361. Eighteen kinds of treasure: secret treasure, profound treasure, mind treasure, wisdom thought treasure, material treasure, life force treasure, minor treasure, crazy treasure, Indian treasure, Tibetan treasure, king treasure, treasure of treasures, mother treasure, neutral treasure, outer treasure, inner treasure, in-between treasure, and wealth.
362. Dokham: the area of Amdo and Kham in Tibet.
363. Sakya and Ngor: monasteries in Tsang. *Sakya* refers to the main Sakya monastery, and *Ngor* here refers to Ngor Ewam Chöden monastery.
364. Bangri, also known as Bangri Jogpo: a holy place in Kongpo discovered by Rigdzin Jatsön Nyingpo, who also established a retreat center there that still exists today.
365. Guide (Tib. kha byang), or treasure guide: an inventory listing details about termas and their locations.
366. Activity consort: Skt. karmamudrā. Tib. le gya. See *Cascading Waterfall of Nectar*, pp, 156–57, 249, 259.

367. The Secret Great Exaltation Cave at Puwo Dongchu is in southern Tibet near Pemakö.
368. That is, the treasures of Red Yamāri, Black Yamāri, and Bhairava that are mentioned in the namthar or life story of Dudul Dorje were apparently not decoded.
369. Rasa Trulnang Temple: the ancient name of the Jokhang in Lhasa.
370. Pemakö: hidden land (Tib. beyul; sbas yul) of Guru Rinpoche.
371. Great flaming ones: wrathful deities of the Nirmāṇakāya.
372. Six kinds of gods of desire: the gods of the heavens of the four great kings; the gods of the heavens free of fighting; the gods of the Heaven of the Thirty-Three; the gods of Tuṣita Heaven; the gods who enjoy their own emanations; and the gods who enjoy the emanations of others.
373. Four extremes of the sense sources of the formless realm: "the four unenlightened states called infinite space, infinite consciousness, nothing whatsoever, and neither presence nor absence" (*Cascading Waterfall of Nectar*, p. 49n66).
374. Supreme deities: Tib. lhag pa'i lha.
375. Lotus Light: the palace at the center of the Glorious Copper-Colored Mountain (Zangdok Palri), the pureland of Guru Rinpoche.
376. Garwang Dudjom Pawo: epithet of Dudjom Lingpa. *Garwang* means "Lord of the Dance"; *Pawo* is translated as "hero."
377. Two-stage path of characteristics: the path of the development stage and completion stage practices. The development stage is with characteristics, and the completion stage is either with characteristics, as in the practice of the wisdom of bliss and emptiness that emphasizes channels, energies, and the sole essence of one's inner vajra body, or the completion stage without characteristics, as in the yoga of abiding in Dharmatā, luminosity, or the way things truly are.
378. Drogmi: the name of a clan. In this passage, *Drogmi* refers to Drogben Khyeuchung Lotsawa, who belonged to this clan.
379. Tertön Dudjom Dorje Drolö is one of the names of Dudjom Lingpa.
380. Harsh eon: In this case, this expression refers to a degenerate time.
381. Two kinds of profound treasure: earth treasures (Tib. sa gter) and wisdom mind treasures (dgongs gter).
382. Nepalese subject: Newari Kālasiddhī, one of the five supreme consorts of Guru Rinpoche.
383. Yarlung Bami: Trisher of the Ba clan, from Yarlung Valley.
384. Jigme Trinle Özer (1745–1831): the first Dodrubchen Rinpoche.
385. Mingyur Namkha Dorje: the fourth Dzogchen Rinpoche.
386. Three treasures: three types of treasures (earth treasures, mind treasures, and pure visions).
387. Dark-Red Yakṣa: Shenpa Marnak, the Protector.
388. Dza: Rāhula, a protector deity.
389. Tsen: a reference to a protector deity, Tsiu Marpo.
390. Dorje Legpa: a protector deity.

391. Dripa Namsal (Skt. Sarvanīvaraṇavikṣambin): a Bodhisattva, one of the Eight Close Sons.

392. Twenty-five disciples of Guru Rinpoche: King Trisong Detsen, Namkhe Nyingpo, Nubchen Sangye Yeshe, Gyalwa Chogyang, Yeshe Tsogyal, Palgyi Yeshe, Langchen Palgyi Senge, Vairotsana, Nyak Jñānakumāra, Yudra Nyingpo, Nanam Dorje Dudjom, Yeshe Yang, Sogpo Lhapal, Nanam Zhang Yeshe De, Kharchen Palgyi Wangchuk, Denma Tsemen, Kawa Paltsek, Shupu Palgyi Senge, Gyalwe Lodrö, Drogben Khyeuchung Lotsawa, Odren Palgyi Wangchuk, Ma Rinchen Chok, Lhalung Palgyi Dorje, Langdro Könchok Jungne, Lasum Gyalwa Jangchub. (This name sequence follows the order given by Kyabje Dudjom Rinpoche in his *History of the Nyingma School.*)

393. Primordial purity: Tib. ka dag. Spontaneous presence: Tib. lhun drup.

394. Treasure replacement: When a treasure is revealed, the treasure revealer puts something else back in the place from which the treasure is taken, as a substitute, not leaving the place empty.

395. Rāhula the Demon: The wrathful protector Rāhula is like a demon to those who harm the teachings of Buddha.

396. Twenty-five characteristics of the result: the five characteristics of enlightened body, the five characteristics of enlightened speech, the five characteristics of enlightened mind, the five characteristics of enlightened qualities, and the five characteristics of enlightened activities.

397. The common vehicles or yānas are the Hīnayāna and Mahāyāna together. The four ways in which the Vajrayāna is more sublime than the common yānas: it is undeluded, it has many methods, it is without hardship, and it is for those of keen faculties.

398. Mansion of Complete Victory of Buddha's Teachings: the palace of Indra, king of the gods, atop Mount Sumeru.

399. Four ways of taking birth: rebirth by karma, as for sentient beings; rebirth by the power of prayers to benefit others and by the power of samādhi, as for Bodhisattvas; and rebirth due to having power over rebirth, as for Buddhas.

400. Three appearances: According to the Secret Mantra tradition, the three appearances are those of the habit of whiteness, which is a subtle cause or seed for the phenomena of the gross physical body to arise; the habit of redness, which is a cause for the subtle phenomena of speech to arise; and the habit of blackness, the combination of white and red, which is the movement of karmic winds and is the cause for the phenomena of subtle mind to arise.

401. Seven branches of union: the seven qualities of a Sambhogakāya Buddha: (1) complete abundance, (2) union, (3) great exaltation, (4) absence of a self-nature, (5) total presence of compassion, (6) being uninterrupted, and (7) being unceasing.

402. Five certainties: the perfect attributes of the Sambhogakāya, which are the perfect teacher, teaching, retinue, place, and time.

403. Jatri Tsenpo (also called Pude Kungyal): ninth in the line of Yarlung kings; a contemporary of the Han Emperor of China (140–85 BCE).
404. Krodhin (Skt.): the name of the thirty-eighth year of the sixty-year cycle (Tib. rabjung). Kyabje Dudjom Rinpoche was born on the twenty-third day of the fourth Tibetan month of that year.
405. Major and minor marks: the thirty-two major and eighty minor marks of excellence that characterize the perfect physical form of a Nirmāṇakāya or Sambhogakāya Buddha.
406. Ngawang Palden Zangpo, a Taglung Kagyu master from whom Kyabje Dudjom Rinpoche received the Bodhisattva vows of both Nāgārjuna's and Asaṅga's lineages. Different from Ngawang Pal Zangpo.
407. Level of the great Noble Ones: sublime beings of the eighth, ninth, and tenth bhūmis.
408. In general, the *Secret Heart Essence* is identical with the Upadeśa Section (man ngag gi sde), the third of the three divisions of the Great Perfection. It refers to the *Quintessential Unexcelled Cycle of Heart Essence* (*yang gsang bla na med pa'i snying thig gi skor*), the fourth of the four divisions of the Upadeśa Section according to the arrangement of Śri Siṃha.
409. The activities, i.e., the four kinds of sublime activity (peaceful, increasing, powerful, and wrathful activities).
410. Eight qualities (of a vajra master): (1) being a guide, (2) with the treasury of knowledge, (3) with all rivers of empowerment complete, (4) holder of upadeśa, (5) with signs of accomplishment, (6) eager, (7) learned in tantra, and (8) skilled in the activities.
411. Threefold vows (Tib. sdom gsum): the precepts, trainings, and samayas of the Prātimokṣa, Bodhisattva, and Secret Mantra teachings.
412. Eight worldly concerns: gain and loss, pleasure and pain, fame and defamation, praise and blame.
413. Flesh of a "seven-birth Brahmin": The flesh of a Brahmin who has died after having been a Brahmin for seven consecutive rebirths is said to be a sacred substance.
414. Six aspects of a master: the general Guru; the Guru who is a guide; the Guru who gives samaya and empowerment; the Guru who restores broken vows; the Guru who liberates one's mind; and the Guru who gives upadeśa and transmissions.
415. Three ways of pleasing the Guru: making material offerings, performing service, and practicing the teachings.
416. Four metaphors: thinking of oneself as someone who is sick, the Dharma as the remedy, one's spiritual teacher as a skillful doctor, and diligent practice as the way to recovery.
417. Five knowledges: five of the twenty-five branch samayas. These are knowing the five skandhas as the five male Buddhas; the five elements as the five female consorts; the five sense faculties as the five male Bodhisattvas; the five sense objects as the five female Bodhisattvas; and the five consciousnesses as the five wisdoms.
418. Six key points of sacred commitments: the ways in which each of the six aspects

of a master must be perceived. The general Guru is respected and seen like a king; the Guru who is a guide is seen like a brother; the Guru who gives samaya and empowerment is seen like a father; the Guru who restores broken vows after transgressions is seen like a mother; the Guru who liberates one's mind is seen like one's eyes; and the Guru who gives upadeśa and transmissions is seen as more precious than one's heart.

419. *Prayer with the Various Names of Dudjom Tulkus*: The disciple Tenzin Chopel requested Kyabje Dudjom Rinpoche to write a prayer containing all the various names of Kyabje Dudjom Rinpoche.
420. Lopön Ngagchang: also known as Do Ngak, who was a ngagpa or nonmonastic tantric practitioner.
421. Godāvarī, located in Nepal, is the holy place of Vajrayogini and one of the twenty-four great sacred places of Ḍākinīs.
422. Supreme mahāpaṇḍita: Khenchen Ngawang Khyentse Norbu.
423. The one bearing the name of Mañjuśrī: Khenchen Manju, also known as Khenchen Jampal Dewe Nyima; Kyabje Dudjom Rinpoche received the prātimokṣa vows from him.
424. Three vows: the precepts, trainings, and samayas of the Prātimokṣa, Bodhisattva, and Secret Mantra teachings.
425. Depending on the practice or a Guru's specific instructions, practitioners may practice until they have completed a requisite number of mantra recitations, or they may recite a mantra for a predetermined time period, or they may practice until certain signs of accomplishment occur.
426. Practice of indestructible longevity: Kyabje Rinpoche undertook the practice at the age of thirty-three.
427. Ten secrets: In the *Guhyagarbha Tantra*, the ten secrets are one of the five main samayas. These ten secrets comprise the four general secrets to be kept, which are (1) profound view, (2) wild conduct, (3) deities' names and dhāraṇīs, and (4) signs of accomplishment; the four middle secrets to be kept, which are (5) place, (6) time, (7) consorts, and (8) substances of spiritual practice; the final secrets to be kept in the end, which are (9) the samayas that are worthy of keeping secret, such as the first and the remainder portions of the feast offering, and (10) the samaya of keeping secret whatever has been told to one by the Lama and vajra brothers and sisters. All ten must be kept secret at all times and on all occasions in the presence of those who are not suitable to receive them, as well as those who are suitable yet have not received empowerment.
428. Previous treasures: any terma teachings revealed by previous masters.
429. Red-faced: a reference to the rosy-cheeked complexions of people living at high altitudes.
430. Khatra is in northeastern India. Mön is identified in some histories of Tibet as any of several places that border Tibet and Nepal, and is sometimes identified as Bhutan. During the reign of Tsongtsen Gampo, Mön was under Tibet's rule.
431. Wish-Fulfilling Lion's Lair: the Senge Samdrub cave where, according to legend,

Guru Rinpoche meditated for three years. Paro Tagtsang is the cliffside temple complex that was built around the cave, in Paro, Bhutan.

432. Wild Subjugator: epithet of Dorje Drolö.
433. King spirits: Tib. gyalpo; rgyal po.
434. Yizhin Palbar: terma statue representing the wisdom body of Guru Rinpoche.
435. *Chim* refers to to Chimpuk Hermitage.
436. Magical being: a reference to Kyabje Dudjom Rinpoche.
437. Gungtang: Mangyul Gungtang, a kingdom of southwestern Tibet under Sakya rule. It lay in an area that was an important gateway between the north and south Himalayas, through which Padmasambhava and Śāntarakṣita arrived in Tibet.
438. Lovely turquoise female dog: Yeshe Tsogyal in disguise.
439. Three masters: Guru Rinpoche, Vimalamitra, and Śīlamañju.
440. According to Lama Tharchin Rinpoche, as given in recorded oral teachings, *Jñāna Vajra* refers to Kyabje Dudjom Jigdral Yeshe Dorje Rinpoche, *Karma Maṇi* refers to Kyabje Thinley Norbu Rinpoche, and *Odi* refers to Orgyen Chemchok Rinpoche.
441. According to Lama Tharchin Rinpoche, the "boy with naturally occurring auspicious marks, born in the Monkey year," could be Kyabje Dudjom Rinpoche's disciple Tulku Jigme Chöying Norbu, who is believed to have attained the Rainbow Body.
442. Reading transmissions: reading scriptural texts aloud to students.
443. "Skillful means and wisdom": Tib. thabs dang shes rab. Skt. upāya and prajñā. This translation follows the usage of Kyabje Thinley Norbu Rinpoche, who has often rendered *shes rab* as "wisdom." Whereas the Tibetan *ye shes* (Skt. jñāna) is translated consistently as "wisdom," *shes rab* (Skt. prajñā) is translated in various ways according to the context and level of teaching. See *Cascading Waterfall of Nectar*, pp. 158–61, which explains that *prajñā* can also be translated as "incisiveness" or "discernment," and that the essence of both prajñā and jñāna is oneness, which is sole Dharmatā. In this volume, *shes rab* is translated as "sublime knowledge" to distinguish it from the translation of *ye shes*.
444. Four ways of gathering disciples: giving of Dharma and resources, kind and gentle speech, consistency between words and deeds, and meaningful conduct. Also called the "four magnetizing qualities."
445. *Way of the Bodhisattva*, chap. 10, verse 49.
446. Qualities of his sublime speech: *speech* in this case refers to both speech that is spoken and speech that is written.
447. Samayasattva and jñānasattva: "Samayasattva (Tib. dam tshig sems dpa') is the tantric vow of the inherent mind of bodhicitta. Jñānasattva (Tib. ye shes sems dpa') is fully enlightened wisdom mind. These terms are connected with rituals. First, one visualizes whatever deity is practiced as the samayasattva, and then, to that deity, fully enlightened Buddhas, or jñānasattva, are invoked from purelands to become indivisible with the samayasattva." *Cascading Waterfall of Nectar*, pp. 177–78, n218.

448. "Granting all that is required at once to the traveler crossing a mountain pass: This granting of all at once is one of the three ways of giving instruction in the Dzogchen tradition, which is mentioned above, given especially to a fortunate practitioner who is about to die. Just as a traveler is given all the directions he needs to cross a pass, the dying being is given all required instructions at once by directly introducing the bardo of Dharmatā that unfolds soon after death.
449. Threefold faith: the three faiths (clear faith, enthusiastic faith, and confident faith).
450. Sixfold power: the six characteristics of an eagle's flight, which are compared to the qualities of stainless samaya: strength, vigor, vision, height, fearlessness, and endurance.
451. Terrestrial pureland: in this case, a reference to Zangdok Palri, the pureland of Guru Rinpoche.
452. The Dundubhi year is the great Drum year, which is also known as the Male Water Dog year, the fifty-sixth year in the sixty-year Jupiter cycle. By traditional Tibetan age reckoning, a person is one year old at birth; thus Kyabje Dudjom Rinpoche (born 1904) was considered to be nineteen in 1922, the Male Water Dog year.
453. According to Tibetan accounts of Buddha Śākyamuni, Devadatta is portrayed as a jealous cousin of Buddha who made various attempts to harm Buddha.
454. As discussed in Kyabje Thinley Norbu Rinpoche's book *The Sole Panacea*, those who undermine and find fault with the Nyingma teachings out of jealousy and ignorance use the names of the two masters Nāgārjuna and Atiśa to defend their position. They claim that the Nyingma lineage of monastic ordination is impure because it came from Nāgārjuna, who received ordination from Saraha, and that Saraha lost his ordination by taking a consort, the arrowsmith's daughter. Atiśa's name is mentioned because Atiśa once said that the third empowerment, which is the prajñā-jñāna abhiṣeka, is not to be received by ordained monks. So, instead of arguing with such people, Kyabje Dudjom Rinpoche held Atiśa's and Nāgārjuna's ultimate life stories to be paramount.
455. The bird called *haṃsa* in Sanskrit (usually translated as "swan") is said to have the power to draw, from a mixture of milk and water, solely the milk, an act symbolic of being able to discern what is important.
456. Quotation from Nāgārjuna's *Tree of Wisdom* (Tib. *lugs kyi bstan bcos shes rab sdong po*), a śāstra on ethical behavior. The original Sanskrit version, *Nītiśāstra-prajñādaṇḍa*, is not extant.
457. King of Mountains: Mount Meru.
458. Buchu Monastery, built in the seventh century, is the oldest Buddhist temple in the Kongpo region of Kham. It is one of the eight "demoness-subduing" temples constructed during the reign of King Songtsen Gampo.
459. Yeshe Nyingpo: Dharma centers established by Kyabje Dudjom Rinpoche in New York City, California, and Oregon.

460. Orgyen Chö Dzong: retreat center established by Kyabje Dudjom Rinpoche in Greenville, NY.
461. Dorje Nyingpo: Dharma center established by Kyabje Dudjom Rinpoche in Paris, France.
462. Orgyen Samye Chöling Meditation and Study Center: established by Kyabje Dudjom Rinpoche in Dordogne, France.
463. Five certain conditions: the conditions of place, time period, beings, occasion, and path. Thinking one can keep vows only in favorable places is the certain condition of place. Thinking one can keep vows only for certain periods, such as a few months or years, is the certain condition of a time period. Thinking that one can keep vows in relation to some beings but not all beings, such as that one should not kill any beings except one's enemy, is the certain condition of sentient beings. Thinking that one can keep vows on certain occasions but not others, such as during famine or war, is the certain condition of occasion. Thinking that one can only keep the gross parts of the trainings and not the subtle training is the certain condition of the path. Whoever was free of these five certain conditions and the four conflicting circumstances were given vows. The Tibetan term for "five certain conditions" is the same as for "five certainties," but the "five certain conditions" refers to the faults of misconceptions related to keeping vows.
464. Four conflicting circumstances: obstacles to sustaining the vows, such as not receiving permission from one's parents; obstacles to the elegance of the vow holder, such as missing parts of the body; obstacles of being in special circumstances, such as being very sick or stricken with sorrow; and obstacles by birth, such as being born with an indefinite gender or androgynous (Tib. ma ning, "neutral").
465. Sublime individuals who uphold the victory banner of the saffron-clad: those who wear the monastic robes of a Buddhist monk, which are traditionally dyed with saffron or ocher.
466. Three bases of purifying the [prātimokṣa] precepts: sojong (Skt. poṣadha), the twice-monthly purification ceremony for restoring vows; yarne (vārṣika), the summer rains retreat; and gagye (pravāraṇā), release from the summer rains retreat.
467. Nyingma Gyubum: collected tantras of the Early Translation school.
468. Sole hero: Tib. dpa' bo gcig pa.
469. Elaborate practice in a large gathering: Tib. tshom bu tshogs sgrub.
470. Exhaustion of Phenomena Beyond Thought (Tib. chos zad blo 'das): the exhaustion of phenomena into their true nature, which is beyond thought.
471. Buddha Radiant Lotus (Tib. pad ma 'od 'bar; Skt. Guru Padmabhasajvala): Padmasambhava's name in the *Könchok Chidu* (*dkon mchog spyi 'dus*) terma cycle of Jatsön Nyingpo.
472. Basis of emanation: the source of emanation. In this case, Kyabje Dudjom Rinpoche is dissolving back into the origin, which is Guru Rinpoche.

473. Drumbeat of Brahma is a Sambhogakāya pureland. Luminous Essence (or Luminous Vajra Essence) is the Dharmakāya pureland.
474. Three blazes: the blazing of blissful warmth in the body, the blazing of potency in speech, and the blazing of realization in the mind.
475. Three gatherings: the gathering of humans during the day, gathering of Ḍākinīs by night, and gathering of food and wealth at all times.
476. Causal and Resultant vehicles: the Causal Vehicle (Skt. Hetuyāna; Tib. rgyu'i theg pa) includes the Hīnayāna and Mahāyāna, which regard the practices of the path as the cause of the result of liberation and enlightenment. The Resultant Vehicle (Skt. Phalayāna; Tib. 'bras bui'i theg pa) is the Vajrayāna, which takes the result of Buddhahood as the path. As Omniscient Rongzompa says, "The meaning of the result vehicle is that everything is primordially enlightened in the state of Dharmatā. The path is also abiding in that way" (*Sole Panacea*, p. 132).
477. Four magnetizing qualities: the four ways of gathering disciples (giving of Dharma and resources, kind and gentle speech, consistency between words and deeds, and meaningful conduct).
478. Eight Herukas: Mahottara (Tib. Chemchok), Hayagrīva, Jigten Chötö, Mātaraḥ (Tib. Mamo Bötong), Möpa Drangak, Vajrakīlaya, Yamāntaka, and Yangdak (Skt. Viśuddha).
479. Fruition teachings: Vajrayāna.
480. Awareness-emptiness: Tib. rig stong.
481. Luminous enclosure: a stage of Dzogchen practice in which the visionary experiences of awareness are continuous day and night, without interruption.
482. Unsurpassed Wisdom: the sixteenth and highest bhūmi according to the Dzogchen teachings. For the eleventh through sixteenth levels, see *Cascading Waterfall of Nectar*, pp. 105, 114–115: All-Pervasive Light (the stage of fully enlightened Buddha), Lotus of Nonattachment; Spontaneously Perfect Vajra Holder, Great Bliss, and Unsurpassed Wisdom. As explained, "These stages are not like steps on a staircase, where one is higher than the other.... The essence of the meaning is free from existing or not existing, so these stages are explained as only one state."
483. Three major hidden lands: Pemakö in Tibet, Denjong in Sikkim, and Khenpa Jong in Bhutan.
484. Six countries of Jambudvīpa where the Holy Dharma was spread: India, China, Tibet, Khotan, Shambhala, and Kailāśa.
485. Six classes of beings: gods, asuras, humans, animals, pretas, and hell beings.
486. Woodpecker (Skt. Śatapatra; Tib. shing rta mo): one of the lives of the Buddha portrayed in the Jātakas.
487. Dorje Nönpo: In Sanskrit, *Dorje Nönpo* is *Vajratīkṣṇa*, an epithet of Mañjuśrī meaning "Sharp Vajra."
488. Kalkī king: the eighth to the thirty-second kings of Shambhala, who hold the teachings of the *Kālacakra Tantra*, which are the teachings of Buddha Śākyamuni passed down from the original seven Dharma kings of Shambhala.

489. In the Vajrayāna tradition, there are thirty-two kings of the kingdom of Shambhala. The first seven are called Dharma kings (Tib. chos rgyal), beginning with Sucandra (a contemporary of the Buddha), and twenty-five are Kalkī kings (Tib. rigden; rigs ldan: "holder of the castes"). Kalkī kings reside upon a lion throne in Kalāpa, the capital city of the kingdom. They are holders of the *Kālacakra Tantra,* which are the teachings of Buddha Śākyamuni passed down from the original seven Dharmarājas of Shambhala.

490. Six countries of Jambudvīpa: the six great countries where the Holy Dharma was propagated: India, China, Tibet, Khotan, Shambhala (Śambhala), and Kailāśa (Kailash).

491. King Mañjuśrī Yaśas (2nd c. BCE) was the first Kalkī king of Shambhala, holder of the *Kālacakra Tantra.*

492. ". . . never any ordinary god!": meaning he is in fact the deity, not a god.

493. Noble Vajra: Here, the meaning of Noble Vajra is "the supreme among the supreme," according to Mipham Rinpoche.

494. Twelve heavenly generals: Kumbhīra, Vajra, Mihira, Aṇḍīra, Anila, Śāṇḍilya, Indra, Pajra, Mahoraga, Kinnara, Chatura, and Vikarāla.

495. Sugata Möpa Taye: the Sugata Adhimukta, Buddha of Boundless Dedication.

496. Transcendent Conqueror: Here, the Buddha is speaking. "Transcendent Conqueror" is the translation of Tib. *bcom ldan 'das* (Skt. *Bhagavān*) and can be used for all Buddhas, including Buddha Śākyamuni.

497. Middle world: A thousand worlds with four continents share a common boundary; and a thousand times such a world constitutes a middle world. A middle world has a thousand times a thousand worlds with four continents, or a million worlds within a billionfold universe.

498. Five sublime states of perception: divine vision; divine hearing; knowing others' thoughts; remembering death, transference, and birth; and knowing miraculous abilities.

499. Three faiths: "the three doors of faith—clear faith, enthusiastic faith, and confident faith" (*Cascading Waterfall of Nectar*, p. 3). Clear faith is inspired by thinking of the great compassion of the Buddhas and great masters. Enthusiastic faith is eagerness to be free of suffering, attain liberation, engage in positive actions, and avoid negative actions. Confident faith arises when we understand the precious qualities of the Three Jewels and the power of their blessings.

500. Sudhana is the central figure in the *Gaṇḍavyūha Sūtra*, the last chapter of the *Avataṃsaka Sūtra*. He was an Indian youth whose search for enlightenment took him on a journey to fifty-three spiritual teachers. He is used as an example of perfect guru devotion.

501. Three kindnesses (of the vajra master): In Sūtra, giving precepts, reading transmissions, and guidance; in Tantra, conferring empowerments, explaining the tantras, and giving upadeśa.

502. Indra's enemies: the asuras.

503. Sky's elephant: a synonym for clouds.

504. From light to the ultimate light: from higher rebirths to enlightenment.
505. Threefold sublime knowing: the sublime knowing through studying, contemplating, and meditating.
506. Swans: The author used the Tibetan term *khor lo'i lag ldan*, meaning "having wheel-like hands," which is a synonym for *swan*. By pervading the full breadth of the ocean's raiment, the swans of the Saṅgha spread Buddha's teachings everywhere.
507. Ocean's raiments: the Earth.
508. Vidyādhara bees: the Secret Mantra Saṅgha, the Vidyādharas of Mahāsandhi (Dzogchen).
509. Branches of troops: Troops on foot, on horses, in chariots, and on elephants correspond to the four boundless wishes.
510. Sixfold greatness: the six perfect aspects of greatness (the greatness of the inviting patron; the greatness of the place of translation; the greatness of the Dharma translators who did the translations; the greatness of the paṇḍitas who guided the translation of the teachings; the greatness of the offering flowers; the greatness of the translated teachings).
511. Charioteers of the three yogas: the prominent masters of the three yogas.
512. Three yogas: the three inner yogas of Mahā, Anu, and Ati.
513. ". . . like gemstone traders": When gem traders find a wish-fulfilling jewel, they wrap the jewel in fine cloth, set it atop a victory banner, and make offerings to it so that the wishes may be granted.
514. Three fetters: the three poisons of desire, hatred, and ignorance.
515. Four abundances: flourishing of the Buddha Dharma, possession of wealth and resources, enjoying the five desirable qualities, and attainment of liberation and enlightenment through relying upon the Dharma.
516. Ten virtues: refraining from the ten nonvirtues, which are the three physical misdeeds of killing, taking what is not given, and engaging in sexual misconduct; the four verbal misdeeds of lying, slandering, using harsh words, and gossiping; and the three mental misdeeds of coveting, having harmful thoughts, and having wrong views. The ten virtues are the opposite of the ten nonvirtues: protecting life, being generous, and engaging in pure conduct; telling the truth, speaking harmoniously, using pleasant speech, and using speech that is in harmony with Dharma; giving alms, thinking only beneficial thoughts, and having faith and belief in the Triple Gems, including accepting previous lives and future lives and believing in karmic cause and result.
517. Seven qualities of higher rebirth: noble family, beautiful bodily form, long life span, no illness, good fortune, abundant wealth, and great intelligence.
518. Noble Eightfold Path: perfect view, perfect intention, perfect speech, perfect action, perfect livelihood, perfect effort, perfect mindfulness, and perfect samādhi.
519. Mahāhimasāgara: the Sambhogahakāya Vairocana. It is said in certain Mahayana sūtras and tantras that there are twenty-five worlds formed on top of one another

and held in the hands of the Sambhogahakāya Vairocana, which are in the evenness mudrā. Our world, the world of forbearance, is the thirteenth of the twenty-five worlds, formed at the heart level of Vairocana.

520. Threefold Buddha: the Three Kāyas (Dharmakāya, Sambhogakāya, and Nirmāṇakāya). The purelands of the Threefold Buddha are the purelands of each of the three Kāyas, such as the Dharmakāya Luminous Vajra Essence, the Sambhogakāya Akaniṣṭha, and the Nirmāṇakāya Zangdok Palri.

521. This stanza contains the eight auspicious symbols: endless knot, golden fish, lotus, victory banner, vase, wheel, conch, umbrella.

522. North country bearing the sound of the unborn syllable ĀḤ: America, beginning with the sound Ah.

523. Six seasons: spring, spring rains, summer, autumn, winter, and late winter.

Bibliography

Selected Works by Kyabje Thinley Norbu Rinpoche

Account of the Great Caitya of Thimbu. Tib. *bdud 'dul mchod rten chen mo'i dkar chag.* Published in Tibetan, Thimphu, Bhutan, 1974. Reprinted in vol. 3 of the *Collected Works of Kyabje Dungse Thinley Norbu Rinpoche.*

Brief Fantasy History of a Himalayan, A: Autobiographical Reflections. Written in English. Boston: Shambhala Publications, 2014.

Cascading Waterfall of Nectar, A. Boston: Shambhala Publications, 2006. Paperback edition with some revisions, 2009. English translation of *khrag thung bdud 'joms gling pa'i gter gsar sngon 'gro shin tu bsdus pa'i 'grel pa go bde chu 'bab tshul du bris pa* (An Easily Understood Commentary Flowing Like a Cascading Waterfall on *The Concise New Treasure Preliminary Practices* of Tragtung Dudjom Lingpa), *tshogs khang pad+ma'i rgyud mang gi don 'grel nyi ma gzhon nu'i 'od zer* (*A Commentary of the Meaning of "The Continuously Blossoming Rosary of the Lotus Assembly Palace" called the Light Rays of the Youthful Sun*) from the *Collected Works of Kyabje Dungse Thinley Norbu Rinpoche*, vol. 2 (2009).

Collected Works of Kyabje Dungse Thinley Norbu Rinpoche. Tib. *skyab rje gdung sras phrin las nor bu'i gsung 'bum.* The three volumes of the *Collected Works* were published in Tibetan in three different places: in Taiwan, by Khandro Pema Chödrön, in 2008, in a hardbound edition; in Thimphu, Bhutan, by Lama Kunzang Wangdi (Lama Nyingkhula), 2009, in a rice paper edition; and in Hong Kong: Tian Ma Publishing, 2009, in a paperback edition.

Dakini Letters, The. Written in English. Publication forthcoming.

Echoes: The Boudhanath Teachings. Taught in Tibetan with Shakya Dorje doing live English translation that was recorded on tape; the live translation was subsequently refined into the written text by Shakya Dorje. Boston: Shambhala Publications, 2016.

Gypsy Gossip and Other Advice. Written in English. Boulder: Shambhala Publications, 2016. The first section was published in 1980 as *Gypsy Gossip*, in a privately printed limited edition.

Magic Dance: The Display of the Self-Nature of the Five Wisdom Ḍākinīs. Boston: Shambhala Publications, 1999. Written in English.

Ruby Rosary Joyfully Accepted by Vidyādharas and Ḍākinīs as the Ornament of a Necklace, The. Tib. *rig 'dzin mkha' 'gro dgyes pa'i mgul rgyan pad ma ra ga'i do shal.* A Commentary on Kyabje Dudjom Rinpoche's *The Pearl Rosary: A Prayer to the Emanations* (*sku 'phreng gsol 'debs muk+ti tig ka'i do shal*). In vol. 1 of the *Collected Works* (Hong Kong: Tian Ma Publishing, 2009).

Small Golden Key to the Treasure of the Various Essential Necessities of General and Extraordinary Buddhist Dharma, The. Boston: Shambhala Publications, 1993. Written in English with the aid of a translator, Lisa Anderson.

Sole Panacea, The: A Brief Commentary on the Seven-Line Prayer to Guru Rinpoche That Cures the Suffering of the Sickness of Karma and Defilement. Boston: Shambhala Publications, 2013. Tib. *tshig bdun gsol 'debs kyi 'grel bsdus las nyon nad kyi du kha sel ba'i bdud rtsi sman gcig ma.* Published privately in Tibetan. An edition of 1,000 copies was privately published in the United States in 2012.

Sunlight Speech That Dispels the Darkness of Doubt: Sublime Prayers, Praises, and Practices of the Nyingma Masters. Compiled and translated into English by Kyabje Thinley Norbu Rinpoche. Boston: Shambhala Publcations, 2015.

Welcoming Flowers from Across the Cleansed Threshold of Hope: An Answer to the Pope's Criticism of Buddhism. Written in English. Boston: Shambhala Publications, 2014.

White Sail: Crossing the Waves of Ocean Mind to the Serene Continent of the Triple Gems. Written in English. Boston: Shambhala Publications, 1992.

Works Cited

Abhidharma Kośa. See *Treasury of Abhidharma.*

Abhidharma Samucchaya (Collection of Abhidharma). Asaṅga. Tib. *chos mngon pa kun las btus pa.*

Abhisamaya Alaṃkāra. See *Ornament of Manifest Realization.*

Abridged Commentary on the "Eighty-Chapter Magical Infinity." Vimalamitra. Tib. *brgyad cu pa'i bsdus 'grel.*

Abridged Kālacakra Tantra. Mañjuśrī Yaśas; compiled by Sucandra. Skt. *Kālacakralaghu-tantra.* Tib. *dus 'khor bsdus rgyud.* Known as the *Abridged Tantra* (*bsdus rgyud*) in contrast to the *Kālacakra Root Tantra* (*rtsa rgyud*).

Abridged Tantra. See *Abridged Kālacakra Tantra.*

Accomplishment of Secrets. Mahāsukha Nātha. Tib. *gsang ba grub pa.*

Amṛta Tantra. Tib. *bdud rtsi'i rgyud.*

Analysis of Haribhadra's "Clear Meaning Commentary on the 'Prajñāpāramitā.'" Katok Dampa Deshek. Tib. *phar phyin seng bzang lugs kyi 'grel pa don gsal rnam 'byed.*

Analytical Commentary on the "Secret Essence Tantra." Buddhaguhya. Tib. *gsang ba snying po la 'grel pa rnam dbye 'grel.* Commentary on the *Guhyagarbha.*

Archenemy Yamāntaka Tantra. Vilāsavajra (Gegpa Dorje). Tib. *gshin rje gshed dgra nag gi rgyud.* Translated into Tibetan by Rongzompa.

Armor Against Darkness: Extensive Commentary on the "Embodiment of Wisdom Mind." Nubchen Sangye Yeshe. Tib. *mdo'i 'grel chen mun pa'i go cha.*

Arrangement Like a Mountain Tantra. Tib. *ri bo brtsegs pa.*

Arrangement of Samayas Tantra. Tib. *dam tshig bkod pa.*

Array of the Path of the "Magical Infinity." King Ja. Skt. *Mayapathavyavastha-pana.* Tib. *sgyu 'phrul lam rnam bkod.*

Avataṃsaka Sūtra (Flower Garland Sūtra). Skt. *Buddhāvataṃsaka-sūtra.* Tib. *mdo phal po che.*

Bhairava Tantra. See *Vajrabhairava Tantra.*

Biography of Joyous Countenance. Tib. *dga' ba'i bzhin gyi rtogs brjod.*

Blue Annals. Gö Lotsawa Zhönu Pal. Tib. *deb ther sngon po.* Famous 2-vol. history of Tibet up to the late 15th c.

Blue Cakrasaṃvara. Tib. *bde mchog sngon mo.*

Blue-Skirted Vajrakīlaya Cycle. Vimalamitra. Tib. *phur pa gsham sngon.*

Bodhicarya Avatāra. See *Way of the Bodhisattva.*

Brief Account of Profound Treasures and Accomplished Treasure Revealers Called "Garland of Lapis Lazuli," A. Jamgön Kongtrul Lodrö Taye. Tib. *zab mo'i gter dang gter ston grub thob ji ltar byon pa'i lo rgyus rin po che baiDUrya'i phreng ba.* A teaching from vol. 1 of the *Great Treasury of Precious Termas.*

Buddhakapāla Tantra (Skullcup of Enlightenment Tantra). Tib. *sangs rgyas thod pa.*

Buddhasamāyoga Tantra. See *Union of All Buddhas.*

Buddhasamāyoga Upadeśa Called "Illuminating the Meaning of the Four Branches." Hūṃkāra. Tib. *sangs rgyas mnyam sbyor gyi man ngag yan lag bzhi'i don snang bar byed pa.*

Cakrasaṃvara Root Tantra. Vilāsavajra (Gegpa Dorje). Tib. *bde mchog rtsa rgyud.* Translated into Tibetan by Rongzompa. The only extant version is the abbreviated *Cakrasaṃvara Concise Tantra* (Skt. *Laghusaṃvara-tantra*; Tib. *bder mchog nyung ngu*).

Candra's Grammar. Candragomin. Skt. *Candravyākaraṇa.* Tib. *sgra tsandra pa yan lag dang bcas pa.* Accompanied by a subsidiary text, the *Varṇa-sūtra.*

Catuḥśataka. See *Four Hundred Stanzas on the Middle Way.*

Catuḥśataka Ṭīkā (Commentary on the Four Hundred). Candrakīrti. Tib. *byang chub sems dpa'i rnal 'byor spyod pa bzhi brgya pa'i rgya cher 'grel pa.* Commentary on Āryadeva's *Four Hundred Stanzas on the Middle Way.*

Clarification of Commitments. Vilāsavajra (Gegpa Dorje). Skt. *Samayavivyakti.* Tib. *dam tshig gsal bkra.*

Classification of Caryātantras. Ngorchen Kunga Zangpo. Tib. *spyod rgyud rnam bzhag.*

Clear Lamp. Candrakīrti. Skt. *Pradīpodyotana.* Tib. *sgron gsal.* A commentary on the *Guhyasamāja Tantra.*

Clear Meaning Commentary on the "Prajñāpāramitā." Haribhadra. Skt. *Sphuṭārthā.* Tib. *'grel pa don gsal.*

Clear Mirror: Accounts of Secret Experiences, Visions of the Magical Display of

Dharmatā. Dudjom Lingpa. Tib. *chos nyid sgyu mar rol pa'i snang lam gsang ba nyams byung gi rtogs brjod gsal ba'i me long*. The autobiography of Dudjom Lingpa. (An English translation has been published, titled *A Clear Mirror: The Visionary Autobiography of a Tibetan Master*. This entry is not a reference to that translation.)

Clear Words. Candrakīrti. Skt. *Prasannapadā*. Tib. *tshig gsal*. A commentary on Nāgārjuna's *Root Verses on the Middle Way Called "Sublime Knowledge."*

Cloud of Dharma Sūtra. Skt. *Dharmamegha-sūtra*. Tib. *mdo sde chos kyi sprin*.

Collected Works of Tsele Natsok Rangdrol. Tib. *rtse le sna tshogs rang grol gyi gsung 'bum skor*.

Collection of All Trainings. Śāntideva. Skt. *Śikṣā-samucchaya*. Tib. *bslab pa kun btus*.

Collection of Discourses. Nāgārjuna. Tib. *gtam gyi tshogs*.

Collection of Hymns. Nāgārjuna. Skt. *Stava-kāya*. Tib. *bstod tshogs*. Four hymns in praise of the Buddha.

Collection of Logical Arguments. Nāgārjuna. Skt. *Yukti-samgraha* or *Yukti-gana*. Tib. *rigs pa'i tshogs*.

Collection of Six Texts on Reasoning. Nāgārjuna. Skt. *Madhyamakayukti-kāya*. Tib. *rigs tshogs drug*. The six texts are *Root Verses on the Middle Way Called "Sublime Knowledge"*; *Refutation of Objections*; *Seventy Stanzas on Emptiness*; *Sixty Stanzas on Reasoning*; *Crushing to Fine Powder*; and *Precious Garland*.

Collection of Sūtras. Śāntideva. Skt. *Sūtra-samucchaya*. Tib. *mdo kun las btus*.

Collection of the Natural State. Nāgārjuna. Tib. *de kho na nyid kyi tshogs*.

Commentarial Notes on the "Mūlamadhyamaka Kārikā." Katok Dampa Deshek. Tib. *dbu ma rsta she'i mchan tik*.

Commentary on "Compilation of All Teachings on Logic." Dharmakīrti. Skt. *Pramāṇa-vārttika*. Tib. *tshad ma rnam 'grel* (Commentary on Logic). Commentary on the *Pramāṇa-samucchaya* by Dignāga.

Commentary on "Compilation of All Teachings on Logic." Dignāga. Skt. *Pramāṇa-samucchaya-vrtti*. Tib. *tshad ma kun las btus pa'i 'grel pa*. Autocommentary.

Commentary on "Compilation of All Teachings on Logic." Īśvarasena. Tib. *tshad ma kun las btus pa'i 'grel pa*. Commentary on the *Pramāṇa-samucchaya* by Dignāga.

Commentary on "Doorway to Speech Like a Sword." Rongzompa. Tib. *smra sgo mtshon cha'i 'drel pa*.

Commentary on "Stages of the Path." Katok Dampa Deshek. Tib. *lam rim 'grel tig*. The title *Stages of the Path* here most likely refers to *Stages of the Path of Magical Infinity* by Buddhaguhya.

Commentary on the "Bhairava Tantra." Rongzompa. Tib. *rdo rje 'jigs byed rgyud kyi 'grel pa*.

Commentary on the "Buddhasamāyoga Tantra." Rongzompa. Tib. *mnyam sbyor gyi 'grel pa*.

Commentary on the Clear Realization of the "Eighty-Chapter Magical Infinity." Nubchen Sangye Yeshe. Tib. *sgyu 'phrul brgyad cu pa'i mngon rtogs 'grel*.

Commentary on the Difficult Points of the "Buddhakapāla Tantra" Called "Jñāna-

vatī." Rāhulabhadra (Saraha). Tib. *dpal sangs rgyas thod pa'i rgyud kyi dka' 'grel ye-shes ldan pa.*

Commentary on the "Earlier Bhūmis." Guṇaprabha. Tib. *sa'i stod 'grel.*

Commentary on the "General Sūtra." King Ja. The *General Sūtra* (Tib. *spyi mdo*) is the *Embodiment of Wisdom Mind* (Tib. *spyi mdo dgongs pa 'dus pa*).

Commentary on the "Guhyagarbha Tantra" Called "Illuminating Lamp of the Core Text." Vimalamitra. Tib. *snying po'i 'grel pa khog gzhung gsal sgron.*

Commentary on the "Lower Realms Purification Tantra." Rongzompa. Tib. *ngan song thams cad yongs su sbyong ba'i rgyud kyi 'grel pa.*

Commentary on the "Moon Lamp Sūtra." Candragomin. Skt. *Candrapradīpa-sūtra-vṛtti.* Tib. *zla ba sgron ma'i 'grel pa.*

Commentary on "Root Verses on the Middle Way Called 'Sublime Knowledge.'" Buddhapālita. Skt. *Mūlamadhyamaka-vṛtti.*

Commentary on "Treasury of Abhidharma." Vasubandhu. Skt. *Abhidharma-kośa-bhāṣya.* Tib. *chos mngon pa mdzod kyi bshad pa.* Autocommentary.

Compilation of All Teachings on Logic. Dignāga. Skt. *Pramāṇa-samucchaya.* Tib. *tshad ma kun las btus pa.*

Complete Gathering of Secrets. Tib. *gsang ba yongs 'dus skor.*

Complete Gathering of the Holy Dharma's Wisdom. Revealed by Dudul Dorje. Tib. *dam chos dgongs pa yongs 'dus.*

Complete Gathering of the Sugatas. Longsal Nyingpo. Tib. *bka' brgyad bde gshegs yongs 'dus chos skor.*

Complete Gathering of Vidyādharas. Tib. *rig 'dzin yongs 'dus skor.*

Complete Vajra Analysis of the Meaning of the Yamāntaka Mantra. Vilāsavajra (Gegpa Dorje). Skt. *Yamāntakamūlamantrārthavajraprabheda.* Tib. *dpal gshin rje gshed po'i rtsa ba'i sngags don rdo rje rab tu 'byed pa.* Translated into Tibetan by Rongzompa.

Concise Commentary on "Vairocana's Awakening." Buddhaguhya. Skt. *Vairocanābhisaṃbodhi-tantra-piṇḍārtha.* Tib. *rnam snang mngon byang gi bsdus 'grel.*

Condensed Meaning of the "Embodiment of Wisdom Mind" Called the "Garland of the White Lotus." Katok Dampa Deshek. Tib. *spyi mdo dgongs 'dus kyi bdus don pad ma dkar po'i phreng ba.*

Crushing to Fine Powder. Nāgārjuna. Skt. *Vaidalyaprakarana.* Tib. *zhib mo rnam 'thag.* One of the texts in Nāgārjuna's *Collection of Six Texts on Reasoning.*

Crystal Cave Chronicles. Revealed by Orgyen Lingpa. Tib. *bka' thang shel brag ma.* Biography of Guru Padmasambhava, also known as the *Pema Kat'ang* (*pad ma bka thang*).

Crystal Rosary of Wrathful Mantras. Tantra transmitted to Śāntigarbha. Tib. *drag sngags shel 'phreng.*

Cycle of the Dharma Guardians Zhanglön and Pomra. Revealed by Dudul Dorje. Tib. *bka' srung zhang blon dang spom ra'i skor.*

Cycle of the Glorious Tiger-Riding Protector. Revealed by Dudul Dorje. Tib. *dpal mgon stag zhon skor.*

Cycle of the Profound Meaning of the Secret Heart Essence. Revealed by Dudul Dorje. Tib. *zab don gsang ba snying thig dpal bde mchog bka' srung phyag bzhi pa'i skor dang bcas pa.* Includes the cycles of *Glorious Cakrasaṃvara* (*dpal bde mchog*) and the *Four-Armed Protector* (*bka' srung phyag bzhi pa*).

Cycle of the Three Yidam Deities: Red Yamari, Black Yamari, and Bhairava. Revealed by Dudul Dorje. Tib. *yi dam dmar nag 'jigs gsum gyi skor.*

Cycles of the Peaceful and Wrathful Deities of the Magical Infinity and of the Eight Heruka Sādhanas, Including Their Protectors. Revealed by Dudul Dorje. Tib. *sgyu 'phrul zhi khro'i skor dang bka' brgyad skor bka' srung bcas.*

Cycles of the Wish-Fulfilling Crown Jewel of the Aural Lineage. Revealed by Dudul Dorje. Tib. snyan brgyud gtsug rgyan yid bzhin nor bu'i skor.

Cycles Tradition of the Great Perfection. Tib. rdzogs chen skor lugs. The tradition of the four cycles of the Upadeśa Class of the Great Perfection: the *Bodylike Outer Cycle* (*lus dang 'dra ba phyi skor*), the *Eyelike Inner Cycle* (*mig dang 'dra ba nang skor*), the *Heartlike Secret Cycle* (*snying dang 'dra ba gsang skor*), and the *Quintessential Supremely Secret Cycle That Resembles Complete Perfection* (*thams cad rdzogs pa dang 'dra ba yang gsang bla na med pa'i skor*).

Dhāraṇī of Secret Relics. Skt. *Guhyadhātu-dhāraṇī.* Tib. *gsang ba ring bsrel gyi gzungs.*

Dhāraṇīs of the Ten Bhūmis. Skt. *Daśabhūmi-dhāraṇī.* Tib. *sa bcu pa'i gzungs.*

Dharma Dharmatā Vibhānga. See *Distinguishing between Dharma and Dharmatā.*

Dharma History of the Early Translation School: The Melodious Sound of Devendra's Great Drum [Proclaiming] *Victory in War.* Kyabje Dudjom Jigdral Yeshe Dorje Rinpoche. Tib. *snga 'gyur ba'i chos 'byung lha dbang g.yul las rgyal ba'i rnga bo che'i sgra dbyangs.* In the *Sungbum* (Collected Works) of Kyabje Dudjom Jigdral Yeshe Dorje Rinpoche (Kalimpong, India: Dupjung Lama, 1979), vol. KA (1). English translation: *The Nyingma School of Tibetan Buddhism: Its Fundamentals and History,* trans. and ed. by Gyurme Dorje and Matthew Kapstein (Boston: Wisdom Publications, 1991). This English translation consists of the two Tibetan volumes combined into one. Book 1 is *Fundamentals of the Nyingma School of Tibetan Buddhism*, which is the translation of vol. 2 (KHA) of the Tibetan edition, *snga 'gyur bstan pa'i rnam bzhag.* Book 2 of the English edition is *History of the Nyingma School of Tibetan Buddhism*, which is the translation of the Tibetan vol. 1 (KA), *rnying ma'i chos 'byung.*

Discourse on the Precious Scriptures. Kawa Paltsek. Tib. *gsung rab rin po che'i gtam.*

Distinguishing between Dharma and Dharmatā. Maitreya, as spoken to Asaṅga. Skt. *Dharmadharmatā-vibhaṅga.* Tib. *chos dang chos nyid rnam'byed.* One of the works in the *Five Treatises of Maitreya.*

Distinguishing between Middle and Extremes. Maitreya, as spoken to Asaṅga. Skt. *Madhyānta-vibhāṅga.* Tib. *dbus mtha' rnam par 'byed pa.* One of the works in the *Five Treatises of Maitreya.*

Dohā Trilogy. See *Dohākośa.*

Dohākośa (Treasury of Dohā). Tib. *do ha'i mdzod.* Saraha. Also called the *Dohā Trilogy*, as the collection of Saraha's spontaneous songs of realization is divided into three sections: the dohā for the king, the dohā for the queen, and the dohā for the subjects.

Doorway to Speech Like a Sword. Smṛtijñāna. Tib. *smra sgo mtshon cha*.

Eight Commands: Gathering of the Sugatas. Compiler: Vairotsana. Tib. *bka' brgyad bde gshegs 'dus pa*.

Eight Mahākāla Tantras. Revealed by Nāgārjuna. Tib. *ma ha ka la'i rgyud bgyad*.

Eight Volumes of Amṛta. Tib. *bdud rtsi bam brgyad*.

Eighty Chapters of Personal Advice. Zurchungpa Sherab Dragpa. Tib. *zhal gyi gdams pa brgyad cu pa*.

Embodiment of the Master's Realization. Sangye Lingpa. Tib. *bla ma dgongs 'dus*.

Embodiment of Wisdom Mind. Tib. *spyi mdo dgongs pa 'dus pa*. The principal text of Anuyoga tantra. Also known as the *General Sūtra* or the *General Sūtra That Gathers All Wisdom*.

Entering the Three Kāyas. Candragomin. Skt. Kāyatrayāvatāra. Tib. *sku gsum la 'jug pa*.

Entering the Way of the Great Vehicle. Rongzompa. Tib. *theg pa chen po'i tshul la 'jug pa*.

Establishing the Authenticity of the Great Heruka Sādhana. Hūṃkāra. Tib. *khrag 'thung chen po'i sgrub thabs yang dag par grub pa*.

Expanded Commentary on the "Later Concentrations." Buddhaguhya. Skt. *Dhyānottarapaṭala-ṭīkā*. Tib. *bsam gtan phyi ma rim par phye ba rgya cher bshad pa*. Commentary on the *Dhyānottara-tantra* (Tantra of Later Concentrations).

Extensive Commentary on "Praise to the Exalted." Prajñāvarman. Tib. *khyad par du 'phags pa'i bstod pa'i rgya cher bshad pa*. Commentary on the hymn attributed to Bhatasiddhi and/or Camkarapati.

Extensive Commentary on *"Praise to the Tathāgata Who Surpasses Worldly Gods."* Prajñāvarman. Tib. *lha las phul du byung bar bstod pa'i rgya cher 'grel pa*. Commentary on the hymn attributed to Bhatasiddhi and/or Camkarapati.

Extensive Commentary on the "Tantra of the All-Doing Great King." Katok Dampa Deshek. Tib. *kun byed rgyal po'i rgyud 'grel chen mo*. Commentary on the *Kūlayarāja-tantra* (Tib. *kun byed rgyal po*).

Extensive, Middling, and Concise Classifications of the Tantras. Katok Dampa Deshek. Tib. *rgyud kyi dbye ba rgyas 'bring bsdus gsum*.

Extensive, Middling, and Concise General Commentaries on the "Lamp for the Eye of Samādhi." Katok Dampa Deshek. Tib. *bsam gtan mig sgron spyi 'grel rgyas 'bring bsdus gsum*.

Extensive Sūtra of Samayas. Rongzompa. Tib. *dam tshig mdo rgyas*.

Extensive Twenty-Five-Chapter Commentary on the "Embodiment of Wisdom Mind." Katok Dampa Deshek. Tib. *mdo'i 'grel chen le'u nyer lnga pa*.

Eye-Opening Commentary on the "Supplementary Magical Infinity." Vimalamitra. Tib. *le lag gi spyan 'grel*.

Five Great Treasuries. Jamgön Kongtrul Lodrö Taye. Tib. *mdzod chen lnga*. (1) *Great Treasury of Precious Termas* (*rin chen gter mdzod chen mo*), (2) *Treasury of Precious Instructions* (*gdams ngag rin po che'i mdzod*), (3) *Treasury of Kagyu Mantras* (*bka' brgyud sngags mdzod*), (4) *Treasury of Extensive Teachings* (*rgya chen bka' mdzod*), and (5) *Treasury of All-Encompassing Knowledge* (*shes bya kun khyab mdzod*).

Five Treatises of Maitreya. Maitreya, as spoken to Asaṅga. Tib. *byams chos sde lnga*. Comprising five individual works listed separately in this bibliography: *Ornament of Manifest Realization*, *Ornament of the Mahāyāna Sūtras*, *Distinguishing between Middle and Extremes*, *Distinguishing between Dharma and Dharmatā*, and *Unsurpassed Continuity*.

Five Treatises on the Yogācāra Levels. Asaṅga. Skt. *Yogācārabhūmipañcavarga*. Tib. *rnal 'byor spyod pa'i sa sde lnga*. (1) *Foundation of the Yogācāra Levels* (*Yogācārabhūmi-vastu*), which includes *Treatise on the Yogācāra Levels* (*Yogācārabhūmi*), *Treatise on the* Śrāvaka *Levels* (Śrāvaka*bhūmi*), and *Treatise on the Bodhisattva Levels* (*Bodhisattvabhūmi*); (2) *Summation of Ascertainment* (*Viniścaya-saṃgrahaṇī*); (3) *Summation of the Ground* (*Vastu-saṃgrahaṇī*); (4) *Summation of Enumerated Categories* (*Paryāya-saṃgrahaṇī*); and (5) *Summation of Training* (*Vivaraṇa-saṃgrahaṇī*).

Fivefold Ritual for Entering All Maṇḍalas. Kukkurāja. Skt. *Sarvamaṇḍalānuvarti-pañcavidhi*. Tib. *dkyil 'khor thams cad kyi rjes su 'jug pa'i cho ga nga pa*.

Flame of Dialectics. Bhāviveka. Skt. *Tarkajvālā*. Tib. *rtog ge 'bar ba*. Autocommentary on Bhāviveka's *Madhyamakahṛdaya-kārikā* (Heart of the Middle Way).

Former Lives of the Buddha. Skt. *Jātakanidāna*. Tib. *skyes pa rabs kyi gleng gzhi*. The standard Pāli collection of jātakas.

Fortunate Eon Sūtra. Skt. *Bhadrakalpika-sūtra*. Tib. *bskal pa bzang po'i mdo*.

Four-Armed Protector. See *Cycle of the Profound Meaning of the Secret Heart Essence*.

Four Branches and Leaves. Ngorchen Kunga Zangpo. Tib. *yal 'dab bzhi pa*. A biography of Rongzompa.

Four Heart Essences. Longchenpa. Tib. *snying thig ya bzhi*. A famous collection of four Dzogchen instructions: the *Vima Nyingtik* (Vimalamitri), the *Lama Yangtik* (Longchenpa), the *Khandro Nyingtik* (Padmasambhava), and the *Khandro Yangtik* (Longchenpa). The collection also includes additional teachings by Longchenpa known as the *Zabmo Yangtik*.

Four Hundred Stanzas on the Middle Way. Āryadeva. Skt. *Catuḥśataka*. Tib. *bzhi brgya pa*.

Four Medical Tantras. Revealed by Drapa Ngönshe. Tib. *rgyud bzhi*. The four texts are the *Root Medical Tantra* (*rtsa rgyud*), the *Explanatory Tantra* (*bshad rgyud*), the *Instructional Tantra* (*man ngag gi rgyud*), and the *Subsequent Tantra* (*phyi ma'i rgyud*).

Four Modes and Fifteen Branches Commentary. Rongzompa. Tib. *tshul bzhi yan lag bco lnga pa*.

Four Modes of Placement. Jñānasūtra; revealed by Vimalamitra. Tib. *bzhag thabs bzhi*.

Fully Enlightened Buddhahood Sūtra of Dharma and Enjoyment. Tib. *chos dang longs spyod mngon par sangs rgyas pa'i mdo.* This scripture appears in citations but seems to be no longer extant as part of any collection.

Garland of Activity Tantra. Tib. *phrin las kyi rgyud karma ma le.*

Gathering of Secrets Tantra. Tib. *thugs rgyud gsang ba 'dus pa.*

General Commentary on the "Embodiment of Wisdom Mind." Katok Dampa Deshek. Tib. *mdo'i spyi don.*

General Outline of Vehicles: The Flower Ornament of General Chö. Katok Dampa Deshek. Tib. *spyi gcod rgyan gyi me tog theg pa spyi chings.*

General Sūtra That Gathers All Wisdom. See *Embodiment of Wisdom Mind.*

General Tantra of Magical Infinity. See *Guhyagarbha: The Root Tantra.*

Glorious Cakrasaṃvara. See *Cycle of the Profound Meaning of the Secret Heart Essence.*

Glorious Four-Faced Protector. Revealed by Dudul Dorje. Tib. *dpal mgon gdong bzhi'i skor.*

Glorious Secret Essence That Ascertains the Absolute Nature Just As It Is. Tib. *dpal gsang ba snying po de kho nan yid nge pa.* See also *Guhyagarbha: The Root Tantra.*

Glorious Supreme Beginning Tantra. Skt. *Paramādyakalparāja.* Tib. *dpal mchog dang po.* The tantra of enlightened qualities.

Goddess Kālī Tantra. Revealed by Nāgārjuna. Skt. *Devikālīpraśaṃsārāja-tantra.* Tib. *lha mo nag mo'i rgyud.*

Gone to Laṅka. Skt. *Laṅkāvatāra-sūtra.* Tib. *lang kar gshegs pa'i mdo.*

Grammar of Morphology. Tönmi Sambhota. Tib. *lung ston pa rtags kyi 'jug pa.*

Great Collection of Teachings on the Path and Its Fruit. Tib. *gsung ngag rin po che lam 'bras bu dang bcas pa.* A collection of teachings in the Sakya tradition, in 43 volumes.

Great Image. Vairotsana; compiled by Yudra Nyingpo and other disciples. Tib. *'dra 'bag chen mo.* According to Ani Jinpa Palmo's preface to her translation of Vairotsana's autobiography, *The Great Image: The Life Story of Vairochana the Translator* (published 2004, with an introduction by Kyabje Thinley Norbu Rinpoche), this version (*'dra 'bag chen mo*) was concealed as a treasure and revealed by Jomo Menmo, while another (*thang yig*) was orally transmitted and edited by Dharma Senge.

Great Treasury of Detailed Explanations. Skt. *Mahāvibhāṣā-śāstra.* Tib. *bye brag bshad mdzod chen mo.* The root Abhidharma text of the Kashmiri Sarvāstivādins. It is extant only in Chinese translation.

Great Treasury of Precious Termas. Compiler: Jamgön Kongtrul Lodrö Taye, assisted by Jamyang Khyentse Wangpo. Tib. *rin chen gter mdzod chen mo.* The largest of the *Five Great Treasuries* of Jamgön Kongtrul the Great (a recent edition consists of 72 volumes). It contains the main terma texts along with their empowerment and guidance texts.

Guhya Mañjuśrī. Vilāsavajra (Gegpa Dorje). Tib. *'jam dpal gsang ldan.* Translated into Tibetan by Rongzompa.

Guhyagarbha: The Root Tantra. Tib. *rtsa rgyud gsang ba snying po.* Among the alternate titles for the *Guhyagarbha Tantra* used in this book are *General Tantra of Magical Infinity* (*spyi rgyud sgyu 'phrul drwa ba*); *Secret Essence Tantra* (*gsang ba snying po* or *gsang snying*); *Glorious Secret Essence That Ascertains the Absolute Nature Just As it Is* (*dpal gsang ba snying po de kho nyid nges pa'i rgyud*); and *Root Tantra of Magical Infinity* (*sgru 'phrul rtsa rgyud*).

Guhyagarbha Tantra. See *Guhyagarbha: The Root Tantra*.

Guhyasamāja Tantra (Tantra of the Secret Assembly). Tib. *gsang ba 'dus pa'i rgyud*.

Guide to the Hidden Land of Pemakö. Revealed by Dudul Dorje. Tib. *sbas yul pad ma bkod pa'i gnas yig*.

Guru Embodiment of Vidyādharas. Revealed by Dudul Dorje. Tib. *bla ma rig 'dzin 'dus pa*.

Guru Tantra. Tib. *bla ma*.

Hayagrīva [Tantra]. Tib. *rta mchog rol pa'i rgyud* (Tantra of the Manifestation of Hayagrīva).

Heap of Jewels. Skt. *Ratnakūṭa*. Tib. *dkon mchog brtsegs pa*. A collection of forty-nine Mahāyāna sūtras on a range of themes.

Heart Essence of the Lake-Born Vajra. Revealed by Kyabje Dudjom Jigdral Yeshe Dorje Rinpoche. Tib. *mtsho skyes thugs thig*. Mind treasure revealed in 1929, focused on Guru Padmasambhava in the form of Guru Tsokye Dorje. It is the main Guru sādhana in the Dudjom Tersar lineage and one of the four main treasure cycles of Kyabje Dudjom Rinpoche.

Heart Essence Triad of Amitāyus, Yangdak Heruka, and Vajrakīlaya. Revealed by Dudul Dorje. Tib. *snying thig tshe gyang phur gsum*.

Heruka Galpo Tantra. Attributed to Hūṃkāra. Tib. *he ru ka gal po*.

Hevajra [Tantra]. Compiled by Vajragarbha. Tib. *dgyes rdor gyi rgyud*.

Hidden Meanings of the "Guyhagarbha Root Tantra" Called "Celebration of Awareness." Khenchen Jampal Dewe Nyima. Tib. *rtsa rgyud gsang ba snying po'i sbas don rig pa'i dga' ston*.

Historical Account of the Origin of the Teaching of Vajrakīlaya Namchak Pudri. Kyabje Dudjom Jigdral Yeshe Dorje Rinpoche. Full title: *A Brief Explanation of the Historical Account of the Origin of the Teaching of Glorious Vajrakīlaya, Dudjom Namchak Pudri, Called the "Celebration for the Ears of Fortunate Ones."* Tib. *gnam lcags spu gri'i lo rgyus chos kyi byung tshul mdo tsam spros pa skal bzang rna ba'i dga' ston*.

History of Treasures. Dudul Dorje. Tib. *gter 'byung*.

Holy Golden Light Sūtra. Skt. *Suvarṇaprabhāsottama-sūtra*. Tib. *gser 'od dam pa'i mdo*.

Holy Teachings of the Heart Essence of the Nirmāṇakāya (together with the practice of Kṣetrapāla). Revealed by Dudul Dorje. Tib. *dam chos sprul sku snying thig bka' srung zhing skyong dang bcas pa*.

Hundred Thousand Quintessential Tantric Texts. Transmitted to Dhanasaṃskṛita. Tib. *rgyud lung 'bum tig*.

Hundred Thousand Verses of Tārā's Perfect Renunciation. Bhatasiddhi. Tib. *sgrol ma mngon par 'byung ba'i rtog pa 'bum pa.*

Hundred-Thousandfold Supreme Awareness Tantra. Skt. *Vidyottama-tantra*. Tib. *Vit+tot mala 'bum sde'i rgyud*. Translated into Tibetan by Padmasambhava and Vairotsana.

Infinity of Pure Wisdom Phenomena. Revealed by Dudjom Lingpa. Tib. *dag snang ye shes drwa ba*. A treasure cycle revealed in 1867. Among other things, it contains the Dudjom Tersar preliminary practices, Tröma Nakmo practices, and Dudjom Lingpa's autobiography, *Clear Mirror*.

Inscribed History of Prophecies. Kyabje Dudjom Jigdral Yeshe Dorje Rinpoche. Tib. *lo rgyus lung gi byang bu*. A short history of prophecies from the *Dorje Drölo* cycle *Quintessential Secret Gathering*.

Introduction to Yoga. Buddhaguhya. Skt. *Tantrārthāvatāra*. Tib. *yo ga la 'jug pa*.

Kālacakra Root Tantra. Skt. *Kālacakramūla-tantra*. Tib. *dus 'khor rtsa rgyud*. The *Kālacakra Root Tantra* is said to have 12,000 verses, but only a part of this tantra that briefly explains empowerments was translated into Tibetan.

Kālacakra Tantra. See *Abridged Kālacakra Tantra*.

King of Samādhi Sūtra. Skt. *Samādhirāja-sūtra*. Tib. *ting nge 'dzin gyi rgyal po'i mdo*. Also known as the *Moon Lamp Sūtra* (Skt. *Candrapradīpa-sūtra;* Tib. *zla ba sgron me'i mdo*).

Kṣetrapāla. See *Holy Teachings of the Heart Essence of the Nirmāṇakāya*.

Lamp for the Eye of Samādhi: Upadeśa of the Great Perfection. Nubchen Sangye Yeshe. Tib. *rdzogs chen gyi man ngag bsam gtan mig sgron*.

Lamp for the Path to Enlightenment. Atiśa. Skt. *Bodhipathapradīpa*. Tib. *byang chub lam gyi sgron ma*.

Lamp of Sublime Knowledge. Bhāviveka. Skt. *Prajñāpradīpa*. Tib. *shes rab sgron me*. Commentary on Nāgārjuna's *Root Verses on the Middle Way Called "Sublime Knowledge"* and countercommentary on Buddhapālita's *Commentary on "Root Verses on the Middle Way Called 'Sublime Knowledge.'"*

Laṅkāvatāra Sūtra. See *Gone to Laṅka*.

Lasso of the Ārya's Method Called "Garland of Lotuses." Tib. *'phags pa zhags pa pad ma'i phreng ba*.

Later Tantra of the Coming of Cakrasaṃvara. Skt. *Saṃvarodayottara-tantra*. Tib. *bde mchog sdom 'byung gi rgyud phyi ma*.

Letter of Praise to the Dharma King of the Three Realms. Chögyal Phagpa. Tib. *khams gsum chos kyi rgyal por bsngags pa'i spring yig*.

Letter to a Disciple. Candragomin. Skt. *Śiṣyalekha*. Tib. *slob spring*.

Letter to a Friend. Nāgārjuna. Skt. *Suhṛllekha*. Tib. *bshes pa'i spring yig*.

Madhyamaka Avatāra (Entering the Middle Way). Candrakīrti. Skt. *Madhyamakāvatāra*. Tib. *dbu ma la 'jug pa*.

Madhyānta Vibhaṅga. See *Distinguishing between Middle and Extremes*.

Magical Infinity of Mañjuśrī. Tib. *'jam dpal sgyu 'phrul drwa ba*.

Magical Infinity of Vairocana. Tib. *rnam snang sgyu 'phrul drwa ba*.

Magical Infinity of Vajrasattva. Tib. *rdo rje sems dpa' sgyu 'phrul drwa ba*. An alternate name for the *Guhyagarbha*. According to the Zur tradition, one of the eight sections of the *Magical Infinity* tantras. According to Longchenpa, however, it is categorized as one of the four sections of the *Magical Infinity*.

Magical Vajra. See *Mirror of All the Magical Infinity Tantras*.

Magnificent Wisdom Lightning Tantra. Tib. *ye shes rnam glog*.

Mahāmāyā Tantra. Tib. *sgyu 'phrul chen po'i rgyud*.

Mahāparinirvāṇa Sūtra (Sūtra on the Great Final Nirvāṇa). Often called the *Nirvāṇa Sūtra*. Tib. *mdo myang 'das*.

Mahāsamaya Sūtra (Great Meeting Sūtra). Tib. *dam tshig chen po'i mdo*.

Mahāyāna Samucchaya. Asaṅga. Tib. *theg pa chen po bsdus pa*.

Main Sādhana Practice. Katok Dampa Deshek. Tib. *sgrub gzhung*. Practice for the *Lasso of Skillful Means* (*thabs kyi zhags pa*).

Mañjuśrī Root Tantra. Skt. *Mañjuśrīmūla-tantra*. Tib. *'jam dpal gyi rtsa ba'i rgyud*.

Mātaraḥ [Tantra]. Tib. *ma mo*.

Mind Class of the Great Perfection. Tib. *rdzogs chen sems kyi sde*.

Minor Transmissions of the Vinaya. Skt. *Vinayakṣudrāgama*. Tib. *'dul ba lung phran tshegs*.

Mirror of All the Vajrasattva Magical Infinity Tantras. Tib. *rdo rje sems dpa' sgyu 'phrul thams cad kyi me long*. According to Longchenpa, one of the eight tantras of the *Magical Infinity of Vajrasattva*. An abbreviated title for this work is *Magical Vajra* (*sgyu 'phrul rdo rje*).

Mirror That Reflects the Treasure Guide of the "Profound Secret Heart Essence of the Ḍākinī," A. Revealed by Dudjom Lingpa. Tib. *zab gsang mkha' 'gro'i snying thig kha byang gsal ba'i Adarsha*.

Moon Lamp Sūtra. See *King of Samādhi Sūtra*.

Mudrā Concentration. Vimalamitra. Skt. *Māyājālamudrādhyāna*. Tib. *phyag rgya bsam gtan*.

Mūlamadhyamaka Prajñā. See *Root Verses on the Middle Way Called "Sublime Knowledge."*

Namchak Pudri (Meteoric Iron Razor That Vanquishes Māra). Revealed by Dudjom Lingpa. Tib. *phur ba gnam lcags spu gri*. Full title: *bdud 'joms gnam lcags spu gri'i thugs sgrub gsang ba rgya can* (Secret Sealed Mind Sādhana of Dudjom Vajrakīlaya Namchak Pudri). A Vajrakīlaya terma practice revealed in 1862 from several treasure sites in East Tibet. Along with the *Pudri Regpung*, it is one of the two main Vajrakīlaya practices of the Dudjom Tersar lineage.

Natural Liberation of Awareness. Tib. *rig pa rang grol*. One of the Seventeen Tantras of the Upadeśa Section of the Great Perfection. Subsidiary to the *Penetration of Sound*.

Nine Cycles of the Formless Ḍākinīs. Tib. *lus med mkha' 'gro skor dgu*.

Noble Shoulder Tantra. Tib. *dpung pa bzang po'i rgyud*.

Notes on "Revealing the Names of Mañjuśrī." Katok Dampa Deshek. Tib. *mtshan brjod mchan.*

Notes on Stages of the Path and Its Condensed Meaning. Katok Dampa Deshek. Tib. *lam rim mchan dang bsdus don.*

Notes on the "Ocean of Magical Manifestations." Katok Dampa Deshek. Tib. *sgyu 'phrul rgya mtsho'i mchan.*

Notes on the "Parkhab Commentary on the 'Guhyagarbha Tantra.'" Katok Dampa Deshek. Tib. *gsang 'grel spar khab mchan.*

Nyingma Gyubum (Nyingma Collected Tantras). Tib. *rnying ma rgyud 'bum.*

Nyingma School of Tibetan Buddhism, The. See *Dharma History of the Early Translation School.*

Nyingtik Yabzhi. See *Four Heart Essences.*

Ocean of Dharma That Embodies All Teachings. Padmasambhava. Tib. *bka' 'dus chos kyi rgya mtsho.*

One Hundred and Fifty Verses of Praise. Aśvaghoṣa. Skt. *Śatapañcāśatkastotra.* Tib. *bstod pa brgya lnga chu pa.*

One Hundred and One Formal Ecclesiastical Acts. Guṇaprabha. Skt. *Ekottarakarmaśataka.* Tib. *las brgya rtsa gcig pa.*

One-Pointed Samādhi Tantra. Skt. *Avalokiteśvarasamādhyeka-tantra.* Tib. *ting 'dzin rtse gcig.*

Opening the Eyes of Prajñā. Vimalamitra. Tib. *shes rab spyan 'byed.*

Oral Instructions of Mañjuśri. Tib. *'jam dpal zhal lung.*

Ornament of Awareness. Gelong Deje. Tib. *rig pa'i rgyan.*

Ornament of Manifest Realization. Maitreya, as spoken to Asaṅga. Skt. *Abhisamayālaṃkāra.* Tib. *mngon rtogs rgyan.* One of the works in the *Five Treatises of Maitreya.*

Ornament of Spontaneous Songs. Jigme Lingpa. Tib. *do ha'i rgyan.*

Ornament of the Mahāyāna Sūtras. Maitreya, as spoken to Asaṅga. Skt. *Sūtrālaṃkāra.* Tib. *mdo sde rgyan.* One of the works in the *Five Treatises of Maitreya.*

Outline of the Path of the Great Perfection. Katok Dampa Deshek. Tib. *rdzogs chen lam gyi khog dbub.*

Pāṇini's Grammar. Pāṇini. Skt. *Aṣṭādhyāyī.* Tib. *sgra pa ni.*

Parkhab Commentary of the Wisdom Mind of Samantabhadra: Notes on All-Inclusive Awareness, the Vajra Adornment. Katok Dampa Deshek. Tib. *kun 'dus rig pa rdo rje bkod pa'i mchan kun bzang dgongs pa'i spar khab.*

Parkhab Commentary on the "Guhyagarbha Tantra." Vilāsavajra (Gegpa Dorje). Tib. *gsang ba snying po'i 'grel pa spar khab.*

Peaceful and Wrathful Deities. Revealed by Pema Lingpa. Full title: Tib. *pad gling zhi thro kun bzang dgongs 'dus* (Embodiment of the Wisdom Mind of Samantabhadra).

Peaceful Practice of Mañjuśrī. Revealed by Dudul Dorje. Tib. 'jam dpal zhi sgrub kyi skor.

Pearl Rosary, The: A Prayer to the Emanations. Kyabje Dudjom Jigdral Yeshe Dorje Rinpoche. Tib. *sku 'phreng gsol 'debs muk+ti ka'i do shal*. In the *Sungbum* (Collected Works) of Kyabje Dudjom Jigdral Yeshe Dorje Rinpoche, vol. 25 (AH). Kalimpong, India: Dupjung Lama, 1979. English translation in *The Ruby Rosary: Joyfully Accepted by Vidyādharas and Ḍākinīs as the Ornament of a Necklace*, trans. Heidi Nevin (Shambhala Publications, 2022).

Penetration of Sound. Tib. *rtsa ba'i rgyud sgra thal 'gyur*. The root tantra of the Seventeen Tantras of the Upadeśa Section of the Great Perfection.

Perfect Collection of All Noble Dharmas Sūtra. Skt. *Dharmasaṃgīti-sūtra*. Tib. *chos thams cad yang dag par sdud pa'i mdo*.

Perfect Conduct: Ascertaining the Three Vows. Ngari Panchen Pema Wangyi Gyalpo. Tib. *sdom gsum rnam nges*.

Perfect Practice of Vajrakīlaya. Vimalamitra. Tib. *phur pa phun sum tshogs pa*.

Play in Full Sūtra. Skt. *Lalitavistara-sūtra*. Tib. *rgya cher rol pa*.

Poison Razor. Tib. *g.za' bdud dug gi spu gri* (Rāhula Demon Poisoned Razor). Invocation prayer to the wrathful protector Rāhula, who is like a demon to those who harm the teachings of Buddha.

Powerful King of Pure Vision. Dudul Dorje. Tib. *dag snang dbang gi rgyal po*.

Prabhāvati (*Luminosity*). Śākyaprabha. Tib. *'od ldan*. Autocommentary on the *Vinaya in Three Hundred Verses*.

Practice Manual of Ārya Tārā Kurukullā. Transmitted by Nāgārjuna. Skt. Ārya-Tārā-kurukullākalpa. Tib. *'phags ma sgrol ma ku ru ku le'i rtog pa*.

Praise to Mañjuśrī with the Tilted Head. Skt. *Bhagavadāryamañjuśrīsādhiṣṭhāna-stuti*. Tib. *'jam dbyangs mjing yon gyi bstod pa*. One of the "four great praises." The other three are *Praise to the Pointing Avalokiteśvara*; *Praise to the Tathāgata Who Surpasses Worldly Gods*; and *Praise to Tārā Who Holds a Flower Garland*.

Praise to Tārā Who Holds a Flower Garland. Tib. *sgrol ma'i bstod pa me tog phreng 'dzin*. One of the "four great praises." The other three are *Praise to Mañjuśrī with the Tilted Head*; *Praise to the Pointing Avalokiteśvara*; and *Praise to the Tathāgata Who Surpasses Worldly Gods*.

Praise to the Exalted. Attributed to Bhatasiddhi and/or Camkarapati. Skt. *Viśeṣa-stava*. Tib. *khyad par 'phags bstod*. Hymn in praise of Buddha Śākyamuni.

Praise to the Pointing Avalokiteśvara. Tib. *thugs rje chen po mdzub ker gyi bstod pa*. One of the "four great praises." The other three are *Praise to Mañjuśrī with the Tilted Head; Praise to the Tathāgata Who Surpasses Worldly Gods;* and *Praise to Tārā Who Holds a Flower Garland*.

Praise to the Tathāgata Who Surpasses Worldly Gods. Attributed to Bhatasiddhi and/or Camkarapati. Skt. *Devātiśayastotra*. Tib. *de bzhin gshegs pa la lha las phul byung du bstod pa*. One of the "four great praises." The other three are *Praise to Mañjuśrī with the Tilted Head*; *Praise to the Pointing Avalokiteśvara*; and *Praise to Tārā Who Holds a Flower Garland*.

Prajñāpāramitā (*Perfection of Sublime Knowledge*). Tib. *sher phyin*. The

Mahāyāna sūtras collected under the title *Prajñāpāramitā* are of varying lengths. They include the *Prajñāpāramitā Sūtra in Eight Thousand Lines* (Skt. *Aṣṭasāhasrikāprajñāpāramitā-sūtra*; Tib. *sher phyin brgyad stong pa*) and the *Prajñāpāramitā Sūtra in One Hundred Thousand Lines* (Skt. *Śatasāhasrikāprajñāpāramitā-sūtra*; Tib. *sher phyin stong phrag brgya pa*).

Pramāṇa Samucchaya. See *Compilation of All Teachings on Logic*.

Pramāṇa Vārttika (Commentary on *Compilation of All Teachings on Logic*). Dharmakīrti. Tib. *tshad ma rnam 'grel*.

Pramāṇa Viniścaya (Ascertainment of Valid Cognition). Dharmakīrti. Tib. *tshad ma rnam par nges pa*.

Pramāṇa Yuktinidhi (Treasury of Valid Cognition). Tib. *tshad ma rigs pa'i gter*. Sakya Paṇḍita. Synthesizes all of Dharmakirti's seven writings on valid cognition.

Prātimokṣa Sūtra (Sūtra on the Vows of Individual Liberation). Tib. *so sor thar pa'i mdo*.

Prayer for Excellent Conduct. Skt. *Bhadracaryapraṇidhāna-rāja*. Tib. *bzang po spyod pa'i smon lam*. From the *Gaṇḍavyūha* chapter of the *Avataṃsaka Sūtra*.

Prayer with the Various Names of Dudjom Tulkus. Kyabje Dudjom Jigdral Yeshe Dorje Rinpoche. Tib. *bdud 'joms sprul sku'i ming gi rnam grangs las brtsams pa'i gsol 'debs*.

Precious Garland. Nāgārjuna. Skt. *Ratnāvalī*. Tib. *rin chen 'phreng ba*. Considered by some scholars to be one of the texts in Nāgārjuna's *Collection of Six Texts on Reasoning*, while others include it in *Collection of Discourses*.

Precious Lamp: An Outline of the "Bodhicarya Avatāra" and Its Condensed Meaning. Katok Dampa Deshek. Tib. *spyod 'jug khog dbub rin chen sgron me dang de'i bdus don*.

Profound Secret Heart Essence of the Ḍakinī. Revealed by Dudjom Lingpa. Tib. *zab gsang mkha' 'gro'i snying thig*. The only Earth Treasure cycle revealed by Dudjom Lingpa, this practice cycle contains the *Khandro Nyingtik* preliminary practices, a Chö practice, and a Vajrakīlaya treasure. This cycle, the *Zabsang Khandro Nyingtik*, formed the basis of the *Namchak Pudri* arrangements.

Profound Teaching Overflowing from the Expanse of Wisdom Mind. Revealed by Dudjom Lingpa. Tib. *zab chos dgongs pa klong rdol*. Treasure cycle containing practices of Avalokiteśvara and Hayagrīva.

Pudri Regpung (Razor That Destroys at a Touch). Tib. *spu gri reg phung*. Revealed by Kyabje Dudjom Jigdral Yeshe Dorje Rinpoche. Vajrakīlaya mind treasure revealed by Kyabje Dudjom Rinpoche in Paro Taktsang, Bhutan, in 1937 and written in 1948. Along with the *Namchak Pudri*, it is one of the two main Vajrakīlaya practices of the Dudjom Tersar lineage.

Quintessential Secret and Unsurpassed Vajrakilaya. Revealed by Ratna Lingpa. Tib. *phur pa yang gsang bla med*.

Rampant Elephant Tantra. Skt. *Hastigajipadama-tantra*. Tib. *glang chen rab 'bog*.

Ratnakūṭa Sūtra. See *Heap of Jewels*.

Record of Profound and Extensive Dharma Teachings Received Called "Precious Lamp." Kyabje Dudjom Jigdral Yeshe Dorje Rinpoche. Tib. *zab pa dang rgya che ba'i dam pa'i chos kyi thob yig rin chen sgron me.*

Red Garuḍa with Wings of Fire. Revealed by Dudul Rolpa Tsal. Tib. *khyung dmar me gshog.*

Refutation of Objections. Nāgārjuna. Skt. *Vigrahavyāvartanī.* Tib. *rtsod bzlog.* One of the texts in Nāgārjuna's *Collection of Six Texts on Reasoning.*

Revealing the Names of Mañjuśrī. Skt. *Mañjuśrīnāmasaṃgīti.* Tib. *jam dpal mtshan brjod.*

Ritual for Cremation. Vimalamitra. Tib. *ro sreg.*

Ritual for Fire Offerings. Vimalamitra. Tib. *sbyin sreg.*

Rituals for Cultivating Bodhicitta. Katok Dampa Deshek. Tib. *byang chub sems bskyed kyi cho ga.*

Root Grammar in Thirty Verses. Tönmi Sambhota. Tib. lung ston pa rtsa ba sum cu pa. Treatise on Tibetan grammar.

Root Tantra of Magical Infinity. See *Guhyagarbha: The Root Tantra.*

Root Tantra of Mañjuśrī. Skt. *Mañjuśrīmūla-tantra.* Tib. *'phags pa 'jam dpal gyi rtsa ba'i rgyud.*

Root Tantra of the Gathering of the Sugatas. Tib. *bder 'dus rtsa rgyud.*

Root Verses on the Middle Way Called "Sublime Knowledge." Nāgārjuna. Skt. *Mūlamadhyamaka-prajñā* or *Prajñā-nāma-mūlamadhyamaka-kārikā.* Tib. *dbu ma rtsa ba'i tshig le'ur byas pa.*

Sādhana of Keen Mañjuśrī. Skt. *Tīkṣṇamañjuśrīsādhana.* Tib. *'jam dpal rnon po.*

Sādhana of Mahādeva. Cycle revealed by Dudul Dorje. Tib. *lha chen sgrub skor.*

Sādhana of Spontaneous Presence. Vilāsavajra (Gegpa Dorje). Skt. *Guhyasamāja-sahajasādhana.* Tib. *lhan skyes sgrub thabs.*

Samantabhadra Grammar Sūtra. Candrakīrti. Skt. *Samantabhadravyākaraṇa.* Tib. *sgra mdo kun tu bzang po.*

Saṃvarodaya Tantra (Tantra of the Coming of Cakrasaṃvara). Compiled by Vajrapāṇi. Tib. *sdom 'byung gi rgyud.*

Sarvabuddhasamāyoga Tantra. Tib. *sku'i rgyud dpal sangs rgyas thams cad mnyam par sbyor ba.* Also known as the *Buddhasamāyoga Tantra.* See *Union of All Buddhas.*

Secret Magical Infinity. Tib. *gsang ba sgyu 'phrul.* Another name for the *Magical Infinity* teaching or cycle.

Secret Moon Essence [Tantra]. Skt. *Candraguhyatilaka.* Tib. *dpal zla gsang thig le.* The tantra of enlightened speech.

Secret Sealed Mind Sādhana of Dudjom Vajrakīlaya Namchak Pudri. See *Namchak Pudri.*

Secret Tantra of the All-Victorious Wrathful Mañjuśrī. Tib. *khro bo rnam par rgyal ba'i rtog pa 'jam dpal gsang ba'i rgyud.*

Secret Wrathful Mañjuśrī Tantra. Tib. *'jam dpal khros pa gsang rgyud.* Mahāyoga Tantra belonging to the Sādhana Section received by Mañjuśrīmitra.

Seed of the Three Faiths: A Supplication to [Dudjom Rinpoche's] *Liberated Life.* Chatral Sangye Dorje. Tib. *rnam thar gsol 'debs dad gsum sa bon.*

Seven Pith Instructions. Śrī Siṃha. Tib. *gzer bu bdun pa.* The final testament of Śrī Siṃha, which he passed on to Jñānasūtra. Title often translated as *The Seven Nails.*

Seven Treasuries. Longchenpa. Tib. *mdzod bdun.* Longchenpa's *Seven Treasuries* include the *Wish-Fulfilling Treasury* (*yid bzhin mdzod*), *Treasury of Pith Instructions* (*man ngag mdzod*), *Treasury of Dharmadhātu* (*chos dbyings mdzod*), *Treasury of Philosophical Tenets* (*grub mtha' mdzod*), *Treasury of the Supreme Vehicle* (*theg mchog mdzod*), *Treasury of Word and Meaning* (*tshig don mdzod*), and *Treasury of the Natural State* (*gnas lugs mdzod*).

Seventy Stanzas on Emptiness. Nāgārjuna. Skt. *Śūnyatāsaptati-kārikā.* Tib. *stong nyid bdun cu.* One of the texts in Nāgārjuna's *Collection of Six Texts on Reasoning.*

Short Commentary on the "Guhyagarbha." Vimalamitra. Tib. *gsang snying 'grel chung.*

Six Arrays of Secret Meaning. Kukkurāja. Skt. *Sadguhyārthadharavyūha.* Tib. *gsang don rnam par dgod pa drug.*

Six Dharmas of Niguma. Tib. *ni gu chos drug.*

Six Meditation Experiences. Mañjuśrīmitra. Tib. *sgom nyams drug.* Instructions of Mañjuśrīmitra to Śrī Siṃha.

Six-Volume Treasure Collection. Jatsön Nyingpo. Tib. *'ja' tshon pod drug.* A collection of termas and writings. Full title: *chos skor 'ja' tshon pod drug* or *gter chen rig 'dzin 'ja' tshon snying po'i zab gter chos mdzod rin po che* (Precious and Profound Wealth of the Great Tertön Rigdzin Jatsön Nyingpo's Dharma Treasury).

Six Yogas of Nāropa. Tib. *na ro chos drug.*

Sixty Stanzas on Reasoning. Nāgārjuna. Skt. *Yuktiṣaṣṭikā-kārikā.* Tib. *rigs pa drug cu pa.* One of the texts in Nāgārjuna's *Collection of Six Texts on Reasoning.*

Sole Essence Sādhana of the Lotus-Born. Revealed by Kyabje Dudjom Jigdral Yeshe Dorje Rinpoche. Tib. *bdud 'joms khrag 'thung pad ma'i srog sgrub zab mo.* Dorje Drolö cycle revealed by Kyabje Dudjom Rinpoche in 1917.

Sprouts of Gold: Summary of Mahāmudrā Guidance. Katok Dampa Deshek. Tib. *phyag chen khrid kyi stong thun gser gyi myu gu.*

Stages of Line Drawing. Vimalamitra. Tib. *thig gi rim pa.*

Stages of Realization of Peaceful and Wrathful Deities. Buddhaguhya. Tib. *zhi ba dang khro bo'i mngon par rtogs pa'i rim pa.*

Stages of the Path of Magical Infinity. Buddhaguhya. Skt. *Māyājālapathakrama.* Tib. *sgyu 'phrul lam rim.* A commentary on the *Guhyagharba.*

Stages of the Path to Enlightenment. Tsongkhapa. Tib. *Lamrim Chenmo*; *byang chub lam rim chen mo.*

Stages of Vajra Activity. Buddhaguhya. Skt. *Māyājālavajrakarmakrama.* Tib. *rdo rje las rim.*

Stainless Light Commentary. Puṇḍārīka (Pema Karpo). Skt. *Vimalaprabha.* Tib. *'grel chen dri ma med pa'i 'od.* Commentary on the *Abridged Kālacakra Tantra.*

Structural Analysis of the "Embodiment of Wisdom Mind" Called "Sunshine of

Excellent Speech." Katok Dampa Deshek. Tib. *'dus pa mdo'i khog dbub legs bshad nyi ma'i snang ba.*

Subduing Haughty Ones. Tib. *'dregs 'dul.* Tantra transmitted to Rambuguhya Devacandra.

Summary of a Venomous Snake. Katok Dampa Deshek. Tib. *dug sbrul gyi stong thun.*

Summary of Empowerments. Katok Dampa Deshek. Tib. *dbang gi stong thun.*

Summary of the "Stages and Paths." Katok Dampa Deshek. Tib. *sa lam stong thun.*

Summary of the Sword. Katok Dampa Deshek. Tib. *ral gri'i stong thun.*

Summary of Training. Katok Dampa Deshek. Tib. *cho ga blsab bya'i stong thun.*

Summary of Upadeśa on the "Lasso of Skillful Means." Katok Dampa Deshek. Tib. *thabs zhags man ngag stong thun.*

Sunlight Heat Longevity Sādhana. Revealed by Dudul Dorje. Tib. *tshe sgrub tsha ba dmar thag.*

Supplementary Tantra. Tib. *le lag.*

Sūtra Alaṃkāra. See *Ornament of the Māhāyana Sūtras.*

Sūtra of Inconceivable Secrets: The Arrangement of the Three Jewels. Skt. *Tathāgatācintyaguhyanirdeśa-sūtra.* Tib. *dkon mchog brtsegs pa'i mdo.* One of the forty-nine sūtras in the *Heap of Jewels* (*Ratnakūṭa*) collection.

Sūtra of Inexhaustible Intelligence. Skt. *Akṣayamatinirdeśa-sūtra.* Tib. *blo gros mi zad pa'i mdo.*

Sūtra of Kṛkin's Prophetic Dream. Skt. *Svapnanirdeśa-sūtra.* Tib. *rgyal po kri kri'i rmi lam lung bstan pa'i mdo.*

Sūtra of Revealing the Five Skandhas. Tib. *phung lnga bstan pa'i mdo.*

Sūtra of Stainless Space. Skt. *Vimalaprabhāparipṛcchā-sūtra.* Tib. *nam mkha' dri ma med pa'i mdo.*

Sūtra of the Dialogue with the Nāga King. Skt. *Sāgaranāgarājaparipṛcchā-sūtra.* Tib. *klu'i rgyal po rgya mtshos zhus pa zhes bya ba theg pa chen po'i mdo.*

Sūtra of the Magical Emanation of the Bodhisattva's Sphere of Activity. Skt. *Satyakaparivarta-sūtra.* Tib. *spyod yul rnam par 'phrul pa'i mdo.*

Sūtra of the Meeting of Father and Son. Skt. *Pitāputrasamāgamana-sūtra.* Tib. *'phags pa yab dang sras mjal ba zhes bya ba theg pa chen po'i mdo.*

Sūtra of the Ornament of Qualities. Skt. *Sarvadharmaguṇavyūha-sūtra.* Tib. *mdo sde yon tan bkod pa.*

Sūtra of the Ritual for Amending Breaches. Skt. *Śakśipūranaśūdraka-sūtra.* Tib. *dpang skong phyag rgya pa'i mdo.*

Sūtra of the River's Play. Skt. *Nānānadī-sūtra.* Tib. *chu klung sna tshogs rol pa'i mdo.*

Sūtra of the Samādhi That Gathers All Merit. Skt. *Sarvapuṇyasamucchayasamādhi-sūtra.* Tib. *bsod nams thams cad bsdus pa'i ting nge 'dzin gyi mdo.*

Sūtra of the Three Heaps. Skt. *Triskandhadharma-sūtra.* Tib. *phung po gsum pa'i mdo.*

Sūtra of the White Lotus of Sublime Dharma. Skt. *Saddharmapuṇḍarīka-sūtra.* Commonly known as the *Lotus Sūtra.* Tib. *dam chos pad ma dkar po.*

Sūtra of the Wise and the Foolish. Skt. *Damamūka-sūtra.* Tib. *mdzangs blun zhes bya ba'i mdo.*

Sūtra of Wisdom Prophecies. Skt. *Saṃdhivyākaraṇa-tantra*. Tib. *dgongs pa lung bstan pa'i rgyud*. This is an Anuyoga tantra, even though the title uses the word *sūtra*.

Sūtra That Elucidates Wisdom Mind. Skt. *Saṃdhinirmocana-sūtra*. Tib. *dgongs pa nges par 'grel pa'i mdo*

Tantra in Eighty Stanzas. Tib. *brgyad bcu pa*.

Tantra in Forty Stanzas. Tib. *bzhi bcu pa*.

Tantra of the Adornment of Wish-Fulfilling Jewels. Tib. *yid bzhin rin po che bkod pa'i rgyud*.

Tantra of the All-Doing Great King. Skt. *Kūlayarāja-tantra*. Tib. *kun byed rgyal po'i rgyud*.

Tantra of the Manifestation of Amṛtakuṇḍalī. Tib. *bdud rtsi rol pa'i rgyud*.

Tantra of the Manifestation of Compassion. Tib. *snying rje rol pa'i rgyud*. Sādhana of Yamantaka.

Tantra of the Manifestation of Hayagrīva. Tib. *rta mchog rol pa'i rgyud*.

Tantra of the Manifestation of Kīlaya. Tib. *phur pa rol pa'i rgyud*. Sādhana of Vajrakīlaya.

Tantra of the Manifestation of the Heruka. Tib. *he ru ka rol pa'i rgyud*.

Tantra of the Perfect Embodiment of the Unexcelled Nature. Tib. *bla med don rdzogs 'dus pa'i rgyud*.

Tantra That Contains the Supreme Path of Skillful Means for Clearly Revealing the Wisdom of Samantabhadra. Tib. *kun bzang ye shes gsal bar ston pa'i thabs kyi lam mchogs 'dus pa'i rgyud*.

Textual Commentary on "Establishing Simultaneous Arising." Skt. *Sahajasiddhi-paddhati*. Tib. *lhan cig skyes grub kyi gzhung 'grel*.

Three-Chapter Tantra. Vilāsavajra (Gegpa Dorje). Skt. *Śrī-Kṛṣṇayamāritantrarāja-trikalpa*. Tib. *rtog pa gsum pa*. Translated into Tibetan by Rongzompa. Full title: *dpal gshin rje gshed nag po'i rgyud kyi rgyal po rtog pa gsum pa*.

Three Roots Mind Sādhana. Tib. *rtsa gsum thugs kyi sgrub pa*.

Three Stages. Vimalamitra. Skt. *Kramatraya*. Tib. *rim pa gsum*. Full title: *sgyu 'phrul dra ba'i man ngag rim pa gsum pa*.

Three Upadeśa on the View and Meditation of the Great Perfection. Rongzompa. Tib. *lhag pa shes rab kyi bslab pa ston byed dzogs pa chen po'i lta sgom man ngag gsum*.

Three Words That Strike the Essence. Garab Dorje. Tib. *tshig gsum gnad du rdeg pa*.

Threefold Lamps That Pacify Suffering. Tib. *zhi byed sgron ma skor gsum*. The lamp of conduct (spyod pa'i sgron ma), lamp of the path (lam gyi sgron ma), and lamp of wisdom mind (thugs kyi sgron ma).

Treasury of Abhidharma. Vasubandhu. Skt. *Abhidharma-kośa*. Tib. *mngon pa mdzod*.

Treasury of Gems: General Analysis of the "Abhidharma Kośa." Katok Dampa Deshek. Tib. *mngon mdzod spyi dpyod*.

Treasury of Precious Instructions. Jamgön Kongtrul Lodrö Taye. Tib. *gdams ngag rin po che'i mdzod*. One of the *Five Great Treasuries* of Jamgön Kongtrul the Great.

Treasury of Precious Qualities: Root Text and Autocommentary. Jigme Lingpa. Tib. *Yönten Dzö*; *yon tan mdzod*.

Treatise on the Yogācāra Levels. Asaṅga. Skt. *Yogācārabhūmi*. Tib. *sa sde'i sna mchan*.

Triangular Fire Pit of Space. Revealed by Kharnakpa of Drum. Tib. *bar snang hom khung ma*.

Trilogy of Dispelling Darkness. Longchenpa. Tib. *gsang snying gi mun sel skor gsum*. Three commentaries on the *Guhyagarbha Root Tantra*: *Dispelling Darkness in the Ten Directions* (*gsang nying 'grel pa phyogs bcu mun sel*); *Dispelling Darkness of the Mind* (*gsang snying spyi don yid kyi mun sel*); and *Dispelling Darkness of Ignorance* (*gsang snying bsdus don ma rig mun sel*).

Trilogy of Natural Liberation. Longchenpa. Tib. *rang grol skor gsum*. The *Natural Liberation of the Nature of Mind* (*sems nyid rang grol*); the *Natural Liberation of Dharmatā* (*chos nyid rang grol*); and the *Natural Liberation of Evenness* (*mnyam nyid rang grol*).

Trilogy of Rest. Longchenpa. Tib. *ngal gso skor gsum*. *Finding Rest in the Nature of the Mind* (*sems nyid ngal gso*); *Finding Rest in Meditation* (*bsam gtan ngal gso*); and *Finding Rest in Illusion* (*sgyu ma ngal gso*).

Trisaṃvara Pravedha (Differentiating the Three Precepts). Sakya Paṇḍita Kunga Gyaltsen Pal Zangpo. Tib. *sdom gsum rab dbye*.

Union of All Buddhas. Skt. *Buddhasamāyoga-tantra*. Tib. *sangs rgyas mnyam sbyor*. The tantra of enlightened body. Also known as the *Sarvabuddhasamāyoga Tantra*.

Unsurpassed Continuity. Maitreya, as spoken to Asaṅga. Skt. *Uttara-tantra*. Also known as the *Mahāyānottaratantraśāstra* (Unsurpassed Continuity of the Mahāyāna). Tib. *rgyud bla ma*. One of the works in the *Five Treatises of Maitreya*.

Uttara Tantra. See *Unsurpassed Continuity*.

Vairocana. As a title mentioned in the text, *Vairocana* refers to the *Tantra of the Awakening of Great Vairocana*: Skt. *Mahāvairocanābhisaṃbodhi-tantra*; Tib. *rnam par snang mdzad ngon par byang chub pa*.

Vajra Essence. Dudjom Lingpa. Tib. *rdo rje snying po*.

Vajra Quitch Grass: Determining Self-Awareness. Katok Dampa Deshek. Tib. *rang rig la bzla ba rdo rje'i tha ram*.

Vajra Tent. Skt. *Vajrapañjara-tantra*. Tib. *rdo rje gur*.

Vajrabhairava Tantra. Tib. *rdo rje 'jigs byed*. Translated into Tibetan by Rongzompa.

Vajraḍāka Tantra. Compiled by Vārāhī. Tib. *rdo rje mkha' 'gro*.

Vajrakīlaya [Tantra]. Tib. *phur pa rol pa'i rgyud* (Tantra of the Manifestation of Kīlaya).

Vajravidāraṇa. Tib. *rdo rje rnam 'joms*.

Vast Magical Display. Tib. *sgyu 'phrul rgyas pa*.

Vast Space Treasury of Dharmatā. Revealed by Dudjom Lingpa. Tib. *chos nyid nam mkha'i klong mdzod*. The major treasure cycle of Dudjom Lingpa, which contains some special Chö practices based on Tröma Nakmo.

Vinaya in Three Hundred Verses. Śākyaprabha. Skt. *Śrāmaṇeratriśata-kārikā*. Tib. *sum brgya pa*. Śākyaprabha's autocommentary is titled *Prabhāvati*.
Vinaya Sūtra. Guṇaprabha. Tib. *'dul ba mdo rtsa*. A root text on Vinaya and its autocommentary.
Way of the Bodhisattva. *Śāntideva*. Skt. *Bodhicaryāvatāra*. Tib. *byang chub sems dpa' i spyod pa la 'jug pa*.
Weapon of Speech That Cuts Through Difficulty. Nubchen Sangye Yeshe. Tib. *dka' gcod smra ba' i mtshon cha*.
Well-Explained Reasoning. Vasubandhu. Skt. *Vyākhyā-yukti*. Tib. *rnam bshad rig pa*.
Whispered Lineage Vajra Bridge. Tib. *snyan brgyud rdo rje zam pa*.
White Lotus of Compassion Sūtra. Skt. *Karuṇāpuṇḍarīka-sūtra*. Tib. *rnying rje pad ma dkar po' i mdo*. A Mahāyāna sūtra that contains an account of how the Buddha first aroused bodhicitta in his former life as the Brahmin Samudrarenu.
White Silver Mirror: A Commentary on the "Prātimokṣa Sūtra" of Bhikṣu Monasticism. Katok Dampa Deshek. Tib. *'dul ba dge slong pha' i so thar mdo 'grel dngul dkar me long*.
Wish-Granting Tree. Kṣemendra. Skt. *Bodhisattvāvadānakalpalatā* (Storehouse of Legends of the Bodhisattvas). Tib. *dpag bsam 'khri shing* (Wish-Granting Tree).
Yangdak Heruka [Tantra]. Tib. *yang dag*.
Yangdak Rulu Golden Rosary. Hūṃkāra. Tib. *yang dag ru lu gser phreng*. The text is believed to be no longer extant.

Index

abandoning and accepting, 72, 275n119
Abhidharma Kośa. See *Treasury of Abhidharma* (Vasubandhu)
Abhidharma Piṭaka, 30–31, 34, 35, 36
Abhidharma Samucchaya (Asaṅga), 42, 137
Abhidharma teachings, 39–40, 50, 52, 272n86
Abhisamaya Alaṃkāra. See *Ornament of Manifest Realization* (Maitreya, as spoken to Asaṅga)
Abridged Commentary on the "Eighty-Chapter Magical Infinity" (Vimalamitra), 85
Abridged Kālacakra Tantra
  chronology of, 112
  compilation of, 69
  five chapters of, 165, 286n296
  Kalkī kings and, 251, 252, 297n488, 298n489
  revelation of, 94, 249
  sādhanas of, 179
  transmission of, 175, 180, 250
Acalā, 49, 135
accomplishment, 76
  common, 81, 84, 277n147
  common and supreme, distinction between, 272n75
  signs of, 75–76, 122, 172, 182
  supreme, xv, 74, 80, 82, 94, 107, 156, 166
Accomplishment of Secrets (Mahāsukha Nātha), 68
Account of the Great Caitya of Thimbu, 16
aggregates, five, 31, 43, 122, 271n63
Agotraka (without lineage), 70, 274n114
Agye Gendun Rabgye, 213
Ajam, 196
Ajanta, 41
Ajātaśatru, King, 33
Akaniṣṭha, 124, 127, 228, 267n6, 275n117
  Buddhahood attained in, 20
  Extraordinary, 67
  Just Barely, 67
  in Name Only, 67
  Nirmāṇakāya, 19
  Sambhogakāya, 14–16, 300n520
  ultimate, 13
  See also Great Akaniṣṭha
Akṣobhya, 15, 19, 84, 85
ālaya, 136, 283n246
Alokabhasvatī, Queen, 89
Amdo, 133, 243, 286n309, 288n343, 289n362
Amitābha, 15, 19
  Dampa Deshek and, 182, 183
  Dharmakāya, 259
  Dudjom Rinpoche and, 210
  emanations of, 77
  family of (lotus), 15, 84, 210, 259
  pureland of, 253, 268n18 (*see also* Sukhāvatī (Great Bliss))
Amitāyus, 79, 116, 220
Amnye Dralkar, 208
Amoghasiddhi, 15, 19, 86
Amṛta Tantra, 238
Amṛtabhaiṣajya, 69
Amṛtakuṇḍalī, 73
analogies and metaphors
  cataracts, 228
  four, 216, 292n416
  Kin of the Sun as, 145
  mirror, 14
  moon escaping from Rāhu, 26, 270n56
  moon's reflection, xvii, 161, 212

analogies and metaphors (*continued*)
moxibustion, 227
sal tree, 165
sky, 13–14
swan separating milk from water, 230, 295n455
uḍumbara flower, 32, 271n65
wisdom arrow, 154, 285n276
Analysis of Haribhadra's "Clear Meaning Commentary on the 'Prajñāpāramitā'" (Katok Dampa Deshek), 181
Analytical Commentary on the "Secret Essence Tantra" (Buddhaguhya), 76
Ānanda, 26, 33, 159, 270n55
Anāthapiṇḍada, 30, 271n61
Anuttaratantra. *See* Unsurpassed Yoga (Anuttarayoga) tantra
Anuyoga sūtras, 108, 176, 210, 287n323
Anuyoga tantras, 71, 89, 97, 107, 279n188, 279n191, 299n512
Anyagotra (indeterminate lineage), 70, 274n114
appearances, 194–95
exhaustion of, 121
sacred, 141
self-arisen, 14
three, 211, 291n400
approach and accomplishment, 85, 165, 220, 277n152, 286n298
Ārāḍa Kālāma, 26, 29
Archenemy Yamāntaka Tantra, 169
Arenemin, King, 142
Arhats
as guardians of teachings, 36
proclaiming false doctrine, 34
in Śākyamuni's retinue, 30, 31–32, 145–46
Armor Against Darkness (Nubchen Sangye Yeshe), 111
Arrangement Like a Mountain Tantra, 73
Arrangement of Samayas Tantra, 73
Array of the Path of the "Magical Infinity" (King Ja), 72
Arrayed in Turquoise Petals pureland, 207
art, science of, 163, 174
Āryadeva, 44–45, 50, 54, 55
attainment of, 92
debates Maticitra, 47–49
Nāgārjuna and, 157
tradition of, 64
works of, 50
Āryas, 271n69
Asaṅga, 44, 55
homage to, 42–43
life story, 40–42
tradition of, 39, 272n72
and Vasubandhu, relationship of, 50–52
works of, 42
Aśoka, King, 34, 79
aspiration prayers, 5, 7, 142, 153, 189, 257–59
Assaji, 149–51, 285n273
astrology, 164–65, 174, 188, 213, 288n351
Aśvagoṣa. *See* Maticitra (Aśvagoṣa)
Atiśa, 133, 175, 179
disciples of, 135
image of, 116
life story, 134–35
Nyingma lineage and, 230, 295n454
Rongzompa and, 166
Atiyoga, xix, 242, 279n188, 299n512
three classes of, 97
transmission of, 107, 210, 279n191
aural lineage, 136, 137
Auspicious Myriad Gate temple, 93
Avalokiteśvara, xxi, 135, 243
Āryadeva's transformation into, 49
Buddhaguhya and, 76
Candragomin and, 61–62
as compiler of tantras, 68
Dudjom Lingpa and, 201
emanations of, 98, 113
lineage of, 67, 69
maṇḍala of, 182
as progenitor of Tibetan race, 97
pureland of, 207
Sambhogakāya, 259
vase consecration of, 194
Avataṃsaka Sūtra, 97, 235, 298n500
awareness, 14
arising of, 89
inner, 163, 165
manifestation of, 197
natural, 237
omniscient, 253
Samantabhadra's, xiv
self-occurring, 67
spontaneously arising, 160
visionary experiences of, 297n481
See also self-awareness
awareness-emptiness, 244

Bamboo Grove, 149, 150–51
Bangri, 192, 289n364
Bangtön Chakyu, 127
barbarians, 6, 249, 251–52
bardo (intermediate state), 166, 286n301, 295n448
Bari Lotsawa (a.k.a. Rinchen Drak), 175–76
Barma Lhatong, 194
beautifully illumined eon, 246, 254
Beautifully Illumined middle world, 254, 298n497
Bejong Ewam Dechen Chökhor Monastery, 233–34, 242
Bengal, 50, 133, 134, 243
Bernakchen Mahākāla, 181
Bhadra, 34
Bhairava, 67, 290n368
Bhakha Tulku Chökyi Gyatso, 194
Bharadvāja, 182
Bhasing charnel ground, 93
Bhatasiddhi, 62–63
Bhāviveka, 59, 64
Bhutan, xx, 212, 222, 238, 240, 243, 293n430, 297n483. *See also* Paro (Bhutan)
Bimbisāra, King, 25, 146
Biography of Joyous Countenance, 33
birth
  four ways of taking, 211, 291n399
  miraculous, 44–45, 77, 92
black magic, 104, 110, 179, 189
Black Powerful One, 102, 279nn185–86
Black Yamāri, 83
Blazing Mountain charnel ground, 89
Bliss-Giving Yellow Ḍākinī, 92
Blue Annals (Gö Lotsawa Zhönu Pal), 162, 173
Blue Cakrasaṃvara, 176
Blue-Skirted Vajrakīlaya Cycle (Vimalamitra), 105
Bodhgayā, 27, 39, 78, 80, 92, 109, 155
Bodhi Tree, 25, 39
Bodhicarya Avatāra. See *Way of the Bodhisattva* (Śāntideva)
bodhicitta, 253, 262
  aspirational, applied, and ultimate, 143, 284n259
  Buddhas' development of, 142, 143, 284n258
  Nāgārjuna's development of, 39
  in Śākyamuni's previous lives, 20
Bodhisattva stages (Skt. *bhūmis*), 20, 237, 268n23
  Akaniṣṭha's appearances on, 67
  eighth (Unwavering), 39, 272n77
  Nāgārjuna's attainment of, 39
  sixteenth (Unsurpassed Wisdom), 244, 297n482
  symbols of, 24
  tenth (Cloud of Dharma), 19, 191, 268n19
  three pure (a.k.a. great bhūmi), 20, 109, 268n25, 280n193
Bodhisattvas, 18, 246
  fulfilled, 16, 67, 268n13
  intentional rebirth of, 187
  resultant, 67, 274n106
  sacred biographies of, 164
  sixty-four skills of, 26
Bodong Chokle Namgyal, 138
body of Great Transference, 93
Body of Light, 81, 92, 93, 112, 180
Bön tradition, 98, 177–78, 179, 278n169
Bönpo Lhabum, 198
Brahmā, 45, 48, 90, 144, 146, 196, 246, 257
  enthronement of, 252
  images of, 116
  realm, 49
  requests Buddha to teach, 28–29
Brahmā Crowned with Conch Shells, 115, 280n202
Brahmadatta, King, 25, 63–64
Brahmins, 272n284
  as guardians of teachings, 36
  seven births of, 216, 292n413
  six practices of, 155, 285n278
  spiritual masters born as, 37, 40, 43, 45, 52, 54, 84
Brief Account of Profound Treasures and Accomplished Treasure Revealers Called "Garland of Lapis Lazuli," A (Jamgön Kongtrul), 93–94
Buchu Sergyi Lhakhang, 234, 295n458
Buddha Adhimukta. *See* Möpa Taye (Buddha Adhimukta)
Buddha Amoghadarśin, 143
Buddha Dīpaṃkara, 20, 24, 254, 256, 269n39

Buddha family, 15
Buddha Kanakamuni, 142, 144, 252, 256, 280n205
Buddha Kāśyapa, 20, 35, 142, 144, 252, 256, 280n205
Buddha King of Myriad Precious Boundless Qualities, 254–55
Buddha Krakucchaṃda, 142, 144, 252, 256, 280n205
Buddha Longevity Cave, 220
Buddha Mahā-Śākyamuni, 19–20
Buddha nature, 253
Buddha of Boundless Dedication. *See* Möpa Taye (Buddha Adhimukta)
Buddha of Boundless Light. *See* Amitābha
Buddha Radiant Lotus (Padmasambhava), 240, 296n471
Buddha Śākyamuni, 135, 144, 230, 253, 256, 268n26, 284n258
  birth of, 23–25, 269n42
  enlightenment of, 20–22, 27–29
  homage to, 3, 11
  in human realm, 269n29
  is requested to teach, 29
  parinirvāṇa of, 31–32
  praise to, 63
  previous lives of, 19–20, 142, 143, 164, 269n39, 297n486
  relics of, 179
  Śāriputra and, xv, 145, 241
  in Secret Mantra transmissions, 65–66, 69, 70, 250, 274n110
  as Supreme Nirmāṇakāya, 93, 278n163
  turns Wheels of Dharma, 30–31, 142
  worshipping, 155–56
Buddha Śikhin, 280n205
Buddha Vairocana, 15, 19, 121, 279n182
  appearance of, 142
  emanation of, 100, 101
  family of, 83
  images of, 116
  Sambhogakāya, 299n519
Buddhaguhya, 75–76, 78, 85, 103, 275n126
Buddhahood
  aspiration for, 258–59
  bardo attainment of, 166, 286n301
  bhūmis and, 268n19
  Śākyamuni's, 29, 30
Buddhajñānapada, 84, 92
Buddhapālita, 59, 64
Buddhas, 15, 232
  enlightened body, speech, and mind of, 94–95
  lineage of, 70, 274n114
  and sentient beings, natures of, 253
  seven of the past, 116, 280n205
  ten powers of, 95, 209, 239, 278n166
  of three times, 116, 280n209
  ways of benefitting beings, 246–48
Buddhasamāyoga. See *Union of All Buddhas Tantra*
Buddhasamāyoga Upadeśa Called "Illuminating the Meaning of the Four Branches" (Hūṃkāra), 85
Buddhaśānti, 76
Buddhasiṃha, 256
Buddhism
  conversions to, 47, 53, 59, 60, 79, 80
  great charioteers of, 97, 278n168
Buddhist Canon. *See* Tripiṭaka
Bumtön, Lama, 180
Busuku Chok, 108

Cakrasaṃvara, 53–54, 67, 175, 176
Cakrasaṃvara Root Tantra, 68, 94, 169, 178, 179
calligraphy, 103
Cāmara, 6, 81, 130, 209, 210, 212, 286n296
Camkarapati, 62–63
Candaka, 25, 26
Candragomin, 59–61, 62, 167
Candrakīrti, 59
  Candragomin and, 61–62
  lineage of, 64
  Nāgārjuna and, 157
  tradition of, 64–65
  works of, 62, 65
Candra's Grammar (Candragomin), 62
Carasiṃha, 137, 283n251
Caryātantra, 68
Cascading Waterfall of Nectar, A (Thinley Norbu)
  on Bodhisattva stages in Dzogchen, 297n482
  on Buddha families, 274n102
  on formless realm, four states, 290n373
  on four demons (māras), 283n253
  on nāda, 274n107
  on translating *ye shes* and *shes rab*, 294n443

on tsok (feast offering), 281n222
on Vajrakāya, 275n124
on wrathful enlightened activity, 276n137
caste, 84, 156, 250, 252. *See also* Brahmins
Catuḥpīṭha, 176
Catuḥśataka. See *Four Hundred Stanzas on the Middle Way* (Āryadeva)
Catuḥśataka Ṭīkā (Candrakīrti), 65
Central Tibet, 176
Dudjom Rinpoche in, 239
Kawa Paltsek's legacy in, 103
Langdarma's sons in, 133
Nubchen Sangye Yeshe in, 108, 109
Nyak Jñānakumāra in, 105
thirteen myriarchies of, 187, 288n342
treasure sites in, 193
turbulence in, 109–11, 209
Upper Zur tradition of, 127, 182
Vairotsana in, 102
Zurpoche in, 113
Chagpori Mountain, 245
Chagrichen, 208
Chakhorchen, King, 245–46
Chal Lotsawa, 161–62
chalk scholar, 45, 48, 272n85
channels, subtle, 17, 113, 114, 176, 177, 192
charnel grounds, 74, 78, 80, 93, 109, 160, 239, 276n134. *See also* Śītavana (Cool Grove)
Chatral Sangye Dorje, xv, xx, 214, 240–45
Che Shakya Gyaltsen, 114
Chenbu Gyare, 184
Cheshak Chok, 113
Chetön Gyanak, 127
Chetsen Kye, 108
Chim Jarok, 104–5, 106, 279n190
Chimpuk Hermitage, 294n435
Chim's Blazing Meteorite, 221, 294n435
China, 105, 206, 297n484, 298n490
artistic traditions of, 163
Dudjom Jigdral Yeshe Dorje in, xx, 240, 243
Dudjom Lingpa in, 207
Padmasambhava in, 81
Sixteen Arhats in, 33
Chö tradition, 137–38, 139, 176, 180, 287n324
Chogden Do Ngak Lingpa, 102
Chogro Lotsawa, 175
Chogtrul Gyurme Dorje, 214
Chögyal Ratna Lingpa. *See* Ratna Lingpa
Chokro Lui Gyaltsen, 134
Chökyi Wangchuk (a.k.a. Guru Chöwang), 131
Chomden Rigpe Raldri, 187
Chulung Dragmar, 208
Chuwori, 129, 133, 282n232
Cittamātra (Mind Only) school, 43, 65, 94
City of Wooden Palisades, 146, 147, 284n270
clairvoyance, 23, 25, 76, 86, 103, 109, 161, 169, 269n36
Clarification of Commitments (Vilāsavajra), 216
Classification of Caryātantras (Ngorchen Kunga Zangpo), 171
Clear Lamp (Candrakīrti), 65
clear light, 88, 114
Clear Mirror (Dudjom Lingpa), 209
Clear Words (Candrakīrti), 59, 65
Cloud of Dharma Sūtra, 157
Coemergent Mahāmudrā, 177
Collected Works of Tsele Natsok Rangdrol, 215
Collection of All Trainings (Śāntideva), 56, 57
Collection of Discourses (Nāgārjuna), 39
Collection of Hymns (Nāgārjuna), 39
Collection of Logical Arguments (Nāgārjuna), 39
Collection of Six Texts on Reasoning (Nāgārjuna), 39
Collection of Sūtras (Śāntideva), 56, 57
Collection of the Natural State (Nāgārjuna), 39
Commentarial Notes on the "Mūlamadhyamaka Kārikā" (Katok Dampa Deshek), 181
Commentary on "Root Verses on the Middle Way Called 'Sublime Knowledge'" (Buddhapālita), 59
Commentary on "Stages of the Path" (Katok Dampa Deshek), 181
Commentary on the "Bhairava Tantra" (Rongzompa), 170
Commentary on the "Buddhasamāyoga Tantra" (Rongzompa), 170
Commentary on the Clear Realization of the "Eighty-Chapter Magical Infinity" (Nubchen Sangye Yeshe), 111

Commentary on the Difficult Points of the "Buddhakapāla Tantra" Called "Jñānavatī" (Saraha), 156
Commentary on the "Doorway to Speech like a Sword" (Rongzompa), 167
Commentary on the "Earlier Bhūmis" (Guṇaprabha), 42–43
Commentary on the "Embodiment of Wisdom Mind" (Nubchen Sangye Yeshe), 111
Commentary on the "General Sūtra" (King Ja), 87
Commentary on the "Guhyagarbha Tantra" Called "Illuminating Lamp of the Core Text" (Vimalamitra), 85
Commentary on the "Lower Realms Purification Tantra" (Rongzompa), 170
Commentary on the "Moon Lamp Sūtra" (Candragomin), 62
Commentary on the "Unsurpassed Magical Infinity" Called "Dispelling Darkness" (Vimalamitra), 85
compassion
  Asaṅga's, 41
  boundless, 7, 257–58
  of Buddhas, 145, 247
  of Dudjom Rinpoche, 211
  Padmasambhava's, 4, 173, 174
  Rongzompa's, 168, 169, 171, 172
  unobstructed, 195
  wrathful, 111
Compilation of All Teachings on Logic (Dignāga), 44, 53
Complete Gathering of Secrets, 221
Complete Gathering of the Holy Dharma's Wisdom (Dudul Dorje), 192
Complete Gathering of the Sugatas (Longsal Nyingpo), 221
Complete Gathering of the Vidyādharas, 221
Complete Vajra Analysis of the Meaning of the Yamāntaka Mantra (Vilāsavajra), 169
completion stage, 88, 97, 111, 114, 136, 210, 224, 290n377
Concise Commentary on "Vairocana's Awakening" (Buddhaguhya), 76
Condensed Meaning of the "Embodiment of Wisdom Mind" Called the "Garland of the White Lotus" (Katok Dampa Deshek), 181
conduct
  fearless, 160, 212
  monastic, immoral, 180
  path of, 149
  pure, 176
  yogic, 78, 83
consciousness, 31, 80, 107, 146, 271n63, 278n174, 281n214. *See also* ālaya; sense consciousnesses
consorts, spiritual
  activity, 75, 84–85, 192, 208
  five supreme, 131, 282n234
  of Padmasambhava, 80
  wisdom, 79
Copper-Colored Mountain (Zangdok Palri), xix, 130, 192, 207, 210, 234, 295n451, 300n520
Crushing to Fine Powder (Nāgārjuna), 39
Crystal Cave, 104
Crystal Cave Chronicles (Orgyen Lingpa), 101
Crystal Rosary of Wrathful Mantras, 86
Cūḍāmaṇi, 52
Cycle of the Dharma Guardians Zhanglön and Pomra (Dudul Dorje), 193
Cycle of the Glorious Tiger-Riding Protector (Dudul Dorje), 193
Cycle of the Profound Meaning of the Secret Heart Essence (Dudul Dorje), 192
Cycles of the Peaceful and Wrathful Deities of the Magical Infinity and of the Eight Heruka Sādhanas, Including Their Protectors (Dudul Dorje), 193
Cycles of the Wish-Fulfilling Crown Jewel of the Aural Lineage (Dudul Dorje), 193

Ḍākas, 93, 229
  Dudjom Lingpa and, 203, 207
  gatherings of, 228, 238
  origin of, 66
  as tantra compilers, 68
  teachings given to, 74, 89
Ḍākinī Mārajitā, 78, 80
Ḍākinī of Infinite Qualities, 92
Ḍākinī Temple, 123
Ḍākinīs, xx, 66, 78
  in dreams, 50
  Dudjom Jigdral Yeshe Dorje and, xix, 226, 229, 241, 243
  Dudjom Lingpa and, 203, 204, 205, 207

entrusted with treasures, 96
flesh-eating, 199
gathering of, 228, 238, 297n475
as guardians, 109
Rongzompa's upadeśa and, 168
script of, 131, 222, 282n235
seals of, releasing, 86–87
secret treasury of, 6, 195, 196
as supreme bliss, 158
as tantra compilers, 68
teachings given to, 74
of three abodes, 78, 275n128
of three Kāyas, 264
tīrthika, 87–88
wisdom, xix, 84, 135–36, 173, 226, 241
wisdom thought of, 70, 274n116
Dakrik Sangwa Nyenpo (Puwo), 208
Dakṣiṇa Stūpa, Śrī, 57, 87
Danak Tsugtor Wangchuk, 127
Danatika River, 92
Darje Palgyi Dragpa, 108
Dark-Red Yakṣa. *See* Shenpa Marnak
Datik Chöshak, 124, 125
De Jampal, 275n126
debates
Āryadeva in, 47–50
between Buddhapālita and Bhāviveka, 59
Candragomin in, 59, 60
between Candragomin and Candrakīrti, 61–62
Dharmakīrti in, 53
Dignāga in, 44
Matricitra in, 45–46, 47–50
Nāgārjuna in, 38, 47
Padmasambhava in, 80
Rongzompa in, 166
Dechen Lingpa. *See* Rongtön Dechen Lingpa
Dechen Teng Temple, 234
degenerate times, xix, 120, 129, 130, 202, 290n380. *See also* five degenerations
Dengyi Yönten Chok, 111
Depa Nagyi Khenchen, 176
Derge, 191, 193, 245
Deshek Phagmo Drupa. *See* Phagmo Drupa Dorje Gyalpo (a.k.a. Deshek/Drogön Phagmo Drupa)
Devadatta, 26, 230, 295n453
Devaputra Adhicitta, 90
development stage, 88, 97, 111, 114, 136, 176, 210, 224, 237, 290n377
Devikoṭa, 82
devotion, 12, 184, 257
to Dharma, 167
Dropukpa's, 126
to Dudjom Rinpoche, xxii, 7, 240, 257
Gorub Lotsawa's, 171
power of, 278n166
Sudhana's, 298n500
to treasure tradition, 130
Zangom Sherab Gyalpo's, 115
Dhanakośa Island, 78, 81, 89, 159, 160
Dhanarakṣita, 108
Dhanasaṃskṛta, 86, 87, 108, 277n158
Dhānyakaṭaka Stūpa. *See* Dakṣiṇa Stūpa, Śrī
Dhāraṇī of Secret Relics, 94
Dhāraṇīs of the Ten Bhūmis, 51
Dharma, four metaphors on, 216, 292n416
Dharma Dharmatā. See *Distinguishing between Dharma and Dharmatā* (Maitreya, as spoken to Asaṅga)
Dharma Guardians, 123, 131, 239, 241
Dharma History of the Early Translation School (Dudjom Rinpoche), 20–21, 231
Dharma Protectors (Dharmapālas), 110, 179, 181–82, 207, 239, 280n202
Dharma treasury of the Ḍākinīs' heart essence, xvii
Dharmabhadra. *See* Rongzom Chökyi Zangpo
Dharmabhodhi, 108
Dharmacitta, 255–57
Dharmadhātu, 67, 159
Dharmagañja (Oḍḍiyāna), 94, 135, 278n164
Dharmakāya, xiv, xxii, 232
attaining, 5, 188
emptiness of, 154, 191, 194–95, 253
for oneself, purpose of, 165
purelands of, 13–14, 267n8, 297n473, 300n520 (*see also* Luminous Vajra Essence pureland)
realizing, 237
and Rupakāya, indivisibility of, 276n140
self-appearances of, 11
speech of, 67
uncompounded, 141

Dharmakīrti, 52–54, 55, 167
Dharmamati, 255–57
Dharmapāla, Paṇḍita, 133
Dharmarāja, 108, 269n29
Dharmatā, xvii, 262
  beholding, 200, 204
  evenness of, 67
  free from elaboration, 5, 188
  manifestations of, 197, 201
  power of, 15
  pureland of, 21
  sky treasure of, 204–5
  sole, 294n443
  yoga of abiding in, 290n377
Dharmodgata, 116
Dhītika, 33
Dhṛtarāṣṭra, King, 143, 254–56, 284n266
Dhumasthira, 87
Dignāga, 43–44, 52, 53, 55, 167
Dīpaṃkara. *See* Atiśa; Buddha Dīpaṃkara
Dīpaṃkarabhadra, 133, 273n99
Discourse on the Precious Scriptures (Kawa Paltsek), 103
Distinguishing between Dharma and Dharmatā (Maitreya, as spoken to Asaṅga), 42, 136
Distinguishing between Middle and Extremes (Maitreya, as spoken to Asaṅga), 42, 136
Dö Khyungpo Hungnying, 170
Dohā Trilogy (*Dohākośa*, Saraha), 155, 156
Dokham, 112, 113, 125, 191, 196, 245, 287n317, 289n362
Dolo Choktrul Jigme Chökyi Nyima, xx
Dolpo Sherab Gyaltsen, 138
Ḍombi Heruka (Ḍombipa), 80, 134
Dome Yungdrung Chagtse, 208
Dongchu River, 193
Dorje Drolö, 294n432
  Dudjom Lingpa as, 12, 198, 199, 290n379
  Padmasambhava as, 223
  practices, 204, 220, 222
Dorje Drolö cycle (Dudjom Lingpa), 222
Dorje Gyaltsen, 177, 178
Dorje Legpa, 202, 290n390
Dorje Lingpa, 102, 131, 282n236
Dorje Nönpo, 6, 249, 297n487
Dorje Nyingpo Dharma center, 234, 296n461
Dorje Wangchuk of Yolchak, 172, 173
Dotön Senge, 170
Dra Palgyi Nyingpo, 108
Dragsum Tsodzong, 236
Drak (Central Tibet), 108, 109, 110
Drak Gyawo, 117, 120–22, 123
Drak Riwoche, 108
Drak Yangzong, 186
Drakar, 189, 245
Drakar Lhachung, 192
Drakar Treldzong, 208
Drakye, Khenpo, 180
Dralha Dargye, 179, 180
Drapa Ngönshe, 103, 279n187
Dravida, 81
Dṛḍhasamādhāna, 246, 269n29
Dregu Geur, 128
Drenka Mukti, 275n126
Dripa Namsal (Skt. Sarvanīvaraṇavikṣambin), 94, 204, 291n391
Dro clan, 107
Dro Kālacakra tradition, 283n100
Drogben Khyeuchung Lotsawa, xvi, 221, 285n286, 290n378
  emanations of, xv, xviii, 212
  homage to, 4
  incarnation of, 191
  life story, 159–60
Drogmi clan, xvi, 160, 198, 285n286, 290n378
Drogmi Lotsawa Shakya Yeshe, 134, 136
Drogön Chögyal Phagpa, xvi, 137, 245, 288n346
  disciples of, 187–88
  homage to, 5
  life story, 186–87
Drogön Phagmo Drupa. *See* Phagmo Drupa Dorje Gyalpo (a.k.a. Deshek/ Drogön Phagmo Drupa)
Dromtön Gyalwe Jungne, 133–34, 135
Dropuk Khandro Duling, 207
Dropuk Temple, 116, 122, 126
Dropukpa. *See* Zur Dropukpa Shakya Senge
Drose Chung, 105, 107
Drubchen Pema Norbu, 194
Drubtop Kharnakpa. *See* Kharnakpa of Drum (a.k.a. Drubtop Kharnakpa)
Druglha Rinchen Teng, 236

Drumbeat of Brahmā pureland, 241, 297n473
Drusha, 108, 280n193
Dudjom Jigdral Yeshe Dorje (Kyabje Rinpoche), xiii, xviii–xix, 253, 261, 262
birth of, 212–13
disciples of, 240
disposition of, 231–32, 243
doubt in, overcoming, 236
early teachers and teachings received, 213–19
enlightened activities of, 233–35
as healer, 237–38
health issues, 239
homage to, 6, 209–10
lifetime successions, sequence of, xiv–xviii, 245–46
meditation practice of, 219–20
names of, xviii, xxii, 12, 213, 267n5
offering verse to, 210–12
passing of, xxii, 239–40
physical appearance, 225–26
renown of, xxi–xxii, 232
Root Gurus of, 219
speech of, sublime, 226–31, 294n446
supplication to, 240–44
teachings and methodology of, 236–37
as threefold emanation, xviii, 212
treasure activity of, xx–xxi, 220, 222–25
wisdom mind of, 232–33
works of, xxi
Dudjom Lingpa, xvii, 197, 241, 245, 262
homage to, 6
life story, 203–9
names and epithets of, 12, 197, 198, 267n5, 290n376, 290n379
prophecies on, 198–202
treasures of, 201–2, 215, 222, 236
Dudjom Namkhe Dorje Tsal, 214, 219
Dudjom tulkus, names of, 216–18
Dudul Dorje, xvi, 245, 289n354
disciples of, 194
homage to, 5
life story, 191–92, 193–94
reincarnation of, 195
treasures of, 190–91, 192–93, 196, 199, 200, 222
Dudul Lhakang, 193
Dudul Nuden Dorje, 196
Dudul Rolpa Tsal, xvii, 6, 195, 196–97, 199, 245
Dungkar Ngedön Gyatso, 214
Duri Namchak Barwa, Mount, 193
Dusum Khyenpa Chökyi Dragpa, first Karmapa, 177
Dza (protector deity), 202, 290n388
Dzamtön Chenpo Drowe Gonpo (Dzamtönpa), 176, 177, 180
Dzogchen Pema Rigdzin, 194, 195

Early Translation school, 65
during Dharma's persecution, 132
doubt in, overcoming, 229–30, 295n454
Dudjom Rinpoche's role in, xiv, xix, xx, 231, 241–42
four teaching streams of, 262
Nyak, Nub, and Zur in, 103–4, 108, 280n192
oral transmission of, 213
Rongzompa and, 170, 172
three main transmission lineages, 66–68
unique lineages of, 97
See also Nyingma tradition
Earth Goddess Tenma, 27, 270nn51–52
earth treasures, xix, 96, 192, 209, 220, 278n167
Earthly Haughty Spirits tantras, 86
ego, belief in, 154, 285n276
eight auspicious symbols, 300
eight chariots of the practice lineage, 183–84, 288n337
eight classes of gods and demons, 172, 223, 287n312
Eight Close Sons, 116, 164, 179, 280n204, 291n391
Eight Commands (Vairotsana), 102
Eight Great Realized Masters, 78, 86, 277n158
eight great treasures of sublime confidence, 173, 287n315
Eight Heruka Sādhanas, 78, 86, 129, 159, 275n130, 277n149, 277n157
empowerments for, 102, 108, 213, 236
maṇḍalas of, 128
Eight Herukas, xxi, 243, 297n478
Eight Mahākāla Tantras (Nāgārjuna), 84
eight subcontinents, 165, 286n296
Eight Volumes of Amṛta, 85, 111
eight worldly concerns, 215, 243, 292n412
eighteen elements, 99, 278n173
Eightfold Path, Noble, 263, 299n518

Eighty Chapters of Personal Advice (Zurchungpa), 123–24
eighty minor marks of excellence, 17–18, 19, 212, 292n405
Ekajaṭī, 109, 193
Embodiment of the Master's Realization (Sangye Lingpa), 213
Embodiment of Wisdom Mind, 71, 108, 112, 113, 114, 211, 279n191
empowerments
  flower toss in, 84, 277n150
  four, 136, 283n247
  four rivers of, 112, 144, 280n197, 284n265
  of *Magical Infinity*, 74
  ripening, 79, 192, 207, 208, 215, 219, 236
  secret, 114
  of sixty-two maṇḍalas, 115
  ten specific, 144, 284n265
  third, 295n454
  twenty-five general, 144, 284n265
  universal awareness, 91
  wisdom, 71
emptiness, 114
  and bliss, union of, 165
  of Dharmakāya, 154, 191, 253
  endowed with most sublime of all aspects, 210
  and interdependent origination, union of, 141
  sealed inconceivability, 159
Endowed with Glory pureland, 19
enlightened activities, 7, 23, 94–95, 99, 212, 253, 258
enlightenment
  five types, 123, 281n217
  three stages of, 21, 269n28
Entering the Three Kāyas (Candragomin), 62
Entering the Way of the Great Vehicle (Rongzompa), 170, 171
Establishing the Authenticity of the Great Heruka Sādhana (Hūṃkāra), 85
eternalism, 161, 196
evenness, 14, 28, 67, 136, 159, 184, 191, 233
Exhaustion of Phenomena Beyond Thought, 240, 296n470
Expanded Commentary on the "Later Concentrations" (Buddhaguhya), 76
Extensive Commentary on "Praise to the Exalted" (Prajñāvarman), 62–63
Extensive Commentary on "Praise to the Tathāgata Who Surpasses Worldly Gods" (Prajñāvarman), 63
Extensive Commentary on the "Tantra of the All-Doing Great King" (Katok Dampa Deshek), 181
Extensive, Middling, and Concise Classifications of the Tantras (Katok Dampa Deshek), 181
Extensive, Middling, and Concise General Commentaries on the "Lamp for the Eye of Samādhi" (Katok Dampa Deshek), 181
Extensive Sūtra of Samayas (Rongzompa), 170
Extensive Twenty-Five-Chapter Commentary on the "Embodiment of Wisdom Mind" (Katok Dampa Deshek), 181
extracted essences, 176, 192, 287n319
Eye-Opening Commentary on the "Supplementary Magical Infinity" (Vimalamitra), 85
eyes
  of Dharma, 126
  five, 281n221
  of wisdom, 70, 274n116

faith
  irreversible, 232
  Maticitra's, 50
  three types, 11, 229, 257, 267n4, 295n449, 298n499
feast offering (tsok), 74, 127, 183, 207, 281n222
fierce tantric practice, 105–7. *See also* wrathful activity
five Buddha families, 67, 141, 187, 259, 273n102, 274n105
five degenerations, 145, 253, 284n267
Five Great Treasuries (Jamgön Kongtrul), xix, 242
five inexhaustible wheels of ornaments, 11, 190, 267n3
five lineages, 70, 274n114
Five Noble Ones, 26–27, 29–30, 271n57
five paths, 117, 280n210
five perfections

of Dharmakāya, 14
of Nirmāṇakāya, 19
of Sambhogakāya, 14–16
Five Treatises of Maitreya, 42, 136. See also *Distinguishing between Dharma and Dharmatā*; *Distinguishing between Middle and Extremes*; *Ornament of Manifest Realization*; *Ornament of the Mahāyāna Sūtras*; *Unsurpassed Continuity*
Five Treatises on the Yogācāra Levels (Asaṅga), 42
five types of beings, 21, 269n30
five visions, 24, 269n41
five wisdom families, 14, 15, 268n10
five wisdoms, 18, 19, 136
Fivefold Ritual for Entering All Maṇḍalas (Kukkurāja), 74
Five-Peaked Mountain (Wutai Shan), 207
Five-Pronged Vajra Cave, 108
Flame of Dialectics (Bhāviveka), 35, 36
form realm, 196
Former Lives of the Buddha, 132
formless realm, 196, 290n373
fortunate eon, xv, xviii, 3, 20, 24, 99, 142, 252–53, 256, 268n26
Fortunate Eon Sūtra, 253
four abundances, 263, 299n515
four activity rituals, 83, 277n145
four boundless wishes, 24, 253, 262, 299n509
Four Branches and Leaves (Ngorchen Kunga Zangpo), 173
four continents, 32, 100, 142, 165, 270n43, 279n181
four demons (māras), 138, 165, 191, 196, 283n253
Four Great Kings, 26, 270n47
four great praises, 61, 62, 63, 64, 273n95
Four Heart Essences (Longchenpa), 213–14
Four Hundred Stanzas on the Middle Way (Āryadeva), 50, 65
Four Medical Tantras (Drapa Ngönshe), 213, 279n187
Four Modes and Fifteen Branches Commentary (Rongzompa), 170
Four Modes of Placement (Jñānasūtra), 93
Four Noble Truths, 28, 30, 270n54, 271n59
four perfectly pure discernments, 167, 172, 286n305
four reliances, 281n214
four seals, 11, 100, 267n1
four states, 165
four sublime activities, 99, 276–77n144, 278n176
four vajras, 165, 286n299
four ways of gathering disciples, 226, 242, 294n444, 297n477
four ways of subduing beings, 21, 22–23, 252, 253, 269n31
Four-Armed Protector. See *Cycle of the Profound Meaning of the Secret Heart Essence* (Dudul Dorje)
fourfold retinue, 30, 32
Frowning Yellow Tārā (Bhṛkuṭi), 76
Fully Enlightened Buddhahood Sūtra of Dharma and Enjoyment, 20

Gampa Pass, 239
Gampo Pön family, 212
Gampopa (a.k.a. Dagpo Lhaje), 136, 177, 182, 184
ganacakra offerings. *See* feast offering (tsok)
Gaṇḍavyūha Sūtra, 298n500
Gaṇeśa, 155
Garab Dorje, 68, 76, 83, 89, 90–92
Garland of Activity Tantra, 73, 275n121
Gartön Tsultrim Zangpo, 166
Garwang Dudjom Pawo. *See* Dudjom Lingpa
Gatekeepers, 179, 287n327
Gathering of Secrets Tantra, 72, 275n121
Gathering of the Sugatas, 86, 87
Gawalung (Puwo), 222
Gegpa/Gegpe Dorje (a.k.a. Vilāsavajra and Līlāvajra), 75, 76, 88–89, 216, 275n122
Gelong Deje, 38
Gelong Sherab, 180
Gelu, Chieftain, 178, 180
Geluk tradition, 273n96
General Commentary on the "Embodiment of Wisdom Mind" (Katok Dampa Deshek), 181
General Outline of Vehicles (Katok Dampa Deshek), 181
General Sūtra That Gathers All Wisdom. See *Embodiment of Wisdom Mind*

General Tantra of Magical Infinity. See *Guhyagarbha: The Root Tantra*
Genghis Khan, 288n342
genyen, twenty-one, 99, 279n180
Gesar of Ling, 179
Gesture Lineage of Vidyādharas, 66, 67, 93, 96, 97
Ghili family, 206
Glorious Cakrasaṃvara. See *Cycle of the Profound Meaning of the Secret Heart Essence*
Glorious Copper-Colored Mountain. *See* Copper-Colored Mountain (Zangdok Palri)
Glorious Four-Faced Protector (Dudul Dorje), 193
Glorious Heruka, xiv, 4, 117, 123, 158–59
Glorious Secret Essence That Ascertains the Absolute Nature Just As It Is. See *Guhyagarbha: The Root Tantra*
Glorious Supreme Beginning Tantra, 73, 113, 275n121
Gö Khugpa. *See* Gö Lhetse (a.k.a. Gö Khugpa Lhetse, Gö Lotsawa Khugpa)
Gö Lhetse (a.k.a. Gö Khugpa Lhetse, Gö Lotsawa Khugpa), 122, 168, 170, 172, 286n307
Gö Lotsawa Zhönu Pal, 134, 162, 171, 173
Gochung Wange, 122
god realms, 69–70, 90, 94
Godāvarī, 217, 293n421
Goddess Kālī Tantra (Nāgārjuna), 84
Gödemchen. *See* Gökyi Demtruchen, Rigdzin (a.k.a. Gödem, Gödemchen)
gods
  of desire, six kinds, 196, 290n372
  at Śākyamuni's birth, 25
  thirteen great, 99, 279n179
  uses of term, 196
  See also eight classes of gods and demons
Gojatsa, 122
Gökyi Demtruchen, Rigdzin (a.k.a. Gödem, Gödemchen), 131, 191
Gomadevī, Princess, 74, 75
Gone to Laṅka Sūtra, 36–37, 175
Gongbur Kyo, 125
Göngyal, Lama, 180
Gonjo Tulku Orgyen Chemchok, xx
Gönpuwa, Je, 172
Gopa, 26
Gorub Lotsawa Gelong Chökyi Sherab, 171, 172
grammar, 43, 107, 213
  Candragomin's skill in, 60, 61, 62
  Dampa Deshek's skill in, 174
  Rongzompa's skill in, 163, 168, 169, 170
  Tönmi Sambhota's study of, 98
Grammar of Morphology (Tönmi Sambhota), 163, 286n294
Great Akaniṣṭha, 15, 66, 268n12
Great Bliss pureland. *See* Sukhāvatī (Great Bliss)
Great Image, The (Vairotsana), 101
Great Mother Prajñāpāramitā, 116, 137
Great Perfection, 16, 114, 224, 280n196
  appearance of, 89–92
  Bodhisattva stages in, 297n482
  concealment of, 92–93
  cycles of, 125, 281n219
  direct introduction to, 214
  Hūṃkāra and, 85
  masters realizing, 198
  Padmasambhava's receipt of, 78
  synonyms of, 274n105
  tantras of, 68–69
  three categories of, 92, 278n162
  three ways of giving instructions in, 227, 295n448
  transmission of, 176, 204
  treasures of, xxi, 243
  Vairotsana's receipt of, 101, 102
Great Secret Early Translation teachings, xiv, xx
Great Secret Luminous Essence, xxii
Great Secret teachings, 6, 21, 89, 210, 214, 218, 262, 264
Great Treasury of Detailed Explanations (Upagupta), 36, 50
Great Treasury of Precious Termas (Jamgön Kongtrul), 93–94, 235–36
Great Wild Shen, 206
Greater Khecara, 54, 273n88
Greater Tibet, 174, 287n317
greatness
  four aspects of, 135
  sixfold, 101, 103, 262, 279n184, 299n510
  ten qualities of, 129, 281n226
Guarī goddesses, 120, 280n212
Guhya Mañjuśrī (Vilāsavajra), 169
Guhyagarbha cycle, 275n126

Guhyagarbha: The Root Tantra, 21, 68, 170, 197, 279n191
  commentaries on, 67, 76, 213, 215, 274n103
  on compassion of teachers and holy ones, 258
  Dropukpa tradition of, 126
  eight sections of, 73–74
  on four ways of subduing, 22–23
  paths in, 122
  on ten secrets, 220, 293n427
Guhyajñāna, Ḍākinī, 78
Guhyasamāja Tantra, 65, 66, 94, 286n306
Guhyasamāja teachings, 156, 157
Guide to the Hidden Land of Pemakö (Dudul Dorje), 193
Guṇaprabha, 42–43, 54, 55, 136
Guru Embodiment of Vidyādharas (Dudul Dorje), 193
Guru Sādhana, xxi, 243
Guru Tantra, 74
Guru Yoga, 129, 225, 257
gurus. *See* spiritual teachers and gurus
Gya Gyeltsul, 170
Gyala Sengdam, 208
Gyalmo Tsawarong, 102
Gyalmorong, 180
Gyalse Norbu Yongdrak, 194
Gyalse Sönam Detsen, xvi, 5, 194–95, 196, 245
Gyalwe Jungne, 133
Gyatön Dorje Gönpo, 127
Gyatön Lodrö, 114
Gyepak Sherab, 108
Gyurme Ngedön Wangpo, 213, 214, 218, 219, 235, 241

Haribhadra, 64
Hayagrīva, 73, 84, 87, 116, 220, 222
Hayagrīva Tantra, 81
healing and medicine, 163, 174, 237–38, 288n350
Heap of Jewels sūtra collection, 184–85, 253
Heart Essence (*Nyingtik*) cycle, 92, 198
Heart Essence of the Lake-Born Vajra (Dudjom Rinpoche), 220
Heart Essence Triad of Amitāyus, Yangdak Heruka, and Vajrakīlaya (Dudul Dorje), 192
heart-son, use of term, 184
Heaven of the Thirty-Three (Trāyastriṃśa), 32, 275n117
hell realms, 31–32, 143, 245
Hepa Chöjung, xvi, 5, 189, 245
Hepo Mountain, 100
Heruka, 73
Heruka Galpo Tantra, 84, 158
Hevajra, 67
Hevajra Tantra (Vajragarbha), 66, 69, 80, 81, 94, 175, 179, 180
hidden lands, 190, 245, 289n355, 297n483
Hidden Meanings of the "Guyhagarbha Root Tantra" Called "Celebration of Awareness" (Jampal Dewe Nyima), 213
Hīnayāna, 103, 143, 182–83, 268n14, 291n397
Historical Account of the Origin of the Teaching of Vajrakīlaya Namchak Pudri (Dudjom Rinpoche), 203–9
History of Treasures (Dudul Dorje), 193
Holy Golden Light Sūtra, 128
Holy Teachings of the Heart Essence of the Nirmāṇakāya (Dudul Dorje), 192
Horpo district, 177–78, 180
Hūṃkāra, xvi, 4, 84–85, 87, 158–59, 245, 277n158
Hūṃkāra (deity), 84
Hundred Thousand Quintessential Tantric Texts, 86
Hundred Thousand Verses of Tārā's Perfect Renunciation (Bhatasiddhi), 63
Hundred-Thousandfold Supreme Awareness Tantra, 86

Ikṣvakus, 24, 269n41
inconceivability, 154, 159, 285n277
India, 35, 297n484, 298n490
  artistic traditions of, 163
  Dudjom Rinpoche's enlightened activity in, 231, 234, 245
  ministers in, 158, 285n281
  Padmasambhava in, 81
  Tibetan masters' travel to, 98, 101, 102, 108, 109, 110, 138
indivisibility, state of, 82, 276n140
Indra, 48, 49, 69, 116, 196, 246, 252, 269n29, 270n47, 289n353
Indrabhūti (a.k.a. Indrabodhi), xvi, 4, 65–66, 77, 88–89, 157–58, 182, 288n334

Indrabhūti (middle). *See* Ja, King
Indrabhūti (younger). *See* Śakraputra (a.k.a. Indrabhūti the Younger)
Infinity of Pure Wisdom Phenomena (Dudjom Lingpa), 201, 209
inner heat (tummo), 113, 176, 283n241
Inscribed History of Prophecies (Dudjom Rinpoche), 220–22
interdependent origination, 141
Introduction to Yoga (Buddhaguhya), 76
Iron Being, 196
irreversible stage, 79, 275n133
Īśvarasena, 44, 52, 53

Ja, King, 70–71, 72, 75, 76, 87, 112, 275n118
Jab Chagpurchen, 193
Jagpa Kagyu lineage, 138
Jālandharipa, 82, 106
Jālandhara Monastery, 35
Jambudvīpa, 24, 269nn40–41
  aspirations for, 263
  Bodhisattvas' appearance in, xvii
  six countries with Dharma in, 246, 249, 297n484, 298n490
  subcontinents of, 286n296
  universal monarchs in, 270n43
  war in, 251–52
Jamgön Kongtrul Lodrö Taye, xix, 94–95, 213, 214, 242. See also *Great Treasury of Precious Termas*
Jampa Namdak, 175
Jampa Puntsok, 193
Jamyang Khyentse Wangpo, 131, 213, 214
Jamyang Yönten, 180
Jang, 177, 179, 180
Jangchub Ö, 133
Jangchub Senge, 176
Jangsem Lodrö Gyaltsen, 214
Jātakas, 297n486. See also *Former Lives of the Buddha*
Jatri Tsenpo, 212, 292n403
Jatsön Nyingpo, Vidyādhara, 192, 236, 282n236, 289n364, 296n471
Jayadeva, 55, 56
Je Fortress, 110
Jedrung Trinle Jampa Jungne. *See* Dudjom Namkhe Dorje Tsal
Jigdral Yeshe Dorje. *See* Dudjom Jigdral Yeshe Dorje (Kyabje Rinpoche)
Jigme Lingpa, 26, 215, 228, 229–30. See also *Treasury of Precious Qualities*
Jigme Trinle Özer, 200, 290n384
Jñānadharmakāya, 136
Jñānagarbha, lineage of, 64
Jñānapada, 66, 283n98
jñānasattva, 227, 294n447
Jñānasūtra, 93
Jo Semo Damo Tsugtorjam, 124
Jomo Yungmo, 119, 120
Jonang Kunpang Tugje Tsöndru, 138
Jowo Śākyamuni statues, 98
Jvalamukhadeva, 269n29

Ka Chok Zhang Trio, 103
Ka Gong Pur Trio, 129
Kadam tradition, 135, 139, 175, 282n240
Kadö Yeshe Nyingpo, 114
Kagyu traditions, xix, 136, 138, 139, 177, 184, 273n96
Kailāśa, 297n484, 298n490
Kailash, Mount, 62, 76, 155, 252, 275n126
Kālacakra (deity), 67
Kālacakra Root Tantra, 250
Kālacakra Tantra. See *Abridged Kālacakra Tantra*
Kālacakra teachings, 66, 274n110, 283n100
Kālacakrapada the Elder, 66, 283n100
Kālacakrapada the Younger (a.k.a. Śrībhadra), 66, 283n100
Kāḷadevala (a.k.a. Asita), 25
Kālagrīva (nāga king), 69
Kalkī kings, xvii–xviii, 6, 249, 250, 297n488, 298n489
Kalyāṇavarman, King, 55
Kam Lotsawa, 175
Kama (spoken) tradition, 275n127, 276n142
  Hayagrīva in, 84
  lineage holder of, use of term, 279n191
  Nyingma, xxi, 231, 236
  on Padmasambhava, 77
  Vajrakīlaya in, 86
  Vajrāmṛita, 85
  Viśuddha Mind in, 84, 277n149
  Yamāntaka in, 83
Kamalaśīla, 64, 108
Kambalapāda. *See* Śakraputra (a.k.a. Indrabhūti the Younger)

Kampo, 175, 176, 183
Kanampa lineage, 212
Kangyur, 179, 214
Kaniṣka, King, 34, 35
Kanthaka (horse), 25, 26
karma
causes of, 154
debts of, 110
dispelling, 257
flesh debts of, 32, 271n64
in Jambudvīpa, 24
perceptions due to, 164, 258
residue of, 184
Karma Chagme, 194
Karma family, 15
karmamudrā (activity consort). *See under* consorts, spiritual
Karṇikavana Temple (Kashmir), 35
Kashmir, 33, 35, 40, 50, 63, 133
Kāśyapa. *See* Mahākāśyapa
Katok Chagtsa Tulku, 214
Katok Dampa Deshek (a.k.a. Deshek Sherab Senge), xvi, 245
appoints regent, 182–83
disciples of, 180
early life, 174–77
homage to, 4, 173–74
at Katok Dorje Den, 177–79
lineage of, 189
passing, 183
scholarship, 176
teaching career, 179–80
works of, 181
Katok Dudul Gyalse Pema Namgyal, 196
Katok Monastery (Katok Dorje Den), xvi, xvii, 4, 287n316
construction of, 178–79
Dampa Deshek at, 176, 177–81
Dudul Dorje at, 193
Dudul Rolpa Tsal at, 197
Gyalse Sönam Detsen at, 195
Katok Tulku Jampal Norbu Tenzin, xxii, 212, 217
Kawa Paltsek, 103, 134
Kāyas
Five, 136, 237
Four, 160, 165, 191, 285n287
perceived, 15–16
See also Three Kāyas
Kecara, 173, 287n313
Khab Gungtang, 161, 285n289
Kham, 103, 133, 162, 286n309, 288n343, 289n362
Dampa Deshek and, 179, 180, 287
Dudjom Lingpa in, 198, 202
Lingje Repa in, 185
Lower Zur tradition of, 127, 182
treasure revealed in, 193
Khandro Nyingtik, 198. See also *Profound Secret Heart Essence of the Ḍākinī* (Dudjom Lingpa)
Kharnakpa of Drum (a.k.a. Drubtop Kharnakpa), xvi, 5, 188–89, 198, 245
Kharsapaṇi Temple, 61
Khatra, 220, 293n430
Khedrub Tsangma Shangtön, 138
Khetsun Zhönu Drub, 138
Khotan, 187, 288n344, 297n484, 298n390
Khugom Chökyi Senge, 138
Khulung Yönten Gyatso, 111, 112
Khyabdal Lhundrub, 195
Khyeuchung Khadingtsel, 80. *See also* Padmasambhava (Guru Rinpoche)
Khyerchu Temple, 189
Khyungpo Naljor, 138
Khyungtsangpa Yeshe Lama, 185
Kīlaya, 77, 81. *See also* Vajrakīlaya
Kin of the Sun (epithet of Śākyamuni), 3, 11, 145, 284n268
King of Samādhi Sūtra, 175
knowledge, sublime (Skt. *prajñā*; Tib. *shes rab*), 24, 29, 62, 269n38, 269n39
of Dudjom Rinpoche, 212
Guṇaprabha's, 54
higher training in, 30, 134, 170
Nāgārjuna's, 39
Rongzompa's, 167
Śāriputra's, xv, 3, 145, 151, 153
self-occurring, 257
threefold, 261, 299n505
and wisdom (*ye shes*), distinguishing, 294n443
Zurpoche's, 114
Kolita. *See* Maudgalyāyana
Könchok Gyalpo, 136
Könchok Gyaltsen, 191
Könchok Rabten, Lama, 213, 222
Kongpo, 104, 180, 192, 208, 215, 234, 236
Kongpo Gyarawa Namkha Chökyi Gyatso, 189

Kongpo Lama Buchu, 182
kośa beings, 89
Kośala, 25
Kriyāyoga/Kriyātantra, 19, 68, 106, 113, 279n188
Kṛṣṇa, 33
Kṛṣṇācārya, 80, 82, 106, 166
Kṛṣṇadhara, xvi, 4, 77, 157–58
Kṣemendra, 164
Kṣetrapāla, 192
Kubera. *See* Vaiśravaṇa (Kubera)
Kublai Khan, 33, 137, 187
Kukkurāja (also Kutarāja), 72, 74, 75, 76
Kukkurāja the Later, 89
Kukkuripa, 66
Kukkuṭapada Mountain, 40
Kula Dzogpa charnel ground, 80, 276n134
Kumāraja, Vidyādhara, 189, 289n352
Kumāravīrabalin, 67
Kunga Gyatso of Derge, 191
Kunga Legpa, 175
Kunkyong Lingpa, 102, 282n236
Kunzang Gatshal, 264
Kunzang Khyabdal Lhundrub, 194
Kusho Gyurme-la, 236
Kuśinagarī, 31, 186, 288n339
Kuvana Monastery (Kashmir), 35
Kyide Nyima Gön, 133
Kyonglung, 125
Kyotön Shakye, 124
Kyotön Sönam Lama, 137

Lachen Gongpa Rabsal, 113
Lalitavajra, King, 63
Lama Ling community, 234
Lamchok Palgyi Dorje, 107–8
Lamp for the Eye of Samādhi (Nubchen Sangye Yeshe), 111
Lamp for the Path to Enlightenment (Atiśa), 175
Lamp of Sublime Knowledge (Bhāviveka), 59
Land of Dreadlocks pureland, 207
Langdarma Udum Tsenpo, 109, 110–11, 112, 132–33
language, study of, 163–65, 286n294. *See also* grammar
Laṅkāvatāra Sūtra. See *Gone to Laṅka Sūtra*
Lantsa script, 162, 285n291
Lapis Lazuli Radiance, 203
Lasso of the Ārya's Method Called "Garland of Lotuses," 73
Later Tantra of the Coming of Cakrasaṃvara, 71
Later Translations. *See* New Translation traditions
Latöpa Könchok Khar, 138
Legden, 116, 123
Legpe Sherab, 133
Len Shakya Jangchub, 125
Len Shakya Zangpo, 125
Letter of Praise to the Dharma King of the Three Realms (Chögyal Phagpa), 188
Letter to a Disciple (Candragomin), 62
Letter to a Friend (Nāgārjuna), 213, 235
Lha Totori Nyenshel, 98
Lhaje Zurpoche. *See* Zurpoche Shakya Jungne
Lhalung Palgyi Dorje, 108, 111
Lhamo Rangjung Gyalmo, 177
Lhasa, 101, 236, 290n369
Lhatsun Namkha Jigme, 194
Lhe charnel ground, 109
Lhodrak Kharchu, 105
Lhundrub Teng Dharma school, 191
liberating instructions, 79, 192, 207, 208, 215, 219, 236
liberation
  four types, 190, 238, 289n360
  individual, 46
  metaphor for, 270–71n56
  path of, 122
  six kinds of, 131, 282n237
Licchavi clan, 70, 97. *See also* Vimalakīrti of Licchavi
life force, 80, 153, 154, 276n135, 285n276
life spans, 24, 142, 197, 253, 254, 256, 269n41, 270n43
life stories, purposes and benefits of, 164
Līlāvajra. *See* Gegpa/Gegpe Dorje (a.k.a. Vilāsavajra and Līlāvajra)
Līlāvajra (Rolpe Dorje), 83, 88–89
Lineage Empowered by Prayer, 96
Lineage of Sealed Treasures from Guru Rinpoche Entrusted to Ḍākinīs, 96
Lineage of Wisdom Prophecies, 96
Ling clan, 191
Ling Lama Tubten Chöjor, 213

Ling Tsang, 177, 179, 180, 194, 287n325
Lingje Repa, xvi, 5, 183, 184–86, 245
Lion of Speech, 4, 160, 161, 170, 201, 286n310
Lochen Dharmaśrī, 215
Loden Chokse, 78. *See also* Padmasambhava (Guru Rinpoche)
Lodrö Taye, xviii, 256
logic and reasoning, 43, 53, 59, 163, 167
Longchen Nyingtik, 257
Longchen Rabjam, 204, 227, 230, 275n120, 289n352
  on major and minor marks, 18–19
  on pureland of Dharmakāya, 14
  works of, 213–14, 215
longevity practices, 220, 293n426
Longsal Nyingpo, 5, 194, 195, 196, 221
Lord of Death, 251
Loro, 185
Lotus Light, pureland of (Palace of Lotus Light), 290n375
  Buddhahood in, 7, 258
  Dudjom Jigdral Yeshe Dorje in, 240
  Dudjom Lingpa in, 209
  leading others to, xx, 6, 195, 196, 199, 243
  replica of, xix
Lotus Mound. *See* Sukhāvatī (Great Bliss)
Lotus-Born (Padmasambhava as), 4, 11, 77, 130, 159–60, 228, 241, 285n285
Lui Wangpo, 136
Lumbinī Grove, 24
Lume tradition, 176
luminous enclosure, 244, 297n481
Luminous One, 20, 268n21
Luminous Vajra Essence pureland, 67, 241, 274n104, 297n473, 300n520
Lūyipa, 94

Ma Rinchen Chok, 108, 132, 134
Ma So Kam trio, 137, 283n252
Machik Labdrön, 137–38
Madhyamaka Avatāra (Candrakīrti), 136
Madhyamaka traditions, 37, 59, 64, 65
Madhyāntha Vibhaṅga. See *Distinguishing between Middle and Extremes* (Maitreya, as spoken to Asaṅga)
Magadha, 25, 27, 29, 40, 54, 56, 63
Magical Infinity of Mañjuśrī, 73, 77, 128
Magical Infinity of Vajrasattva, 73. See also *Guhyagarbha: The Root Tantra*
Magical Infinity tantras, 72, 74, 75, 76, 78
  commentaries on, 85
  maṇḍala of, 182
  sādhanas of, 179
  transmission of, 104, 107, 113, 114, 121, 176, 279n191
  See also *Guhyagarbha: The Root Tantra*
Magical Vajra. See *Mirror of All the Vajrasattva Magical Infinity Tantras*
magical/miraculous powers, xvii, 82, 89
  Chögyal Phagpa's, 187
  Dampa Deshek's, 182
  of disciples of Zurpoche, 117
  Dudjom Lingpa's, 203
  Kharnakpa of Drum's, xvi
  Maudgalyāna's, 145–46, 150
  Nyak Jñānakumāra's, 104, 106
  Padmasambhava's, 79, 80, 99–100
  Rongzompa's, 172
  Śakraputra's, 88
  Śāntideva's, 56, 57
  Saraha's, 154–55
  Smṛtijñāna's, 161
  Vairotsana's, 101
  Vimalamitra's, 105
  Zurchungpa's, 121, 122–24
Magnificent Wisdom Lightning Tantra, 73
Mahābodhi Temple, 63, 156
Mahādeva, 34
Mahāhimasāgara, 263, 299n519
Mahākarmendraṇī (Lekyi Wangmoche), Ḍākinī, 86–87, 277n157
Mahākāśyapa, 32, 33–34, 36
Mahāmāyā Tantra, 66
Mahāmāyūrī, 37, 38
Mahāmudrā
  basis, path, and fruition, 154
  four yogas of, 154, 184
  masters attaining, 74, 85, 86, 157, 252
  transmission of, 180
  See also Coemergent Mahāmudrā
Mahāmudrā (Padampa Sangye), 137
Mahāmudrā Chö, 138
Mahāpadma, King, 25, 34
Mahāparinirvāṇa Sūtra, 127
Mahāprajāpatī Gautamī, 25, 30, 31, 270n44
Mahāsamaya Sūtra, 179
Mahāsaṃghika tradition, 34–35
Mahāsiddhas, xv, 66, 82, 94, 129, 164, 172

Mahāyāna, 182–83
caste of, 250
causal, 268n14
and Hīnayāna, differences between, 143
spreading of, 42
teachings in, 19
treasure of, 15, 16
uncommon tradition, 103
and Vajrayāna, distinctions in, 291n397
Mahāyāna Samucchaya (Asaṅga), 42
Mahāyāna sūtras
compilation of, 35
disappearance and revival of, 93–94
variations in, 23
Mahāyoga, 279n188, 299n512
development stage in, 210
divisions of, 97
Dudjom Rinpoche's practice of, 220
eighteen great tantras of, 72–74, 275n120, 275n121
oral transmission lineage of, 72–83
origin of, 72
transmission of, 107, 279n191
Treasure tradition of, 86
Maheśvara, 58, 155–56, 246
Maheśvara Temple, 45
Mahottara Heruka, 67, 86–87
Main Sādhana Practice (Katok Dampa Deshek), 181
Maitreya
Asaṅga and, 40, 41–42, 51
as compiler of Mahāyāna, 36
disciples of, 39
as future Buddha, 142, 144, 253
maṇḍala of, 182
as regent, 24
teachings by, 175
See also *Five Treatises of Maitreya*
Maitreyanātha, 36
Maitripa, 138
Malaya, Mount, 70, 77, 83, 92
Malaya Pureland, 116
mamos, 70, 96, 127, 274n115, 287n312
Manasarovar, Lake, 155
Maṇḍala That Encompasses All of Buddha's Words, 144, 284n265
maṇḍalas
of Amṛta Quality, 104, 279n189
Cakrasaṃvara, 182, 184
of Deity Assembly, 75
Eight Herukas, 128
Guhyasamāja, 156
of Magical Infinity, 182
of Maheśvara, 58
of peaceful and wrathful Buddhas, self-appearing, 67
of peaceful and wrathful deities, 14
of Pema Garwang and Yamāntaka, 109
seen by Dampa Deshek, 182
sixty-two, 115
of Three Noble Protectors, 182
twenty-one, 116
Unsurpassed Quintessential Secret Heart Essence, 218
Vajradhātu, 76, 275n125
of wrathful deities, 19
of Yangdak Heruka, 84, 86, 111, 115, 182
Mandāravā, Princess, 79
Mandya, 65
Mangyul, 99, 278n177
Mangyul Gungtang, 223, 294n437
Manifest Joy pureland, 19, 85
Manifestation of Hayagrīva, 84
Mañjuśrī (a.k.a. Mañjughoṣa), 4, 108, 109
Āryadeva and, 45
Buddhaguhya and, 75–76
Candrakīrti and, 62, 65
as compiler of Mahāyāna, 36
as compiler of tantras, 68
Dignāga and, 43, 44
Dudjom Lingpa and, 201, 204
emanations of, xvii, 5, 98, 165, 167, 186
epithets of, 249, 286n310, 297n487
forms of, 69
lineage of, 67
maṇḍala of, 182
Mañjuśrīmitra and, 83, 92
Nāgārjuna and, 38
Śāntideva and, 55, 56
Smṛtijñāna and, 160–61
statue of, tilting head, 61
sword of, 58, 273n93
Mañjuśrī Root Tantra, 37, 54, 187
Mañjuśrī Yaśas, 250–51, 298n491
Mañjuśrīmitra, 83, 87, 92, 277n158
Mañjuśrīmitra the Younger, 92
Mañjuśrī-Yamāntaka, 83
Mansion of Complete Victory of Buddha's Teachings, 210, 291n398

mantras
  Essence of Interdependence, 202
  rulu, 115, 280n201
  six-syllable, 177, 182
  wrathful, 80, 83, 111, 189, 276n138
Mar, 205
Mar Śākyamuni, 132–33
Māra, 27, 270n52
Māra's daughters, 27–28
Maratika Cave, 79
Mardo Tashi Gakhyil, 207
Margyen, Queen, 105
Marpa Chökyi Wangchuk (a.k.a. Marpa Dowa), 170, 171, 172
Marpa Lotsawa, 134, 136, 286n306
Master's Realization, xxi, 243
Mātaraḥ Tantra, 81
Mātaraḥ tantras, 86, 87, 109, 172
Maticitra (Aśvagoṣa), 45–46, 47–50, 61, 168, 272n85
Matok Jangbar, 123
Matyaupayika (rakṣa), 70
Maudgalyāyana, 30, 145–46
  Assaji and, 149–51
  hell realm journey of, 31–32
  passing of, 33
  renunciation of, 146–49
Māyādevī, Queen, 24, 25, 269n41, 270n49
Mayul Orgyen Pezha, 208
Medicine Buddha, 203, 213
Menmo (noblewoman), 184–85
merit, 42, 218, 249, 253, 254, 261, 262
Meru, Mount, 25, 68, 100, 165
Middle Way. *See* Madhyamaka traditions
Mikchung Wangsen, 122
Milarepa, 136, 162, 176
mind
  ordinary, 173, 188, 210–11, 281n214
  proper engagement of, 234
  subduing, importance of, 182–83
Mind Class, 107, 113, 279n191, 285n282
mind treasures, xxi, 96, 209, 220, 222, 243, 278n167
Mindrolling Vajra Holder Namdrol Gyatso, 213, 214, 219
Mingyur Namkha Dorje, 200, 290n385
ministers, outer and inner, 157, 285n281
Minling Terchen Gyurme Dorje, 214, 215, 227
Minor Transmissions of the Vinaya, 34, 35
Minyak, 175, 177, 179, 180, 287n318
Minyak Khyungdrak, 117
Mipham Gönpo Gyalwa Jampa. *See* Maitreya
Mipham Rinpoche, 165, 173, 213, 214–15, 230, 298n493
Mirror of All the Vajrasattva Magical Infinity Tantras, 15, 71, 126
Mirror That Reflects the Treasure Guide of the "Profound Secret Heart Essence of the Ḍākinī" (Dudjom Lingpa), 205
Mön, 220, 221, 222, 293n430
monasticism, 34
  Dudjom Rinpoche's support for, 234–35
  guarding Dharma, role of in, 36
  reversing ordination in, 149
  three stages of ordination in, 113, 280n198
  in Tibet, 100–101, 133 (*see also* "seven men to be tested")
moon, hare-marked, 161, 285n290
Möpa Taye (Buddha Adhimukta), 298n495
  homage to, 6–7
  prophecies about, xv, xvii, xviii, 142, 144, 244
  story of, 252, 253, 256
mother tantras, 122, 279n191
Mṛgajā, 26
Mudrā Concentration (Vimalamitra), 85
mudrā samādhi, 121, 281n215
Muksang, 191
Mūlamadhyamaka Prajñā. See *Root Verses on the Middle Way Called "Sublime Knowledge"*
Mūlasarvāstivāda tradition, 34–35
Mūlasarvāstivāda Vinaya, 270n55
Mune Tsenpo, 105, 132
Munīndrakṛṣṇa, 44
Murub Tsenpo, 132
Muruṇḍaka, Mount, 89
Murwa Tsurtön. *See* Tsurtön Wangyi Dorje
Mutik Tsenpo, 132, 200

Na Cave, 105
Nabhika Ananta, King, 25
Nabun Dzong, 193
nāda, 68, 274n107

Nāga, the elder, 34
Nāgabodhi, 157
Nāgārjuna, 55, 66, 277n158
  Āryadeva and, 44, 45
  life span of, 277n148
  life story, 37–39
  Maticitra and, 46–47, 50
  in nāga realm, 39, 94
  Nyingma lineage and, 230, 295n454
  oral instructions of, 134
  prophecies on, 36–37
  Saraha and, 156–57
  tantras revealed by, 84
  tradition of, 64, 272n72
  treasure revealed to, 87
  works of, 39, 59, 213, 231, 235, 295n456
nāgas, 32, 39, 66, 68, 69, 76, 78, 94
Nagpo Khar, 188
Nairātmyā, 136, 283n245
Nālandā University, 32, 147
  Āryadeva at, 47–50
  Buddhaguhya at, 75
  Candragomin at, 61
  Candrakīrti at, 65
  Dignāga at, 43
  establishment of, 156
  Hūṃkāra at, 84
  Maticitra at, 46
  Nāgārjuna at, 38
  Śāntideva at, 56
  Vasubandhu at, 50, 52
Namchak Pudri (Dudjom Lingpa), 205, 223
Namchö Mingyur Dorje, 194
Namde Ösung, 133
Namgyal Drolma, 212
Namkha De, 113
Namkhe Nyingpo, 131
Nanam Dorje Dudjom, 131
Nanda, 25, 26, 34
Napuwa Lingje Repa Pema Dorje. *See* Lingje Repa
Narlungrong, 166
Nāropa, 134, 136, 138, 161, 273n99
Nartang Monastery, 176, 187
Natural Liberation of Awareness Tantra, 214
Nayagrodha Cave, 33
Nepal, xvi, 52, 80, 238, 245
  artistic traditions of, 163
  Dudjom Dorje in, xx, 239, 240, 243
  Hūṃkāra's birth in, 84, 245
  language of, 286n300
  Tibetan masters' travel to, 108, 110
Nerañjanā River, 27
New Tantra tradition, 183–84
New Translation traditions, 65, 134, 169, 171, 180, 183–84, 273n96
New Treasure tradition, xxi
Newari Kālasiddhī, 200, 290n382
Ngadak Drak, 115
Ngagchang, Lopön, 217, 293n420
Ngagchang Tsedrub Tharchin. *See* Tharchin Rinpoche
Ngagtsun Gedun Gyatso, 214
Ngakha Darchung, 170
Ngala Tagtse, 202
Ngari, 133, 278n177, 286n309, 287n317
Ngari Panchen Pema Wangyi Gyalpo, 213
Ngaröl Taktse, 205
Ngawang Khyentse Norbu, Khenchen, 293n422
Ngawang Pal Zangpo, 214, 292n406
Ngawang Palden Zangpo, 213, 217, 292n406
Ngayab Pelri retreat center, 242
Ngok Loden Sherab, 124
Ngor Ewam Chöden Monastery, 192, 289n363
Ngorchen Kunga Zangpo, 171, 173
Ngulgö Mountain, 205
Ngulpunang, 191
Niguma, 138
nihilism, 31, 59, 161
Nila River, 81
Nine Cycles of the Formless Ḍākinīs, 176
Nine Island Lake, 109
Nirmāṇakāyas
  compassion of, 258
  emanations of, 21, 90, 91, 108, 113, 119, 124, 166, 218, 244
  great flaming ones of, 195, 290n371
  natural, 11
  nonabiding, 239–40
  purelands of, 19, 300n520
  supreme, 16–18, 93, 269n29, 278n163
  types of, xiv, xvii, 22, 166, 286n302
Nobkyi Putak Pudrak, 193
Noble Shoulder Tantra, 99
Noble Vajra, 251, 298n493

nonduality, designations for, 14
Notes on "Revealing the Names of Mañjuśrī" (Katok Dampa Deshek), 181
Notes on "Stages of the Path" and Its Condensed Meaning (Katok Dampa Deshek), 181
Notes on the "Ocean of Magical Manifestations" (Katok Dampa Deshek), 181
Notes on the "Parkhab Commentary on the 'Guhyagarbha Tantra'" (Katok Dampa Deshek), 181
Nub clan, 108, 203
Nubchen Sangye Yeshe, 108–12, 131, 179
Nuden Dorje Chang (Vajradhara), xv, xvii, 245
  homage to, 3
  lineage of, 66–68, 276n142
  state of, 69, 74, 75, 274n111, 276n140, 277n154
  story of, 142, 143–45
  teachings from, 138
nuns
  as Arhats, 31
  in Śākyamuni's retinue, 30
  Sudharma, 90, 91
Nyagchen Yeshe Zhönu, 103, 131
Nyak Getön, 104, 105, 106, 107
Nyak Jñānakumāra, 104–8, 134
Nyang River, 101
Nyang Yeshe Jungne, 113
Nyangben Tingdzin Zangpo, 131
Nyangnak Dowo, 127
Nyangpo, 191–92
Nyangral Nyima Özer, 131
Nyarong Khenchen Jampal Dewe Nyima (a.k.a. Pende Özer), 213, 219, 293n423
Nyatri Tsenpo, royal succession of, 97–98
Nyemo, 101, 110
Nyemo Ramang, 138
Nyenak Wangdrak, 113–14
Nyenchen Palyang, 107
Nyetön Chöseng, 127
Nyingma Gyubum, 236, 296n467
Nyingma tradition, 176
  Dampa Deshek in, 180
  Dudul Dorje and, 193
  on hidden lands, 289n355
  Kama of, xxi, 231, 236
  masters of, xvi
  nine yānas in, 120, 163, 224, 262, 280n211
  preservation of, xxi
  translation in, 134
  Zur family lineages in, 112
  See also Early Translation school
Nyingpo Drupa, 138
Nyoshul Lungtok Tenpe Nyima, 214

obscurations
  three, 78, 275n129
  two, 253
Ocean of Dharma That Embodies All Teachings (Padmasambhava), 79
Oḍḍiyāna, 65–66
  Dudjom Lingpa in, 207
  Indrabhūti in, 157, 158
  ordination in, 75
  Padmasambhava in, 77–78, 79, 81, 160
  Śakraputra in, 87–89
  teachings in, 68, 74, 76
Odren Palgyi Zhönu, 106–7, 108
offerings
  to gurus, 114
  human, 63–64
  material, 103
  returning, 118
  to Three Jewels, 77, 157
  torma, 114
Ölmo Tsel, 109
Öme Tsel, 109
omniscience, 3, 23, 30, 129, 139, 141, 163, 187, 235, 261
Önchangdo Tashi Gepel temple, 132
One Hundred and Fifty Verses of Praise (Aśvaghoṣa), 61
One Hundred and One Formal Ecclesiastical Acts (Guṇaprabha), 54
one taste, xv, xxii, 7, 21, 67, 121, 232, 258, 259
One-Pointed Samādhi Tantra, 73
Opening the Eyes of Prajñā (Vimalamitra), 85
Oral Instructions of Mañjuśrī, 92
Orgyen Chemchok Rinpoche, 294n440
Orgyen Chö Dzong retreat center, 234, 296n460
Orgyen Chönjor Gyatso, 213, 219
Orgyen Garwang Drodul Lingpa Tsal/Orgyen Drodul Lingpa. *See* Dudjom Jigdral Yeshe Dorje (Kyabje Rinpoche)

Orgyen Lingpa, 131, 199, 212, 282n236
Orgyen Rigdzin, Lama, 214
Orgyen Tendzin, 192
Ornament of Awareness (Gelong Deje), 38
Ornament of Manifest Realization (Maitreya, as spoken to Asaṅga), 42, 136
Ornament of the Mahāyāna Sūtras (Maitreya, as spoken to Asaṅga), 22, 42, 136, 211
Outline of the Path of the Great Perfection (Katok Dampa Deshek), 181

Padampa Sangye, 125–26, 137
Padma (lotus) family, 15, 84, 210, 259
Padma Tötreng Tsal, 79, 218. *See also* Padmasambhava (Guru Rinpoche)
Padmakāra. *See* Lotus-Born (Padmasambhava as)
Padmanarteśvara, 67
Padmasambhava (Guru Rinpoche), 4, 11, 12, 162, 277n156, 277n157, 294n439
  arrival in Tibet, 99–100, 294n437
  as basis of emanation, 240, 296n472
  birth of, 158
  Dampa Deshek and, 182
  Dudjom Jigdral Yeshe Dorje and, xiii, xviii, xix, xxii, 209–10, 212, 213, 222, 228–29, 243
  Dudjom Lingpa and, 200–201, 204, 205, 206, 207, 208
  five supreme consorts of, 131, 282n234, 290n382
  incarnations of, 199, 200
  instructions of, 172
  life stories, 77–82, 127–29, 160, 164
  names of, 77, 78, 79, 80, 159, 240, 285n285, 296n471
  as Nirmāṇakāya, 259
  Nubchen Sangye Yeshe and, 108
  Nyak Jñānakumāra and, 104
  regents of, 196
  teachers of, 76, 78
  in Treasure tradition, 86, 87, 96, 129–31, 191, 202
  twenty-five disciples of, xvi, 204, 212, 291n329
  Vairotsana and, 102, 103
  visualizing, 225
Pagor Lönchen Phagpa, 111
Palace of Lotus Light. *See* Lotus Light, pureland of (Palace of Lotus Light)
Palace of Perfect Purity, 254–55
Palden Lhamo, 116, 132, 175, 179
Palgyi Chökhor, 175
pañcalika brocades, 45, 272n84
Pañcaśṛṅga, King, 44
Pangka Darchungwa, 122
Pāṇini's Grammar, 61
Paramādyakalparāja. See *Glorious Supreme Beginning Tantra*
Parbuwa Lodrö Senge, 184
Parkhab Commentary of the Wisdom Mind of Samantabhadra (Katok Dampa Deshek), 181
Parkhab Commentary on the "Guhyagarbha Tantra" (Vilāsavajra), 75, 113, 181
Paro (Bhutan), 188–89, 245
Paro Tagtsang, 220, 221, 222, 293n431
parrot scholar, 45, 48
Path and Its Fruit (lamdre), 137, 175, 180
Path of Secret Mantra and Its Fruit practice, 136
path of training, 253
Patrul Chökkyi Wangpo (Patrul Rinpoche), 227, 234
Pawang Gyeleb "Site of Eight Boulders," 179
Peaceful Practice of Mañjuśrī (Dudul Dorje), 193
Peaceful and Wrathful Ḍākinī cycles, 220
peaceful and wrathful deities, 14, 118, 189, 190, 281m215
Peaceful and Wrathful Deities (Pema Lingpa), 189, 236
Peaceful and Wrathful Guru cycles, 220
peaceful deities, nine signs of, 14, 267n9
Pearl Necklace (Dudjom Rinpoche), xiv–xv, 3–7
Pema Dragpo, 5, 194, 195, 198
Pema Garwang, 109
Pema Gyalpo, 79. *See also* Padmasambhava (Guru Rinpoche)
Pema Gyurme Gyatso, 215
Pema Khandro, xx
Pema Kyi (noblewoman), 192
Pema Lingpa, 189, 214, 236, 282n236
Pema Ösal Do Ngak Lingpa. *See* Jamyang Khyentse Wangpo

Pema Ösal Pal Zangpo, xix–xx
Pema Tendzin, Lama, 213
Pema Yungdrung Tangmar, 177
Pemakö, xviii, 193, 194, 290n370
  Dudjom Rinpoche in, 212, 213, 233–34, 241, 245
  guidebook to, 221
  opening, 208, 209
Pende Özer. *See* Nyarong Khenchen Jampal Dewe Nyima (a.k.a. Pende Özer)
Penetration of Sound Tantra, 214
Pengyi Khangngön, 119
Penyul Gyal, 176
perception, 226, 247, 271n63
  direct, 64
  disciples', xiv, xvii, 145, 160, 206, 233
  dualistic, 159, 188, 210
  five sublime states of, 255, 298n498
  karmic, 164, 258
  worldly, 64
Perfect Collection of All Noble Dharmas Sūtra, 82
Perfect Conduct (Pema Wangyi Gyalpo), 213
Perfect Practice of Vajrakīlaya (Vimalamitra), 105
Perfectly Adorned world realm, 254
performing arts, 164
Personally Heard Teachings Given by Voice Lineage, 66, 81, 93, 96, 97
Phagmo Drupa Dorje Gyalpo (a.k.a. Deshek/Drogön Phagmo Drupa), xvi, 175, 183, 184, 185
Phagmodru, 185–86
phenomena
  compounded, 32
  dualistic perception of, 188
  exhaustion of, 121, 122, 232, 240
philosophical scriptures, eighteen renowned, 136–37
Phuntsok Gyaltsen, 264
Play in Full Sūtra, 143
Play of Great Joy charnel ground, 239
Pobpa Taye. *See* Katok Dampa Deshek (a.k.a. Deshek Sherab Senge)
poetry, 163–64
Poison Razor invocation prayer, 206
Por Shedrak, 194
poṣadha purification, 24
Potala pureland, 207
Potalaka, Mount, 76
Powerful King of Pure Vision (Dudul Dorje), 192
Prabhāhasti (king and ācarya), 76, 78, 86, 277n158
Prabhāvati (*Luminosity*, Śākyaprabha), 54, 55
Prabhāvatī, Ḍākinī, 77
Practice Manual of Ārya Tārā Kurukullā (Nāgārjuna), 84
Praise to Mañjuśrī with the Tilted Head, 61, 273n95
Praise to Tārā Who Holds a Flower Garland, 63, 64, 273n95
Praise to the Exalted, 63
Praise to the Pointing Avalokiteśvara, 61, 273n95
Praise to the Tathāgata Who Surpasses Worldly Gods, 62, 63, 273n95
Prajñābhāva. *See* Garab Dorje
Prajñāpāramitā in One Hundred Thousand Lines, 94
Prajñāpāramitā Sūtra, 42, 138
Prajñāpāramitā Sūtra in Eight Thousand Lines, 174–75
Prajñāpāramitā teachings, 39, 65
Prajñāvarman, 62, 63
Prakaśalaṃkara, 108
Pramāṇa Samucchaya. See *Compilation of All Teachings on Logic*
Pramāṇa Vārttika (Dharmakīrti), 137
Pramāṇa Viniścaya (Dharmakīrti), 137
Pramāṇa Yuktinidhi (Sakya Paṇḍita), 137
Prāsaṅgika Madhyamaka, 64, 65
Prasannaśīla, 40
Prasenajit, King, 25
Pratimokṣa Sūtra, 34, 136
Pratyekabuddhas, 70, 152, 237, 246, 254, 274n114
Prayer for Excellent Conduct, 15–16
Prayer with the Various Names of Dudjom Tulkus (Dudjom Rinpoche), xxii, 216–18, 293n219
Precious Advice for Bringing Realization onto the Path teaching (Padampa Sangye), 137
Precious Garland (Nāgārjuna), 39
Precious Lamp (Katok Dampa Deshek), 181

primordial purity, 204
Profound Secret Heart Essence of the Ḍākinī (Dudjom Lingpa), 202, 209
Profound Teaching Overflowing from the Expanse of Wisdom Mind (Dudjom Lingpa), 201, 209
Profound View tradition, 36–37, 213, 229, 272n72
prophecies
  on Buddhaguhya, 76
  on Buddhas to come, 143–44
  by Ḍākinīs, xxi, xxii, 93, 115
  on Dampa Deshek, 176, 177
  on Dharma in Tibet, 98, 278n171
  on Dharmakīrti, 54
  on Drak Gyawo, 120
  on Dudjom Jigdral Yeshe Dorje, xviii, xx, xxii, 212, 235–36, 241
  on Dudjom Lingpa, 198–202, 208
  Dudul Dorje and, 191, 192, 193
  on Garab Dorje, 92
  on hidden lands, 190, 289n355
  on Kharnakpa, 188
  on King Ja, 71
  on Langdarma, 132
  on Maticitra, 49–50
  on Nāgārjuna, 36–37
  on Nubchen Sangye Yeshe, 108, 109
  on Padmasambhava, 77, 79, 127–28, 159
  on Śākyamuni, 24, 25, 254, 269n39
  on Saraha, 154–55
  on Secret Mantra, 69, 70, 71–72
  on Vimalamitra, 101
Pu Ridak Dzongpuk, 208
Pudri Regpung (Dudjom Rinpoche), 222–24
Pukung/Puktrul Tulku Rinpoche Gyurme Ngedön Wangpo. *See* Gyurme Ngedön Wangpo
Puṇḍariki, Kalkī King, 250, 251
Puṇyadhara, King, 80
Puṇyakīrti, 54, 55, 76
pure abodes, 15, 19, 268n11
pure perception, xxi, 175, 181, 213
Pure Vision cycle, 209
pure visions, 96, 278n167
  Dudjom Jigdral Yeshe Dorje's, 243
  Dudjom Lingpa's, 204
  Dudul Dorje's, 191
Puri Dagdzong Cave, 192
Puri Shelgyi Yangdrom, 192–93
Pūrṇa Kāśyapa, 31–32
Pūrṇopasanti, Ḍākinī, 68
Puwo, 193, 208, 212, 222
Puwo Dongchu, 192

Quintessential Secret and Unsurpassed Vajrakīlaya (Ratna Lingpa), 192
Quintessential Secret Gathering cycle, 221
Quintessential Unexcelled Cycle of Heart Essence, 292n408

Ra Lotsawa Dorje Dragpa, 175, 184
race, 24, 225
Rāhu Razor's Wrathful Mantras, 189
Rāhula, 28, 32, 155, 156, 270n55
Rāhula (protector), 189, 206, 291n395
Rāhulabhadra. *See* Saraha
Rainbow Body, 66, 122, 176, 180, 208, 294n441
Rājagṛha, 33, 36, 149, 150
Rakṣasavarma, 26
Ralpachen, King, 110, 132
Rambuguhya Devacandra, 86, 87, 277n158
Ramoche Temple, 98
Rampant Elephant Tantra, 73
Rangjung Gyalmo, Śrī Devi, 181, 193
Rangjung Rigpe Dorje, sixteenth Karmapa, xxii
Rangrung Menpa, 199
Rasa Trulnang Temple (now Jokhang Temple), 98, 193, 244–45, 290n369
Rashakpa, Tertön, 198
Ratna (jewel) family, 15, 85
Ratna Lingpa, xviii, 192, 212
Ratna Senge, 176
Ratnagarbha (formerly Sagaragarbha), 142
Ratnakūṭa Sūtra. See *Heap of Jewels* sūtra collection
Ratnasambhava, 15, 19, 85
Raudra Cakrin, Kalkī King, xvii–xviii, 249–50, 251
rebirth
  four ways of taking, 211, 291n399
  power over, 209
  seven qualities of higher, 263, 299n517
Rechungpa, 176, 185
Record of Profound and Extensive Dharma Teachings Received Called "Precious Lamp" (Dudjom Rinpoche), 219

Red Garuḍa with Wings of Fire (Dudul Rolpa Tsal), 197
Refutation of Objections (Nāgārjuna), 39
Rekhe, 196
Repa Zhiwa Ö, 176
Reting Monastery, 175
Revealing the Names of Mañjuśrī, 61, 75
Rich Adornment pureland, 15, 19
Richly Adorned world system, 143, 245, 246
Rigdzin Sangpuk (treasure site), 193
Rigzang Dorje, 244
Rinchen Zangpo, 133, 134
Ritual for Cremation (Vimalamitra), 85
Ritual for Fire Offerings (Vimalamitra), 85
Rituals for Cultivating Bodhicitta (Katok Dampa Deshek), 181
Riwoche, 194
Rok Shakya Jungne, 114, 115
Rongben Rinchen Tsultrim, 166
Rongtön Dechen Lingpa, 103, 196
Rongzom Chökyi Zangpo, xvi, 173, 230, 245, 286n308
  disciples of, 172
  doubt and slander toward, 170, 171
  homage to, 4
  life span, 172
  life stories, 165–68, 170, 171–72
  on result vehicle, 297n476
  scholarship of, 162–63, 168, 170–71
  translations of, 169
  works of, 167, 168–69, 170
Root Grammar in Thirty Verses (Tönmi Sambhota), 163, 286n294
Root Tantra of Magical Infinity. See *Guhyagarbha: The Root Tantra*
Root Tantra of Mañjuśrī. See *Mañjuśrī Root Tantra*
Root Tantra of the Gathering of the Sugatas, 68
Root Verses on the Middle Way Called "Sublime Knowledge" (Nāgārjuna), 39, 65, 136
Ṛṣi Bhāṣita, 76
Ruby Rosary Joyfully Accepted by Vidyādharas and Ḍākinīs as the Ornament of a Necklace, xiv–xv, 264
Rudra, 48, 67
Rupakāyas, 14, 154, 165, 267n7
sacred commitments, 237
  five knowledges in, 216, 292n417
  six key points of, 216, 292n418
  sixfold power of stainless, 229, 295n450
  ten secrets of, 220, 293n427
Ṣaḍānana (Six-Faced One), 83
Sādhana of Keen Mañjuśrī, 55
Sādhana of Mahādeva (Dudul Dorje), 193
Sādhana of Spontaneous Presence (Vilāsavajra), 75
Sagama (laywoman), 30
Sahā world system, 128, 281n225
Sahor, 72, 76, 78, 79, 99
Sakara, 94
Śakrabhūti (a.k.a. Uparāja), 74
Śakraputra (a.k.a. Indrabhūti the Younger), 74, 87–89
Śākya clan, 25, 150, 250
Śākya Kalyāṇamitra, 157
Śākya Licchavis, 97. *See also* Licchavi clan
Sakya Lochen, 122
Sakya Monastery, 192, 289n363
Sakya Paṇḍita Kunga Gyaltsen Pal Zangpo, 133, 137
Sakya tradition, xvi, 136–37, 139, 191, 273n96, 283n249
Śākyadevī, Princess, 80
Śākyaprabha, 54–55, 76
Śākyaśrī (Śākyaśrībhadra), 64, 133
sal trees and flowers, 4, 32, 143, 162, 165, 284n258
samādhis
  of dharma stream, 42, 167
  of five enlightenments, 123, 281n217
  of flowing river of nonmeditation, 204
  fourth, 28
  free of characteristics, 88
  higher training in, 170
  of nothingness, 26
  of peak of existence, 26
Samantabhadra, xiv, 11, 288n349
  attaining, 188
  as compiler of Mahāyāna, 36
  Dharmakāya, 160, 225
  emanation of, 98
  manifestation of, 144–45
  prophecy of, 101
  Sambhogakāya, 14
  three lineages of, 224
  as Vajradhara, 66

Samantabhadra (*continued*)
  wisdom mind of, xvii, 6, 197
Samantabhadra Grammar Sūtra (Candrakīrti), 62
Samantabhadra Guru Padmasambhava, xxii
Samantabhadrī, 3, 141, 280n204, 288n349
samaya substances, 5, 190, 237–38, 243, 289n359
samayas. *See* sacred commitments
samayasattva, 227, 294n447
Sambhogakāya, 11
  appearance as Nirmāṇakāya, xvii
  five certainties of, 212, 262, 291n402
  purelands of, 14–16, 67, 297n473, 300n520
  seven qualities of, 291n401
Samding Monastery, 138
Sāṃkhya school, 53
Saṃmitīya school, 34–35
Saṃvarodaya Tantra (Vajrapāṇi), 69
Samye Monastery, 115, 179
  construction of, 100
  Dudjom Rinpoche at, 236
  Lingje Repa at, 186
  translation at, 101
  treasures at, 193, 279n187
Śāṇavāsika, 33
Sangchen Ösal Namdrol Chöling, 234
Sangen, 189, 196, 197
Saṅgha, eighteen divisions of, 34–35
Saṅgha counting stick, 179, 288n331
Saṅghabhadra, 40, 50, 52
Sanglung Nagpo charnel grounds, 109
Sangye Lama, 131, 198
Sangye Lingpa, 198, 199, 213, 236, 282n236
Sangye Pema Shepa Drodul Rigdzin Trinley Drupe De. *See* Pema Ösal Pal Zangpo
Śaṅkarakuta Stūpa, 86, 89
Sanskrit, 166, 167, 171, 173
Śāntamati, 254
Śāntarakṣita, 64
  invited to Tibet, 99, 294n437
  masters ordained by, 101, 103, 104
  precept lineage of, 234–35
  at Samye, 100
Śāntideva, 55–59, 171, 232, 273n90. See also *Way of the Bodhisattva*
Śāntigarbha, 86, 87, 108, 277n158
Śāntiprabha, 54, 55, 76
Saraha, xv, 66, 204, 205, 245, 272n78, 295n454
  Dampa Deshek and, 182
  homage to, 3
  Hūṃkāra and, 84
  life story, 154–56
  Nāgārjuna and, 36, 38
  Padmasambhava as, 80
  supreme accomplishment of, 94
  teachings of, 153–54
Sarasvatī, 131
Śārikā, 146
Śāriputra, xv, 30, 145, 245
  Assaji and, 149–51
  birth of, 146–47
  birthplace of, 156
  hell realm journey of, 31–32
  homage to, 3
  and Maudgalyāyana, relationship between, 14147
  passing of, 33
  past karma of, 151–53
  renunciation of, 147, 149
Sarma tradition. *See* New Translation traditions
Saroruhavajra. *See* Padmasambhava (Guru Rinpoche)
Sarvabuddhasamāyoga Tantra. See *Union of All Buddhas Tantra*
Sarvajñānamitra (a.k.a. Sarvaprada), 63–64
Sarvanīvaraṇavikṣambin
  See Dripa Namsal (Skt. Sarvanīvaraṇavikṣambin)
Sarvāstivada order, 100
Sarvāstivadin Vinaya, 54
Śāstra tradition, 36, 272n73
śāstras, three features of authors, 230–31
Śatānīka, King, 25
Saurāṣṭra, 55
Sautrāntika school, 36
sciences
  five, 39, 98, 272n76
  ten, 162–65
Second Buddha, use of expression, 159, 285n285
Secret Essence Tantra. See *Guhyagarbha: The Root Tantra*
Secret Great Exaltation Cave, 192, 290n367

Secret Heart Essence, 214, 292n408
Secret Magical Infinity. See *Magical Infinity* tantras
Secret Mantra New/Later Translation tradition, 65–66, 165
Secret Mantra of the Early Translations, 165
Secret Mantra Vajrayāna, 113, 156, 235, 274n113
  and common vehicles, distinctions between, 210, 291n397
  Early Translation school on origins of, 66–72
  New Translation schools on origins of, 65–66
  on signs and marks, 16, 18–19
  in Tibet, 160
Secret Moon Essence Tantra, 72, 74, 81, 275n121
Secret Sealed Mind Sādhana of Dudjom Vajrakīlaya Namchak Pudri. See *Namchak Pudri* (Dudjom Lingpa)
Secret Tantra of the All-Victorious Wrathful Mañjuśrī, 171
Secret Wrathful Mañjuśrī Tantra, 83
Seed of the Three Faiths (Chatral Sangye Dorje), xv, 240–45
self-awareness, 21, 280n197, 284n265
selflessness, 191, 285n276
semantics, 164
Senge Zangpo, 175
sense consciousnesses, 67, 278n173, 292n417
sentient beings, 232, 254
  Buddhas' compassion for, 145
  endless, 256
  pervaded by Dharmakāya, 253
  places of, determining factors in, 258
  ripening, 22, 269n34
  subduing, 6, 21, 22–23, 245, 246, 252, 253, 269n31
  treasure of satisfying, 95
Serachok, 193
Serlingpa, Jowo, 134
Setrom Gyatso Bar, 170
seven branches of union, 211, 240, 291n401
"seven men to be tested," 100, 101–2, 103, 112, 279n183
Seven Patriarchs of the Teachings, 32, 33
Seven Pith Instructions (Śrī Siṃha), 93
seven precious materials, 144, 255, 284n261
seven precious royal emblems, 143, 284n260
seven riches, 190, 289n358
Seven Treasuries (Longchenpa), 214, 215
Seventy Stanzas on Emptiness (Nāgārjuna), 39
Shadrak Dorjechen, 205
Shamar Rinpoche, the eighth, 195
Shambhala, 297n484, 298n490
  kings of, xvii–xviii, 6, 245–46, 249–50, 297n488, 298n489
  teachings from, 66, 68
Shangpa Kagyu. *See* Zhangpa (Shangpa) Kagyu
Shar, Nub, and Gung Trio, 188, 288n347
Sharkampo, 177
Sheldrak, 129
Shenpa Marnak, 202, 239, 290n387
Sherab Senge. *See* Katok Dampa Deshek (a.k.a. Deshek Sherab Senge)
Sherab Tsultrim, 114
Shingtakchen, 32
Shinje Dongkha, 193
Short Commentary on the "Guhyagarbha" (Vimalamitra), 85
Siddhārtha, 25, 26. *See also* Buddha Śākyamuni
Śikhin, King. *See* Padmasambhava (Guru Rinpoche)
Śīlamañju, 294n439
Siljin charnel ground, 93
Siṃhanāda, 80. *See also* Padmasambhava (Guru Rinpoche)
Siṃhaputra, 89
Siṃharāja, 74
Sindhu Kingdom, 207
Śītavana (Cool Grove), 78, 86, 92, 207, 238
Śiva, 45, 49, 62, 196, 272n85
Six Arrays of Secret Meaning (Kukkurāja), 74
six Buddha Munis, 21, 269n29
Six Dharmas of Niguma, 138
Six Meditation Experiences (Mañjuśrīmitra), 92
six ornaments and two supreme ones, 55
six pāramitās , 242, 284n259

six realms/classes of beings, 21, 246–47, 269n29, 269n33, 297n485
Six Scholarly Gatekeepers, 66, 283n99
Six Yogas of Nāropa, 180
Sixteen Great Arhats, 32–33
sixth Buddha family, 66, 273n102, 277n154
Sixty Stanzas on Reasoning (Nāgārjuna), 39
Six-Volume Treasure Collection (Jatsön Nyingpo), 236
skillful means, 113, 114, 122, 138, 141, 161, 226, 294n443
Smṛtijñāna, xvi, 4, 160–62, 166, 245
So Yeshe Wangchuck, 111–12
Sogpo Palgyi Yeshe, 106–7, 108
sogpos (blacksmiths), 106
Sokyadeva, disciples of, 108
sole essence, 192, 285n277, 290n377
Sole Essence Sādhana of the Lotus-Born (Dudjom Rinpoche), 222
Sole Essence Upadeśa class, 92–93
sole hero, unelaborate practice of, 238
Sole Panacea (Thinley Norbu), 295n455
Sönam Tsemo, 175
songs of realization, 181, 183
Songtsen Gampo, King, 98, 132, 234, 295n458
sorcerers, signs of, 106
Sosadvipa charnel ground, 78, 92
space, xvii, 21, 95, 154, 159
spiritual friends, 55, 273n91
spiritual teachers and gurus
  Buddhas and, 211
  nonhuman, 6, 197
  qualities of, 233
  relying on, 216
  six aspects of, 216, 292n414, 292n418
  three kindnesses of, 259, 298n501
  three spheres of activity of, xvi
  three ways of pleasing, 216, 236, 292n415
  vajra masters, eight qualities of, 215, 292n410
spontaneous presence, 67, 204
Sprouts of Gold (Katok Dampa Deshek), 181
Śrāvakas, 20, 36, 70, 156, 237, 246, 254, 274n114
Śrāvastī, 35
Śrī Dharmapāla, 52, 133
Śrī Gupta, 64
Sri Lanka, 71–72
Śrī Parvata Mountain, 39, 45, 46, 48, 58, 84, 156, 221, 272n78, 277n148
Śrī Siṃha, 78, 92–93, 101, 102, 108, 292n408
Stages of Line Drawing (Vimalamitra), 85
Stages of Realization of Peaceful and Wrathful Deities (Buddhaguhya), 76
Stages of the Path of Magical Infinity (Buddhaguhya), 74–75, 85, 114, 215
Stages of the Path to Enlightenment (Tsongkhapa), 180
Stages of Vajra Activity (Buddhaguhya), 76
Stainless Light Commentary (Puṇḍārīka), 251
Sthavira school, 20, 34–35
Sthiramati, 34, 35
Stone Stūpa of Ratsak, 193
Structural Analysis of the "Embodiment of Wisdom Mind" Called "Sunshine of Excellent Speech" (Katok Dampa Deshek), 181
Stūpa of Great Purity, 26, 270n48
Subduing Haughty Ones, 86
Sucandra, King, 69, 249, 250, 251, 274n110, 298n489
Sudarśana, 33
Śuddhodana, King, 24, 25, 26, 269n41
Sudhana, 258, 298n500
Sudharma, 90, 91
suffering, four great rivers of, 26, 270n46
Sujātā, 27
Sukhasiddhi, 138
Sukhāvatī (Great Bliss), xix, 19, 37, 117, 183, 268n18, 272n74, 288n336
Sukṣmadirga, 166
Summary of a Venomous Snake (Katok Dampa Deshek), 181
Summary of Empowerments (Katok Dampa Deshek), 181
Summary of the "Stages and Paths" (Katok Dampa Deshek), 181
Summary of the Sword (Katok Dampa Deshek), 181
Summary of Training (Katok Dampa Deshek), 181
Summary of Upadeśa on the Lasso of Skillful Means (Katok Dampa Deshek), 181
Sumpa Repa, 185

Sumpa Yebar, 122
Sunlight Heat Longevity Sādhana (Dudul Dorje), 193
Supplementary Tantra, 74
Suprabuddha, King, 26, 270n49
Supreme Perfect Activity pureland, 19
Śūrpaṇakhā, 152–53. *See also* Śāriputra
Sūryakiraṇā, Ḍākinī, 92
Sūryaprakāśa, Mount, 91
Sūryaraśmi, 80. *See also* Padmasambhava (Guru Rinpoche)
Sūryaratha, 250–51
Sutönpa Legpe Drönme, 111
Sūtra Alaṃkāra. See *Ornament of the Mahāyāna Sūtras*
Sūtra lineage, 107, 108, 125, 279n191
Sūtra of Inconceivable Secrets, 13, 36
Sūtra of Inexhaustible Intelligence, 51
Sutra of Kṛkin's Prophetic Dream, 35
Sūtra of Revealing the Five Skandhas, 94
Sūtra of Stainless Space, 211
Sūtra of the Dialogue with the Nāga King, 94–95
Sūtra of the Magical Emanation of the Bodhisattva's Sphere of Activity, 79
Sūtra of the Meeting of Father and Son, 22
Sūtra of the Ornament of Qualities, 31
Sūtra of the Ritual for Amending Breaches, 98
Sūtra of the River's Play, 95–96
Sūtra of the Samādhi That Gathers All Merit, 95
Sūtra of the Three Heaps, 143
Sūtra of the White Lotus of Sublime Dharma, 22
Sūtra of the Wise and the Foolish, 94
Sūtra of Wisdom Prophecies, 69
Sūtra Piṭaka, 30, 33, 35, 36
Sūtra That Elucidates Wisdom Mind, 175
Suvarṇimadroṇa , 154, 155
Svabhavikakāya, 136, 275n124, 285n287
svāstikas, 18, 268n17
Svātantrika Madhyamaka, 64
Svetaketu, 24
Swayambhunath stūpa, 39
swift walking, 102
Swirling Amṛta (gatekeeper), 116

Tagzang Palgyi Dorje, 107
Tail-Fan Island (Ngayab Ling), xix, xx
Taizong, Emperor, 33
Taklung Tarpa Tashipal, 184
Takṣaka (nāga king), 39, 69–70
Takṣilā, 25
Tangtong Gyalpo, 244–45
Tantra in Eighty Stanzas, 74
Tantra in Forty Stanzas, 74
Tantra of the Adornment of Wish-Fulfilling Jewels, 21
Tantra of the All-Doing Great King, 13–14
Tantra of the Awakening of Great Vairocana, 113
Tantra of the Manifestation of Amṛtakuṇḍalī, 73
Tantra of the Manifestation of Compassion, 73
Tantra of the Manifestation of Hayagrīva, 73
Tantra of the Manifestation of Kīlaya, 73
Tantra of the Manifestation of the Heruka, 73
Tantra of the Perfect Embodiment of the Unexcelled Nature, 128
Tantra That Contains the Supreme Path of Skillful Means for Clearly Revealing the Wisdom of Samantabhadra, 71–72
tantras
  compilation and concealment of, 94
  explanatory and aural, 92
  four classes of, 81, 103, 133, 276n139, 279n188
  six classes of, 103, 279n188
  written, authorization for, 91–92
Tārā, 61, 76, 135
  emanation of, 46
  images of, 62, 64, 205
  maṇḍala of, 182
  offerings to, 45
  as progenitor of Tibetan race, 97
  pureland of, 207
  visions of, 63, 64
Tārā Who Protects from the Eight Fears, 116, 280n206
Tashi Tsegpa Pal, 133
Tashi Tseten, 191–92
Tashö Kyilkhor Tang, 193
Teaching on the Unfathomable Secrets of the Tathāgatas, 253–57
Temple of Powerful Strength, 63
ten directions, 21, 269n32

ten powers, 95, 209, 239, 278n166
ten qualities of purity, 129, 281n227
ten secrets, 220, 293n427
ten transgressions, 34, 271n71
ten virtues, 263, 299n516
Tengyur, 179
Terchen Tagsham Dorje, 195
Terdak Lingpa, 102, 131, 282n236
Terma (treasure) tradition, 276n142
  as Buddha's Speech, 93–96
  of Mahāyoga, 86
  potency of, 96–97
  seal of secrecy in, 207
  three special lineages of, 96
  treasure locations, 95, 129, 221–22
  treasure types, 96, 190, 199, 200, 278n167, 289n361, 290n381, 290n386
Textual Commentary on "Establishing Simultaneous Arising," 87
Tharchin Rinpoche, xxiii, 264
Thinley Norbu Rinpoche, xv, xx, 294n440
thirty-two major marks of excellence, 19, 212, 292n405
  common vehicle on, 16–17, 268n15
  Secret Mantra on, 18–19
three blazes, 241, 297n474
Three Councils, 33–35, 93
three defilements, 80, 276n138. *See also* three poisons/fetters
Three Families, 116, 204, 280n207
three gatherings, 241, 297n475
three higher trainings, 135, 170
Three Jewels, 33, 61, 77, 95, 157, 196, 271n67
Three Kāyas, 19, 136, 262, 268n20
  indivisibility of, 275n124
  perfecting, 158
  purelands of, 264, 300n520
  self-manifest array of, 67
  teacher and retinue, 259
three mudrās, 135, 283n243
three planes (Tib. *sa gsum*), 11, 48, 181, 250, 267n2, 285n280
three poisons/fetters, 80, 246, 263, 276n138, 299n514
three realms, 90, 154, 159, 210, 246, 278n161, 288n348
Three Roots, 190, 196, 200, 289n357
  Dudjom Rinpoche's practice of, 220
  sādhana practices of, xxi
  treasure teachings on, 205, 207
Three Roots Mind Sādhana, 221
three secrets, 184, 210, 288n338
Three Stages (Vimalamitra), 85
three sweets, 144, 284n263
Three Upadeśa on the View and Meditation of the Great Perfection (Rongzompa), 170
three "useless men," 120, 122, 124
three whites, 144, 284n262
Three Words That Strike the Essence (Garab Dorje), 92
three worlds (Tib. *'jig rten gsum*), 156, 267n2, 285n280, 288n348
Three Yidam Deities (Dudul Dorje), 193, 290n368
Three-Chapter Tantra (Vilāsavajra), 169
threefold knowledge, 54, 273n89
Threefold Lamps That Pacify Suffering (Padampa Sangye), 137
Tibet, 221, 297n484, 298n490
  alphabet of, 98
  artistic traditions of, 163
  Bön tradition in, 98
  Buddhist revival in, xix, 133–39
  council in, 128
  crown jewel and two earrings of, 162
  demonic ruling spirits of, 97, 278n169
  Dharma's arrival in, 98, 160
  Dharma's persecution in, 110–11, 132–33
  imperial law's collapse in, 109–10
  monasticism established in, 100–101
  people of, origins of, 97
  provinces of, 170, 187, 286n309, 288n343
  sacred geography of, 129, 282n228–32
  Sakya rule in, 137
Tibetan Buddhism
  four major schools of, 139
  spread of, 183
  on Third Council, 35
Tilopa, 135–36, 283n241
Tingri, 125
tīrthikas, 40, 83, 272n79
  conversion of, 91
  Ḍākinīs as, 87–88
  debates with, 43–44, 45–46, 47–50, 60
  Padmasambhava's subjugation of, 80, 81
  Śāntideva and, 57, 58–59
  six teachers, 149
Tiṣya, 146

Toding Temple, 133
Togden Tenpa Rabgye, 214
Tongtsab Jangchub, 114
Tönmi Sambhota, 98, 163, 286n294, 286n303
Tönyön Samdrub, 176
Tradruk Temple, 98, 101
Tragtung Dudjom Lingpa. *See* Dudjom Lingpa
Tragtung Dudul Dorje. *See* Dudul Dorje
Tragtung Nagpo, disciples of, 108
Transcendent Conqueror, 254, 298n496
transference (Tib. *'pho ba*), 82, 283n241
translation and translators, 100, 101–3, 104, 105, 107, 128, 132, 160, 169, 262
transmissions
  from nonhuman teachers, xvii, 6, 197
  reading, 225, 236, 294n442
  for rivers of, 104
treasure caskets, 86–87, 131
treasure guides, 192, 205, 289n365
treasure replacement, 205, 291n394
Treasury of Abhidharma (Vasubandhu), 52
Treasury of Gems: General Analysis of the "Abhidharma Kośa" (Katok Dampa Deshek), 181
"Treasury of Gems of the Threefold Faith," xiii
Treasury of Precious Instructions (Jamgön Kongtrul), 214
Treasury of Precious Qualities (Jigme Lingpa), 215, 233, 246
Treasury Prophecy (Orgyen Dechen Lingpa), 212
Treatise on the Yogācāra Levels (Asaṅga), 42
Tree of Wisdom (Nāgārjuna), 231, 295n456
Trengpo Sherab Özer, 102
Triangular Fire Pit of Space (Kharnakpa of Drum), 189
Trilogy of Dispelling Darkness (Longchenpa), 215
Trilogy of Natural Liberation (Longchenpa), 215
Trilogy of Rest (Longchenpa), 215
Trime Kunga, 131
Trime Lhunpo, 131
Trime Özer, 131
Tripiṭaka, 33–35, 42, 56, 135, 236, 271n70
Trisaṃvara Pravedha (Sakya Paṇḍita), 137
Trisong Detsen, King, xviii, xxii, 128
  dates, 112, 278n171
  incarnations of, 200
  reign of, 98–104
  sons of, 132
  treasure concealed by, 131
Tritsun Bhṛkuṭi Devi, Princess, 98
Tröma, Great Wrathful Mother, 204
Trompa Gyen, Princess, 200
Tromzil Tromkaryak, 193
Trowo Tumdrak Barwa, 198
Trulshik Rinpoche, 218
Tsamtön Gocha, 170
Tsang, 113, 118, 166, 175, 180, 184, 192, 245
Tsang Rabsal, 133
Tsangben Legdrub, 102
Tsangpa Chitön, 127
Tsangpa Gyare, 186
Tsangpo River, 101, 113, 123
Tsangtön Dorje Gyaltsen, 180, 182–83
Tsari, 177, 180, 192
Tsawa Drodak, 192
Tsedrub Tharchin. *See* Tharchin Rinpoche
Tsepongza, Queen, 104
Tsewang Norbu, 196
Tsilupa, 66, 94
Tsiu Marpo (Tsen), 202, 290n389
Tso Pema Orgyen Heruka Nyingmapa Gompa, 234
Tsokchen Dupa, 182
Tsuglak Palge, 108
Tsultrim Rinchen, 177
Tsurtön Wangyi Dorje, 167, 286n306
Tulku Jigme Chöying Norbu, 294n441
Tulku Sangye of Putö Pulung Monastery, 214
Turquoise Lake Place, 192
Tuṣita Heaven, 23–24, 42, 68, 175, 275n117
twelve deeds of Buddhas, 23, 116, 269n37
twelve heavenly generals, 251, 298n494
twelve links of interdependence, 99, 278n174
twelve Tenma sisters (a.k.a. twelve Mātaraḥ), 86, 99, 277n156, 279n178
twenty-five characteristics of the result, 210, 291n396
two accumulations, 20, 29, 189, 196, 253, 268n22
two benefits, 22, 269n35

two stages, 84, 85, 197, 222, 277n151, 290n377. *See also* completion stage; development stage

U, 175, 180
Udāyana, 25
Udraka Rāmaputra, 26, 29
Ugpa Lungpa (Owl Valley), Lama of. *See* Zurpoche Shakya Jungne
Ulkamukha (yakṣa), 69, 70
ultimate truth, xiv, 5, 188
Umā, 45, 146, 155, 285n279
Union of All Buddhas Tantra, 71, 72, 74, 115, 170, 275n121
universal monarchs, 25, 68, 142, 143, 254, 262, 270n43
Unsurpassed Continuity (Maitreya, as spoken to Asaṅga), 23, 42, 136
Unsurpassed Yoga (Anuttarayoga) tantra, 67, 68, 76, 81, 279n188
Upa Chöseng, 127
Upa Dosal, 108
Upadeśa for Seeing with Naked Awareness (Padampa Sangye), 137
Upadeśa Section (Tib. *man ngag gi sde*), 97, 102, 107, 113, 210, 214, 274n105, 281n219, 292n408. *See also* Sole Essence Upadeśa class
Upagupta, 33, 50
Upajīvaka, 29
Upāli, 33, 176, 287n321
Uparāja, King, 72, 87, 89, 91
Upatantra, 279n188
Upatiṣya. *See* Śāriputra
Upayoga, 19, 106
uṣṇīṣa, 17, 268n15
Uṣṇīṣavijayā, 51, 52, 283n87
U-Tsang, 133, 186, 286n309, 287n317, 288n343. *See also* Central Tibet
Uttara Tantra. See *Unsurpassed Continuity*
Uyukpa Dawa Samten, 170

Vaibhāṣika school, 52
Vairocana. See *Tantra of the Awakening of Great Vairocana*
Vairotsana, 100, 134, 227, 279n187
  cave of, 178, 180
  emanation of, 214
  instructions of, 172
  Katok Dorje Den and, 176
  life story, 101–2
  rebirths of, 102–3
  transmissions from, 104
  treasure concealed by, 131
  and Vairocana, distinction between, 279n182
Vaiśālī, 25, 34
Vaiśravaṇa (Kubera), 146, 207, 270n47, 284n271
vajra body, 79, 84, 165, 290n377
Vajra family, 15, 84
Vajra Heruka, 85
vajra mind, 68, 211, 274n109
Vajra Queen, 67
Vajra Quitch Grass (Katok Dampa Deshek), 181
Vajra Seat, 27, 270n50
vajra song of yearning (Dudjom Rinpoche), 228–29, 495n452
Vajra (*Vajracchedika*) *Sūtra*, 269n39
Vajra Tent Tantra, 175
Vajrabhairava, 83
Vajrabhairava Tantra, 66, 169
Vajracaṇḍikā, 175
Vajraḍāka Tantra (Vārāhī), 69
Vajradhara. *See* Nuden Dorje Chang (Vajradhara)
Vajradharma, 68, 86
Vajradhātu Ḍākinī Who Enjoys Worldly Bliss, 91–92
Vajragarbha, 68, 69
Vajrahāsya, 76
Vajrakāya, 75, 275n124
Vajrakīlaya, 73, 129, 172
  Dharma Protector of, 196
  Dudjom Rinpoche's practice of, 222
  eight masters of, 107–8
  maṇḍalas of, 182
  Nyak Jñānakumāra and, 104
  practitioners' marks, 106
  in Sakya tradition, 175
  treasure teachings of, 207, 220, 243
  vision of, 86
  and Yangdak Heruka combined, 81, 115
  See also *Pudri Regpung* (Dudjom Rinpoche)
Vajrakīlaya scriptures, xxi, 73, 80, 86, 87
Vajrakīlaya Tantra, 81
Vajrakumāra. *See* Vajrakīlaya

Vajrapāṇi, 254, 257
  aspiration of, 189
  as compiler of Mahāyāna, 36
  as compiler of tantras, 68–69
  Dudjom Lingpa and, 202
  emanations of, 123, 125, 126, 132, 250
  lineage of, 67
  maṇḍala of, 182
  Nubchen Sangye Yeshe and, 109
  prophecy on, 144
  pureland of, 207
  in Secret Mantra, role of, 66, 70, 72
  transmissions of, 87, 89, 135
Vajrasattva, 19, 71, 72, 90, 91, 121, 277n157
Vajratīkṣṇa (form of Mañjuśrī), 69
Vajravārāhī, 78, 134, 175, 287n313
Vajravidāraṇa, 113
Vajrayoginī, 222
valid cognition, 44, 163
Vārāhī, 69, 182, 212
Vārāṇasī, 27, 29–30, 75, 76, 108, 155
Vareṇdra, 59, 60
Varuṇa, 146, 270n47
Vast Conduct tradition, 36, 39, 213, 229, 272n72
Vast Magical Display, 74
Vast Space Treasury of Dharmatā (Dudjom Lingpa), 202
Vasubandhu, 54, 55, 167
  Dignāga and, 43
  life story, 40, 50–52
  works of, 52, 231
Vasudhara, 108
Vasukalpa, King, 66
Vātsīputra, 35
Vātsīputrīya school, 43
Vedas, 24, 38, 63, 83, 84, 146, 147, 167, 276n143
Vehicle of Mantra. *See* Secret Mantra Vajrayāna
  Bodhisattva (Bodhisattvayāna), 20, 253, 280n211
  Causal, 69, 242, 297n476
  certain, 69, 274n113
  common, 16–18, 33–35, 268n14, 291n397
  nine, 120, 163, 224, 262, 280n211
  Resultant, 242, 297n476
  three guiding, 69, 274n112
Vehicles of Characteristics, 20, 113, 128, 156, 180, 268n27, 280n199
Vemacitra, 246, 269n29
Vidarbha, 36, 37
Vidyādharas, 229
  Completely Accomplished, 191
  eight, 128, 204, 277n157
  Fully Ripened, 79, 275n131
  gatherings of, 228
  Immortal, 79, 275n132
  Mahāmudrā, 80, 191
  nāga, 69
  with Power Over Life, 80
  spontaneously accomplished, 117
  Supreme, 79, 86
view, meditation, and conduct, 232
Vikramaśīla University, 66, 133, 134, 137, 283n98
Vilāsavajra. *See* Gegpa/Gegpe Dorje (a.k.a. Vilāsavajra and Līlāvajra)
Vimalakīrti of Licchavi, 70, 72, 87
Vimalamitra, 103, 104, 277n158, 279n191, 294n439
  disciples of, 108
  emanation of, 214
  instructions of, 172
  life story, 85
  Nyak Jñānakumāra and, 105–6
  teachings received by, 93
  in Treasure Tradition, 87, 131
  works of, 85
Vimalasvabhāva Mountain, 36
Vinaya in Three Hundred Verses (Śākyaprabha), 55
Vinaya lineages, 133
Vinaya Piṭaka, 30, 33, 35, 36, 54
Vinaya Sūtra (Guṇaprabha), 54, 136
Vināyaka Dhṛtarāṣṭra, 20
Vināyaka Sādhukāra, 20
Vindhya, Mount, 43
Vīras, 78, 275n128
Vīrasena, King, 34
Virūpa, 38, 80, 82, 136, 182
Vīryabhadra (formerly Śāṅkara), 156
Vīryaprabha, 185
Viṣṇu, 45, 196, 252, 272n85
visionary experiences, 119, 227, 244, 297n481
Viśuddha Mind, 4, 84, 158, 159, 277n149, 285n282
Viśuddhamati, 256
Viśvāmitra, 25–26

vital-essence syllable, 110
Vivarta script, 167, 286n303
vows and precepts
  eight of lay ordination, 94, 278n165
  five certain conditions of, 234, 296n463
  four conflicting circumstances, 234, 296n464
  prātimokṣa, 217, 288n331, 293n423, 296n466
  Siddhartha's, 27
  three bases of purifying, 235, 296n466
  three/threefold, 215, 219, 234, 292n411, 293n424
  See also sacred commitments
Vulture Peak, 30, 33, 271n60

Way of the Bodhisattva (Śāntideva), 56, 213, 226, 247–48
Wazhab Senge Drakar (a.k.a. Dra Chakhung), 203, 245
Weapon of Speech That Cuts Through Difficulty (Nubchen Sangye Yeshe), 111
Well-Explained Reasoning (Vasubandhu), 231
Wencheng Kongjo, Princess, 98
Wensermo, 116
Wheel of Dharma, 29
  of Secret Mantra, 67, 68
  three turnings of, 30–31
Wheel of Life, 116, 280n208
Whispered Lineage Vajra Bridge, 107
White Lotus of Compassion Sūtra, 154–55
White Silver Mirror (Katok Dampa Deshek), 181
Wild Subjugator. *See* Dorje Drolö
wind disease, 188, 288n350
winds, 113, 176, 177, 192, 218, 291n400
wisdom
  accumulating, 253
  appearances of, 15–16
  discerning, 161
  luminous, 195
  nondual, 188, 210, 239
  perfection of, 191
  self-appearing, xiv
  of self-awareness, 21
  seven pure thoughts, 70
  skillful means and, 226, 294n443
  supreme, 4, 158, 159
Wisdom Mind Lineage of the Victorious Ones, 66–67, 93, 96, 97, 197
wisdom permission, 44, 272n83
wisdom presence, fearless, 86
Wish-Fulfilling Jewel Dhāraṇī of Avalokiteśvara, 98
wish-fulfilling jewels, 77, 136, 157, 158, 247, 248, 262, 299n513
Wish-Fulfilling Lion's Lair, 220, 293n431
Wish-Granting Tree (Kṣemendra), 164
wolf spirits, life-supporting, 106, 107, 279n190
women
  five attributes of wise, 146–47
  teaching Dharma to, 184–85
Wönpori, 136, 283n248
Woodpecker (Śatapatra), 246, 297n486
words of truth, 86, 183
world of forbearance, 263, 299–300n519
world systems, 165
wrathful activity, 80, 106, 110–11, 175, 189, 197, 198, 276n138
wrathful deities
  maṇḍala of, 19
  nine expressions of, 14, 267n9
  of Nirmāṇakāya, 195, 290n371
Wrathful Guru sādhana, 222
Wrathful Hayagrīva, 116
Wrathful Mantra Incantations tantras, 86, 87, 102, 277n159
wrong view, 24, 75, 198, 299n516

Yak Dorje Dzinpa, 172
Yakchar Ngönmo, 199
yakṣas, 40, 68, 69
Yama, 270n47
Yamāntaka, 73, 83, 87, 109, 110–11, 175
Yamarāja, 172
Yangdak Heruka, 87, 116, 158, 285n282
  emanations of, 112
  maṇḍalas of, 84, 86, 111, 115, 182
  mantra of, 280n201
Yangdak Heruka practice, 80–81, 114, 277n149. *See also* Viśuddha Mind
Yangdak Heruka Tantra, 81, 114
Yangdak Heruka temple, 123
Yangdak Rulu Golden Rosary (Hūṃkāra), 85
Yangkheng, Lama, 125
Yangkhye Lama of Shab, 170, 172

Yangleshö Cave, 80, 86, 225
Yangzong sacred site, 109, 129
Yardrok, 104, 105
Yardzong (a.k.a. Sarmo), 112
Yarlung, 104, 292n403
Yarlung Bami, 200, 290n383
Yarlung Namolung, 113
Yaśasvī Varapāla, 69–70
Yaśodharā, 25, 26, 270n49
Yazi sword, 179, 287n329
Yeshe Nyingpo Dharma centers, 234, 295n459
Yeshe Ö, 133
Yeshe Tsogyal, 103, 130, 218
  as compiler, 131
  Dudjom Jigdral Yeshe Dorje and, 223, 224–25, 294n438
  Dudjom Lingpa and, 205, 208
  speech emanation of, xviii, 212
Yeshe Yang, 200
Yizhin Palbar, 221, 294n434
Yo Gejung, 132–33
Yogācāra Madhyamaka, 64
Yogatantras, 19, 68, 76, 78, 86, 97, 106, 122, 279n188
Yoginī Cinto, 135, 283n242
Yogurt Drinker, 5, 189, 289n353
Yönpu Chöje lineage, 212
Yönten Bum, 180
Yönten Taye Dragpa, 256
Yudra Nyingpo, 102, 104, 279n191
Yumbu Lagang Palace, 98
Yungdrung Rinchen Terne, 109
Yutön Horpo, 127
Yutso, 193
Yutso Rinchen Drak, 192
Zangom Sherab Gyalpo, 115, 117
Zangdok Palri. *See* Copper-Colored Mountain (Zangdok Palri)
Zangdok Palri Monastery (Kalimpong), 234
Zangdok Palri Monastery (Kongpo), 234
Zangri Kharmar, 137, 176
Zangtsa Sönam Gyaltsen, 187
Zhang, 100, 118, 138
Zhang Göchung, 117
Zhang Gyalwe Yönten, 108
Zhang Lotsawa, 184
Zhang Zhung, 81, 133
Zhangpa (Shangpa) Kagyu, 138, 283n255
Zhangtön, 127
Zhije tradition, 137, 176, 180, 287n324
Zhong Zhong Temple, 138, 283n254
Zhugi Dorje Gombu, 108–9
Zhutön Sönam Shakya, 114
Zilnön Namkhe Dorje (a.k.a. Dechen Zilnön Dorje), 214, 219
Zombie Sukhasiddhi. *See* Garab Dorje
Zur Dropukpa Shakya Senge, 112, 123, 124–27, 179
Zur traditions, 112, 127, 176, 182, 213, 274n103, 275n120, 287n322
Zurchungpa Sherab Dragpa, 112
  disciples of, 124
  Dropukpa and, 124–25
  life story, 117, 118–24
  at Zurpoche's passing, 117
Zurnak Khorlo, 127
Zurpoche Shakya Jungne, 176, 179
  disciples of, 117–18
  life story, 112–17
  Zurchungpa and, 118–20, 122